JOHN CALVIN AND THE GROUNDING
OF INTERPRETATION

CALVIN'S FIRST COMMENTARIES

BY

R. WARD HOLDER

BRILL

LEIDEN · BOSTON

2006

On the cover: John Calvin [in his study]. Photo: American Vision Collection.

This book is printed on acid-free paper.

Library of Congress Cataloging-in-Publication Data

A C.I.P. record for this book is available from the Library of Congress.

ISSN   1573-5664
ISBN   90 04 14926 0

© *Copyright 2006 by Koninklijke Brill NV, Leiden, The Netherlands*
Koninklijke Brill NV incorporates the imprints Brill Academic Publishers,
Martinus Nijhoff Publishers and VSP

PRINTED IN THE NETHERLANDS

For

John and Thomas

Joshua 24.15

"Ego autem et domus mea serviemus Domino"

110

$$\begin{array}{r} 2\overset{6}{7}\overset{1}{7} \\ 139 \\ \hline 138 \end{array}$$

TABLE OF CONTENTS

ACKNOWLEDGEMENTS

In preparing this book for publication, I have benefited from the help of several institutions, colleagues, and friends. This is my opportunity to offer my gratitude. This book would have been impossible to complete without the generous support of four different institutions. A Dissertation Fellowship from Boston College allowed the timely completion of the first incarnation of this work. A Summer Grant from Stonehill College allowed me to spend time with the collection at the H. Henry Meeter Center at Calvin College; and Saint Anselm College also granted me a Summer Grant which allowed me time to reflect and write. Finally, the H. Henry Meeter Center at Calvin College provided the backbone for research, and its director Karin Maag and curator Paul Fields were untiring in their helpfulness and generous with their time.

The greatest debts I have incurred in the years of working on this are owed to the many friends and colleagues who have been my confidantes, encouragers, and sounding boards. I was set on this path by two mentors at Princeton Theological Seminary, Edward A. Dowey, Jr., whose example led me always deeper into Calvin, and Karlfried Froehlich, my advisor who first demonstrated to me the depths available in examining the exegetical traditions of the Church. Their example still inspires me. Mark Burrows began as my preceptor, developed into my friend, and became my dissertation director—one who convinced me to write the thesis that was in me, rather than that which I thought was "scholarly." My dissertation readers offered specific insights without which I could hardly have progressed. James Weiss was instrumental in pushing for a greater engagement with humanism; Willemien Otten led me to a far better understanding of the richness of the medieval heritage that Calvin inherited; and Robin Jensen both reminded me to be careful about what the Reformers were doing with the patristic heritage, and taught me with her special knack of asking the simple and profound questions. To my whole committee, I cannot be grateful enough for what they taught me about teaching and scholarship, even now their dedication humbles me and reminds me that part of our journey is incurring debts which we can never repay.

The members of the Writer's Group at Saint Anselm College afforded me the chance to bounce ideas off generous and responsive colleagues—I owe special thanks to Dante Scala, Don Cox, Beth Salerno, Brother Isaac Murphy, and Alex Inglis. A chance meeting with Randall Zachman at the Sixteenth Century Studies Conference turned into a decade of dialogue on Calvin's theology and biblical interpretation both at informal settings and at conferences. Conversations with Karen Spierling, Darlene Flaming, Robert A. Johnson, Jr., Barbara Pitkin, Gary Neal Hansen, Richard Muller, John Thompson, and Irena Backus have all enriched the book. Finally, David Whitford and Bruce Gordon have read earlier drafts, and made valuable comments that clarified my rhetoric, and my thought. Their help was encouragement and challenge, and an exercise in grace. In all of these, I am reminded that the scholarly process is best conceived as a conversation, and I am grateful to all my conversation partners.

CHAPTER ONE

READERS AND READINGS

John Calvin interpreted the Bible. He was one of the premier biblical interpreters in an age which highly valued biblical interpretation.[1]
That fact alone should make it worthwhile to understand his interpretive efforts deeply. However, in approaching John Calvin's exegetical
writings, the unwary reader frequently finds a mystery wrapped in a
paradox, illumined by all-too-darkened mirrors. First, there is the question of the nature of Calvin's writings on scripture. In a sense, almost
all of Calvin's work can be categorized as an interpretation of scripture.
He wrote the *Institutes* as a help to understanding scripture, and the
work is full of quotations from scripture. He preached and lectured on
scripture, and certainly some of his treatises are his exposition of scripture's witness on a particular topic. Most particularly, he commented on
most of the books of the Bible. His commentaries were eagerly awaited
by friends and colleagues. Calvin himself thought that his commentaries were the integral, but not only, component of his interpretation
of scripture.

But those commentaries can offer special challenges to readers. At
times, they are difficult because of their changes in genre, shifting
almost abruptly from what might be called a verse-by-verse commentary to a lengthy discussion of a particular theological topic, and just

---

[1] Frederic Farrar, in his Bampton lectures of 1885, stated that "the greatest exegete
and theologian of the Reformation was undoubtedly Calvin. ... {H} is commentaries,
almost alone among those of his epoch, are still a living force." *History of Interpretation* (Grand Rapids: Baker Book House, 1961), 342–343. More modern thinkers continue to find Calvin in the forefront. Basil Hall wrote that "Calvin's resources as an
exegete made him superior to all his contemporaries if we allow his purposes in exegesis to be sufficient.", in "Biblical Scholarship: Editions and Commentaries" in *The
Cambridge History of the Bible*, vol. 3, edited by S.L. Greenslade (Cambridge: Cambridge
University Press, 1963), 89. Werner Jeanrond has termed the Protestant Reformation a
"hermeneutical event," and consistently lists Calvin as a paradigmatic figure. *Theological
Hermeneutics: Development and Significance* (New York: Crossroad Publishing, 1991), 30–35.
David Steinmetz wrote "Although Calvin considered himself to be primarily an interpreter of the Bible and although his sermons and commentaries outnumber in length
and quantity his systematic and polemical writings, far more is known about Calvin as
a systematic or polemical theologian than as an interpreter of the Bible. What makes

as quickly back again. Calvin's interpretation, although intended to aid understanding, can become a labyrinth in which the unprepared reader quickly becomes lost.

Beyond the problem of reading the commentaries is the difficulty of categorizing Calvin's effort.[2] How shall we understand Calvin's interpretive efforts? Was Calvin the fore-runner of modern historical-critical method? If so, how can his tendencies to see the whole of scripture as carrying a unitive message be understood? Or was Calvin's religious consciousness basically medieval, formed by popular piety from his youth, explaining the strongly conservative slant in some of his writings? This position will not bear the scrutiny of scholarship that sees in Calvin's work great affinities to the methods and spirit of the Renaissance. Can Calvin even be seen as the quintessential Reformer, carrying out faithfully the Protestant credo of *sola scriptura* in his efforts at interpretation and polemic? This conception suffocates under the frequent patristic citations in Calvin's commentaries.

These competing approaches to Calvin leave us with the unsatisfying picture of a thinker dangling between the suspensions of the past and the anticipations of the future.[3] Calvin has been portrayed as a man who "needed to strike a balance between the two sides of himself."[4] For some analysts, one of those two forces was a profoundly traditional impulse, presented as an effort to build up instruments of cultural and spiritual control, and the second was a stubborn originality, rebelling at the constriction of those very structures![5] Other scholars have noted the eclecticism in Calvin's interpretive approach.[6] Both scholastic and a variety of humanistic approaches appear in Calvin's

---

this situation particularly ironic is that Calvin regarded his primary theological work, the Institutes of the Christian Religion, as a handbook or introduction for beginners to study Scripture." *Calvin in Context* (Oxford: Oxford University Press, 1995), 64.

[2] Alexandre Ganoczy and Stefan Scheld have found that in Calvin's interpretation one finds a mixture of simple, dispassionate explication of the historical sense of the text with barely restrained impulsiveness toward the didactic meaning. *Die Hermeneutik Calvins: Geistesgeschichtliche Voraussetzungen und Grundzüge* (Wiesbaden: Franz Steiner Verlag GMBH, 1983), 7.

[3] Bernard Cottret's recent biography of Calvin proclaimed that Calvin "had one foot in the fifteenth century, the other in the seventeenth." *Calvin: A Biography*, translated by M. Wallace McDonald (Grand Rapids: Eerdmans, 2000), 345–346.

[4] William Bouwsma, *John Calvin: A Sixteenth Century Portrait* (Oxford: Oxford University Press, 1988), 48.

[5] Bouwsma, 48.

[6] Michael L. Monheit, "Young Calvin, Textual Interpretation and Roman Law." *Bibliotheque d'humanisme et renaissance: travaux et documents.* 59, No. 2, (1997): 277.

early legal work.[7] On the other hand, one scholar who has examined Calvin's humanism and his biblical commentary, argues that Calvin's conscious choice for a different style of rhetoric implicitly critiques the humanistic rhetoric with a biblical rhetoric.[8] Other scholars, in searching for Calvin's hermeneutic choice, have found him "bound by a mindset" which was essentially medieval.[9]

This confusion is mirrored by the issue of a fractured Augustinianism in Calvin's approach to scripture and theology. Calvin's dependence upon and allegiance to Augustine has been well noted.[10] Though some have preferred to be more careful, and speak of Calvin being influenced by a *schola Augustiniana moderna*,[11] the point remains that Calvin is consciously Augustinian. However, if Calvin's Augustinianism can be established, the question should be posed about Calvin's rejection of allegory, one of Augustine's favorite exegetical tools. Why would Calvin so consciously reach for Augustine as a source of true Christian doctrine, while just as consciously discarding his interpretive method? Our intention is to approach the questions of the "divided Calvin" and of his method of receiving Augustine through his Pauline commentaries. Many of the difficulties in grasping the coherence of Calvin's interpretation of scripture, and how that interpretation works with his doctrine, may be solved by a methodological possibility.

Calvin saw the interpretation of scripture as a key component to the Christian life, but one fraught with peril. His awareness of this peril is expressed in two prefaces Calvin wrote about the functioning of his theology as a preparation to read the scripture.

> It has been my purpose in this labor to prepare and furnish candidates in sacred theology for the reading of the divine Word, that they might be able both to have easy entrance into it and to advance in it unhindered. For it seems to me that I have provided a summary of religion in all its parts, and have arranged it in such an order so that should anyone rightly grasp it, it will not be difficult for him to establish what he

---

[7] Monheit, 281.

[8] Richard C. Gamble, "Exposition and Method in Calvin." *Westminster Theological Journal* 49 (1987): 153–165.

[9] Hans-Joachim Kraus, "Calvin's Exegetical Principles." *Interpretation* 31 (1977): 18.

[10] Luchesius Smits, *Saint Augustin dans L'œuvre de Jean Calvin* (Assen: Van Gorcum & Comp., 1957); Lange van Ravenswaay, *Augustinus totus noster: Das Augustinverständnis bei Johannes Calvin* (Göttingen: Vandenhoeck & Ruprecht, 1990); Anthony N.S. Lane, *John Calvin: Student of the Church Fathers* (Grand Rapids: Baker Book House, 1999).

[11] Alister McGrath, *A Life of John Calvin: A Study in the Shaping of Western Culture* (Cambridge, MA: Blackwell Publishers, 1990), 43–47.

ought particularly to seek in Scripture, and also to what goal he ought
to refer its contents. Having paved the way, should I then publish any
commentaries on Scripture, I shall always condense them, because I shall
have no need to undertake long dogmatic disputations, nor to digress
into commonplaces. For this reason, the pious reader will be spared
great annoyance and boredom, provided he approaches fortified with
a knowledge of the present work, as a necessary instrument.[12]

In order that my readers may better profit from this present work, I
wish to demonstrate briefly the utility which they may take from it. For,
in doing this, I will demonstrate to them the purpose to which they
should bend and direct their intention in reading it. Although the Holy
Scripture contains a perfect doctrine, to which one can add nothing;
because our Lord meant to display the infinite treasures of his wisdom
in it, on the other hand a person who has not had much practice in it
has good reason for some guidance and direction, in order to know what
he ought to look for in it, so that he will not wander here and there, but
will hold to a sure path, in order that he might attain the goal to which
the Holy Spirit calls him. Thus, the responsibility of those who have
received from God more ample light than others is to help the simple
in this issue, as if lending them a hand, in order to conduct them and
help them to find the sum of what God wished to teach us in his Word.
Now, that cannot be better done in the Scriptures than by treating the
principal and most consequential matters, which are comprised in the
Christian philosophy. For he who knows these things will be prepared to
profit more in the school of God in one day than another will in three
months. This is because that one knows well to what he should refer each
sentence, and has this rule for grasping all that is presented to him.

Seeing then that it is very necessary to help in this fashion those who
desire to be instructed in the doctrine of salvation, consequently, I was

---

[12] Joannis Calvini, *Opera Selecta*, in 5 volumes, 3rd ed., edited by Peter Barth and Wilhelm Niesel (Munich: Christian Kaiser, 1967). Vol. 3.6.18–31. Although I have consulted
the standard translations, and especially that of Ford Lewis Battles in the *Library of Christian Classics*, all translations of Calvin's work are my own. I shall use standard published
translations for other figures. Further, my capitalization shall reflect that of the text.
When "Gospel" is capitalized, the reader may assume that it is so in the text. "Porro
hoc mihi in isto labore propositum fuit, sacrae Theologiae candidatos ad divini verbi
lectionem ita praeparare et instruere, ut et facilem ad eam aditum habere, et inoffenso
in ea gradu pergere queant; siquidem religionis summam omnibus partibus sic mihi
complexus esse videor, et eo quoque ordine digessisse, ut siquis eam recte tenuerit, ei
non sit difficile statuere et quid potissimum quaerere in Scriptura, et quem in scopum
quicquid in ea continetur referre debeat. Itaque, hac veluti strata via, siquas posthac
Scripturae enarrationes edidero, quia non necesse habebo de dogmatibus longas disputationes instituere, et in locos communes evagari: eas compendio semper astringam.
Ea ratione, magna molestia et fastidio pius lector sublevabitur: modo praesentis operis
cognitione, quasi necessario instrumento, praemunitus accedat."

forced, according to the faculty that the Lord has given me, to undertake this task. This has been my goal in composing the present book.[13]

For students of Calvin, few passages are more often seen and so infrequently read. Both of these passages are taken from the prefaces to Calvin's *Institutes of the Christian Religion*. The first was the preface entitled "John Calvin to the Reader." It introduced the 1539 edition of Calvin's *Institutes*, and was appended to all further Latin editions.[14] The second was the preface to the French edition of 1560. The choice of the first preface is clear. Calvin composed it directly at the time of his writing of his first commentary on the epistle to the Romans. But clearly, the 1560 is written years later, after much of Calvin's commenting upon scripture is finished. Why supply it? These are chosen because they bracket Calvin's career as a commentator, the greatest part of his interpretive work having been published between these two prefaces. Although there are significant differences between the two, meaningful commonalities also can be detected, and in these, Calvin sets out a number of issues for interpretation of the scriptures.

---

[13] OS, 3.7.15–40. "A fin que les Lecteurs puissent mieux faire leur proffit de ce present livre, ie leur veux bien monstrer en brief, l'utilité qu'ilz auront a en prendre. Car, en ce faisant, ie leur monstreray le but, auquel ils devront tendre et diriger leur intention, en le lisant. Combien que la saincte Escriture contienne une doctrine parfaicte, a laquelle on ne peut rien adiouster: comme en icelle nostre Seigneur a voulu desployer les Thresors infiniz de sa Sapience: toutesfois une personne, qui n'y sera pas fort exercitée, a bon mestier de quelque conduicte et addresse, pour sçavoir ce quelle y doibt cercher: a fin de ne s'esgarer point çà et là, mais de tenir une certaine voye, pour attaindre tousiours a la fin, ou le Sainct Esprit l'appelle. Pourtant l'office de ceux qui ont receu plus ample lumiere de Dieu que les autres, est, de subvenir aux simples en cest endroict: et quasi leur prester la main, pour les conduire et les ayder a trouver la somme de ce que Dieu nous a voulu enseigner en sa parolle. Or cela ne se peut mieux faire par Escritures, qu'en traictant les matieres principales et de consequence, lesquelles sont comprinses en la Philosophie Chrestienne. Car celuy qui en aura l'intelligence, sera preparé a proffiter en l'eschole de Dieu en un iour, plus qu'un autre en trois mois: d'autant qu'il sçait a peu pres, ou il doibt rapporter une chascune sentence: et ha sa reigle pour compasser tout ce qui luy est presenté. Voyant donc que cestoit une chose tant necessaire, que d'ayder en ceste façon ceux qui desirent d'estre instruictz en la doctrine de salut, ie me suis efforcé, selon la faculté que le Seigneur m'a donnée, de m'employer a ce faire: et a ceste fin i'ay composé ce present livre."

[14] The date of the origin of this preface explains the reference, which seems odd to the modern reader, that Calvin may publish commentaries on scripture—he had not at this time seen his Romans commentary (1540) go to press. An analysis of the function of the prefaces, and the history of their redaction, can be found in Serene Jones, *Calvin and the Rhetoric of Piety*, Columbia Series in Reformed Theology (Louisville: Westminster John Knox Press, 1995), 46–58.

First, although the high regard which Calvin had for scripture is
evident, he does not believe that it was a book which can be entered
without some fear of becoming lost.[15] The reader's eye is drawn not
only to the affirmations of Calvin's own work, or the importance of
scripture, but also to the negative terms. "*Inoffenso*" alerts us that the
scripture contains not only a stumbling block to Jews and foolishness
to Greeks, but also opportunities for the unwary to fall. If Calvin
was concerned to instruct the learned readers—candidates in sacred
theology, then he was tacitly acknowledging that even prepared readers
occasionally misunderstand scripture.[16]

This becomes even more clear in the French *Argument de Present Livre*
of 1560. The scripture contains "*les Thresors infiniz de sa* (the Lord's) *Sapience.*" But like so many treasures of epic lore, the treasure is guarded
by a labyrinth.[17] The prudent treasure seeker seeks out a guide, so that
"*a fin de ne s'esgarer point cà et là, mais de tenir une certaine voye, pour attaindre
tousiours a la fin, ou le Sainct Esprit l'appelle.*" If the rewards are immense,
the risks seem commensurate. Scripture, for Calvin, offers a difficult
task, which is properly essayed only after becoming equipped with the
Christian philosophy. Obviously, the too simple "*sola scriptura*" formulation must be narrowly circumscribed, if Calvin's reforming impulse
is to fit that rubric.[18] John Calvin, who taught that "Holy Scripture
contains a perfect doctrine," believed that that perfect doctrine could
more profitably be approached from a stance which would highlight

---

[15] Randall C. Zachman has discussed this in his "'Do You Understand What You
Are Reading?' Calvin's Guidance for the Reading of Scripture" *Scottish Journal of
Theology* 54 (2001): 3.
[16] The issue of the historical context of the struggle to understand the Bible in the
late middle ages is addressed by Ganoczy and Scheld, *Die Hermeneutik Calvins* (9–12).
They concentrate upon the Franciscan struggle over the issue of poverty, and how that
issue became a flashpoint for the question of primacy of Church or scripture, going so
far as to assert that the result was a critical separation of Church from scripture (21).
[17] William Bouwsma has drawn out Calvin's concern for the labyrinth in his biography of the Reformer. See *John Calvin: A Sixteenth Century Portrait* (Oxford: Oxford University Press, 1988), especially 45–48.
[18] Max Engammare denies the possibility of a true "sola scriptura" formula because
of Calvin's carelessness in citation during his sermons in his "Calvin connaissait-il la
Bible? Les citations de l'Ecriture dans ses sermons sur la Genese." *Bulletin de la Societe de
l'Histoire du Protestantisme Francais* 141 (1995): 183, "C'est que le principe du sola Scriptura
n'existe pas de facto. Il est confronté aux hommes qui lisent l'Écriture, la comprennent
et l'expliquent. La négation de la subjectivité du lecture, quand bien même celui-ci est
un réformateur d'importance et d'influence, quand bien même le livre qu'il lit est la
Bible, reste théorique."

the chief matters in the "Christian philosophy."[19] This Christian philosophy, then, becomes his lens through which to view the scriptures correctly.[20] Without the Christian philosophy, one can too easily become lost, Calvin's first issue of interpretation.

The second point is a corollary to the first, that there is a particular content that is to be found in the scriptures. This seems too obvious, every book contains content to be found. But beyond that, Calvin seems to state that there is a particular interpretation which is correct, a certain message which demands to be extracted from within scripture. The *Institutes* were to serve as a guide to the perplexed, a roadmap to the journey into the scriptures. Thus, one must know how to understand and refer the words of scripture before one takes on the task of reading scripture. Quite simply, Calvin was consciously giving a key to the scriptures to his readers. The claim of *sola scriptura* is becoming more and more nuanced.

Further, Calvin made it clear that correct interpretation is related to religion. The key is the "summary of religion in all its parts", which is both theological and practical. The point of reading scripture is to adapt oneself to its purpose, or rather the purpose of its ultimate author. He assumed that this interpretation of the Bible will be integrally related to the Christian religion. This second issue is that of knowing the correct content of scripture.

---

[19] The element of intrigue involved in Calvin's use of the term Christian philosophy does not wholly lie within the bailiwick of students of Calviniana. The term "Christian philosophy," is not a neutral term, or a phrase free from historical baggage. Perhaps it is found most famously in the work of the French medievalist, Etienne Gilson. In an essay entitled "What Is Christian Philosophy?" Gilson surveys the history of the term. He determines that although the term had originally been defined in contradistinction to "philosophy," this usage, Gilson states, can still be used profitably. Gilson does not include Calvin in his consideration of Christian philosophy. In a bibliographical essay at the end of his "*L'Esprit de la Philosophie Medievale*," Gilson considers the history of the notion of a Christian philosophy. Beginning with Augustine, and proceeding through figures such as Erasmus, Balzac, and even Feuerbach, Gilson completely ignores Calvin's name. In fact, when the index is searched, one finds only three mentions of Calvin, each time, the Reformer is found placed in a negative context. Gilson pointedly does not include John Calvin in his notion of a Christian philosophy. Presuming that this is a choice on his part, the reason seems to be their vastly different ideas of the character of Christian philosophy. For Gilson, the content of that philosophy is a certain search for truth, for Calvin, it is a search for edifying piety.

[20] Wilhelm Niesel writes in his summary of Calvin's theology that "the aim of Calvin's theology seems to be not an unfolding of "*philosophia humana*" but an exposition of the "*philosophia christiana*" which God gives us in the Bible." Wilhelm Niesel, *The Theology of Calvin*, translated by Harold Knight (Philadelphia: Westminster Press, 1956), 24.

Thirdly, Calvin believed that his key to the scriptures has come from the scriptures. He was so insistent on this point that he invited his readers to check his theology against the testimony of scripture so as to assure themselves of his veracity, or perhaps to remain founded upon the testimony of the words of scripture.[21] There was no self-justifying principle or foundational effort in this program. However, the difficulty is apparent. If reading the *Institutes* was a preparatory exercise to ready the reader to understand scripture, how then could that reader be able to break from that original conditioning, if Calvin has mis-understood some portion of scripture, and carried that mis-understanding into the *Institutes*? Further, if Calvin has argued persuasively, will the possibility even exist to tear aside the curtain of his rhetoric, to have a fuller access to the revelation concealed within?[22] The spectre of the personality of the interpreter outweighing the testimony of scripture will force this study to consider Calvin's effort carefully. Calvin set up a movement from scripture to doctrine to scripture, but one can only prepare for reading the scripture by knowing doctrine! This issue of the circular motion from scripture to doctrine and back to scripture was Calvin's third point.

Finally, there is the question of the end or goal (*scopus*) toward which Calvin was directing this effort. This might be addressed as the question of action or contemplation. In short, what did Calvin hope would occur in the mind of his readers when they read the *Institutes*? Is it simply that he desired his audience to be well prepared to read the scriptures? Did he seek to impart an intellectual understanding of the Christian religion? The answer to both these questions must be "no." Calvin made it clear from the very beginning, in the prefaces, that he was serving the "doing" of Christianity. He wanted to prepare candidates for sacred theology—pastors. But that preparation was always in

---

[21] OS 3.8.25–27. "Above all, my reader should have recourse to Scripture in order to consider the testimonies that I put forward from it." "Sur toutes choses, if fauldra auoir en recommandation, de recourir a l'Escriture, pour considerer les tesmoingages que i'en allegue."

[22] Harold Bloom has considered the task of interpretation as the task of "misreading," an effort in misprision. He denotes the stronger interpretation as a "strong reading," and characterizes it as one that insists upon its own exclusive and complete truth claim. Harold Bloom, *Kabbalah and Criticism* (New York: Seabury Press, 1975), 95–126. This obviously raises the problem of error. If Calvin makes a strong mis-reading, claiming to have finished the course on a particular scriptural passage or motif, can his reader break free from that spell to claim another reading, in the case that Calvin was finally wrong?

service of the Church. Moreover, the purpose of the *Institutes* as a guide
to the scriptures was not, finally, to supply the world with well-read people. Rather, it was the inculcation of the Christian religion in the hearts
of his readers.[23] Calvin was concerned with the living out of the Christian life, and with moving readers to do so correctly. In fact, the whole
point of reading scripture was not for polemic battle, nor for university advancement. Rather, it was to press toward "the goal to which the
Holy Spirit calls." Calvin's fourth issue was the goal of interpretation,
or the application of scripture's witness.

It may be seen, then, that Calvin set out (at least) these four issues in
his prefaces. First, he was concerned about the problem of wandering
in the labyrinth of the scriptures. Secondly, he supplied a lens through
which the reader was to understand the meanings of scripture. Thirdly,
he set up a circular relationship, fraught with difficulties, between his
doctrine and the scriptures. Fourthly and finally, he expressed a desire
for his readers to apply themselves to the doing of Christianity.

Armed with these issues, how should a study proceed? When one
surveys the field of Calvin studies over the past few decades, various
options are available.[24] Yet those diverse efforts have failed to come to

---

[23] Serene Jones, in her *Calvin and the Rhetoric of Piety*, Columbia Series in Reformed
Theology (Louisville: Westminster John Knox Press, 1995), introduction and chapter 1,
says dispositional—I believe that we mean the same thing.

[24] An (incomplete) survey of the literature on Calvin's biblical interpretation demonstrates its popularity in the later twentieth century. Some of the more significant efforts
have been H. Jackson Forstman, *Word and Spirit: Calvin's Doctrine of Biblical Authority*
(Stanford, CA: Stanford University Press, 1962); Hans Frei, *The Eclipse of Biblical Narrative: A Study in Eighteenth and Nineteenth Century Hermeneutics* (New Haven, Yale University
Press, 1974), 19–37; Hans-Joachim Kraus, "Calvin's Exegetical Principles," *Interpretation*
31 (1977): 8–18; Alexandre Ganoczy and Klaus Müller, *Calvins Handschriftliche Annotationen zu Chrysostomus: Ein Beitrag zur Hermeneutik Calvins* (Wiesbaden: Franz Steiner Verlag
GMBH, 1981); Ganoczy and Stefan Scheld, *Die Hermeneutik Calvins: Geistesgeschichtliche
Voraussetzungen und Grundzüge* (Wiesbaden: Franz Steiner Verlag GMBH, 1983); Richard
C. Gamble, "*Brevitas et Facilitas*: Toward an Understanding of Calvin's Hermeneutic," *Westminster Theological Journal* 47 (1985): 1–17; Gamble, "Exposition and Method
in Calvin," *Westminster Theological Journal* 49 (1987): 153–165; Roland M. Frye, "Calvin's
Theological Use of Figurative Language," *John Calvin and the Church*, 172–194, edited
by Timothy George (Louisville: Westminster John Knox Press, 1991); George Stroup,
"Narrative in Calvin's Hermeneutic," *John Calvin and the Church*, 158–171; John Thomp-
son, *The Daughters of Sarah: Women in Regular and Exceptional Roles in the Exegesis of Calvin,
His Predecessors, and His Contemporaries* (Geneve: Librairie Droz, 1992); Peter Opitz, *Calvins
Theologische Hermeneutik* (Neukirchen-Vluyn: Neukirchener, 1994); David L. Puckett, *John
Calvin's Exegesis of the Old Testament*, Columbia Series in Reformed Theology (Louisville:
Westminster John Knox Press, 1995); and Barbara Pitkin, *What Pure Eyes Could See:
Calvin's Doctrine of Faith in Its Exegetical Context* (Oxford: Oxford University Press, 1999).

any conclusive unity. Since 1971, when T.H.L. Parker sparked the attention of the world of Calvin scholarship to Calvin as a biblical expositor, there have been literally dozens of studies upon Calvin's exegesis, hermeneutics, and biblical interpretation.[25] Further contributions have come from chapters in works that take on other topics in Calvin's thought. Yet basic questions of Calvin's understanding of the Bible simply have not been satisfactorily answered.

This work examines how some of the difficulties inherent in understanding Calvin's interpretation of the scripture can be more fruitfully addressed through a re-examination of the terms "hermeneutics" and "exegesis." The differentiation between hermeneutical principles and exegetical practices or rules, demonstrated most clearly from the work of Karlfried Froehlich, is vital to understanding both Calvin's continuities and discontinuities with the patristic and medieval tradition.[26] This method also shows promise of creating greater understanding of Calvin's mind, and of how his work is a coherent complex, rather than a jumble of competing and contradictory impulses. When properly understood, this difference allows greater clarity in understanding both Calvin's critical reception of tradition and his attempts at reframing the basic religious content of Christianity to meet the needs of the sixteenth century.[27] In examining Calvin's scriptural interpretation through the application of these tools, Calvin's work is seen as a grasping of the Christian *religio*, re-framed for the historical circumstances of the mid-sixteenth century. Thus, Calvin sets out edification (*ædificatio*), as the heart of the theological task, and the driving force behind scriptural interpretation is the search for God's truth, always done in and through the faith community, most obviously seen as the visible Church, the congregation(s) of Geneva.

I will argue that this method of interpretation holds out significant possibilities for seeing Calvin as a coherent thinker and interpreter of scripture. Doctrinal efforts have looked directly at the theological

---

[25] T.H.L.Parker, *Calvin's New Testament Commentaries* (London: SCM Press, 1971).

[26] Karlfried Froehlich, *Biblical Interpretation in the Early Church*, translated and edited by Karlfried Froehlich (Philadelphia: Fortress Press, 1984).

[27] An illuminating example of the aporia from which I hope to rescue Calvin's thought can be seen in Michael Monheit's "Young Calvin, Textual Interpretation and Roman Law." *Bibliotheque d'humanisme et renaissance: travaux et documents.* 59, No. 2, (1997): 263–282. Monheit notes that Calvin's interpretive practice betrays "mutually contradictory habits of interpretation," (281), and suggests that Calvin simply does not realize what he is doing.

output of Calvin's engagement with scripture. While this can be enormously helpful in pointing out the parallels between the *Institutes* and
various commentaries, it does not see the actual work of interpretation. Likewise, those analytical efforts which have concentrated upon
Calvin's interpretive practices have pointed out what Calvin did, but
have not always been able to argue why he did so. The most significant
advances in the recent decades of Calvin scholarship have frequently
come from the application of the history of exegesis method.[28] This
has been an extraordinary tool for demonstrating the balance between
the originality of a particular commentator and that which has been
taken from the interpretive and doctrinal tradition. In this study, while
drawing from these various approaches, we shall be asking a different
question. Rather than pursuing those influences that informed Calvin's
interpretation, we shall be seeking to find the principles and rules that
he employed in his commentaries, above all his exegesis of the Pauline
letters.

The most important place to begin with Calvin's interpretive project
is at the beginning. Calvin's Pauline commentaries were both his first
commentaries and the first he would revise, and it is here that he begins
to hone his craft of biblical interpretation.[29] Calvin comes to the first
commentary with some ideas about what he should avoid, and what
virtues his commentary should pursue, but only a close examination of
the texts enables us to determine in what measure he realized those
ideas.[30] Further, these are from a crucial period in his life. Though
Romans is published in 1540, Calvin was certainly writing it in 1539.
He may have had the idea of a set of commentaries on the Pauline
epistles as early as 1535.[31] When he completed that set, he revised

---

[28] See, for example, David C. Steinmetz, *Calvin in Context* (Oxford: Oxford University
Press, 1995); John Thompson, *The Daughters of Sarah: Women in Regular and Exceptional
Roles in the Exegesis of Calvin, His Predecessors, and His Contemporaries* (Geneve: Librairie
Droz, 1992); and Barbara Pitkin, *What Pure Eyes Could See: Calvin's Doctrine of Faith in Its
Exegetical Context* (Oxford: Oxford University Press, 1999).

[29] Calvin commented upon the Pauline corpus and Hebrews between 1540 and 1551.
See T.H.L. Parker, *Calvin's New Testament Commentaries*, 2nd ed. (Louisville: Westminster
John Knox Press, 1993), chapters 1 & 2.

[30] See his introductory epistle to Simon Grynaeus.

[31] T.H.L. Parker, Calvin's New Testament Commentaries, 2nd ed., "It therefore
seems certain that from at least as early as 1539, possibly by 1535 or 1536, Calvin
planned a set of commentaries on the Pauline corpus. This is confirmed in general
by the order in which he wrote and published his commentaries. He worked his way
steadily through the epistles in their canonical order and did not publish others until
this set was completed." 16.

them (somewhat) and published them, including Hebrews, in 1551. In this period Calvin moves from being the young scholar-pastor who is banished from Geneva, brilliant but inexperienced, to being one of the recognized leaders of an international religious movement, fully capable of maneuvering through the political minefields of Geneva and of Switzerland.[32] Further, by studying Calvin's Pauline commentaries, we are selecting a division that he himself acknowledged. Therefore, along with appropriate citations from the *Institutes*, it makes sense for us to commence our examination here.

Should this study succeed in grasping the strands of both hermeneutical principles and exegetical rules in Calvin's earliest commenting, there would be a finer platform upon which to stand to survey the rest of his interpretive corpus. It may be that Calvin's methods of and principles for interpreting scripture never change, it may be that they change drastically as he turns to different material and eventually the Old Testament. This question can only be answered through a detailed examination of the principles set down in the earliest commentaries. Such an investigation also fills a gap in the scholarship as to date there is no full-length study of Calvin's Pauline commentaries.[33] Thus, the

---

[32] As well, by concentrating upon a wider range of commentaries, this method avoids the pitfalls which Alexandre Ganoczy and Stefan Scheld saw in the work of their predecessors, who went too far in specializing—"Die größere Ausführlichkeit ihrer Belege geht jedoch Hand in Hand mit einer spezifizierung der Thematik." *Die Hermeneutik Calvins: Geistesgeschichtliche Voraussetzungen und Grundzüge* (Wiesbaden: Franz Steiner Verlag GMBH, 1983), 2.

[33] This seems a strange oversight in the literature. At present, several studies have been published upon Calvin's exegesis of the Old Testament, including Peter Opitz, *Calvins Theologische Hermeneutik* (Neukirchen-Vluyn: Neukirchener, 1994); David L. Puckett, *John Calvin's Exegesis of the Old Testament*, Columbia Series in Reformed Theology (Louisville: Westminster John Knox Press, 1995); Susan Schreiner, *Where Shall Wisdom Be Found? Calvin's Exegesis of Job from Medieval and Modern Perspectives* (Chicago: University of Chicago Press, 1994); Richard A. Muller, "The Hermeneutic of Promise and Fulfillment in Calvin's Exegesis of the Old Testament Prophecies of the Kingdom," In *The Bible in the 16th Century*, edited by David Steinmetz (Durham: Duke University Press, 1990, 68–82). Alexandre Ganoczy and Stefan Scheld's *Die Hermeneutik Calvins: Geistesgeschichtliche Voraussetzungen und Grundzüge* (Wiesbaden: Franz Steiner Verlag GMBH, 1983), is brilliant, but draws broadly upon Calvin's entire corpus, and does not allow for the kind of historically narrow study that will begin the process of ascertaining whether Calvin's exegesis develops across his life's work. In terms of New Testament studies, several briefer studies have been written, but none which consider Calvin's first set of commentaries as a whole, nor one which differentiates between hermeneutical principles and exegetical rules. Some studies include Benoît Girard, *Rhétorique et Théologique: Calvin, Le Commentaire de L'Epître aux Romains* (Paris: Éditions Beauchesne, 1979); Hubert Goudineau, "Luther et Calvin commentatuers de l'epitre aux Romains: Une compara-

task of this study begins narrowly, and broadens. To begin, this study is about how Calvin conceived the process of finding God's truth from the scripture. But in laying the groundwork for understanding what Calvin intended and attempted to do in interpreting the scripture, the way that scripture permeated his thought will necessitate consideration of Calvin's reception of traditional readings, the nature of authority, the sense of history, the place of the application of edifying doctrine, and the function of the Church, both as a trans-historical phenomenon, and as the gathered body of believers.

A Moment for Method

If Calvin posed a Christian doctrinal prejudice as the correct way to read scripture, how did he do so? In other words, how did Calvin use the Christian tradition in his approach to the scripture? What is the best manner in which to follow this question? Is the answer only possible by tracing out the various influences in his commentaries, and in his major theological treatises? Is it a matter of deciding who his favorite exegetes were, and demonstrating either an explicit knowledge of or dependence upon them? Such studies could be written. One might argue that only the rigorous historical studies of dependence are of use in understanding Calvin's use of the tradition.[34] However, all this would demonstrate would be historical dependence upon certain authors. That is a worthy task, but will not achieve the stated goal of this study. How can one get at Calvin's acceptance or rejection of the doctrinal and exegetical traditions available to him in the first half of the sixteenth century? As a guide, what we must consider is what was *possible* for this man in this time to think.[35] With that in hand, we shall aim at an ideal of understanding.

The attempt has been made to consider Calvin as a pre-critical type, as a reader for whom the literal and figural sense cohered.[36] But

---

ison." *Positions Lutheriennes*, 44, (1996): 16–52; Elsie Anne McKee, "Calvin's Exegesis of Romans 12:8–Social, Accidental, or Theological," *Calvin Theological Journal* 23 (1988): 6–18.

[34] A.N.S. Lane, "Calvin's Use of the Fathers and the Medievals." *Calvin Theological Journal*, April, 1981, 149–151.

[35] Lucien Febvre, *The Problem of Unbelief in the Sixteenth Century: The Religion of Rabelais*, trans. Beatrice Gottlieb (Cambridge: Harvard University Press, 1982), 16.

[36] Hans Frei, *The Eclipse of Biblical Narrative: A Study in Eighteenth and Nineteenth Cen-*

what does this mean for his reception of a tradition of reading? What
does this mean for the way he handled the scriptures, especially those
non-narrative portions of the scripture? Further, though this method of
understanding Calvin is suggestively rich, it does not give much insight
into his frequent use of the tradition. For this reason, I have selected
another option. In this study, I will make the effort to consider interpretation as guided by hermeneutic principles, in which large frameworks
color, and in fact pre-make, some if not all of the choices of interpretation; and of rules, which govern the methodology chosen to explicate
the chosen texts.

I take this method particularly from the work of Karlfried Froehlich.
It is his differentiation between the principles of hermeneutics and the
rules of exegeis which sets out part of the methodological apparatus for
this study. In 1984, Froehlich wrote that

> Patristic hermeneutics (from the Greek *hermeneuein*, to explain, interpret)
> concerns itself with the developing principles and rules for a proper
> understanding of the Bible in the early Christian church. The *principles*
> reflect the theological framework in which the Biblical writings were
> interpreted by different groups and individuals at various times; they
> always included the basic conviction that God's revelation in Jesus Christ
> was central to God's plan of salvation (*oikonomia*) but they left room
> for different readings of major themes such as Israel and the church,
> eschatology, ethics, even Christology, anthropology, and soteriology. The
> *rules* reflect the methodology by which the language of Biblical revelation
> was scrutinized so that it would yield insight into God's *oikonomia* and
> its ramifications for the life of the community; they were often taken
> over from the literary culture of the surrounding world but were then
> developed into new, creative paradigms of literary analysis.[37]

For Froehlich, the difference between hermeneutics and exegesis is crucial to understanding a pre-modern interpreter. What then, will be our
working definition of hermeneutical principles, and exegetical practices
or rules? Principles are the deeper term. These are core conceptions
which the interpreter brings to the task of interpretation, basic presuppositions which the encounter with the text is rather unlikely to
change. If the human consciousness can be conceived as a web, these

---

tury Hermeneutics (New Haven: Yale University Press, 1974), 37. Frei's work on Calvin's
exegesis, which he sets out as a benchmark against which to consider the subsequent
hermeneutical horizons, is enormously suggestive. However, because he is concentrating upon the function of narrative, rather than doctrinal/paranetic discourse, the rele-
vance of his work in the present study is limited.

[37] Karlfried Froehlich, *Biblical Interpretation in the Early Church*, 1.

would be most central, and thus most difficult to reach and change. As the web moves through changes, the outside is constantly being rewoven, as it tatters upon the experiences which the subject encounters. But the basic core principles remain widely constant.[38] As we are seeking to explicate the work of a Christian theologian, these principles will be expressed theologically, though this is not a necessary characteristic of hermeneutic principles—it would in fact be quite remarkable to express the principles of a modern scientist using the language of theology. Further, hermeneutic principles work at such a depth in the subject that they are frequently neither conscious nor articulated. They are part of "the structure of reality" for that person, so are below the level of comment.

Exegetical practices have to do with the method of extricating meaning from a text. Thus, what has passed for the history of exegesis, or history of interpretation, frequently deals only with exegetical practices. Terms such as allegory, literal sense, *sensus germanus*, typology, αναγογη, historical-critical, and philological normally belong to this division. These have the character of tools, the choice of which is as culturally conditioned as the choice of clothing.[39] Interpreters choose a certain set of practices or rules so as to be intelligible to a particular audience, and because they find those practices most useful.[40]

It is frequently difficult to draw clear degrees of separation between principles of hermeneutics and rules of exegesis. This is especially true in authors who stand before the hermeneutical "turn to the subject" of the early portion of the last century. However, although the difficulties in teasing apart the hermeneutical principles and exegetical rules in the thought of any given author are extraordinarily difficult, the possible reward is exceptional. By achieving some clarity on these questions, one may arrive at a tool which supplies another window on the mind

---

[38] Should they not, in this paradigm, the subject would be schizophrenic.

[39] Thus, for example, I differ from Richard C. Gamble's "*Brevitas et Facilitas*: Toward an Understanding of Calvin's Hermeneutic." *Westminster Theological Journal* 47 (1985): 1–17. Gamble posits that brevity is a principle of Calvin's hermeneutic. I offer that it is instead an exegetical practice, adopted for the sake of the audience. In a sense, we do not disagree, because what we mean by hermeneutics and exegesis are fundamentally different.

[40] One normally does not think about interpreters "choosing" their rules of exegesis. But that this is so is nicely laid out in M.L. Monheit's "Young Calvin, Textual Interpretation and Roman Law." *Bibliotheque d'humanisme et renaissance: travaux et documents.* 59, No. 2, (1997): 263–282; where Monheit points out the various models of interpretation opened to Calvin by his teachers, and his subsequent use of them.

of a particular author. In the case of a given theologian, the tool may
even act as a new trajectory of inquiry into discerning how his or her
theology coheres internally, as well as how it relates to the antecedent
and subsequent traditions within the Church.

This is the sort of tool I am attempting to develop, hone, and use
in the present study. It is my contention that Calvin's reception of
tradition concerned the notion of a basic acceptance of the traditional
hermeneutical horizon, while adopting some new rules which give the
superficial appearance of lack of agreement with the tradition in which
he stood. By demonstrating the differences between his principles and
rules, it will be possible to observe how his thought coheres to the broad
tradition which preceded him, while at the same time he transforms
that tradition. Further, by understanding this dynamic, some historical
questions are given a different venue, in which, I will argue, they are
easier to decide.

A key example of this will be in the way that Calvin engages the
doctrine and biblical interpretion of Augustine and Chrysostom. It is
recognized that Augustine is in many ways Calvin's favorite among the
patristic authors. But just as clearly, Chrysostom receives more praise
from Calvin as a biblical commentator. Calvin even began to prepare
an edition of Chrysostom as an aid to reading the Bible for simple
readers.[41] I will argue that Calvin turned to Augustine for a doctrinal-
hermeneutical lens, but adopted instead Chrysostom's method of reading the scriptures. To demonstrate the terminology of this work, Augustine generally was the principal influence in Calvin's hermeneutic,
Chrysostom was the greater authority in Calvin's exegesis.

Thus, one of the goals of this study will be to determine Calvin's
hermeneutical principles, and delineate them from his exegetical practices. Having demonstrated that, the horizon toward which he drives
both his interpretive enterprise and his constructive theology will become clearer. But some mention of that horizon needs to be made now,
to clarify that material which will come later.

What is the horizon which Calvin accepted? For that matter, what
is "horizon," in the first place? The "horizon" which is invoked here
is the historically effected consciousness.[42] Only by recognizing one's

---

[41] Ian Hazlett, "Calvin's Latin Preface to His Proposed French Edition of Chrysostom's Homilies: Translation and Commentary." in *Humanism and Reform: The Church in
Europe, England, and Scotland, 1400–1643* (Cambridge: Basil Blackwell, 1991), 129–150.
[42] The theory of the horizon is common in the modern discussion of hermeneutical

own stance within the stream of historical tradition, and accepting the effective weight of that tradition, can the interpreter of a historical text deal meaningfully with the text from the stance which he or she cannot escape. From within that stream, the possibility appears of true Christian exegesis and exegetical theology which is neither obscurantist echoing of earlier formulations, nor ultra-modern jettisoning of the whole of the Christian tradition, and thus perhaps of the faith.[43]

This openness to the weight of tradition, as we shall see, is frequent in Calvin's interpretation. This interaction with the tradition is neither stultifying nor stodgy, but instead makes possible the whole enterprise of Christian dogmatics which is both in contact with the tradition and making authentic progress possible. The possibility of having a stance within history, facing its claim, is critical for any connection to the Christian faith for the theologian faced with the reality of reclaiming a time and experience that is not immediately his own.[44] For it is only history which can tell the sixteenth century person that the Church in which he stands has a right to claim that it is the same Church that is described in the New Testament documents. Doctrine cannot do so, since it has changed too radically. The words of confessions cannot do so, they do not mean the same to moderns of different world views from the original framers. Only genuine history, which makes a lively demand upon the historian-theologian, can speak to this need.

Calvin's horizon was actually a double horizon. In the first case, Calvin used the model of the early Church, and especially the New Testament community, as a measure by which to determine the ortho-

---

theory, and is especially prevalent in the work of Hans-Georg Gadamer. See his *Truth and Method.*, 2nd rev. edition, translated and revised by Joel Weinsheimer and Donald G. Marshall (New York: Crossroad Publishing, 1989), 361.

[43] Friedrich Schleiermacher, in considering the dogmatic task, asserted that two elements, the common and the peculiar or original, needed to interpenetrate each other for Christian doctrine to avoid stagnation as antiquarianism, or simple ultra-modernism (*Christian Faith*, §25).

[44] Mark Burrows has considered this difficulty in "Jean Gerson on the 'Traditioned Sense' of Scripture as an Argument for an Ecclesial Hermeneutic," in *Biblical Hermeneutics in Historical Perspective*, 152–172, edited by Mark Burrows and Paul Rorem (Grand Rapids: Eerdmans, 1991), esp. 160–164. In this consideration of an "ecclesial hermeneutic" option given by Gerson to answer the difficulty of reaching the proper interpretation of the literal sense, Burrows finds that Gerson's answer of a privileged stance of the primitive church in some ways pre-figures the Reformer's position. However, he does not equate the two, suggesting that the Reformer's hermeneutical stance would be more correctly called a "creedal exegesis." n. 56, 172.

doxy and orthopraxy of later instances of the Church. Calvin's second horizon was the Church of the present and future. This first horizon is necessary to understand Calvin's relationship to the antecedent doctrinal and exegetical traditions. Otherwise, the call for *sola scriptura* may be understood absolutely, and the spectre of individual interpretation arises.[45] This individual interpretation is not allowed by Calvin in either the contemporary situation, nor within the lengthy stream of the Church's proclamation of the truth. Thes two might be considered as the horizontal (contemporary situation), and vertical (Church's tradition), axes. Calvin never permitted a particular individual the task of authoritative interpretation. In this horizontal stance, he stands between two streams of thought that tend in that direction.[46] On the one hand stood Rome, with an individual bishop of Rome as the arbiter of "correct interpretation" of the scriptures.[47] On the other hand, stand (some of) the radical Reformers, who could argue a more explicit *sola scriptura* principle than the magisterial reformers conceived. Finding the guarantee of the correctness of an interpretation to be only the testimony of the Holy Spirit in the mind of the individual goes too far for Calvin.

Similarly, when turning to the vertical consideration of the problem of scriptural interpretation, Calvin again rejected individual authority. In his interpretation, Calvin always felt constrained to answer the questions which had normally been put to various passages of scripture by an antecedent exegetical tradition. His interpretive writings are

---

[45] Gerhard Ebeling makes this point in his "'Sola Scriptura, and Tradition," in *The Word of God and Tradition: Historical Studies Interpreting the Divisions of Christianity*, translated by S.H. Hooke (Philadelphia: Fortress Press, 1968), 102–147. Ebeling demonstrates that the idea of *sola scriptura* as meaning that only the Bible was authoritative and subject to individual interpretation is not in the mind of the Reformers.

[46] The theme of Calvin as standing or balancing between two poles is rather common, though helpful. For a fuller development of this, see Ford Lewis Battles, "God Was Accommodating Himself to Human Capacity," *Interpretation* 31 (1977): 19–38; and Donald McKim, "John Calvin: A Theologian for an Age of Limits." *Readings in Calvin's Theology*, ed. by Donald K. McKim (Grand Rapids: Baker Book House, 1984), 291–310.

[47] I do not wish to suggest, by any means, that this was a monolithic or universally accepted position. Rather, I am stating that the position of the pope as final arbiter of scriptural interpretation would not have been an unfamiliar theory in the first half of the sixteenth century. An extraordinary exception is noted in the case of Jean Gerson, by Mark Burrows, in "Jean Gerson on the 'Traditioned Sense' of Scripture as an Argument for an Ecclesial Hermeneutic," in *Biblical Hermeneutics in Historical Perspective*, edited by Mark Burrows and Paul Rorem (Grand Rapids: Eerdmans, 1991), 152–172. See esp. 161–167, and the defining of a "hermeneutic of tradition."

full of allusions to and discussions of earlier exegetes.[48] The reason is that Calvin did not accord himself a privilege he denied to all other individuals. Instead, the goal is the doctrine of the Church.

To get into the problem of the vertical axis, is simply to re-name one of the motivating questions behind this study. In Calvin, we find a theologian who finds great value in the historical traditions of interpretation of the Church, and yet one who could reject portions of that history, or language about that history, with vigorous finality.[49] Calvin denied what the Council of Trent will call the second source of authority, "tradition."[50] Further, when discussing the instance of a council that went awry, Calvin spared little ink in demonstrating how wrong that council had been.[51] Yet, Calvin shows an overall deference to the ecumenical councils, and the way in which the early Church sets the tone for later obedience to Christ.[52] As the study progresses, I will demonstrate that so far as Calvin was concerned, the Church's doctrine relates to the tradition in the same way as an actual building stands in relation to a first plan or blue-print, except when corrected by the plain sense of Scripture. Calvin was unwilling to depart from the exegetical choices made by his favorite patristic exegetes, unless moved by a clarifying motive. In all this, Calvin exhibited a veneration for contact with the Church which may even shock those who too easily have seen Calvin as less than catholic.

So, in the vertical axis, or historical stream, Calvin did not allow individual authority to become the final arbiter. Not even Augustine,

---

[48] See, for instance, David Steinmetz, "Calvin Among the Thomists: Exegesis of Romans 9," in *Biblical Hermeneutics in Historical Perspective*, edited by Mark Burrows and Paul Rorem (Grand Rapids: Eerdmans, 1991), 198–214, where Steinmetz lays out convincingly that Calvin's exegesis is as often traditionally motivated as it is contextually.

[49] Concerning Calvin's reception of the greatest early historian, Eusebius, see Irena Backus, "Calvin's Judgment of Eusebius of Caesarea." *Sixteenth Century Journal* 22 (1991): 419–437.

[50] The fourth session of Trent stated that "all saving truth and rules of conduct … are contained in the written books and in the unwritten traditions, which, received by the apostles from the mouth of Christ himself, or from the apostles themselves, have come down to us, transmitted as it were from hand to hand." *The Canons and Decrees of Trent*, ed. and trans. H.J. Schroeder (St. Louis: 1941), 17, 296.

[51] James Payton sets out the development of Calvin's understanding and his final position well in his "Calvin and the Legitimation of Icons: His Treatment of the Seventh Ecumenical Council," *Archiv für Reformationsgeschichte* 84 (1993):222–241.

[52] Consider, for instance, Calvin's reception of the ecumenical councils. He writes in the 1559 *Institutes* that "Indeed, I venerate them from my heart, and I wish that they be honored by all." "Veneror enim ea ex animo, suoque in honore apud omnes esse cupio." OS 5,151, 7–8. ICR, IV.ix.1.

arguably Calvin's favorite theologian, was given that authority. No single person's thought about the scripture's message, at any point along the historical spectrum, can be called finally binding. Not Augustine, nor even Calvin himself. For Calvin believed that God has richly divided the knowledge of scripture, so as to encourage human joint discernment. No one has a perfect knowledge of scripture's meaning.[53]

Thus, we find Calvin creating a complex series of interpretive moves, whereby he sets out the defining of Christian truth, or the grounding of interpretation. Three interpenetrating phenomena act as foci, or stress points. Each one makes definite contributions, but those particular contributions are held in dynamic tension by the other two. Further, each one is a workplace of the Holy Spirit. The three are scripture, history, and the Church. This is the ground of interpretation, and the compass from which true direction toward the final Christian horizon is found.

Calvin and Scripture

The definitive consideration of Calvin's use of the terms scripture, gospel, and doctrine has yet to be written.[54] A partial explanation for this gap is the general acceptance that these terms in Calvin are familiar and static. Further, Calvin's shifting usage of terms may have caused some to shy away from this subject out of fear that it is an

---

[53] Calvin, Commentary on Romans, Argument. *Iohannis Calvini Commentarius in Epistolam Pauli ad Romanos*, edited by T.H.L. Parker (Leiden: E.J. Brill, 1981), 3.107–110. "God has never so dignified His servants with the blessing that each possessed a full and perfect understanding of every part of their subject. Without a doubt, his plan was first that we would be kept humble, and also that we should continue to have communication with our brothers." "Nunquam enim tanto beneficio servos suos dignatus est Deus, ut singuli plena perfectaque omni ex parte intelligentia praediti essent. nec dubium quin eo consilio, ut nos in humilitate primum, deinde communicationis fraternae studio retineret."

[54] See Edward A. Dowey, Jr., *The Knowledge of God in Calvin's Theology*, 3rd ed. (Grand Rapids: Wm. B. Eerdmans, 1994), 153–164. Dowey argues that in Calvin's theology there is an unreconciled variance between his idea of the acceptance of scripture and salvation through Christ. "... he must be judged to have two not entirely reconcilable theological explanations of the faithful man's knowledge of God's revelation. This flaw can be described, although he never used the terms, as a discrepancy between the so-called formal and material principles of the Reformation: the authority of Scripture and justification by faith in Christ." (161) Dowey maintains that Calvin finds two objects of faith, Christ and scripture, and does not consider fully the necessary ramifications of such a position.

enormous undertaking that carries no promise of a return. However, it is essential that these terms be examined in order for us to understand the ways in which Calvin's theology operates.

Scriptura sacra: The literature is clear that Calvin held a functionalist canon, as evidenced by his arguments for the canonicity of the book of Hebrews.[55] For Calvin, the content of the Bible, that is, the number of its books, was set. His dispute with Castellio supports this approach. Even in the case of a book upon which Calvin may not have wished to comment, such as the book of Revelation, excising it from the canon was not an option. However, his approach to that scripture has not yet been fully understood. Did Calvin hold that the scripture was not only the self-authenticating, but also self-interpreting?

The answer to this must be set out in the negative. Calvin began his French preface to the *Institutes* of 1560 with the statement that "Although the Holy Scripture contains a perfect doctrine, to which one can add nothing," and goes on to argue for the need for direction in the scripture. But note his verb choice in the crucial passage. "*Combien que la saincte Escriture contienne une doctrine parfaicte.*"[56] Calvin choses *contenir*, meaning "to contain", to argue that scripture *contains* a perfect doctrine but is not itself doctrine.

Evangelium: "Gospel" remained a central term in Calvin's vocabulary throughout his writings. The most cursory consideration of only a few of his works finds him speaking of the gospel both frequently and warmly. But Calvin used the term with more sophistication than is generally acknowledged. One can find in his work a variety of uses of the term gospel, a deliberation on the doctrine of the gospel,[57] a consideration on the whole goal or end of the gospel,[58] a warning that the bad character of ministers through the cunning of Satan can

---

[55] Calvin takes on the arguments immediately in his Hebrews Argumentum. "Ego vero eam inter Apostolicas, sine controversia amplector; nec dubito Satanae artificio fuisse quondam factrum ut illi authoritatem quidam detraherent. Nullus enim est ex Sacris libris qui de Christ sacerdotio tam luculente disserat, unici quod morte sua obtulit, sacrifii vim dignitatemque tam magnifice extollat, de caerenius explicet Chrstum esse finem Legis." *Ioannis Calvini Opera Exegetica, Commentarius in Epistolam ad Hebraeos*, ed. T.H.L. Parker, (Geneva: Droz, 1996), 11. See also Parker's Introduction, xiii–xv.

[56] OS 3.7.18–19.

[57] Comm. I Thessalonians, 1.9, CO 52.144. "Ergo huc tendit evangelii doctrina, ut nos in cultum obsequiumque Dei traducat."

[58] Comm. I Corinthians 1.8, CO 49.313. "Nam hic finis est evangelii, ut Christus noster fiat, ac nos in eis corpus inseramur."

bring the gospel into disrepute,[59] and even such a strikingly unexpected term usage as Paul's gospel.[60] The question then stands begging, what did Calvin intend to signify by his use of the term "gospel," or is his usage so unsystematic as to be an eternal twisting labyrinth waiting to ensnare the unwary scholar, a labyrinth whose exit has perhaps even been covered over?

For Calvin, the gospel is defined as the manifestation of Christ, and the term functions rhetorically as the message or meaning of the scripture, or of a scriptural author, rather than the words of scripture. This is in accord with his definition in the *Institutes*: "I take the gospel as the clear manifestation of the mystery of Christ."[61] In this way, Calvin could occasionally identify the gospel as not being in the words, but in their meanings, and thereby avoid biblicism.

Doctrina is a central concern of this study. Again, one faces the familiar problem of Calvin's nuanced rhetorical use of the term. Sometimes, he can savagely denounce "doctrines" as the wind which comes from men. At other times, he asserts "Hence the purpose of the doctrine of the gospel is to lead us into worship and submission to God."[62] This is a particularly telling example, as it demonstrates a differentiation in Calvin's mind between the gospel and doctrine. Again, he will speak of the need for constant attention to doctrine.[63]

For Calvin, *doctrina* is the taught form of faith. It is closely linked purposely to God's revelation in the scriptures, so that *doctrina* always takes on the character of application of interpretation.[64] This is the

---

[59] Comm II Corinthians 6.3, *Ioannis Calvini Opera Exegetica, Commentarii in Secundum Pauli Epistolam ad Corinthios*, edited by Helmut Feld (Geneva: Droz, 1994), 109.18–19. "Hic enim est astus Satanae: quaerere aliquid vitii in ministris, quod in Evangelii infamiam redundet."

[60] Comm. II Timothy, theme, CO 52.342. Argumentum. "Postea brevem evangelii sui summam complexus, Timotheo praecipit ut eam aliis quoque tradat, et curet ad posteros propagari."

[61] OS 3.399.26–27, ICR II.ix.2, "Evangelium accipio pro clara mysterii Christi manifestatione."

[62] Comm. I Thessalonians 1.9. CO 52.144. "Ergo huc tendit evangelii doctrina, ut nos in cultum obsequiumque Dei traducat."

[63] Comm I Thessalonians 3.10. CO 52.158. "Hence it is still clear how necessary it our constant attention to doctrine; for teachers (doctors) were not set apart in order actually to bring men to faith in Christ in one day, but in order to perfect the faith which is unformed." "Hinc etiam patet quam necessaria sit nobis doctrinae assiduitas: neque enim in hoc tantum ordinati sunt doctores ut uno die vel mense homines adducant ad fidem Christi, sed ut fidem inchoatam perficiant."

[64] Neuser comments that "Der Begriff Lehre (doctrina) wird von ihm in der Institutio sehrt häufig verwendet. Die Lehre wird meistens himmlische Lehre (doctrina

teaching which must edify, and when understood, has a dispositional force.[65] *Doctrina* is a knowledge that when duly understood, becomes a driving force within the life of the hearer. Calvin wrote, "And this especially is to be observed, we are summoned to a knowledge of God: not one which is content with empty speculation and merely flies in the brain, but that which will be solid and fruitful if we rightly understand it, and if it takes root in the heart."[66] The word play in which Calvin opposes brain (*cerebro*) and heart (*corde*), is significant. Knowledge in the brain flies about, while that of the heart takes deep root. Calvin claimed that the act of perception in the brain or psychological center is insufficient for a Christian life. Instead, he demanded a knowledge that takes root so deeply that it compels action.

Scripture, comprising the sixty-six books of the Old and New Testaments, is the carrier of the message of salvation, and of God's will. It is the vehicle of the gospel, which is the message of salvation. Gospel contains the whole of the message of Jesus Christ, and his benefits. It tells of both salvation and of sanctification. That message, however, must be applied, and that is the role of doctrine. In order to be true, doctrine must pass the test of edification, since any actual application of the message of salvation into a particular community must build that community up into Christ. A particular doctrine may change as the needs of the particular community and the vagaries of history change, but the objective principle, holy scripture, remains the same, and the central core of its message, the gospel, remains recognizably constant.

---

coelestis) genannt. Damit wird klargestellt, daß sie aus der Scrhift und also von Gott stammt. Der doctrina coelestis entspricht das verbum dei. Doctrina ist vie verbum Dei ein Allgemeinbegriff, dessen Bezug zur heiligen Schrift und zur Verkündigung der Erklärung bedarf." "Calvins Verständnis der Heiligen Schrift," in *Calvinus Sacrae Scripturae Professor*, International Congress on Calvin Research, edited by Wilhelm Neuser (Grand Rapids: Eerdmans, 1994), 55.

[65] For a consideration of the dispositional character of Calvin's theology and rhetoric, see Jones, 13–30.

[66] OS 3.53.10–14. ICR I.v.9. "Atque hic rursus observandum est, invitari nos ad Dei notitiam, non quae inani speculatione contenta in cerebro tantum volitet, sed quae solida futura sit et fructuosa si rite percipiatur a nobis, radicemque agat in corde."

Calvin and History

Calvin believed that understanding an historical document, including a biblical text, required knowledge of the contextual circumstances to which it spoke. On the other hand, such sophistication never prevented Calvin from appreciating the trans-historical message of the gospel carried within the tradition. Calvin, in fact, was a traditionalist. "If Calvin has such a value for traditional exegesis, why is his own exegesis so clearly non-traditional?" This question may be given different forms, such as "If Calvin's doctrine is clearly Augustinian, why is his exegesis so clearly not?" This question needs to be further nuanced. Is Calvin's doctrine truly Augustinian? For that matter, what is signified by the term "Augustinian?" Since 1957 and the publication of Luchesius Smits' magisterial study of Calvin's use of Augustine's thought,[67] Calvin has been regarded as standing within the "broad augustinian tradition."[68] Although certain points in his thought are demonstrably mediated through other readers of Augustine, such as Luther,[69] or can be more profitably considered as coming from other sources,[70] Calvin's theology

---

[67] Luchesius Smits, *Saint Augustin dans L'œuvre de Jean Calvin* (Assen: Van Gorcum Comp., 1957).

[68] The term "augustinian" or Augustinian, has come to carry far too many connotations to be used with confidence of referent quality. That there were different streams of thought in the Middle Ages which claimed, either correctly or incorrectly, to be based in Augustine's theology, is a commonplace. The question can be asked whether this is a useful distinction. I cannot answer that question here, but feel that it is. Certainly Calvin believed that his theology was a correct resumption of the doctrine of the church fathers, and especially of Augustine's. The term "broad Augustinian tradition," is coined here to refer to a stream of Christian thought which is recognizable by a high doctrine of grace, a dependence upon scriptural and rhetorical rather than logical proofs, and a radical doctrine of sin.

[69] Alexandre Ganoczy, in the most complete study of Calvin's early thought outside of Doumergue, discusses eight particular sources for Calvin's early work, i.e., the work up to and including the first edition of the Institutes. He considers the most important to be Luther, Melanchthon, Zwingli, Bucer, Gratian, Lombard, Lefèvre, and Erasmus. Obviously, at least six of these sources would offer "readings" of Augustine to Calvin. *The Young Calvin*, trans. David Foxgrover and Wade Provo (Philadelphia: Westminster Press, 1987), 133–181.

[70] Sources are a particular and perennial problem in Calvin's writing. Since he does not cite regularly nor fully, a cottage industry has arisen in tracing his sources and influences, both in particular works and in his theology as a whole. This process of tracking sources is further complicated by his ongoing reading and development, clearly visible through the various editions of his *Institutes* and commentaries. On this issue, see Ganoczy, 133–181; A.N.S. Lane, "Calvin's Use of the Fathers and the Medievals," *Calvin Theological Journal*, April, 1981, 149–200; Lane, "Calvin's Sources

so frequently echoes the bishop of Hippo that few scholars would debate Calvin's overall debt to Augustine.[71]

But how can this study move so quickly from a consideration of tradition, to that of Augustine? Simply put, Calvin accepted the broad normative character of Augustine's theology as setting out patristic orthodoxy. When Calvin spoke of Augustine, though he did so polemically, he frequently was addressing a broad orthodoxy which may never have existed.[72] In particular cases, Calvin could and did criticize Augustine ferociously. But in general, he presented Augustine as a particularly clear instance of a consensus that he believed existed among the fathers.

However, while Calvin owed a tremendous debt to Augustine, and even some later Augustinians, this doctrinal dependence was frequently obscured in his more exegetical works.[73] This concealment may be considered under three causes. First, Calvin's exegetical method was self-consciously almost wholly different from that of his pre-Reformation Augustinian predecessors. He bitterly railed against any use of the tool of allegory, and vigorously chided those who might still consider it a useful device. Secondly, Calvin mentioned his forebearers far less often in his commentaries than in his more doctrinal works, giving the (false) impression that he is simply interpreting the text with the help of a very small dependence on Erasmus' New Testament.[74] Thirdly, Calvin frequently disagreed explicitly with Augustine or other prominent Augustinians in his commentaries.[75]

---

of Saint Bernard." *Archiv für Reformationsgeschichte* 67 (1976):253–283; Alister McGrath, "John Calvin and Late Mediaeval Thought: A Study in Late Mediaeval Influences upon Calvin's Theological Development," *Archiv für Reformationsgeschichte* 77 (1986): 58–78; and Karl Reuter, *Das Grundverständnis der Theologie Calvins: unter Einbezeihung ihrer geschichtlichen Abhangigkeiten* (Neukirchen-Vluyn, 1963).

[71] A.N.S. Lane, "Calvin's Use of the Fathers and the Medievals," Appendix II, 201–205.

[72] A.N.S. Lane, "Calvin's Use of the Fathers and the Medievals," 159.

[73] A.N.S. Lane, "Calvin's Use of the Fathers and the Medievals," 201–205. Lane includes an extraordinarily helpful appendix of works cited in the 1559 *Institutes*. Although it is clear that Augustine holds the pride of place, Augustinian theologians such as Anselm, Bernard, Cassiodorus, Gregory the Great, and Aquinas are also mentioned.

[74] David Steinmetz has adequately proven that regardless the amount of explicit citation, Calvin's commentaries display a mind which feels constrained to consider the tradition of commenting, as well as the text upon which commentary is being made. See his *Calvin in Context* (Oxford: Oxford University Press, 1995), which collects several of his most important articles on this topic.

[75] Calvin most often disagrees with Augustine's exegetical or interpretive moves. This will prove to be a significant point.

Thus, a set of questions presents itself. If Calvin was within the "broad augustinian tradition," why did his exegesis differ so radically from his pre-Reformation predecessors? Can it be that the last forty years of Calvin scholarship needs to be re-considered, that Calvin is not an Augustinian? No. Even within Calvin's commentaries, the doctrinal points on which Calvin chose to draw parallels with Augustine are too frequent to be ignored. Thus, the question is not "Is Calvin an Augustinian?" but, rather, "Why did Calvin depart so radically from the exegetical models that generated the doctrinal mold which he wishes to hold? Why did Calvin hold Augustine's doctrine while rejecting his exegesis?"

How did Calvin use the Christian tradition in his approach to scripture? For that matter, what effective voice can a scholar who advocates *ad fontes* give to an intervening interpretive tradition? A first step is a determination of Calvin's own approach to scripture. This must be followed by an examination of the relationship between scripture and doctrine. If Calvin is able to differentiate between exegesis and doctrine from his main model, Augustine, then that suggests a certain instrumental character to the tool of the exegetical model. This must be addressed with some vigor, or the proper foundation for considering his relation to the antecedent tradition will not exist.

Calvin's adoption of a traditional doctrinal horizon is far more significant to the consideration of the exegetical basis of his theology than the rejection of the rule of allegory, which many later scholars have seen as his major contribution to the art of interpretation. In this opposition of poles, or placement within a circle, Calvin can be seen accepting the traditional and doctrinal approach to the scriptures, while constantly judging that approach by the living voice speaking from the scripture.

Calvin and the Church

In 1543, only returned from Strasbourg two years, Calvin had come to believe that one of the key virtues of the Reformers was the re-introduction of particular knowledge of the scriptures.[76] In fact, this "rescue" of the body of believers from the "deep darkness" of ignorance

---

[76] This is not to argue that the pre-Reformation believer was without knowledge of the scriptures. But her reading of them in the vernacular, and struggling with their meaning, would have been far more rare than it became in the Reformation.

of the scriptures became central to Calvin's understanding of the visible Church.[77] The Church, for Calvin, is a set of readers of scripture.

However, the Church must be considered under two headings. First, the Church is a historical and mystical entity, enlivened and guarded by the Holy Spirit. Secondly, the Church is the present body of the faithful, working to understand the will of God and bring it about, however imperfectly, in this particular time and place. For this reason, the contemporary Church never abandons the lessons of the historical Church, but neither can it slavishly ape them. Rather, as we shall demonstrate, it must have the courage to transform the message in order to apply it in changed historical circumstance, guided by the testimony of the Holy Spirit, and the witness of Scripture.

Conclusion

The table is now set. Several points, though not presently clear, are involved in this study. First, Calvin used a theological hermeneutic in his approach to and work from the scriptures. He did this unconsciously, but often enough to demonstrate analyzable patterns. Demonstrating these hermeneutical principles will be the focus of the second chapter. Secondly, Calvin employed a set of exegetical rules to help explicate the text, rules which frequently bear the mark of his humanistic training. Revealing those rules and setting forth their working will be the focus of the third chapter.

The fourth chapter will consider the end or horizon toward which Calvin drove his interpretive project. It is here that we will see Calvin's effort at receiving the doctrinal and interpretive traditions of the Church, and his transformation of them. The specific case of Calvin's relationship to Augustine will be taken up in the fifth chapter. I will argue that Calvin can and does critique Augustine and Augustinians, especially in their exegetical procedures. In doing so, he differentiates clearly between an approval of Augustinian doctrine and formation, and a general denial of Augustinian exegetical styles. This aligns closely

---

[77] Of course, this was not an issue which Calvin could claim solely for those who accepted his teaching. Erasmus had earlier desired that all people, even the lowliest women read the Gospels and the Pauline Epistles. Erasmus, "The *Paraclesis*" in *Desiderius Erasmus: Christian Humanism and the Reformation, Selected Writings*, ed. John C. Olin (Gloucester: Peter Smith, 1973), 97.

to the difference between hermeneutic principles and exegetical rules. After that is set, I will make an argument about Calvin's transformative model for reception of the whole of tradition, this will be the subject of the sixth chapter. In the final chapter, I will consider again the circle of scripture, history and the Church that Calvin uses as the key to the interpretation of the scripture, and will offer that this dynamic tension also provides a more helpful starting point from which to approach Calvin's theology in general.

CHAPTER TWO

HERMENEUTICAL PRINCIPLES

Calvin's work as a doctrinal theologian has always been recognized as having an enormous influence, especially in countries where Reformed denominations held particular sway.[1] Today, that recognition has extended more particularly towards Calvin's exegetical work.[2] Through pioneering work performed in the last four decades, Calvin is widely recognized as one of the more celebrated scripture scholars of the sixteenth century.[3] However, that recognition has not brought full agreement on some of the foundational issues in Calvin's interpretive work. Modern scholars have argued about Calvin's hermeneutics, his relation to the previous exegetical traditions, and his exegetical/doctrinal goals.[4]

---

[1] For example, David Steinmetz writes "In short, although Calvinism is not the only ingredient in American intellectual and religious history, it is such an important ingredient that no one can claim to understand American history and culture without some appreciation of its Calvinist heritage." *Calvin in Context* (Oxford: Oxford University Press, 1995), 5.

[2] Steinmetz points out the irony of the late-modern recognition of Calvin as a biblical interpreter, when he notes that Calvin saw even his major theological work, the *Institutes*, as a guide to scripture. See his *Calvin in Context*, 64.

[3] See T.H.L. Parker, *Calvin's New Testament Commentaries* 1st ed., 1971, 2d ed., (Louisville: Westminster John Knox Press, 1993); *Calvin's Preaching* (Louisville: Westminster/John Knox Press, 1992); *Calvin's Old Testament Commentaries* (Edinburgh: T. & T. Clark, 1986); *Commentaries on Romans: 1532–1542* (Edinburgh: T. & T. Clark, 1986), esp. 71–77. Parker wrote in 1971 that it was a "strange task" to have to defend the importance of Calvin's commentaries, and by extension his biblical work in general. Parker's bewilderment is even more understandable when the *Institutes* itself is considered. On page after page, the biblical quotations literally swarm through the text, diverting the eye and mind from a too-easy grasp of the flow of Calvin's rhetoric. One noteworthy predecessor to Parker is Frederic Farrar's opinion of Calvin in his Bampton Lectures of 1885, published as *History of Interpretation* (New York: E.P. Dutton, 1886), 342–352.

[4] Besides, and because of Parker, the literature upon Calvin's hermeneutics or exegesis has become vastly popular over the last three decades. A sense of the trends can be gained from the following works, listed chronologically. Emil G. Kraeling, *The Old Testament Since the Reformation* (London: Lutterworth Press, 1955); H. Jackson Forstman, *Word and Spirit: Calvin's Doctrine of Biblical Authority* (Stanford, CA: Stanford University Press, 1962); Hans Frei, *The Eclipse of Biblical Narrative: A Study in Eighteenth and Nineteenth Century Hermeneutics* (New Haven, Yale University Press, 1974), 19–37; Alexandre Ganoczy and Stefan Scheld, *Die Hermeneutik Calvins: Geistesgeschichtliche Voraussetzungen und Grundzüge* (Wiesbaden: Franz Steiner Verlag GMBH, 1983); Richard C. Gamble, "*Brevitas et Facil-*

Little work has been done to consider the relationship between his doc-trine, represented in such works as the *Institutes* and the treatises, and his more strictly exegetical work.[5] It is to this part of the study that we now turn. I propose to consider Calvin's approach to scripture, his reception

---

itas: Toward an Understanding of Calvin's Hermeneutic." *Westminster Theological Journal* 47 (1985): 1–17; Gamble, "Exposition and Method in Calvin." *Westminster Theological Journal* 49 (1987): 153–165; Roland M. Frye, "Calvin's Theological Use of Figurative Language." *John Calvin and the Church*, edited by Timothy George (Louisville: Westminster John Knox Press, 1991), 172–194; George Stroup, "Narrative in Calvin's Hermeneutic," *John Calvin and the Church*, 158–171; David L. Puckett, *John Calvin's Exegesis of the Old Testament* Columbia Series in Reformed Theology. (Louisville: Westminster John Knox Press, 1995); Max Engammare, "Calvin connaissait-il la Bible?" *Bulletin de la Societe de L'Histoire du Protestantisme Francais* 141 (1995): 163–184; Erik A. de Boer, "Hermeneutische Schlüssel zur alttestamentlichen Prophetie in Calvins Hesekiel predigten." *Calvinus Sacrae Scripturae Professor*, International Congress on Calvin Research, edited by Wilhelm Neuser (Grand Rapids: Eerdmans, 1994), 199–208; Hans Helmut Esser, "Die Lehre vom 'testimonium Spiritus Sancti internum' bei Calvin innerhalb seiner Lehre von der Heiligen Schrift." *Verbindliches Zeugnis. Vol. 2: Schriftauslegung-Lehramt-Rezeption, edited by Wolfhart Pannenberg. Dialog der Kirchen 9* (Freiburg im Breisgau: Herder; Gottingen: Vandenhoeck & Ruprecht, 1995), 246–258; Vincent Bru, "La notion d'accommodation divine chez Calvin: Ses implications theologiques et exegetiques." *La Revue Reformee* 49 (1998): 79–91; Jean-Marc Berthoud, "La formation des pasteurs et la predication de Calvin." *La revue reformee* 49 (1998): 19–44. Another way of measuring this could be to compare Parker's bewilderment with the lack of attention to Calvin's interpretive work in 1971, to Alexandre Ganoczy and Stefan Scheld's statement in 1983 that "Das Schrift- und Auslegungsverständnis Calvins ist schon mehrfach Gegenstand wissenschaftlicher Untersuchungen gewesen." *Die Hermeneutik Calvins: Geistesgeschichtliche Voraussetzungen und Grundzüge* (Wiesbaden: Franz Steiner Verlag GMBH, 1983), 1.

On exegetical traditions, some of the most significant work done here can fre-quently either be attributed to the pen or the influence of David Steinmetz. See especially David C. Steinmetz, *Calvin in Context* (Oxford: Oxford University Press, 1995), this gathers together some of Professor Steinmetz' more trenchant essays; Susan Schreiner, "'Through a Mirror Dimly': Calvin's Sermons on Job." *Calvin Theological Journal* 21 (1986): 175–193; Schreiner, *Where Shall Wisdom Be Found? Calvin's Exegesis of Job from Medieval and Modern Perspectives* (Chicago: University of Chicago Press, 1994); John Thompson, *The Daughters of Sarah: Women in Regular and Exceptional Roles in the Exegesis of Calvin, His Predecessors, and His Contemporaries* (Geneve: Librairie Droz, 1992). Beyond this school, Alexandre Ganoczy and Stefan Scheld's *Die Hermeneutik Calvins: Geistesgeschichtliche Voraussetzungen und Grundzüge* includes a significant overview of the development of medieval hermeneutics, 9–47; see also Robert H. Ayers, "The View of Medieval Biblical Exegesis in Calvin's Institutes," *Perspectives in Religious Studies* 7 (1980): 188–193.

   [5] A significant exception is the work of Ganoczy and Scheld, *Die Hermeneutik Calvins*, which bluntly puts forward an extraordinarily doctrinal hermeneutic. "Unsere Unter-suchung wird verdeutlichen, daß sich Calvin sehr wohl darum bemüht, die Auslegung im Sinne der 'analogia fidei' durchzuführen, wobei das Apostolicum, nach dessen Grundstruktur in überraschender Weise sein Argument des Epheserbriefkommentars augfgebaut ist." 4.

of the Church's exegetical tradition, and the relation of those two elements to his doctrine, under three headings. The first is a consideration of Calvin's hermeneutic.[6] The second, the subject of the next chapter, is a discussion of some of the particular habits Calvin uses when he does exegesis. The third, discussed in the fourth chapter, is a suggestion of the goal toward which Calvin drives all of his hermeneutical principles and exegetical practices.

To begin, it is essential to revist the issue of hermeneutical principles and exegetical rules or practices, and to emphasize the distinction between them that informs this study of Calvin's work.[7] Although often used interchangeably by many scholars, hermeneutics refers to principles while exegesis to interpretive practice.[8] Hermeneutics illuminate

---

[6] Hans-Joachim Kraus has set out Calvin's hermeneutics in his "Calvins exegetische Prinzipien." *Zeitschrift für Kirchengeschichte*, 79, (1968): 329–341, translated as "Calvin's Exegetical Principles." *Interpretation* 31 (1977): 8–18. Several problems exist with this work. First, Kraus provides very little recourse to the commentaries, depending too much on the *Institutes*. Second, there is no differentiation between principles of hermeneutics and practices of exegesis. Finally, the model for the study has been an unfortunately modern stance that Calvin is understood as important for what he contributes to the later history of exegesis, from the perspective of the twentieth century. Kraus supplies eight principles. These are 1) Clarity and brevity; 2) Intention of the author; 3) Circumstances; 4) Real meaning; 5) Context; 6) Going beyond the literal wording; 7) Metaphorical expressions; 8) Scope of Christ. Richard Muller has considered this work carefully in his "The Hermeneutic of Promise and Fulfillment in Calvin's Exegesis of the Old Testament Prophecies of the Kingdom," In *The Bible in the 16th Century*, edited by David Steinmetz (Durham: Duke University Press, 1990), 68–82. I shall consider the portions of Kraus' work throughout my exposition of Calvin's hermeneutics and exegesis.

[7] Alexandre Ganoczy and Stefan Scheld have argued that Calvin clearly approaches the scripture, as all interpreters do, with presuppositions about its meaning which are not grounded in the particular text. *Die Hermeneutik Calvins*, 4. Though I argue for a broader understanding of textual grounding, the point does support my contention of a hermeneutic schema.

[8] This is a unique distinction in Calvin scholarship. Because of my dependence upon it, I depart from some of the more significant articles and monographs on Calvin's hermeneutics and exegesis. Frequently, this is because those works are not attempting to delineate between hermeneutics and exegesis, or do not recognize a difference between those terms. Thus, Richard C. Gamble, in his "*Brevitas et Facilitas*: Toward an Understanding of Calvin's Hermeneutic." *Westminster Theological Journal* 47 (1985): 1–17, sees Calvin copying the rhetoric of the scriptures themselves. (15) While this is a profound observation, it does not help to consider the continuity of Calvin's theology, based on his understanding of the scripture, with those who held different exegetical methods. Further, if this states the whole case, one needs to question the order of the scriptures. Calvin states that Romans is the key to the scriptures, but why place the key so late? Gamble's "Exposition and Method in Calvin," *Westminster Theological Journal* 49 (1987): 153–165 does not further the consideration of

deep conceptions that the person brings to the task of interpretation, basic pre-suppositions that remain unchanged by the encounter with the text.[9] Though such conceptions are below the level of notice, they are detectable to the later historian.[10]

Exegetical rules, on the other hand, concern the manner in which a person deals with specific issues in texts. Frequently, scholarship on historical biblical interpretation has concentrated upon these exegetical practices.[11] The terminology is highly specialized, using specific language such as allegory, literal sense, *sensus germanus*, typology, and αναγογη. The key to the necessity of the hermeneutics/exegesis discussion is that once the scholar has discovered the exegetical rules used by a particular author the task remains to determine *why* he or she has done so!

Calvin's hermeneutic, but adopts Gamble's earlier posture, and places it within the *via media*, a theory of Calvin's theology characterized by avoiding paired extremes. J.L.M. Haire's "John Calvin as an Expositor." *Irish Biblical Studies* 4 (1982): 2–16 is too brief to make a contribution, while Hans-Joachim Kraus' "Calvin's Exegetical Principles," mixes principles and rules. Alexandre Ganoczy and Stefan Scheld have constructed the most significant effort in their *Die Hermeneutik Calvins: Geistesgeschichtliche Voraussetzungen und Grundzüge* (Wiesbaden: Franz Steiner Verlag GMBH, 1983), and this work will be continually referred to throughout this chapter. But Ganoczy and Scheld do not differentiate between practices and principles—considering *Schriftzeugnis und Geistzeugnis* alongside *Textkritik*. Other studies have not attempted to set out Calvin's whole hermeneutic, but have concentrated upon a specific aspect or text. They will be cited in due course. Finally, Thomas F. Torrances's lengthy monograph, *The Hermeneutics of John Calvin*, (Edinburgh: Scottish Academic Press, 1988), deserves mention, as soundly setting out a particular propaedeutic for considering Calvin's hermeneutics. However, since most of the effort is spent on preliminary discussions, perhaps this more correctly deserves the title of *Calvin's Epistemology*.

[9] Though I am proposing a methodology which employs a distinction which is not standard in Calvin studies, this does not mean that others have not seen certain items of greater permanence and power in Calvin's approach to the scripture, which I take to be hermeneutic principles. For instance, Brian G. Armstrong, depending upon the Psalms commentary, notes Calvin's employment of the dual-authorship principle of hermeneutics, and the importance of holding the Spirit together with the Word. See his "Report on the seminar: An investigation of Calvin's principles of Biblical interpretation." *Hervormde teologiese studies*, 54, No. 1–2, (1998): 133–142.

[10] Thus, the necessity of demonstration. This difficulty occasionally bedevils scholars, who find wonderful ideas in Calvin's thought or work, only to be unable to demonstrate them. See the discussion of Alexandre Ganoczy and Stefan Scheld, *Die Hermeneutik Calvins*, 2–3.

[11] See Karlfried Froehlich's 1996 Warfield Lecture, published as "'Aminadab's Chariot': The Predicament of Biblical Interpretation," in *Princeton Seminary Bulletin*, 18, 1997, 262–278. See especially his discussion and rejection of the study of historical interpretation only through rules, 273–276.

Our purpose is to offer an understanding of the relationship between Calvin's theological hermeneutics and his exegetical rules. This is not straightforward, and I am mindful that the distinction between the two can be both artificial and heuristic.[12] Calvin did not set out a system that he then rigorously followed. Nor did he make conscious choices of how his hermeneutical principles might have primacy over his exegetical rules—to say so would conflict with our understanding of hermeneutical principles as generally existing below the surface of consciousness. However, when we examine the two levels separately, certain key issues stand out in greater relief, allowing greater understanding.[13]

The most important text for Calvin's hermeneutics was his dedicatory epistle to Simon Grynaeus, which was appended to the first edition of his first published scriptural commentary, the commentary on Romans.[14] Calvin wrote to Grynaeus about the task of the interpreter, and possible contemporary models for interpretation.[15] Despite prais-

---

[12] Alexandre Ganoczy writes "Eine Hermeneutik ohne Exegese würde in der Luft hängen …" "Hermeneutische Korrelationen bei Calvin." *Reformatio Ecclesiae. Beitrage zu Kirchlichen Reformbemuhungen von der Alten Kirche bis zur Neuzeit. Festgabe fur Erwin Iserloh,* hrsg. von Remigius Baumer (Zurich: Schoningh, 1980), 617.

[13] Richard C. Gamble noted in 1988 that "… there has been, till now, no in-depth study in the English language of the relationship between Calvin's theology and his exegetical method." "Calvin as Theologian and Exegete: Is There Anything New?" *Calvin Theological Journal* 23 (1988): 193.

[14] I must note here that this is simply a setting out of Calvin's hermeneutical principles. This is expressly not an effort to demonstrate that his hermeneutic principles differentiate him from those of patristic or medieval authors. See Richard A. Muller's "The Hermeneutic of Promise and Fulfillment in Calvin's Exegesis of the Old Testament Prophecies of the Kingdom," 68–82 in *The Bible in the 16th Century,* edited by David Steinmetz, (Durham: Duke University Press, 1990), 69.

[15] Calvin notes that he will say nothing of the ancients, then specifies those who have done the principal work. Comm. Romans, Dedicatory epistle, *Iohannis Calvini Commentarius in Epistolam Pauli ad Romanos,* edited by T.H.L. Parker, (Leiden: E.J. Brill, 1981), 2.41–59. "I will remain silent about the ancient commentators, whose piety, erudition, sanctity and age have secured them such great authority that we should not despise anything which they have produced. To those who are alive today, nothing will be gained in mentioning them all by name. Concerning those who have done the most distinguished work, I will give my opinion. Philip Melanchthon, on account of the extraordinary character of his learning, and his industriousness and the deftness which he brings to all the types of disciplines in which he excels, more than those who have published commentaries before him, has given much light. But since it is clear that his only object was to discuss the points which were especially worthy of observation, he therefore remains at length on these, and passes by many things which can perplex those of common understanding. Bullinger came next, who for his merit has gained great approval. Bullinger explained doctrine with such facility, and for this he has been widely approved. Finally there comes Bucer, who spoke the last word on the subject

ing much that is admirable in the work of his contemporary reforming commentators, Calvin had found deficiencies that he hoped to address in his own work.[16] Calvin set out his own ideal, writing that "Because it is almost his [the interpreter's] only responsibility to make accessi-

---

with the publication of his writings. Because he is a man of such profound erudition, and such great knowledge of a variety of things, in addition possessed of such ability of discernment, being widely read, and having so many other talents in which he is excelled by hardly anyone at the present day, this one is superior to very many. He especially should be praised that no one in memory has been more exacting or diligent in interpreting scripture than he." "De veteribus sileo: quibus pietas, eruditio, sanctimonia, aetas denique tantum authoritatis fecit, ut nihil quod ab ipsis profectum sit, contemnere debeamus. Ac eos etiam qui hodie vivunt, nominatim omnes commemorare nihil attinet. De iis qui praecipuam operam navarunt, dicam quod sentio. Philippus Melanchthon pro singulari et doctrina, et industria, et dexteritate qua in omni disciplinarum genere pollet, prae iis qui ante ipsum in publicum prodierant, multum lucis intulit. Sed quia illi propositum modo fuisse apparet, quae in primis essent animadversione digna, excutere: in iis dum immoratur, multa consulto praeterit quae vulgare ingenium fatigare nonnihil possint. Sequutus est Bullingerus, qui et ipse magnam suo merito laudem adeptus est. habuit enim coniunctam cum doctrina facilitatem, qua se magnopere approbavit. Tandem Bucerus, lucubrationibus suis emissis, veluti colophonem imposuit. Siquidem vir ille (ut nosti) praeter reconditam eruditionem, copiosamque multarum rerum scientiam, praeter ingenii perspicaciam, multam lectionem, aliasque multas ac varias virtutes quibus a nemine fere hodie vincitur, cum paucis est conferendus, plurimos antecellit: hanc sibi propriam laudem habet, quod nullus hac memoria exactiore diligentia in Scripturae interpretatione versatus est."

[16] Calvin does not note any other commentators by name, though Parker makes it clear that he is aware of other patterns of exegetical method open to him, noting those of Aquinas, Nicholas of Lyra, Faber Stapulensis, and Erasmus. T.H.L. Parker, *Calvin's New Testament Commentaries*, 2nd ed., 97–99.

Comm. Romans, Dedicatory epistle, Ad Romanos 2.68–3.79. "In addition, I had hoped that by using a different kind of writing I would not be accused of envy, which was my primary fear. Philip indeed attained what he wished by demonstrating the principal points which were necessary. He passed over many things which are not to be neglected, because of his primary occupation. He did not wish to prevent others from examining them also. Bucer is more wordy than is helpful for people who have other matters with which to deal are able to read quickly, and he is more profound than the more humble and less intelligent and attentive readers are able to grasp. For whatever the topic he takes up, so many ideas are suggested as at hand by his incredible and ingenius fecundity of mind, that he does not know how to take the tablet from his hand. Since, therefore, the former author has not followed into every detail, while the latter has done so at greater length than can be read in a short time, it did not seem to me that what I wished to do had the appearance of jealousy." "Ad haec, sperabam fore ut in diverso scribendi genere nulla aemulationis invidia premerer, quae mihi in primis timenda erat. Philippus enim quod voluit adeptus est, ut maxime necessaria capita illustraret. Multa quae negligenda non sunt, dum in illis primis occupatus praetermisit, noluit alios impedire quin ea quoque excuterent. Bucerus et prolixior est quam ut ab hominibus aliis occupationibus districtis raptim legi: et sublimior quam ab humilibus et non valde attentis intelligi facile queat. Nam ad cuiuscunque argumenti tractationem se contulit, tam multa illi ad manum suggeruntur

ble the mind of the writer whom he has undertaken to explicate, he wanders away from that aim, or at least strays outside his goals, by the extent to which he leads his readers away from that meaning."[17] This passage reveals an ideal neither ideologically nor theologically cast. Rather, the effort concentrates totally upon the understanding of the mind of the writer. Perhaps this hermeneutical principle helps to explain the frequently mentioned "modern" character of Calvin's commentaries.[18] Concentrating upon a classical model of interpretation, he anticipates Schleiermacher by more than two hundred fifty years.[19]

---

ab incredibili, qua pollet, ingenii foecunditate, ut manum de tabula tollere nesciat. Quum ergo alter non omnia sit persequutus, alter fusius sit persequutus quam ut exiguo tempore perlegi possint: nullam aemulationis speciem habere institutum meum mihi videbatur." Calvin does not mention Bullinger in the list of shortcomings. This fact has led Fritz Büsser to theorize that Calvin uses Bullinger as his model exegete. See his "Bullinger as Calvin's Model in Biblical Exposition: An Examination of Calvin's Preface to the Epistle to the Romans," 64–95 in *In Honor of John Calvin, 1509–1564*, edited by E.J. Furcha (Montreal: Faculty of Religious Studies, McGill University, 1987). Büsser's extensive claims are modified in Joel Kok's "Heinrich Bullinger's Exegetical Method: The Model for Calvin?" in *Biblical Interpretation in the Era of the Reformation*, edited by Richard A. Muller and John L. Thompson (Grand Rapids: Eerdmans, 1996), 241–254.

[17] Comm. Romans, Dedicatory epistle. "Et sane quum hoc sit prope unicum illius officium, mentem scriptoris, quem explicandum sumpsit, patefacere: quantum ab ea lectores abduxit, tantundem a scopo suo aberrat, vel certe a suis finibus quodammodo evagatur."

[18] Frederic W. Farrar, *History of Interpretation*. New York, Dutton, 1886. Reprint edition (Grand Rapids, Baker Book House, 1961), 343–345. Without going into great detail here, an interjection on Calvin's reception by later generations might be helpful. Frequently, 19th and 20th century biblical scholars have seen in Calvin's work a true value, in those portions which seem to anticipate the historical-critical method. This view then characterizes Calvin as standing at a nexus in history, and explains some of his non-anticipatory themes as "hold-overs" from the medieval period. This project seems to be some of the most Whiggish history possible, and is unhelpful for understanding Calvin. Far better, as Richard Muller states in "The Hermeneutic of Promise and Fulfillment in Calvin's Exegesis of the Old Testament Prophecies of the Kingdom," *The Bible in the 16th Century*, edited by David Steinmetz, (Durham: Duke University Press, 1990), 68–82, (69) "Finally, I submit that any discussion of Calvin's exegetical principles that tends to distinguish the 'critical' principles with which Calvin adumbrates modern exegesis from the few embarrassing 'precritical' principles remaining in Calvin's method has missed the crucial historical question of how all of Calvin's exegetical and hermeneutical principles came to belong to one fairly consistent whole."

[19] Calvin "anticipates" Schleiermacher's insistence upon the nature of hermeneutics as the unfolding of the mind of the author. Although Calvin never states a hermeneutic as systematically as Schleiermacher, at various points within his work one can see the same kind of processes as those which the "Father of hermeneutics" will later set down as a system.

Although the Romans dedication is the *locus classicus* for the issue of hermeneutics in John Calvin's work, I shall delay a detailed consideration of its significance.[20] As the dedication itself makes clear, this text contains thoughts about which Calvin had been ruminating and holding discussions for years. To understand its import more fully, one has to explore the very principles in Calvin's thought upon which this text is built, and without which it makes no sense.[21] We shall consider seven essential hermeneutic principles in Calvin's writing: hierarchical epistemology, scripture's authority, divine accommodation, the unity of the scripture's testimony, interpretation's goal, the hermeneutical circle, and edification.

Hierarchical Epistemology

Calvin's caution concerning the possibilities of human reason is well known. His objections take the form of scorn for those who might attempt to reach spiritual truth by un-aided human powers. His diatribes against the philosophers frequently make his criticisms seem more polemically eager than thoughtful. Concerning the knowledge of God, for example, Calvin states that it is clear "how willingly has the whole race of philosophers shown their absurdity and obtuseness. For if we spare the others, who talk so foolishly, Plato, the most religious of all and the most sober, even vanishes in his round globe."[22] Calvin found that even the most wise philosophers could not compare to the "sacred reading," that has within itself the power to move the very heart of the reader.[23] The power of scripture is that it carries the gospel, ensured

---

[20] Indeed, Richard Muller criticizes several scholars for the over-dependence upon this particular passage. "The Hermeneutic of Promise and Fulfillment in Calvin's Exegesis of the Old Testament Prophecies of the Kingdom" *The Bible in the 16th Century*, edited by David Steinmetz, (Durham: Duke University Press, 1990), 69.

[21] Thus, eventually we shall see that although Calvin and Schleiermacher describe the process of interpretation in almost exactly the same words, the different foundations for those words give very different meanings to the seemingly nearly identical statements.

[22] OS 3.55.25–29. ICR I.v.11. "Quam prolixe suam in hac parte stoliditatem ac insulsitatem prodidit tota Philosophorum natio? Nam ut aliis parcamus, qui multo absurdius ineptiunt: Plato inter omnes religiosissimus, et maxime sobrius, ipse quoque in rotundo suo globo evanescit."

[23] OS 3.72.29–40. ICR I.viii.1. "Now this power which is particularly that of the Scripture is clear from the fact that of human writings, however artfully refined, none have the force to influence us in such a manner. Read Demosthenes or Cicero; read

by the Holy Spirit's presence, so that its words can transport the soul. God's purpose in the scriptural teaching of his infinite and spiritual essence, Calvin states, is to refute even subtle speculations of secular philosophy.[24] Even those who have attained the intellectual first rank cannot reach the eminence that is natural to the gospel.[25]

Calvin was not simply anti-philosophical, hating the works of philosophers and philosophy in general.[26] If that were true, would he have required logic to be taught in the Genevan Academy?[27] Rather, he

---

Plato, Aristotle, and others of that cohort. I will confess that they will astonish you, entice you, please you, move you, enrapture you in wonderful measure. From there, take yourself from them to this sacred reading. Then, in spite of yourself, it will vividly affect you, it will penetrate your heart, it will sink into your marrow, that, compared with its deep impression, such power as the Orators and Philosophers have will nearly vanish. Therefore, it is clear to see that the sacred Scriptures breathe something divine, that excells all gifts and graces of human industry." "Haec autem virtus quam propria sit Scripturae, inde liquet, quod ex humanis scriptis quamlibet artificiose expolitis, nullum omnino perinde ad nos afficiendos valet. Lege Demosthene, aut Ciceronem: lege Platonem, Aristotelem, aut alios quosvis ex illa cohorte: mirum in modum, fateor, te allicient, oblectabunt, movebunt, rapient: verum inde si ad sacram istam lectionem te conferas, velis nolis ita vivide te afficiet, ita cor tuum penetrabit, ita medullis insidebit, ut prae istius sensus efficacia, vis illa Rhetorum ac Philosophorum prope evanescat; ut promptum sit, perspicere, divinum quiddam spirare sacras Scripturas, quae omnes humanae industriae dotes ac gratias tanto intervallo superent."

[24] OS 3.108.23–25. ICR, I.xiii.1. "The infinite and spiritual essence of God is handed on by the Scriptures and should suffice, not only to destroy popular delusions, but also to refute the arguments of profane Philosophy." "Quod de immensa et spirituali Dei essentia traditur in Scripturis, non modo ad evertenda vulgi deliria, sed etiam ad refutandas profanae Philosophiae argutias valere debet."

[25] Comm. I Corinthians 2.7, CO 49.337 "Indeed the gospel towers over human ingenius grasp, therefore they who are reputed to be above others intellectually may raise their eyes as high as possible, but they will never reach its height." "Ita enim supereminet humani ingenii perspicaciam evangelium, ut quamlibet sursum oculos attollant qui prae aliis ingeniosi putantur, ad eius altitudinem nunquam perveniant." Ganoczy and Scheld note that Calvin shared his high opinion of the gospel, and of its authors, with others of his day. Erasmus found Paul to be the pinnacle of antique civilization, placing him even above Cicero. *Die Hermeneutik Calvins*, 46.

[26] Robert H. Ayers has asserted of Calvin that "In short, there is as high regard for reason in Calvin as there is in Augustine and Aquinas." See his "Language, Logic and Reason in Calvin's *Institutes*." *Religious Studies* 16 (1980): 285. For a fuller examination of Calvin's attitude towards and use of the classical philosophers, see Charles Partee's *Calvin and Classical Philosophy* (Leiden: E.J. Brill, 1977).

[27] For the specifics on Calvin's vision of the usefulness of logic or dialectic, and the sources for the classes in the Genevan Academy, see Irena Backus, "L'Enseignement de la Logique à L'Académie de Genève entre 1559 et 1565." *Revue de Théologie et de Philosophie* 111 (1979): 153–163. Backus also points out a rather late (1557) shift of Calvin's thought on the use of Aristotelian categories for the elucidation of the Trinity, especially in the *Institutes*. Though this did not affect the earlier Pauline commentaries, it does

wished to turn the question of wisdom and philosophy clearly towards obedience to Christ. Thus, in the commentary on I Corinthians, Calvin writes:

> For all the knowledge and understanding a man has is mere vanity unless it is upheld by true wisdom; and it is worth nothing more for comprehending spiritual teaching than the eye of the blind for discerning colors. Both of these things must be carefully noted, that all knowledge of the sciences is vapor where it passes away from the heavenly science of Christ; and that man with all his cunning is as capable of understanding by his own powers the mysteries of God as donkey is capable of understanding a concert.[28]

The interesting point about this passage is that Calvin is neither denigrating human philosophizing, nor human reason. He is addressing the true purpose of knowledge or understanding, and the real foundation of human knowledge. Calvin is not moving back to an Aristotelian self-evident principle, his foundation is instead true wisdom. The phrase "true wisdom" (*vera sapientia*) draws the reader to the opening sentence of the *Institutes*.[29] It was that basis of "true and solid wisdom" (*vera ac solida sapientia*) that Calvin was seeking, the only place from which epistemology could be safely grounded.[30] Reason, and the fruits of reason, have their place. However, that place does not command a privilege over revealed wisdom.

----

demonstrate Calvin's willingness to use appropriate tools to make his points clear. Irena Backus, "'Aristotelianism' in some of Calvin's and Beza's expository and exegetical writings on the doctrine of the trinity, with particular reference to the terms ουσια and υποστασις." *Histoire de l'exégèse au XVIe siècle. Textes du Colloque International tenu a Genève en 1976.* Rèunis par Olivier Fatio et Pierre Fraenkel (Genève: Librairie Droz, 1978), 351–360.

[28] Comm. I Cor. 1.20, CO 49.324–325. "Nam et mera est vanitas quidquid scit homo ac intelligit, nisi vera sapientia fulciatur: et nihilo plus valet ad comprehensionem spiritualis doctrinae quam caeci oculus ad colores discernendos. Utrumque istorum diligenter notandum, quod fumus est omnium scientiarum cognitio, ubi abest coelestis Christi scientia: et homo cum toto suo acumine perinde est stupidus ad intelligenda per se Dei mysteria atque asinus ineptus est ad symphoniam."

[29] OS 3.31.1–3. ICR, I.i.1 "Almost all the wisdom we possess, that is to say, true and sound wisdom, consists of two parts: the knowledge of God and of ourselves." "Tota fere sapientiae nostrae summa, quae vera demum ac solida sapientia censeri debeat, duabus partibus constat, Dei cognitione et nostri."

[30] Compare Charles Trinkaus' "Renaissance Problems in Calvin's Theology," in *The Scope of Renaissance Humanism*, (Ann Arbor: University of Michigan Press, 1983), 317–340, where Trinkaus lays out how Calvin's ethic supports Calvin's epistemology which rests upon a duality of God and humanity.

This instrumental view allows Calvin to give high praise to the fruits of reason. Human reason can even occasionally ascend to consider the truths that are more properly above its grasp, but cannot provide the necessary controls to ensure that its investigations are carefully and correctly considered. Reason is "not too senseless to be able to taste something of things above, however it is more negligent about investigating these."[31] Calvin divides reason, giving it various depths of penetration according to its subject matter: "This therefore, is the distinction: that there is one kind of understanding of things of this earth; another of those of heaven. I call 'things of this earth' those which do not pertain to God or his kingdom, to true righteousness, or to the blessedness of the future life; but those which have their reason and relationship with regard to the present life and are, in a sense, contained within its bounds."[32]

Thus, Calvin was simply fulfilling his own division when he comments from I Corinthians 3 that "Further, the apostle does not require us in his words to renounce wholly the discretion which is either ours by nature or acquired by long experience, only recalls us to the position that we yield it to God, so that all our wisdom might be founded upon his word."[33] Calvin wished, quite explicitly, to consider the various arts as maid-servants. He cautioned against making them mistresses.[34] Perhaps this tells us something faintly autobiographical about the man who had set off on the career of a humanist, only to find himself both converted and drawn along another road.

Finally, Calvin suggests that the search for knowledge is blocked by God for a purpose. The fact that no one has the knowledge to penetrate within all of the scriptures is, for Calvin, an evidence of God's providen-

---

[31] OS 3.256.15–17. ICR, II.ii.13; "non ita stupida est quin exiguum quiddam et de superioribus delibet, utcunque negligentius illis percontandis vacet."

[32] OS 3.256.21–27. ICR, II.ii.13. "Sit ergo haec distinctio, esse aliam quidem rerum terrenarum intelligentiam, aliam vero caelestium. Res terrenas voco, quae ad Deum regnumque eius, ad veram iustitiam, ad futurae vitae beatitudinem non pertingunt: sed cum vita praesenti rationem relationemque habent, et quodammodo intra eius fines continentur."

[33] Comm. I Corinthians 3.18, CO 49.359. "Porro his verbis non requirit apostolus ut prudentiae vel nobis a natura insitae, vel longo usu collectae renuntiemus in totum: sed tantum ut eam redigamus in Dei obsequium, ne quid sapiamus nisi ex eius verbo."

[34] Comm. I Cor. 3.19, CO 49.359. "quare pedisequas esse oportet, non dominas." The Latin here is difficult to translate to get Calvin's meaning. Literally, it means have the sciences be servants, rather than masters. But the genders and the medieval background of theology as the "queen of the sciences," suggests more.

tial care. In the first place, this division of understanding kept scholars humble. In the second, it drove them to constant mutual intercourse, which they might have otherwise abandoned.[35] Thus, Calvin's epistemology denied reason the highest place when dealing with spiritual matters, although reason has significant uses within its own sphere.[36] Second, the true foundation of knowledge of the higher realities, or true wisdom, is to be found through the scriptures.[37]

Scripture's Authority

If true wisdom is only to be founded upon the scriptures, or rather the gospel message which comes from the scriptures, how is the believer to find solace that the scriptures are true? This is the question of the authority of scripture.[38] For Calvin, the scripture is its own guarantor through the power of the Holy Spirit.[39] It is important to note that for Calvin, the nature of the case is that scripture has the nature of an Aristotelian first principle, not in the sense of it being self-evident to the rational mind, but in being that beyond which one cannot

[35] Comm. Romans Dedication, Ad Romanos 3.109–110.

[36] Francis Higman asserts that for Calvin, experience functions in a nuanced manner, even in its engagement with scripture. He writes "En fait Calvin fait appel à l'expérience surtout quand elle conforme les données de la Bible." "Calvin et L'Expérience." *Experience, Coutume Tradition au Temps de la Renaissance*, edited by Marie T. Jones-Davies (Paris: Editions Klincksieck, 1992), 254.

[37] This is not to say that Calvin is always careful about his handling of the scriptures. Especially in the case of the sermons, as Max Engammare has pointed out, Calvin frequently cites a scripture which is different from that of the actual scripture. "Calvin connaissait-il la Bible? Les citations de l'Ecriture dans ses sermons sur la Genese." *Bulletin de la Societe de l'Histoire du Protestantisme Francais* 141 (1995): 163–184.

[38] The literature on this is vast, and cumbersome. See Dowey, *The Knowledge of God in Calvin's Theology*, 3rd ed. (Grand Rapids: Eerdmans, 1994), 89–124 for a roadmap through the traditional arguments.

[39] Richard C. Gamble has perhaps gone too far in claiming "Calvin acknowledges no greater source of authority than the Bible." "Calvin as Theologian and Exegete: Is There Anything New?" *Calvin Theological Journal* 23 (1988): 181. This statement confuses the authority of scripture and that of its source, God.

W. Robert Godfrey notes that "The real self-authenticating character of the Bible was found in the work of the Spirit, who first inspired it and then applied it to the believer." "'Beyond the Sphere of our Judgment': Calvin and the Confirmation of Scripture." *The Westminster Theological Journal*, 58, No. 1, (1996): 31. H. Jackson Forstman supplies this summation, "Authority for the Christian faith, for the reliable knowledge of God and man, is to be found in a reciprocal relation of word and Spirit." *Word and Spirit: Calvin's Doctrine of Biblical Authority* (Stanford, CA: Stanford University Press, 1962), 18.

go.[40] It cannot be independently grounded. Independent arguments can be given for its validity, but these have a secondary, ancillary character.

Further, the scripture must be known first in order for the believer to grasp other revelations of God. The natural knowledge of God is not only insufficient for salvation, but human minds, darkened by sin, cannot even truly grasp it prior to receiving the message of scripture.[41] Calvin writes in his 1559 *Institutes* that, "Just as old or half-blind, and those with dull vision, if you put before them the most beautiful volume, although they may know it to be some kind of writing, they will hardly be able to form two words. However, give the use of glasses and they will begin to read distinctly; in that same way Scripture, gathering up the otherwise confused knowledge of God in our minds, having rolled away our dullness, clearly makes plain to us the true God."[42] Commenting earlier upon Romans 1, Calvin had less helpfully stated that humans are blind, but not too blind (*Caeterum non ita caeci sumus*).[43] In any case, whatever evidence God has granted to humans in creation,[44] Calvin was certain that it cannot truly be appropriated before they are aided by scripture.[45]

Scripture functions as objectively valid and true only for those who hear the Spirit.[46] The proof of scripture as God's word comes not

---

[40] Dowey asserts that "In the very nature of the case, Calvin cannot be described as validating to us the Scripture as the word of God, since God alone can do that." *The Knowledge of God in Calvin's Theology*, 3rd ed. (Grand Rapids, MI: Wm. B. Eerdmans, 1994), 88.

[41] Pierre Berthoud states that it is only the Word of God and the Holy Spirit which allows the re-establishment of the personal relationship of the believer and the heavenly Father. "La Connaissance De Dieu Chez Jean Calvin." *La Revue Reformee* 47 (1996): 43–50.

[42] OS 3.60.25–30. ICR I.vi.1 "nempe sicuti senes, vel lippi, et quicunque oculis caligant, si vel pulcherrimum volumen illis obiicias, quanvis agnoscant esse aliquid scriptum, vix tamen duas voces contexere poterunt: specillis autem interpositis adiuti, distincte legere incipient: ita Scriptura confusam alioqui Dei notitiam in mentibus nostris colligens, discussa caligine liquido nobis verum Deum ostendit."

[43] Comm. Romans 1.20. Ad Romanos 30.50 51.

[44] The most recent and thorough consideration of the natural knowledge of God in Calvin's thought is Susan E. Schreiner's *The Theater of His Glory: Nature and the Natural Order in the Thought of John Calvin*. Studies in Historical Theology (Durham: Labyrinth Press, 1991).

[45] David Steinmetz has considered this exegetical choice of Calvin's, and pointed out the "highly original" character of his treatment of Romans 1.18–32 in "Calvin and the Natural Knowledge of God" in *Calvin in Context* (Oxford: Oxford University Press, 1995), 23–39.

[46] Richard Muller makes this point well in stating that "A keen balance of ... sub-

because of the beauty or purity or protection of the text, but because God witnesses to the message of the scripture through the internal testimony of the Spirit.[47] Calvin's understanding of scripture is preserved from aridity by virtue of its role as a sacramental Word.[48] The verity of scripture in matters of faith about the higher realities is only for the believer, because only the believer hears and feels the Spirit who spoke to and through the prophets.[49] This is a doctrine of double revelation.

------

jective and objective elements appears, therefore, both in Calvin's doctrine of scripture and in his description of faith." "The Foundation of Calvin's Theology: Scripture as Revealing God's Word." *Duke Divinity School Review* 44 (1979): 15.

[47] OS 3.70.2–8, ICR I.vii.4. "For just as God alone is the correct witness for his own word, in the same way it cannot be that the word will be ascertained before faith in the hearts of men until it is sealed by the internal testimony of the Spirit. Therefore just as the Spirit spoke by the mouth of the prophets, it is necessary that it should penetrate our hearts in order to persuade us that they delivered faithfully the message which was divinely given." "Nam sicuti Deus solus de se idoneus est testis in suo sermone: ita etiam non ante fidem reperiet sermo in hominum cordibus quam interiore Spiritus testimonio obsignetur. Idem ergo Spiritus qui per os Prophetarum loquutus est, in corda nostra penetret necesse est, ut persuadeat fideliter protulisse quod divinitus erat mandatum."

[48] Brian A. Gerrish makes this point in his *Grace and Gratitude: The Eucharistic Theology of John Calvin* (Philadelphia: Fortress Press, 1993), chapter 3. Though Gerrish finds the sacramental character most strongly located in the preached Word, there are passages in Calvin's commentaries where Calvin suggests that same character for the read form of the revelation. For an earlier view on the sacramental functioning of preaching in Calvin and the Reformation, see Heiko Oberman, "Preaching and the Word in the Reformation." *Theology Today* 18 (1961/1962): 16–29.

[49] Comm. II Timothy 3.16. CO 52.383. "This is the principle which distinguishes our religion from all others, that we know that God has spoken to us and are truly persuaded that the prophets did not speak from their own sense, but they were organs of the holy spirit, and revealed only that which they had been commanded from heaven. All those who desire to profit from the Scriptures must especially accept this as a settled principle, that the Law and the prophets are not human teachings handed on by men, but are dictated by the holy spirit. If anyone object and ask how this can be known, I respond that it is by the revelation of the same spirit both to disciples and doctors that God is shown as its author. Neither Moses nor the prophets produced with their own temerity what we have received from their hands, but, speaking by God's impulse, they boldly and intrepidly testified the truth that it was the mouth of the Lord that spoke through them. Therefore, that same spirit who made Moses and the prophets certain of their vocation now also bears witness to our hearts that He has made use of them as ministers through whom to teach us. It is hardly a miracle that many should doubt the authority of Scripture. For although the majesty of God is demonstrated in it, only those who have been enlightened by the holy spirit have eyes to see what should have been obvious to all, but which is in fact apparent only to the elect. This is the meaning of the first clause, that we owe to the scripture the same reverence as we owe to God, since it has come only from him and has nothing of humanity mixed with it." "Hoc principium est quod religionem nostram ab aliis omnibus discernit, quod scimus Deum nobis loquutum esse, certoque persuasi simus, non ex suo sensu

The Spirit who spoke to the prophets and apostles and caused them to write down the scriptures is the same Spirit who testifies to the truth and authority of the scriptures in the hearts of believers, for the life of the contemporary Church.[50]

Does this mean that Calvin holds a position that the inspiration of the text of scripture is its guarantor of truth? By no means. Rather, Calvin follows the logic of his doctrine of revelation to establish a doctrine of inspiration.[51] But what of that doctrine of inspiration? Does Calvin maintain some form of the mechanistic authors-as-tools theory which would justify a theory of verbal inspiration? Although that question will be taken up later, for now it is possible to say that in Calvin's usage, there are too many instances of both authors as amanuenses, and considerations of particular author's styles to answer either in the affirmative or negative. Calvin respects both authorial levels in the scripture—a subject we shall elaborate on in the section "The Mind of the Author."

---

loquutos esse prophetas, sed ut erant spiritus sancti organa, tantum protulisse quae coelitus mandata fuerant. Quisquis ergo vult in scripturis proficere, hoc secum inprimis constituat, legem et prophetias non esse doctrinam hominum arbitrio proditam: sed a spiritu sancto dictatam. Si quis obiiciat, undenam id sciri possit: respondeo, eiusdem spiritus revelatione tam discipulis quam doctoribus Deum patefieri autorem. Neque enim Moses et prophetae temere prodiderunt quae habemus ex eorum manu: sed quum Dei impulsu loquerentur, confidenter ac intrepide, u res erat, testati sunt os Domini loquutum esse. Idem ergo spiritus, qui Mosen et prophetas vocationis suae reddidit certiores, nunc quoque testatur cordibus nostris, eorum se ministerio usum esse ad nos docendos. Itaque non mirum si plerique de autore scripturae dubitent. Nam utcunque illic Dei maiestas se ostendat: non tamen habent oculos nisi qui sunt a spiritu sancto illuminati, ut cernant quod omnibus quidem esse debebat, solis tamen electis est conspicuum. Hoc prius est membrum: eandem scripturae reverentiam deberi quam Deo deferimus, quia ab eo solo manavit, nec quidqam humani habet admistum."

[50] Alexandre Ganoczy and Stefan Scheld point out that the hearer of the Word of God must be enlightened by the same Spirit who inspired the prophets and apostles. See their *Die Hermeneutik Calvins*, 93 ff. Hans Helmut Eßer notes that Calvin generated this doctrine under the dual pressure of rejection of Roman and Radical understandings of scripture. "Die Lehre vom 'testimonium Spiritus Sancti internum' bei Calvin innerhalb seiner Lehre von der Heiligen Schrift." *Verbindliches Zeugnis Vol 2: Schriftauslegung-Lehramt-Rezeption* edited by Wolfhart Pannenberg, Dialog der Kirchen 9 (Freiburg im Breisgau: Herder; Gottingen: Vandenhoeck & Ruprecht, 1995), 246–258.

[51] Dowey, 89–90. "There is, strictly speaking, no independent doctrine of inspiration in Calvin's *Institutes*. His teaching about the historical origin and providential preservation of the sacred books is carried along by his doctrine of the living and present witness of the Spirit to the truth of the contemporary Bible. Calvin does not accept the Bible as revelation because it has somehow objectively been proved to be inspired. On the contrary, he finds the Bible to be a revelation of God, then he makes the corollary assertion that its writers were inspired, as they asserted, by God."

One final question must be asked before we move further in contemplating Calvin's principles for understanding that scripture. Given the strength of Calvin's polemic against those who would turn away from the scriptures to find other independent sources of revelation, can Calvin be faulted for proposing scripture as the object of faith, rather than the gospel, or more importantly, the Christ? Does Calvin, in his zeal for the word of God, fail to raise his eyes from the *signum* to the *res*?

This is a legitimate concern. Some have found Calvin to be at least unclear upon this point.[52] To answer this, two points need to be raised. The first is that Calvin lived in the first half of the sixteenth century, and generally faced opponents over the interpretation of scripture who were just as willing as he to state that the Bible was to be believed. They may have wished to change from Calvin's stance, his Roman opponents added that the Bible was to be believed because the Church said so; his Radical opponents argued about whose task it was to interpret the Bible. To state it another way, Calvin had no reason to consider whether the scripture might not be the object of faith. Some of the same scholars who have raised this issue have noted this historical truth.[53]

The second point to be raised is that although Calvin's thought on the issue of the belief in the scriptures is occasional, and rarely on the point of whether faith is in the scripture, or in Christ, in those instances where he speaks of the scripture, the gospel, and the Christ, the relationship becomes clearer. Generally speaking, for Calvin the scriptures are the repository of God's particular revelation to humankind. The gospel is the core of that scripture, its deepest message, and the gospel points toward the mysteries of Christ. Christ remains the head of the Church, and the mystical body into which the believer is to be engrafted. Though this is not always consistent, there is a strong tendency in this direction. But that tendency does not make clear all of God's ways of communicating to humans. Calvin turns to that issue when he considers God's accommodation.

---

[52] Dowey argues that in Calvin's theology there is an unreconciled variance between his idea of the acceptance of scripture and salvation through Christ. "... he must be judged to have two not entirely reconcilable theological explanations of the faithful man's knowledge of God's revelation. This flaw can be described, although he never used the terms, as a discrepancy between the so-called formal and material principles of the Reformation: the authority of Scripture and justification by faith in Christ." 161.

[53] Dowey, 162.

God's Accommodation

To appreciate the depth of God's love for humanity in Calvin's theology, one needs to understand that the whole of God's self-revealing,
especially through the scripture, stands as a sort of divine move toward
humanity, a move of accommodation. The term "accommodation"
has become rather celebrated in Calvin studies in recent decades.[54]
Although not without its own problems, the term seems to cover a variety of significant impulses in Calvin's thought.[55] It has been defined as
"the process by which God reduces or adjusts to human capacities what
he wills to reveal of the infinite mysteries of his being, which by their
very nature are beyond the powers of the mind of man to grasp."[56] This

---

[54] In 1952, Edward Dowey spent a chapter discussing it, Dowey, 3–7. Only two years
earlier, Wendel noted the use, but did not discuss accommodation as an independent
issue; *Calvin: Origins and Development of His Religious Thought*, translated by Philip Mairet,
(Durham, NC: Labyrinth Press, 1987), 229–230. By 1962, Forstman was terming accommodation as "perhaps [his] most widely used exegetical tool." *Word and Spirit: Calvin's
Doctrine of Biblical Authority*, (Stanford, CA: Stanford University Press, 1962), 13. The
most widely cited study of Calvin's use of accommodation in English is that of Ford
Lewis Battles, "God Was Accommodating Himself to Human Capacity." *Interpretation*
31 (1977): 19–38. Olivier Millet has weighed in by dedicating a section of his magisterial volume, *Calvin et la dynamique de la parole: Etude de Rhétorique réformée* (Geneve: H.
Champion, 1992), 247–256, where he concludes that for Calvin, the accommodation of
God is an omnipresent phenomenon, without which special revelation is not able to
be understood. Stephen Benin has considered the history of accommodation in Jewish
and Christian thought in *The Footprints of God: Divine Accommodation in Jewish and Christian
Thought*, (Albany, NY: SUNY Press, 1993). Vincent Bru's "La notion d'accommodation
divine chez Calvin: Ses implications theologiques et exegetiques." *La Revue Reformee*
49 (1998): 79–91, considers the various ways in which accommodation is essential to
the relationship between God and humanity. Finally, David F. Wright has considered
accommodation in Calvin in several articles. See his "Calvin's Pentateuchal Criticism:
Equity, Hardness of Heart, and Divine Accommodation in the Mosaic Harmony Commentary." *Calvin Theological Journal* 21 (1986): 33–50; "Accommodation and Barbarity in
John Calvin's Old Testament Commentaries." *Understanding Prophets and Poets: Essays in
Honor of George Wishart Anderson*, 413–427, edited by A. Graeme Auld, (Sheffield: Journal
for the Study of the Old Testament Press, 1993); and most recently in his "Calvin's
Accommodating God." *Calvinus Sincerioris Religionis Vindex*, edited by Wilhelm Neuser
and Brian Armstrong, (Kirksville, MO: Sixteenth Century Journal Publishers, 1997),
3–20. This last article contains a brief overview of the literature.

[55] Inexplicably, Alexandre Ganoczy and Stefan Scheld in *Die Hermeneutik Calvins*
ignore this facet of Calvin's interpretation.

[56] Dowey, 3. Although Wright calls this "rather too systematic and … highfalutin
to be wholly satisfactory," "Calvin's Accommodating God," 5, he later states that this
definition is quite to the point, 16, when asserting that accommodation has to do with
more than scripture alone. Any definition can be picked at, Dowey's seems sufficient to
cover Calvin's usage.

definition drives toward all forms of God's revelation, and can be considered in all forms of revelation.[57] However, it is particularly relevant to the interpretation of the scripture.

In the interpretation of scripture, Calvin used the principle of accommodation to resolve inconsistencies within scripture.[58] For instance, Calvin could by use of this instrument resolve some of the issues presented by the anthropomorphic and anthropopathic portions of scripture.[59] He also could negotiate his way through the morass of what seems to be permitted anarchy in patriarchal sexual mores. Calvin judged the patriarchs rather harshly, having little difficulty in condemning transgressions of what he believed was a trans-historical moral code. Calvin "displays a remarkable readiness to read the narratives just as they stand, while agreeing with most earlier and contemporary commentators that the patriarchal misdeeds set no precedent."[60]

Calvin claimed that it is necessary for God to accommodate the immensity of the divine wisdom to the relative puniness of human understanding.[61] This is not an innovation for him, the tradition makes full use of this theme.[62] What is significant for this study is the centrality that Calvin gives to this issue. Although suggestions are made that this allows Calvin to treat accommodation as a Reformation-acceptable substitute for allegory,[63] the greater issue for Calvin's principles for

---

[57] Compare Battles, "God Was Accommodating Himself to Human Capacity." *Interpretation* 31 (1977): 19–38. "Calvin makes this principle a consistent basis for his handling not only of Scripture but of every avenue of relationship between God and man." (20) Thus, the most important moment of revelation, the incarnation, still has some character of accommodation to limited capacity in it, otherwise, the fullness of God would obliterate the receiving eyes of the faithful. As well, God's revelation in the created sphere might have been unbearably beautiful, insupportably breathtaking, so as to provide not insight and manifestation, but only tears of pain.

[58] Battles, 20–21. Battles lists four paradigmatic instances. (1) God's nature, in which biblical language attributes physical features to the deity—ICR I.xiii.1; (2) Problem of the creation of angels not mentioned in the creation account—ICR I.xiv.3; (3) Fortuitous chance awaits all humanity—ICR I.xvi.9; (4) God's repentance—ICR I.xvii.12.

[59] OS 3.109.11–18, ICR I.xiii.1.

[60] Wright, "Accommodation and Barbarity in John Calvin's Old Testament Commentaries," 415. See also John Thompson's "The Immoralities of the Patriarchs in the History of Exegesis: A Reappraisal of Calvin's Position." *Calvin Theological Journal* 26 (1991): 9–46.

[61] ICR I.xiii.1, OS 3.109. 15–18. "Proinde tales loquendi formae non tam ad liquidum exprimunt qualis sit Deus, quam eius notitiam tenuitati nostrae accommodant; quod ut fiat, longe infra eius altitudinem descendere necesse est."

[62] See Benin, *The Footprints of God: Divine Accommodation in Jewish and Christian Thought.*

[63] This position is stated by David F. Wright, "Calvin's Accommodating God," 18, and he makes a strong case for this.

handling scripture and revelation in general is that not only does this tell the believer something about God in relation to humans, but also reminds the believer that it is God who is always initiating the move toward the believer.[64] It is God who is attempting to find appropriate ways to disclose an infinite divinity to a finite creation. This changes the basic view of God, and fits with Calvin's dictum to avoid the question of what God is, to concentrate upon the issue of who God is to us.[65] Further, this would be true even in the case of very particular peoples. If a nation was harsh, or barbaric, God did not turn away from them, but accommodated the divine revelation to what can be stood by those people at that time.[66] The difficulty, both for the interpreter of scripture, and for the believer, is that at times, this can present stories or cases in scripture where the possible doctrinal or moral implications are incorrect. It must be remembered that none of Calvin's hermeneutical principles stand in isolation, but all are in a state of reflexive tension, always effecting the others to achieve a position of creative force.

Finally, one more oddity of the use of accommodation needs to be considered. Calvin speaks of God "lisping" or "prattling," (*quodammodo balbutire*).[67] But instead of piling up more instances of Calvin's usage, consider for a moment that single passage. God is speaking to us as babysitters speak to babies "*ceu nutrices solent cum infantibus*," adapting by condescension to our level.[68] However, when we explore the minds of babies, we do not expect to discover that they realize that the

---

[64] Peter Opitz notes this by stating "Als sich akkommodierendes Wort besteht Gottes Wort immer aus menschlichen Worten, denn Gott spricht menschlich zum Menschen." *Calvins Theologische Hermeneutik*, (Neukirchen-Vluyn: Neukirchener, 1994), 110.

[65] OS 3.35.11–14. ICR I.ii.2. "What is God? Men who pose this question are merely toying with idle speculations. It is more important for us to know of what sort he is and what is consistent with his nature." "Itaque frigidis tantum speculationibus ludunt quibus in hac quaestione insistere propositum est, quid sit Deus: quum intersit nostra potius, qualis sit, et quid eius naturae conveniat scire."

[66] Wright notes that Calvin can rage against the barbarous nature of the Israelites, calling them "utterly barbaric," Exod. 21.7 11, CO 24:650, CTS III:80–81; and considers that the treatment of Achan seems to be harsh, savage and barbaric (*durum, immane, barbarum)* Joshua 7.24–26 CO 25:479–480, CTS:117. He states that "Calvin's dilemma here is not untypical of his response to numerous aspects of the early books of the Old Testament. Too often what he finds is inconsistent with an external objective standard of measurement which he calls 'equity' (*aequitas*), a compound of natural law, the law engraved on the human conscience and the 'law of the nations' (*lex gentium)*" "Accommodation and Barbarity in John Calvin's Old Testament Commentaries," 421.

[67] OS 3.109.15. ICR I.xiii.1.

[68] OS 3.109.14. ICR I.xiii.1.

speech of their sitters is accommodated. When we give explanations to children of complicated phenomena, and oversimplify so as even to mis-represent, we do not believe that they are catching us in our mis-representation, and realizing that we are condescending. But in the scriptures, God has given enough clues that humans are able to realize that God's language is accommodated. Here stands another testimony to God's revealing and God's hiding. Even in the hiding which God must do so as to reveal something to humanity, there is no deception, but rather another pedagogy, another lesson.[69]

Although the principle of accommodation is frequently associated more closely with the Old Testament, and its more frequent anthropomorphisms, such as God walking in the Garden, the Pauline commentaries also show Calvin maintaining this concept.[70] In Romans 1.19, commenting upon "because what is known of God," Calvin observes that God lays down rules beyond which the prudent will not attempt to go.[71] He explains "What the word signifies is that it is not possible to grasp with our minds fully God's greatness, but that there are certain limits within which men ought to restrain themselves, just as God accommodates to our capacity every declaration he makes of himself. Only fools, therefore, want to know what God is."[72] Here Calvin has taken the opportunity, through the "what is known," to lay down his principle.

That the principle of accommodation is more of an effort at revelation than of hiding is made clear in Calvin's comment upon I Corinthians 2.7. Paul has told the Corinthians that the apostles "speak God's wisdom in a mystery, a hidden mystery, which God chose before the worlds for our glory." Calvin's interpretation immediately takes up the

---

[69] Here, I take direct issue with Wright's position in "Calvin's Accommodating God," 18ff. Wright notes that the "revealed God is always still for Calvin the partly hidden God ... We must make do with the prattling of God until hereafter he speaks to us face to face." 19. But the wonder is that God tells us that. God does not lie, does not allow humans to believe that they are facing the real and full knowledge. Perhaps the burden of living with a knowledge that is received through a glass and dimly is a great burden. But it is not an unwarned burden.

[70] For instance, three of four of Wright's cited articles specifically aim only at Old Testament texts, as does Thompson's study.

[71] Comm Romans 1.19, Ad Romanos 29.24. "quod notum est Dei."

[72] Comm. Romans 1.19, Ad Romanos 29.22–25. "Quo verbo significat, Deum quantus est, minime posse mente nostra capi: sed aliquem esse modum intra quem se cohibere debeant homines: sicuti Deus ad modulum nostrum attemperat quicquid de se testatur. Delirant ergo quicunque scire appetunt quid sit Deus."

danger of a "too-hidden" character of the message of God, a hidden-
ness which would frighten away believers. Calvin writes

> Because Paul had said that the gospel is a hidden thing there was a
> danger that believers, hearing this, and being frightened by the difficulty,
> might run away from it and lose heart. Therefore he faces this danger
> and declares that nevertheless the gospel had been appointed for us, for
> our enjoyment of it. Lest anyone, I say, might consider that the hidden
> wisdom has nothing to do with him, or even that it is wrong for him to
> look at it, because it is not within the range of human comprehension,
> Paul teaches that it has been imparted to us by the eternal purpose of
> God. Yet he had something greater in mind, for by a tacit comparison
> he places in the clearer light the grace which has been laid open for us
> by the coming of Christ, and which puts us in a higher position than
> our fathers who lived under the Law. ... First of all, then, he argues
> from what God has ordained. For if God established everything to some
> purpose, it follows that we will lose nothing in hearing the gospel, which
> he intended for us, for when he speaks to us he accommodates Himself
> to our capacity. What Isaiah says relates to this (45.19): 'For I have not
> spoken in a hiding place, or in a dark corner. Not in vain did I say to the
> seed of Jacob, "Seek me".'[73]

Calvin thus can find his support for accommodation within scripture,
and not only use it as a hermeneutical principle, but also as an encouragement to engagement with the scriptures. The God that the believer
follows is hidden in a mystery, but not a mystery so deep that the reading of the scripture is not profitable, nor is the mystery so dark as to
leave the believer without direction in doctrine and life's actions.

Similarly, expounding Ephesians 4.10, Calvin assumes the principle
of accommodation in explaining the biblical language. Commenting
on Christ's physical and non-physical position, (a phrase which already
demonstrates the difficulty at hand), Calvin writes "When Christ is said
to be in heaven, we should not understand that to mean that he resides
among the spheres and numbers the stars. Instead, heaven signifies a

---

[73] Comm. I Cor. 2.7, CO 49.337. "Quia dixerat Paulus evangelium rem esse arcanam, periculum erat ne hoc audito fideles, difficultate terriri, refugerent ac desponder-
ent animos. Ergo occurrit huic periculo, ut eo fruamur. Ne quis, inquam, latentem sapientiam nihil ad se pertinere ducat: aut etiam nefas humano captui exposita: communi-
catam nobis aeterno Dei consilio esse docet. Quamquam altius quoque respexit: tacita
enim comparatione amplificat gratiam, quae Christi adventum patefacta nos patribus,
qui sub lege vixerunt, excellentiores reddit. ... Primum autem ab ordinatione Dei argu-
mentatur: nam si Deus nihil frustra statuit, sequitur nos operam non perfituros in audiendo evangelio quod nobis destinavit: se enim modulo nostro attemperat, quum nobis
loquitur. Atque huc pertinet illud Iesaiae (45, 19): Non in latebris loquiutus sum, neque
in obscuro angulo. Non frustra dixi semini Iacob, quaerite me."

place greater than all the spheres, which was fixed upon for the Son of
God after his resurrection. Properly speaking, that is not a place outside
the world, but we cannot speak of the kingdom of God except in our
own custom."[74] It is impossible for human speech to encompass some
of the realities which God's will and power make possible. Therefore,
though our customs of our speech (*loqui more nostro*) cannot give a good
approximation of the reality toward which they point, we must use
them while constantly correcting ourselves so far as possible.[75] This will
always require recourse to scripture.

Unity of the Two Testaments

But which scriptures gave access to true and sound wisdom? Was there
a portion of the sacred writings which surpassed all others?[76] Many
would correctly cite Romans as Calvin's key book of the scripture. But
was Romans so important as to negate the importance of other portions

---

[74] Comm. Ephesians 4.10, Ad Ephesios 226.19–23. "Nam quum dicitur Christus in
caelo esse, non sic accipere debemus, quasi resideat inter sphaeras, ut stellas numeret,
sed illic caelum significat sphaeris omnibus superiorem, qui post resurrectionem Filio
Dei est destinatus. Non quod proprie locus sit extra mundum, sed quia de regno Dei
loqui nisi more nostro non possumus."

[75] This raises an interesting point. Does Calvin speak about the impossibility of
God's realities being represented in human speech, or only in the "customs of human
speech?" In other words, is the problem one of incommensurability, or one of proper
speech? Both are problems. However, Calvin makes it sufficiently clear that the difficulty which God is addressing through accommodation is one of incommensurability.
As a good rhetorician and with a mind always to the education of the Church, however, Calvin must keep in mind that the regular patterns of colloquial speech are even
less correct about the realities of God. This is something the pastor-teacher can never
forget, since it represents the "classroom conditions" from which he or she will not
escape.

[76] In point of fact, there was. Calvin privileges Romans, as did many Reformers. He
wrote "Therefore, it will be better for me to come now to the argument itself. This will
establish beyond any controversy that among other exceptional endowments the Epistle has one in particular which is never estimated highly enough. It is this—that if the
true understanding of it is followed, we will have an open door to all the most concealed
treasures of Scripture." Ad Romanos, Argumentum, 5.6–11. "Ergo iam ad argumentum
ipsum transire satius fuerit: unde citra controversiam protinus constabit, praeter pluri-
mas alias, et eas eximias dotes, hanc ei proprie competere, quae nunquam pro dignitate
satis aestimetur: quod siquis veram eius intelligentiam sit assequutus, ad reconditissimos
quosque Scripturae thesauros adeundos habeat apertas fores." Alexandre Ganoczy and
Stefan Scheld have pointed out that Calvin's own historical situation was that of being
born into the rebirth of European humanistic Paulinism. *Die Hermeneutik Calvins* (22–46),
and "Forschungsansatze zur Hermeneutik Calvins: Calvin als paulinischer Theologe."

of scripture?[77] Further was there for Calvin an unprofitable portion of scripture which could be passed over? That John Calvin held for a basic unity between the Old Testament and New Testament has become a commonplace.[78] This was his solution to the ancient exegetical question of the relationship between the Old and New Testaments. Various possibilities, both orthodox and heretical, had been suggested almost from the beginning of Christian history.[79] Marcion had suggested that the two testaments have only the relationship of opposition. Origen's solution of systematic allegorizing answered that claim, and became the most generally accepted resolution in the Western Church.[80] However, although Calvin might have agreed with the impulse that led Origen to promulgate his rule of interpretation, that the Spirit places within the text of scripture impossible events, in order to spur on the godly interpreter, the possibility for abuse that such a non-restrictive method allowed seemed too indulgent to him.[81] In this manner, might not all

---

Lecture given at the Europäischer Kongress für Calvinforschung, Amsterdam, Sept. 16–19, 1974; John Thompson has pointed out that Calvin's Paulinism was so significant that it might drive his interpretation of the Old Testament to extreme positions, not taken by his contemporaries. See his "Hagar, Victim or Villian? Three Sixteenth-Century Views." *The Catholic Biblical Quarterly* 59 (1997): 213–233.

[77] Bernard Cottret argues that it does not—that there is in Calvin's thought a bifurcation represented by the books of Romans and Hebrews, which bear an equal importance in the Reformation. See his *Calvin: A Biography*, 71–72.

[78] The point is made by E.A. Dowey Jr., *The Knowledge of God in Calvin's Theology*, 164–166; by Wilhelm Niesel, *The Theology of Calvin*, translated by Harold Knight, (Philadelphia: Westminster Press, 1956), 104–109; by Edmond Grin. "L'Unite des deux Testaments Selon Calvin." *Theologische Zeitschrift*, 17, (1961): 175–186; and François Wendel, *Calvin: Origins and Development of His Religious Thought*, 208–214. Some have even accused Calvin of Christianizing the Old Testament. Kraeling states that he "practically closes his eyes to the new moral values in the preaching of Jesus and reduces Him to the level of a correct intepreter of Moses." Emil Kraeling, *The Old Testament Since the Reformation*, (London: Lutterworth Press, 1955), 25. Alexandre Ganoczy and Stefan Scheld point out the relation of Christ to the law almost as soon as they turn to the consideration proper of Calvin's own extension of the hermeneutics of the reformers. *Die Hermeneutik Calvins*, 91.

[79] For background, see Beryl Smalley, *The Study of the Bible in the Middle Ages*, 2nd ed., (Notre Dame: Notre Dame University Press, 1952), 1–36 and *Cambridge History of the Bible: From the Beginnings to Jerome*, edited by P.R. Ackroyd and C.F. Evans, (Cambridge: Cambridge University Press, 1970), 412–488.

[80] The Antiochene school provided a significant option, which did not flower immediately. See *Cambridge History of the Bible: From the Beginnings to Jerome*, edited by P.R. Ackroyd and C.F. Evans, (Cambridge: Cambridge University Press, 1970), 489–509.

[81] Origen, *On First Principles*, Bk IV.ii.8, in Karlfried Froehlich, *Biblical Interpretation in the Early Church*, Sources of Early Christian Thought, William G. Rusch, series ed. (Philadelphia: Fortress Press, 1984), 62–63. "One must also be aware of another feature.

difficult passages of scripture be only allegories? Calvin's solution was to understand the Old Testament wholly as a Christian book, with the same goal as the New Testament, but differing in clarity. Calvin conceived of the religion of the Old Testament not as an expression of the religious laws and customs of the Jews, but from the first line to the last it preaches about Christ.[82] Calvin pronounces that "The covenant given by God to all the patriarchs differs so little from ours in substance and reality that the two are wholly one and the same."[83] The covenants differ only in the manner of dispensation.[84]

This position allowed Calvin some flexibility to maneuver around difficult texts from the Old Testament, while denying neither the historical particularity of the Israelite covenant,[85] nor the basic unity between

---

Since the (Spirit's) primary goal was to present the logical system of spiritual realities by means of events that happened and things that were to be done, the Word used actual historical events wherever they could be accommodated to these mystical (meanings), hiding the deeper sense from the multitude. But where the recorded actions of a specific person did not fit the account of the inner coherence of intelligible realities in terms of the deeper mystical meaning, Scripture has woven into the historical narrative some feature which did not happen; sometimes the event is an impossibility; sometimes, though possible, it actually did not happen. Sometimes only a few phrases which are not true in the bodily sense are inserted, sometimes more. We must assume an analogous situation in regard to the law. Frequently one can find commandments which are useful in themselves and appropriate for the time of legislation. Sometimes, however, their usefulness is not self-evident. At other times, even impossible things are commanded; such instances challenge the more skillful and inquisitive to devote themselves to a painstaking examination of the text and become seriously convinced that a sense worthy of God needs to be sought in these commandments."

[82] Wilhelm Niesel, *The Theology of Calvin*, 105. Richard Muller has asserted that the method of Calvin's maintenance of the connection between the Old and New Testament is a hermeneutic of promise and fulfillment, strictly retained. See his "The Hermeneutic of Promise and Fulfillment in Calvin's Exegesis of the Old Testament Prophecies of the Kingdom," In *The Bible in the 16th Century*, edited by David Steinmetz (Durham: Duke University Press, 1990), 68–82.

[83] OS 3.404.5–7. ICR, II.x.2. "Patrum omnium foedus adeo substantia et re ipsa nihil a nostro differt, ut unum prorsus atque idem sit."

[84] Wilhelm Neuser states that "Das Verhältnis von Altem und Neuem Testament ist das der Steigerung vom Positiv zum Komparativ." "Calvins Verständnis der Heiligen Schrift," in *Calvinus Sacrae Scripturae Professor*. International Congress on Calvin Research, edited by Wilhelm Neuser, (Grand Rapids: Eerdmans, 1994), 43.

[85] Calvin could be extremely vigorous about the historical particularity of the ancient Israelites. The Decalogue is given because of the forgetfulness of the people of Israel, and their hardheartedness. As well, God allows particular sins for a time because of Israelite barbarity. See the treatments of Israelite specificity in John Hesselink's "John Calvin on the Law and Christian Freedom." *Ex Auditu* 11 (1995): 77–89; and in John Thompson's "The Immoralities of the Patriarchs in the History of Exegesis: A Reappraisal of Calvin's Position." *Calvin Theological Journal* 26 (1991): 9–46.

their religion and the Christian religion. Calvin saw the function of the institutions of the Old Covenant as representing the greater clarity under shadows, or as aids to children. "From that series of observations that we have gathered together, it is possible to see that the law was added about four hundred years after the death of Abraham, but that this was not done to lead the chosen people away from Christ; but instead to hold their souls in suspense until his advent: to enkindle their desire, and confirm their expectation, in order that they might not weaken from too long a delay."[86]

Four points of organic union can be discerned functioning in Calvin's thought to bind the message of the Old Testament to that of the New. The first point of union between the two Testaments is the Church. Calvin believes that the Church was prefigured in the Old Testament—in fact, that the Old Testament community constituted a genuine Church.

> Those people (the Israelites) were a figure of the christian church in such a way that they were also a true church. Just as their circumstances so delineated ours, so too the permanent condition of a church was there. The promises given to it sketched the gospel in such a way that it was included in them. Just as their sacraments served to give a figure of ours, this was in order that they were true sacraments with a present effectiveness applying to their day. To sum up, those who made a proper use of the sacraments in those days were endowed with the same spirit of faith as we are.[87]

The Israelites were a Church. They had the gospel and the sacraments, or adumbrations of those which contained the substance of the gospel and sacraments. Further, the function of gospel and sacraments, that of representing Christ to the hearer, is substantially, if not wholly clearly, retained within the elements of the Israelite religion. Calvin leaves no doubt that the Jews turned to Christ through God's will: "God wanted

---

[86] OS 3.326.22–27. ICR, II.vii.1. "Ex continua illa, quam retulimus, serie colligere licet Legem non ideo post mortem Abrahae quadringentis circiter annis fuisse superadditam, ut electum populum a Christo abduceret: imo ut suspensos teneret animos usque ad eius adventum, accenderet etiam eius desiderium, et in expectatione confirmaret ne longiore mora deficerent."

[87] Comm. I Corinthians 10:11, CO 49.460. "Sic enim fuit populus ille christiana ecclesiae figura, ut vera etiam ecclesia fuerit: sic eius conditio nostram delineavit, ut esset tamen iam tunc proprius ecclesiae status: sic promissiones illi datae evangelium adumbrarunt, ut inclusum continerent: sic eorum sacramenta nostris figurandis serviebant, ut tamen pro illo quoque tempore vera sacramenta forent praesentis efficaciae: denique eodem spiritu fidei nobiscum praediti fuerunt qui et doctrina et signis tunc rite usi sunt."

the Jews so steeped in these prophecies that they might correctly turn
their eyes to Christ in order to seek deliverance."[88]

The second joint property of the two Testaments is the covenant.
The covenant of the Old Testament is substantially the same as the
covenant of grace which Christ came into the world to proclaim. The
only difference between the promise to the patriarchs and the promise
to the disciples of Jesus was the mode of ministry (*administratio tamen
variat*).[89] There are three crucial similarities between the two covenants.
First, the goal set before the Israelites was not temporal prosperity
but adoption into the hope of immortality. Secondly, the covenant was
supported totally by the free gift of God, and not by any merit of their
own. Thirdly, Calvin even states that the Israelites had and knew Christ
as Mediator, and he joined them to God and his promises.[90]

The first notion, that the goal was not simply mortal and temporal,
Calvin supports with passages from Paul. In Romans 1.2–3, the apostle
writes that God had "promised beforehand through his prophets in the
holy scriptures the gospel concerning his Son," placing the promise
of Christ back into the time of the Old Covenant community. The
promise was of Christ, not a poor worldly inheritance. The second and
third ideas, that the covenant was supported totally by the mercy and
grace of God, and that the Israelites knew Christ, Calvin braces with
New Testament texts–always referring to Christ. He quotes John 8.56,
Christ's statement that "Abraham rejoiced that he was to see my day."
If Abraham knew the day of Christ, certainly all the following patriarchs knew of him. Calvin interprets Hebrews 13.8–that Christ remains
yesterday, today, and forever, as speaking not only of the divinity of
Christ, but also of his power, the power of salvation, perpetually available to believers.[91] The patriarchs knew Christ, in his person, and his
power, just as the New Testament witnesses knew him. Through Christ
came belief, and participation in the covenant.

Calvin forged a third link between the two Testaments in his concept
of the relation of law and gospel. It can be seen that Calvin's view of
the unity of the substance of the two Testaments opposed, or at least
substantially modified, Luther's attitude towards the Old Testament.

---

[88] OS 3.325.3–4. ICR, II.vi.4; "His vaticiniis ita imbui voluit Deus Iudaeos, ut
liberationis petendae causa, recta oculos ad Christum converterent."
[89] OS 3.404.7. ICR, II.x.2.
[90] OS 3.404.20–22. ICR., II.x.2.
[91] OS 3.406.9–11. ICR, II.x.4.

While Luther did not deny that the Old Testament contains gospel, he believed that the New Testament was the real book of gospel, and that the Old Testament was of a more provisional nature. Also, some of Luther's beliefs about the Old Testament were determined by a dialectic between law and gospel.[92] Calvin, when speaking of the law, does not dwell upon its provisional nature, but rather on its true relation to gospel. The law is a type of the gospel to come.[93] The law holds people in expectation of Christ's incarnation–although at his coming there will be far more light.[94] There is no essential difference between the law and gospel for Calvin. Any provisional nature which is credited to the law is not essential, but rather historical.[95] The law was the device which God chose to make himself known to the people until he decided to reveal himself more fully. The difference between the law and the gospel is not that they oppose each other, rather "the Gospel points with its finger what the Law foreshadowed under types."[96]

Because of Calvin's view of the continuity and basic congruence between the law and the gospel, the reformer is able to posit his famous third use of the law. The discussion of the uses of the law precede the exposition of the Decalogue in the 1559 edition of the *Institutes*, "in a manner appropriate to the covenant setting."[97] The law is the gift of God, through the covenant setting–and the covenant always points to Christ. The third use of the law its proper goal or end or aim, finds its place among believers in whose hearts the Spirit of God already lives and reigns.[98] Calvin claims that the law is the best instrument for the guidance of the believer. The believer already knows Christ, and yet the law is presented as a help, a free gift from God to aid the believer in his or her struggle to learn the nature of the Lord's will.

The last and most important point which Calvin raises to bind the two Testaments together is the figure of Christ. The law was given

---

[92] Klaas Runia, "Hermeneutic of the Reformers." *Calvin Theological Journal*, 19 (1984): 142.

[93] Ganoczy and Scheld remark that "Schon im Gesetz des Alten Bundes war Christus nähmlich als ewiges Weisheitswort des Vaters geheimnisvoll und verborgen gegenwärtig und wirksam." Alexandre Ganoczy and Stefan Scheld, *Die Hermeneutik Calvins*, 91.

[94] OS 3.398.18–20. ICR, II.ix.1.

[95] Runia, 142.

[96] OS III.401.20–21. ICR, II.ix.3. "Evangelium digito monstrat quod Lex sub typis adumbravit."

[97] ICR, II.vii.6. n. 9.

[98] OS III.337.23–25. ICR, II.vii.12. "proprium finem".

to hold the expectant people together until Christ would come–it was pointing always to Christ. The Redeemer was promised to the chosen people under the law.[99] All worship that is right, which pleases God, always looks to Christ. Christ comes under the law–thereby fulfilling the law, as he abrogated the curse of the law. Christ is the fulfillment of the covenant, the incarnation of the promise which was made to the patriarchs. All the promises given to believers, at any time, are given in Christ.[100] Christ is the head of the Church, both Old and New Testament communities looked to Christ as the head of the body. Christ, literally, is the bridge between the Old and New Testaments. Calvin sees Christ as the point of convergence of the messages of the two Testaments, and the other points of intersection are subordinate to that convergence.[101] It is in directing the reader's attention to Christ that the scriptures of both the Old and New Testaments fulfill their purpose, anything else, and they are in some sense perverted. Therefore, Calvin could remark that "What therefore is said of the Law applies to the whole of Scripture, everything that is not taken as referring to Christ, its one aim and centre (*ad unicum scopum*) it is twisted and perverted."[102]

Calvin was not so simple to see only that the Old and New Testaments had things in common—he also noticed the differences between the two. He is quick to admit this, writing "I freely admit the differences which are related in Scripture, but still hold that they do not derogate in any way from its established unity."[103] Calvin enumerates the differences as four, but allows that if anyone would make the differences five, he would not mind. Rather, he is only worried about the nature of the differences. The nature, he asserts, is always and only in the manner of dispensation, never in the substance.[104]

---

[99] OS 3.321.17. ICR, II.vi.1.

[100] Comm. II Corinthians 1.20, Secundam ad Corinthios, 30.14–16. "I answer that all the promises given to believers from the beginning of the world had their foundation in Christ." "Respondeo, quaecunque ab initio mundi promissiones datae sunt fidelibus, in Christo fuisse fundatas."

[101] For a more extended treatment, see I. John Hesselink's "John Calvin on the Law and Christian Freedom." *Ex Auditu* 11 (1995): esp. 77–80.

[102] Comm. II Corinthians 3.16, Secundam ad Corinthios, 63.6–64.2. "Quod autem de Lege dicitur, ad totam Scripturam patet: nempe ubi ad Christum non dirigitur tanquam ad unicum scopum, perperam torqueri ac perverti."

[103] OS 3.423.5–7. ICR, II.xi.1. "Ego vero libenter recipio quae in Scriptura commemorantur differentias: sed ita ut nihil constitutae iam unitati derogent:" (It can be seen from this statement alone that the principles of interpretation must proceed the search in the scripture).

[104] The differences are as follows. 1. Calvin's first difference is that the Lord of old

Throughout his exposition of the differences between the two Testaments, Calvin held fast to the dictum that the differences pertained only to the dispensation of the message of scripture, never to the substance of the message.[105] No contradiction between the intent of the two could ever exist if they were understood correctly. This cannot be overstated.[106] For Calvin, the functional unity of the two testaments is a result of a more basic statement of his theology and theological hermeneutics. That statement is "God is the same yesterday and today, and always acts toward humanity in the same manner." God speaks with one voice through the whole of the scripture, so that scripture cannot finally contradict itself.[107] With that as a touchstone of his theology, any other relationship between the Old and New Testaments would be preposterous, positing a God who used to have a different relation-

---

willed that his people direct and elevate their minds to the heavenly heritage; yet, to nourish them better in this hope, he displayed it for them to see and taste under earthly benefits. Now, the gospel has more plainly revealed the grace of the future life, so the Lord leads our minds to meditate upon it directly, laying aside the lower mode of training which was used with the Israelites. (II.xi.1) Calvin here argues against those who would contend that Israel's heritage was only earthly. Calvin disputes this position, holding that the earthly reward of the Israelites was not the end in itself, but only the manner in which the Lord wished to raise their eyes to their final heavenly blessedness. (2) The second difference between the Old and New Testaments consist is figures: that, in the absence of the reality, it showed but an image and shadow in place of the substance; the New Testament reveals the very substance of truth as present.(II.xi.4) (3) The third difference is that the Old Testament is literal, of the letter, while the New is spiritual. (II.xi.8) (4) The fourth difference which Calvin admits is that the Old Testament struck consciences by the yoke of bondage, while the New by its spirit of liberality emancipates them into freedom (II.xi.9).

[105] Brian Armstrong asserts "What is important to note is that his commitment to the unity of the Biblical message, Old and New Testament, nearly necessitates frequent typological interpretations." "Exegetical and Theological Principles in Calvin's Preaching, with Special Attention to his Sermons on the Psalms." *Ordenlich und Fruchtbar. Festschrift für Willem van't Spijker Anlasslich seines Abschieds als Professor der Theologische Universitat Apeldoorn* (Leiden: J.J. Groen en Zoon, 1997), 199. This assertion has the added benefit of demonstrating a case for Calvin's hermeneutical stance taking priority over his understanding of what exegetical tool to use.

[106] Interestingly, Heinrich Bullinger was even more emphatic in his linking of the Old and New Testaments, even going so far in *Der alte Glaube* as to state that the Old Testament is a text to which the New Testament is an exposition. See Edward A. Dowey's "The Old Faith: Comments on One of Heinrich Bullinger's Most Distinctive Treatises," *Erbe and Auftrag: Festschrift für Wilhelm Heinrich Neuser zum 65 Geburtstag*, edited by W. van 't Spijker (Kampen, Netherlands: J H Kok, 1991), 270–278.

[107] Hans-Joachim Kraus will state this, though with seeming dismay. "It will also become evident that the Geneva Reformer, for all his significant and effective ap-

ship to his followers than he does now. This can also be seen in the realization that the final import of the whole scripture was the manifestation of Christ. The whole of scripture, thus, is tied together not only by a single author who is the Holy Spirit, but also by its single message, who is Christ, sent from the one fountain of all goods, God the Father.[108]

Having established this principle, we might ask what is its effect? Certainly, Calvin held for the scripture's basic unity, and that unity is a significant help to understanding the revelation of God.[109] But beyond that, this move allows Calvin to identify, at least in part, the search for the meaning of the scriptures with the search for knowing the mind and will of God for humans.

The Mind of the Author

In writing to Grynaeus about the task of the interpreter, John Calvin had argued that "Because it is almost his [the interpreter's] only responsibility to make accessible the mind of the writer whom he has undertaken to explicate, he wanders away from that aim, or at least strays outside his goals, by the extent to which he leads his readers away from that meaning."[110] The apparent clarity of Calvin's principle here would seem to make the consideration of this principle rather short. Calvin has laid out his belief with characteristic brevity and clarity. However, two points immediately spring to mind. First, and perhaps more problematically, why is it *almost (prope)* his only task? What other task, or consideration might come to bear? Secondly, who is the writer? For the consideration of scripture, this is not a straightforward question in Calvin's thought. For Calvin, there is always a two-fold author,

---

proaches, was yet bound by a doctrinal mindset that was oriented to the unity and inner harmony of Scripture." "Calvin's Exegetical Principles," 18.

[108] Brian Gerrish organizes Calvin's theology around the fatherhood of God in his *Grace and Gratitude: The Eucharistic Theology of John Calvin*, (Philadelphia: Fortress Press, 1993).

[109] Even in the process of his critique, Kraus notes that finding unity in the Word of God is a significant theological goal. "Calvin's Exegetical Principles," 18.

[110] Romans, Introductory epistle, Ad Romanos, 1.9–12. "Et sane quum hoc sit prope unicum illius officium, mentem scriptoris, quem explicandum sumpsit, patefacere: quantum ab ea lectores abducit, tantundem a scopo suo aberrat, vel certe a suis finibus quodammodo evagatur."

the Holy Spirit, and the human author.[111] Following Calvin, it seems that the order of teaching demands that we consider the Holy Spirit's authorship first.

The Holy Spirit's connection to scripture is indissoluble. It is only by the office of the Holy Spirit that absolute certainty can be gained in matters of divine truth.[112] Calvin will call the Spirit the author of scripture, and will allude to scripture by declaring that the Holy Spirit expressly declares something.[113] Further, Calvin frequently uses the term *dictare* for God's inspiring act. In his commentary on John's gospel, Calvin writes that God's action is imperious with his scribes. "Therefore he dictated to the four Evangelists what they should write, in order that among them, each had his own part, but the whole formed one integrated body."[114] It fulfilled perfectly Calvin's dictum of finding out the mind of the author that he then suggests the blending of the four gospels in order to allow ourselves to be taught as if by mouth (*ore simul*). In this context, there is no doubt that the mouth referred to is that of the Lord.

The Holy Spirit is the inspiring agent of the authors of the scriptures. Calvin calls the apostles "certain and authentic scribes of the Holy

---

[111] Perhaps the best review of the two minds at work in the production of the biblical text, that of the Holy Spirit and that of the human author, is found in David Puckett's *John Calvin's Exegesis of the Old Testament*, (Louisville: Westminster John Knox Press, 1995), 26–37. See also Brian G. Armstrong's "Report on the seminar: An investigation of Calvin's principles of Biblical interpretation." *Hervormde teologiese studies*, 54, No. 1–2, (1998): 133–142.

[112] Comm. II Corinthians 1.21, Secundam ad Corinthios, 32.15–19. "Since everything that God says is perfectly certain, he wants us to receive it into our souls with a firm and stable acceptance. Then, it is to be noted that, since this degree of certainty is beyond the capacity of the human mind, this is the office of the holy Spirit to confirm in us what God promises in his word." "Nam sicuti certo certius est, quicquid loquitur Deus, ita vult illud firmo stabilique assensu in animis nostris esse constitutum. Deinde notandum est, quum eiusmodi certitudo res sit humanae mentis captu superior, hoc esse Spiritus sancti officium, nobis intus confirmare, quod Deus verbo suo promittit."

[113] OS 3.204.4–7. ICR, I.xvii.2. "As if the things we teach were figments of our brain, and were not distinctly asserted by the Spirit, and repeated in innumerable forms of expression." "Quasi vero cerebri nostri figmentum sit quod docemus: ac non ubique idem diserte pronuntiet Spiritus, et innumeris loquendi formis repetat."

[114] Commentary on John, Argumentum. *In Evangelium Secundum Johannem Commentarius Pars Prior*, edited by Helmut Feld (Geneve: Droz, 1997), 9.3–7. "Sic ergo quatuor Euangelistis dictavit, quod scriberent, ut distributis inter ipsos partibus, corpus unum integrum absolveret. Nunc ergo nostrum est quatuor ita mutuo inter se nexu coniungere, ut nos patiamur quasi uno omnium ore simul doceri."

Spirit."[115] Second, the authority of scripture is based, first and foremost, on the inner testimony of the Spirit.[116] To avoid a dependence on human institutions, even the Church, Calvin finds the certainty of faith only through the Spirit. Calvin will even consider the possibility that the Holy Spirit works without the agreement or knowledge of the writer, characterizing the author as a medium.[117]

However, the human authors of the books of the Bible are not simple automatons. They maintained their own marks of style, and the peculiarities of their textual manner, which the trained textual critic must discern. In considering Ezekiel, Calvin writes that "His language has evidently an exotic sense, this is because since those who are in exile naturally pick up many faults of language. Further, the prophet was not worried about elegance and polish, but, as he had been accustomed to common language, that is the way he spoke."[118]

This attention to the language and style of the human author holds true in the New Testament. For instance, Calvin's reasoning about the authorship of the letter to the Hebrews is absolutely tied to a consideration of the language, and the substance of the message.[119] Calvin sees in Paul's writing itself a chance for the pastor, especially, to be instructed in the ways of ministry. Constantly, Calvin is explaining the Paul's reasoning and motives according to the pastoral situation, that

---

[115] OS 5.141.13. ICR, IV.viii.9. "certi et authentici Spiritus sancti amanuenses." This passage has been used to buttress arguments that Calvin held a doctrine of verbal inerrancy, and has also been a battleground of those who fought against such a position. The LCC edition, for instance, immediately notes that this particular location contains language that is uncharacteristic of the rest of the *Institutes*, and directs the reader to authors who support other views. This argument is outside the scope of this chapter—instead, the passage is quoted to demonstrate that it is the Holy Spirit who inspired the scriptural authors. For an overview of this, see H. Jackson Forstman's *Word and Spirit*, 49–65.

[116] Dowey, 106.

[117] Comm. I Corinthians 13.3, CO 49.509. "But the spirit is seen here predicting, through the mouth of Paul, the persecutions that were to come." "Sed videtur spiritus hic per os Pauli de futuri persequutionibus vaticinatus fuisse."

[118] Comm Ezek. 2.3 CO 40.63. "Nam sermo eius spirat aliquid exoticum. Fieri enim non potuit quin contraherent multa linguae vitia quum essent in exilio. Et propheta non fuit curiosus elegantiae et nitoris. Sicuti ergo iam ad sermonem vulgarem assueverat, it loquutus est."

[119] Obviously, Calvin also does consider Paul's style. His reasoning for not attributing Hebrews to Paul is the lack of Pauline language. See T.H.L. Parker's introductory essay to *Ioannis Calvini Opera Exegetica, Commentarius in Epistolam ad Hebraeos*, edited by T.H.L. Parker. (Geneva: Droz, 1996), xiv–xv.

is to say, according to the needs of the people.[120] Paul becomes, in Calvin's hands, a paradigm not only of faith, but of pastoral practice.[121]

In Paul's case, Calvin occasionally preferred to consider the apostle's chosen rhetoric. In the case of the church at Corinth, Calvin understood the author as choosing a non-eloquent style for two reasons. The first was the more immediate, satisfying the particular pastoral need. The Corinthians were afflicted with "itching ears," and were overly excited by human eloquence.[122] Thus, their need was for a simpler fare, a solid meal, without the delicate sweets.[123] Otherwise, like children, they would have eaten only the dessert, and left the bulk of the nutrition behind. The second reason held permanent validity, for Calvin. This is that "... the Cross of Christ is made void, not only by the wisdom of the world, but also by the brilliance of words."[124]

I wish to examine this particular passage further, for it beautifully illustrates both the possibilities inherent in Calvin's two-fold author

---

[120] For examples of this tendency, see Calvin's comments on Romans 3.5, Galatians 3.18, Philippians 3.12, Ephesians 1.16, I Thessalonians 4.15, and II Thessalonians 2.5. Calvin's practice stands in sharp contrast to Deborah Kuller Shuger's contention that "Renaissance biblical scholarship evinces almost no interest in the intentions, motives, or inner life of either the biblical writers or the texts' sacred personae. Subjectivity dissolves into language and culture–that is, into philological and historical analysis." Shuger, *The Renaissance Bible: Scholarship, Sacrifice, and Subjectivity*, (Berkeley: University of California Press, 1994), 45. This error is more confusing as Shuger is not claiming a Renaissance against Reformation division, so Calvin would certainly count in her field of research. It may be that the subjectivity which she sees dissolving is available in Reformed rhetoric about Paul's motives, and the practical lessons to be learned there.

[121] I have written on Calvin's habit of seeing the Pauline epistles as rich sites for gaining knowledge about pastoral practice in my "Calvin's Exegetical Pastor." In *Calvin and the Company of Pastors: Calvin Studies Society Papers, 2003*, edited by David Foxgrover (Grand Rapids: CRC Publications, 2004), 179–209; and about Paul as a paradigm of pastoral practice for Calvin in "Paul as Calvin's (Ambivalent) Pastoral Model," In *Dutch Review of Church History* (Leiden: Brill, 2004), 284–298.

[122] Comm I Corinthians 1.17 (see below).

[123] This care for the pastoral personality and style of the human author more closely links Calvin to some of the issues of other humanists. See James D. Tracy, "*Ad Fontes*: The Humanist Understanding of Scripture as Nourishment for the Soul." 252–267 In *Christian Spirituality: High Middle Ages and Reformation*, edited by Jill Raitt with Bernard McGinn and John Meyendorff. World Spirituality: An Encyclopedic History of the Religious Quest, vol. 17, (New York: Crossroad, 1988), 255–256. For a conflicting view, see Deborah Kuller Shuger's *The Renaissance Bible: Scholarship, Sacrifice, and Subjectivity*, (Berkeley: University of California Press, 1994).

[124] Comm I Corinthians 1.17 (see below).

scheme, and the difficulties in grasping the strands within Calvin's rhetoric to penetrate to the hermeneutical principle of the dual authorship.

> The second question is a little more difficult. He says that the cross of Christ is emptied, if it is mixed with the wisdom of words. My answer to that is to consider to whom Paul is speaking. For the ears of the Corinthians were itching with foolish desire for pompous language. Because of this they needed to be called back to the humility of the cross more than others, in order to learn that they would embrace the bare Christ, and the gospel in its simplicity, free from any embellishment. And yet I think that in some way this passage has a perpetual message, that the cross of Christ is made empty, not only by the wisdom of the world, but also by the splendor of words. For the preaching of Christ crucified is bare and simple; therefore it should not to be obscured by embellishment. The characteristic work of the gospel is to drive back the wisdom of the world into order, that, dispossessed of our own sense we become completely docile, and do not offer to know, or even desire to know anything but what the Lord himself teaches. As far as the wisdom of the flesh is concerned, we shall have to discuss, soon, on how it is opposed to Christ. But it is necessary to touch upon eloquence here, a little.
>
> We see that from the beginning God has so ordained, that the gospel should be handled stripped bare of any support from eloquence. Surely the one who formed the tongues of men for eloquence, could have been skilled in speech if he wanted. That is possible, but he rejected that. I can find two most important reasons for his rejection. The first is that in rude and unpolished words, the greatness and the majesty of his truth would be all that much more apparent, and the efficacy of the spirit might penetrate the hearts of men, by itself, without external aids. The second reason is that our obedience and teachableness is better tested, and at the same time, he instructs us in true humility. For the Lord admits only little ones to his school. Therefore the only ones with the capacity for heavenly wisdom are those who are content with the preaching of the cross, in a crude way, and do not wish that Christ be covered with a mask. Therefore the teaching of the gospel had to be made to serve the purpose of drawing believers away from all conceit and arrogance.[125]

---

[125] Comm. I Corinthians, 1.17, CO 49.321. "Secunda quaestio paulo plus habet difficultatis: dicit enim exinaniri Christi crucem, si qua sermonis sapientia admisceatur. Respondeo, considerandum esse quos alloquatur Paulus. Pruriebant Corinthiorum aures stulta cupiditate magniloquentiae: prae aliis ergo ad crucis humilitatem revocandi erant, ut discerent nudum Christum et simplex evangelium absque fuco ullo amplecti. Quamquam hanc sententiam quodammodo perpetuam esse fateor, Christi crucem exinaniri non tantum mundana sapientia, sed verborum quoque splendore. Christi enim crucifixi praedicatio simplex est ac nuda: obfuscari ergo verborum fuco non debet. Evangelii proprium est, mundi sapientiam sic in ordinem redigere, ut proprio sensu

There are three conceptual divisions in the text. First is Paul's pastoral styling. The second and third divisions are grouped together by Calvin as God's message given through the chosen pedagogy. God's very choice of a manner of teaching carries a particular message, which is unchanging.

The first division concerns Paul's choice of styles, according to his analysis of the pastoral needs of his particular audience. Calvin was absolutely clear that the key to understanding Paul's choice is to remember to whom this is addressed.[126] Context can never be discarded, but occasionally it is only the entrance into a problem. Throughout his exposition of the first epistle to the church at Corinth, Calvin constantly reminds his readers of the worldly nature of the Corinthians. They were the kind of people easily impressed with outward and empty displays.[127] Paul's pastoral prescription to such a people was to be exactly what they do not want. There is no sense from Calvin that Paul is acting here at the special prompting of the Spirit, but rather that he was a good pastor, choosing the correct tone and substance for the particular audience.

The second and third divisions have to do completely with God's authorship. This portion Calvin sets apart as having a "permanent validity." Calvin reaches this understanding through considering the nature of the language of the Gospel.[128] Since God could have chosen

---

vacui dociles nos tantum praebeamus, nec aliud scire nos putemus, aut etiam appetamus, quam quod Dominus ipse docet. De sapientia carnis fusius mox tractandum erit, qualiter Christo repugnet: de eloquentia paucis hic perstringam quantum locus requirit. Videmus Deum ita ab initio ordinasse, ut evangelium omni eloquentiae subsidio nudum administraretur. Qui linguas hominum format ad facundiam, non posset ipse disertus esse si vellet? quum posset, noluit. Cur noluerit, duas potissimum rationes invenio: altera est ut in rudi et impolito sermone magis conspicua appareret veritatis suae maiestas, et sola spiritus efficacia absque externis adminiculis in hominum animos penetraret. Altera vero, ut nostram obedientiam ac docilitatem melius experiretur, et simul ad veram humilitatem erudiret. Solos enim parvulos in scholam suam admittit Dominus: ergo illi demum coelestis sapientiae sint capaces, qui praedicatione crucis in speciem abiecta contenti larvatum Christum nequaquam desiderant. Ideo in hunc finem evangelii doctrinam attemperari oportuit, ut ab omni fastu et altitudine abstraherentur fideles."

[126] Comm. I Corinthians 1.17, CO 49.321.

[127] Comm. I Corinthians 2.3, CO 49.334.

[128] It is interesting that this whole discussion depends on a nominalistic distinction between what God could have done (*potentia dei absoluta*), and what God did (*potentia dei ordinata*). David Steinmetz, in his "Calvin and the Absolute Power of God" in *Calvin in Context* (Oxford: Oxford University Press, 1995), 40–52, argues that Calvin does not hold, especially in his exegesis, a place for this distinction. After surveying some of

to present the gospel in the most eloquent, most perfect speech, and did not, there must be reasons available for such a choice. Calvin gives two, corresponding to the second and third conceptual divisions.

The second division has to do with the proclamation and protection of the majesty of God's truth. God's truth is clearer in simple language. Moreover, the power of that truth, that is, the efficacy of the Holy Spirit, is seen to be free of need of persuasive human language to attain its ends. The third division concerns the qualities which the Lord wishes to inculcate in believers. Believers are to come as obedient and teachable children.[129] In this way, they are both tested as to our willingness to receive the yoke of God, and are exercised in the "teaching of true humility."[130]

Following Calvin, the first division stands, in a certain way, over against the unity of the second and third divisions. Thus, they are distributed according to the mind most active behind their appearance. It would seem that one could state that the specific, contingent, pastorally functioning portion of the text might be accredited to Paul, and the trans-historically permanent functional portion assigned to the divine author.

So then, what is the relationship between the authorial levels of the text, that of the human author, and that of the divine? One might say that "it is as easy–one should probably say easier–for Calvin to speak

---

the characteristic doctrines, such as miracles, providence and predestination, Steinmetz concludes that Calvin was opposed to the very distinction as such (50). However, here we see Calvin using the very distinction between what God could have done and what God did, Steinmetz's functional distinction between the two powers (42). As much as Calvin is uncomfortable with the discussions about *potentia ordinata* and *potentia absoluta*, he does betray the influence of certain typical forms of nominalistic thought, here and in other places. Other scholars, who have seen Calvin as much more influenced by nominalistic and/or scotistic thought, support these tendencies. See Alister McGrath, *A Life of John Calvin: A Study in the Shaping of Western Culture*, (Cambridge, MA: Blackwell Publishers, 1990), 40–47. I wish to put forward another possibility, however. Steinmetz's article revolves around whether Calvin held out for the theological use of the distinction. It may be that Calvin was not comfortable with that. However, in the present pericope, Calvin is finding an edifying and educational use, which he finds extremely useful. That these two positions are not fully reconcilable demonstrates Calvin's theological method of "right teaching" even more clearly. Properly used, the distinction is an occasion for edification. Incorrectly used, it only leads to perilous speculation.

[129] Randall C. Zachman brought this facet of Calvin's thought, his imploring believers to cultivate a teachable nature, to my attention. See his "'Do You Understand What You Are Reading?' Calvin's Guidance for the Reading of Scripture" *Scottish Journal of Theology* 54 (2001): 1–20, esp. 13–19.

[130] Comm. I Cor 1.17, CO 49.321. CNTC 9.34. "ad veram humilitatem erudiret."

of the scriptures as the writings of the Spirit as to think of them as the product of the men who actually moved the pens."[131] But from the analysis of the I Corinthians passage, it seems that there is instead a true duality of office in the writing of the scripture.[132] The text points to a human author, who is pastoral, and conventional. In that same text, the Spirit works to record God's timeless truths. Beyond this, there remains some overlap. The overlap must be preserved, for Calvin speaks of the writers of the scripture, or even the scripture itself, as using a method of being guided in what is said by the capacity of their audience.[133] Further, Calvin allows his human authors some leeway in the context of their particular situations. Thus, Paul, when speaking to the Corinthians, will emphasize those parts of a particular doctrine which are most salutary for the Corinthians, and may not cover all possible portions of that topic.[134]

To demonstrate this case, consider Calvin's interpretation of I Corinthians 11.3. Calvin is concerned to demonstrate how Paul could have placed man over the woman, without Christ's position as Head being usurped.[135] Calvin realizes that the passage seems to contradict Gala-

---

[131] H. Jackson Forstman, *Word and Spirit: Calvin's Doctrine of Biblical Authority*, 50.

[132] Ganoczy and Scheld point to this, *Die Hermeneutik Calvins*, 7. Heiko Oberman has pointed out a different "double operation of the Holy Spirit," which refers to the preaching of the Word by the preacher and the opening of the hearts of the congregation. These are analytically separate, though logically connected divisions. Heiko Oberman, "Preaching and the Word in the Reformation." *Theology Today* 18 (1961/1962): 16–29.

[133] Comm. I Cor. 10.3, CO 49.453. "The custom of scripture is, when dealing with the sacraments, or other things for that matter, the method is to be guided in what they say by the capacity of the people, with whom they are dealing. Thus, they do not speak with respect to the nature of the thing, but with the sense of the audience." "Scripturae mos est, quum de sacramentis aut aliis rebus disserit, interdum pro captu auditorum loqui: atque ita non rei naturam respicit, sed quid perperam sentiant auditores." However, Calvin does circumscribe this principle with the qualifier that gives the most significant examples as mysterious—the sacraments.

[134] Comm. I Cor. 10.7, CO 49.458. "Doubtless he chose what was most suited for Corinthians." "Nempe elegit quod maxime Corinthiis congruebat."

[135] Comm. I Cor. 11.3, CO 49.474. "In the passage that follows, there is more difficulty. Here, the man is placed in an intermediate position between Christ and the woman, so that Christ is not the head of the woman. Yet elsewhere, it is the same apostle who teaches in Galatians 3.28 that 'in Christ there is no male or female.' Why has he kept this difference here? I answer that the solution depends on the circumstances of the passages. When the difference between man and woman is negated, he is considering the spiritual kingdom of Christ, where persons are not respected, and are not taken into consideration, for it has nothing to do with the body, nothing to do with human external relationships with each other, but it is concerned wholly with the spirit. That is

tians 3.28, and believes himself to be constrained to resolve that difficulty. He did so by differentiating between the two contexts. The Galatians passage speaks to the spiritual kingdom, the Corinthians passage
speaks to the sphere of ecclesiastical polity.[136] But Calvin has already
definitely determined that polity is a matter of convention and even *adiaphora*.[137] The implication from this interpretation is that the placing of
the man over the woman is purely a matter of convention, and a partic-

---

the reason that he declares that there is even no difference between 'a slave' and 'a free
man.' At the same time, however, he does not touch the civil order and also the distinctions in honors, for it is not possible to get along without such in ordinary everyday life.
In this passage the dispute is concerned with external appearance and decorum, which
is part of ecclesiastical polity. Therefore, so far as spiritual union is concerned, before
God and inwardly in their conscience, Christ is the head of both the man and woman
without any distinction, because no respect is given to male or female. On the other
hand, as far as external composition of society and social order are concerned, the man
follows Christ, and the woman the man, so that they do not stand on the same level, but
this inequality exists." "In eo quod sequitur, plus est aliquanto difficultatis. Hic ponitur
vir medius inter Christum et mulierem, ita ut caput mulieris non sit Christus. Atqui
alibi docet idem apostolus (Galat. 3, 28), in Christo non esse masculum nec feminam.
Cur ergo hic statuit discrimen quod illic tollit? Respondeo, solutionem pendere ex locorum circumstantia. Quum mulierem a viro differre negat, tractat de spirituali Christi
regno, ubi personae non aestimantur, nec in rationem veniunt: nihil enim ad corpus,
nihil ad externam hominum societatem, sed totum in spiritu situm est. Qua ratione
etiam servi et liberi nullam esse differentiam testatur. Neque tamen civilem ordinem
interea confundit, aut honorum distinctiones, quibus non potest carere communis haec
vita. Hic vero disputat de externa honestate atque decoro, quae pars est politiae eccle-
siasticae. Ergo quantum ad spiritualem coniunctionem, coram Deo et intus in conscientia, Christus caput est viri ac mulieris absque discrimine: quia illic neque masculi
neque feminae habetur respectus. Quantum ad externam compositionem et decorum
politicum, Christum vir et virum mulier sequitur: ita ut non sit idem gradus, sed locum
habeat inaequalitas ista."
   [136] I Corinthians 11.3, CO 49.474.
   [137] I Corinthians 11.2, CO 49.473. "Now, I do not deny that some of the traditions of
the apostles were not written down, but I do not concede that these were elements of
doctrine, nor were they things necessary for salvation. What were they? Those things
pertaining to order and polity. We know that each church is free to set up the form of
polity that is useful for it, and is to its advantage, because the Lord has given no certain
prescriptions about this. Thus, Paul who first founded the church at Corinth, gave form
to it by pious and honest institutions, in order that things would be done decently
and in order, as is set forth in chapter 14." "Ego autem non nego quin aliquae fuerint
apostolorum traditiones non scriptae: sed non concedo fuisse doctrinae partes, nec de
rebus ad salutem necessariis. Quid igitur? quae pertinerent ad ordinem et politiam.
Scimus enim unicuique ecclesiae liberum esse, politiae formam instituere sibi aptam
et utilem: quia Dominus nihil certi praescripserit. Ita Paulus ecclesiae Corinthiacae
primus fundator, institutis quoque piis et honestis eam formaverat, ut decenter et ordine
illic agerentur omnia: sicuti praecipiet cap. 14."

ular strategy of Paul's for preventing the Corinthian church from facing scandals caused by too great a departure from the moral conventions of the wider society.

Further, Calvin, in his consideration of I Corinthians 11.14, demonstrates a contextual sophistication about historical texts, and the circumstances which distance the first audience from a latter one.[138] Calvin makes a strong argument in favor of understanding "natural" as that which is conventional, in the reading of this passage. The sixteenth-century Frenchman represents Paul as sharing that popular misconception.[139] Here, Calvin places before the reader the truth that a particular human is unable to escape his own historical circumstances. This is certainly different from the Holy Spirit, which has no historical circumstances *per se.*

Thus, when Calvin seeks to uncover the mind of the author in scripture, he is attempting to have access to the divine mind, the Holy Spirit's intention.[140] He does so, however, through the medium of the mind of the human author. This allows him to see historically contextual passages in scripture which are only contingently relevant, while maintaining an overall unity of message and meaning. Further, it is a necessary step. One can come to know the mind of a human author

---

[138] I Corinthians 11.14, CO 49.478. "Again, he proposes nature before them as the model of propriety. What, however, he calls 'natural' was what was accepted by common consent and usage at that time, at least among the Greeks, for long hair was not always shameful among men." "Iterum naturam illis decori magistram proponit. Quod autem omnium consensu et consuetudine receptum tunc erat, et quidem apud Graecos, vocat naturale: nam viris non semper fuit coma dedecori." That sophistication becomes even greater when one realizes that the key term here is φυσις, a term which Calvin handles quite differently in Romans 1.26.

[139] I differ here with Alexandre Ganoczy's claim in his address of 1974, given at Amsterdam to the Europäischer Kongress für Calvinforschung, "Forschungsansatze zur Hermeneutik Calvins: Calvin als paulinischer Theologe." Ganoczy stated that "Dis Aussagen der Schrift sind als solche einfache und eindeutige Kundgebungen des Willens Gottes. Den Gedanken, daß in der Schrift selbst vielfältige, geschichtlich bedinte Meinungen über das ewige Wort Gottes zur Sprache kommen und die Schrift auf diese Weise natürlich vieldeutig ist, hätte Calvin wohl als Blasphemie und Frivolität angesehen." This is impossible to reconcile with Calvin's obvious discomfort at Paul's confusion of nature with convention. Calvin could and did find errors of fact and historically conditioned opinions in the scripture—but at the hands of the human author, not the Holy Spirit.

[140] Obviously, I am disagreeing with Han-Joachim Kraus, who lists this principle, but restricts it to the human author, 13. This is to read far too much of a modern historical-critical mindset into Calvin.

through his writings. The analogies are not too strained, when shifting from one era to another, since the human consciousness remains reasonably constant. No such direct and immediate access to the divine mind is possible. God has already accommodated the divine mind so as to use human speech, and the ministry of human pastors. Further, God has been forced to hide what cannot be understood, and babble to the ears of human children. Access through so many veils to the mind of the divine author is impossible. Instead, the possibility is held out to understand the mind of the human author, inspired to place messages in his words which would be of value for the directing of the Christian life on earth, and the directing of the believer's journey to heaven, and through that avenue to approach to the meanings God intended for believers.

Finally, there is the issue of the "almost."[141] One wonders whether this is simply Calvin's normal caution when making sweeping statements; the form of the statement rings with a familiar timbre to the reader whose ears have become accustomed to the rhythm of the beginning of the *Institutes*. Although such an issue cannot ever be definitively decided either in the affirmative or negative, I would suggest that this "almost" would contain two particular items. The first would be the knowledge of the given audience and context, the second, the background of correct Christian teaching. But both of these lead us into the next section, that of hermeneutical circles.

Hermeneutical Circles

To raise the notion of John Calvin clearly holding the idea of hermeneutical circles raises questions, and possibly gives as many scholars alarm as it does pleasure. It certainly may be argued that in some senses, John Calvin anticipates some of the more salient insights into the art of interpretation of his spiritual heir, Friedrich Schleiermacher.[142] His insistence that almost the only task of the interpreter is to explain

---

[141] Romans, introductory epistle, Ad Romanos, 1.

[142] Brian Gerrish has considered the relationship of Calvin and Schleiermacher more than any other single scholar. See especially his "From Calvin to Schleiermacher: The Theme and Shape of Christian Dogmatics." In *Continuing the Reformation: Essays on Modern Religious Thought* (Chicago: University of Chicago Press, 1993), 178–195; "Theology within the Limits of Piety Alone: Schleiermacher and Calvin's Notion of God." In *The Old Protestantism and the New: Essays on the Reformation Heritage* (Edinburgh:

the mind of the author closely parallels Schleiermacher's dictum that the task of the interpreter is to come to know the mind of the author better than he knew it himself.[143] However, the differences between Calvin's work and Schleiermacher's remind us not to attempt to draw out more than there is to be found. Calvin certainly never set out to write down a general theory of interpretation, nor, after the Seneca commentary, do we find him again indulging in specific interpretive works on texts other than scriptural books.

The model of the hermeneutical circle, especially as it is proposed by Heidegger, is one of the more helpful heuristic tools available for grasping what Calvin was attempting in the task of interpretation.[144] Heidegger lays out the basic thesis that to engage in the process of understanding, some pre-understanding must already be at work. "Any interpretation which is to contribute understanding, must already have understood what is to be interpreted."[145] Functionally similar statements are found throughout the Christian tradition. Augustine makes several such statements in *De Doctrina Christiana*, setting up the two-fold hermeneutic of love of God and of neighbor, a standard which is found within scripture, as the key to understanding scripture.[146] Bonaventure, in the *Prologue* to his *Breviloquium*, states that "By knowing and loving Christ, by being confirmed in faith and rooted ... in love, we can know the

---

T.&T. Clark Limited, 1982), 196–207; and "Schleiermacher and the Reformation: A Question of Doctrinal Development," In *The Old Protestantism and the New: Essays on the Reformation Heritage*, 179–195.

[143] Friedrich Schleiermacher, *Hermeneutics: Handwritten Manuscripts*, edited by Heinz Kimmerle, translated by James Duke and Jack Forstman, (Atlanta: Scholars Press, 1977), 69. "One must understand as well as and better than the author."

[144] Martin Heidegger, *Being and Time*, translated by John Macquarrie and Edward Robinson, (San Francisco: Harper and Row, 1962), 194. Heidegger characterizes the circle of understanding as the guise for the most primordial kind of knowing. To attempt to escape this condition of human knowing is a possibility which Heidegger dismisses, and a possibility which Calvin would have denied as idolatrous.

[145] Heidegger, 194.

[146] Augustine, *On Christian Doctrine*, translated by D.W. Robertson, (Indianapolis: Bobbs-Merrill, 1954), 87–88. III.x.14. "Generally, this method consists in this: that whatever appears in the divine Word that does not literally pertain to virtuous behavior or to the truth of faith you must take to be figurative. Virtuous behavior pertains to the love of God and of one's neighbor; the truth of faith pertains to a knowledge of God and of one's neighbor." *De Doctrina Christiana*, edited by Martin Joseph, (Turnholt: Brepols, 1962), III.x.14. "Et iste omnino modus est, ut quicquid in sermone diuino neque ad morum honestatem neque ad fidei ueritatem proprie referri potest, figuratum esse cognoscas. Morum honestas ad diligendum deum et proximum, fidei ueritas ad cognoscendum deum et proximum pertinet."

breadth, length, height, and depth of Scripture, ..."[147] At some level, the act of knowing Christ necessarily contains either hearing or reading the New Testament. Thus, the reader knows and loves a central figure out of a book which then helps the reader understand the book! This circularity, which so bothers minds conditioned by the Enlightenment, was apparently not a cause for concern for the medievals or Reformers. So it should not be too surprising that some of the statements from the "Purpose of the Present Work" make no sense without something like a hermeneutical circle.[148]

There are five circles which Calvin sees as particularly important as he attempts to understand the particular books of the scripture. These are (1) orthodox Christian doctrine and scripture; (2) the specific passage and the entire book; (3) the specific book and the corpus of that author; (4) the specific book or passage and the entirety of scripture; (5) the specific passage's message and the life of faith in Geneva and the world. Obviously, circles two through four are various levels within a particular set of the part/whole circle. Furthermore, the various circles to which he pays attention mutually enrich one another, and help him to come to an understanding of the meaning of various passages.

1. *From Christian Doctrine to Scripture and Back*

Calvin calls his *Institutes* "... a key to open access to all the children of God.", a key that unlocks the door to a right understanding of scripture.[149] But why should Christians need any key at all? If, as Calvin claims, scripture contains "a perfect doctrine, to which one can add nothing,"[150] then what is left for the Christian pastor to do but make

---

[147] Bonaventure, The Breviloquium—Prologue, 4. *The Works of Bonaventure*, v. II., translated by José de Vinck, (St. Anthony Guild Press, 1963), 4.

[148] We should also note that this is not the only possibility in the sixteenth century. Girolamo Zanchi proposed that a key to the scriptures as well. But for him, it was the theory of analogy, taken from a basically philosophical investigation of the names of God, which supplied the key. Thus, the hermeneutic key in Zanchi was supplied from outside of the scripture, rather than from within it. See Harm Goris, "Thomism in Zanchi's Doctrine of God," in *Reformation and Scholasticism: An Ecumenical Enterprise*, edited by Willem J. van Asselt and Eef Dekker (Grand Rapids: Baker Book House, 2001), esp. 126–133.

[149] *Argument du Present Livre*, OS 3.8.5–6. "une clef et ouverture, pour donner acces a tous enfans de Dieu ..."

[150] *Argument du Present Livre*, OS 3.7.19–20. "une doctrine parfaicte, a laquelle on ne peut rien adiouster."

sure that believers are reading the scripture?[151] Simply put, Calvin believed that the coming to the scriptures involved more than the willingness to be instructed, or even receiving the gift of the Holy Spirit's insight.[152] One can make a mistake, either in referring a particular passage incorrectly, or in misunderstanding the correct context for application of the message of scripture. Further, Calvin claimed that he is keeping longer doctrinal disputes out of the commentaries.[153] Thus, one must come to the scripture having already received some instruction in doctrine. Doctrine, drawn from scripture, is the guide to reading the scripture.[154] That this is a circular notion does not seem to have bothered Calvin.[155] Rather, he saw the *Institutes* as a summary of Christian teaching,[156] that could serve as a guide to the book it sought to explain. While this may seem prejudicial to those who read with modern eyes, it certainly was Calvin's ideal. The whole of the *Institutes* serves this purpose. Calvin wrote his purpose in the 1560 French edition of the *Institutes*.[157] The point is clarified by the longer quotation.

---

[151] Calvin takes up this very point in his comments upon II Timothy 2.15. Without rehearsing the whole argument, basically Calvin points out that the pastor is like a father guiding children in their most efficient reception of the scriptural nourishment.

[152] This is not to belittle the Holy Spirit's role in a believer's reading of the scriptures, which will be covered later.

[153] If one looks too briefly at the length of Calvin's commentaries, one may reckon that he failed. However, as Ganoczy and Scheld point out, there is a difference between those doctrinal points which Calvin includes and those which are left for the *Institutes*. Those longer arguments which are more tangentially related to the text are left for other venues, those which are pertinent to its thrust are retained. See *Die Hermeneutik Calvins*, 169–170.

[154] Francois Wendel asserted that Calvin shifted his original focus of the *Institutes*, that of giving "a succinct exposition of the reformed doctrine," to that of being "a properly dogmatic introduction to the reading of Holy Scripture." *Calvin: Origins and Development of His Religious Thought*, 146.

[155] Alexandre Ganoczy has described this as a circle from the scripture to the *Institutes* to the scripture. Alexandre Ganoczy, "Calvin als palulinischer Theologe," in *Calvinus Theologus*, ed. Willhelm Neuser (Neukirchen: Neukirchener Verlag, 1976), 39–69. See also his "Exegese und Systematik" in "Hermeneutische Korrelationen bei Calvin." *Reformatio Ecclesiae. Beitrage zu Kirchlichen Reformbemuhungen von der Alten Kirche bis zur Neuzeit. Festgabe fur Erwin Iserloh*, hrsg. von Remigius Baumer (Zurich: Schoningh, 1980), 617–620.

[156] *Argument du Present Livre*, OS 3.8.18–19.

[157] Richard Muller has pointed out that this introduction is not, in fact, in the 1560 French edition, in his "Calvin's 'Argument du livre' (1541): An Erratum to the McNeill and Battles 'Institutes.'" *Sixteenth Century Journal* 29 (1998): 35–38. Though Muller's arguments are persuasive, I present it as such for ease of use for English readers.

In order that my readers may better profit from this present work, I wish to demonstrate briefly the utility which they may take from it. For, in doing this, I will demonstrate to them the purpose to which they should bend and direct their intention in reading it. Although the Holy Scripture contains a perfect doctrine, to which one can add nothing; because our Lord meant to display the infinite treasures of his wisdom in it, on the other hand a person who has not had much practice in it has good reason for some guidance and direction, in order to know what he ought to look for in it, so that he will not wander here and there, but will hold to a sure path, in order that he might attain the goal to which the Holy Spirit calls him. Thus, the responsibility of those who have received from God more ample light than others is to help the simple in this issue, as if lending them a hand, in order to conduct them and help them to find the sum of what God wished to teach us in his word. Now, that cannot be better done in the Scriptures than by treating the principal and most consequential matters, which are comprised in the Christian Philosophy. For he who knows these things will be prepared to profit more in the school of God in one day than another will in three months. This is because that one knows somewhat well to what he should refer each sentence, and has this rule for grasping all that is presented to him.

Seeing then that it is very necessary to help in this fashion those who desire to be instructed in the doctrine of salvation, consequently, I was forced, according to the faculty that the Lord has given me, to undertake this task. This has been my goal in composing the present book. First of all I put it into Latin so as to serve all men of learning, from whatever nation they came; then after that, desiring to communicate what could come to fruition for our French nation, I have also translated it into our language. I do not want to give too favorable an appraisal concerning it, nor do I want to declare how profitable reading it could be, for I fear seeming to value my work too highly. Nevertheless, I can promise that it can be a key to open access for all children of God into a good and right understanding of holy Scripture. Thus, if from now on our Lord gives me the means and opportunity of writing some commentaries, I will use the greatest possible brevity, because there will be no need for me to make long digressions, seeing that I have here treated at length almost all the points pertinent to Christianity. Since we must recognize that all truth and sane doctrine proceed from God, I will in all simplicity dare fearlessly to protest what I think of this work; I shall recognize that it is more God's than mine. Therefore, truly, any praise for it should be given to him.

Thus, I urge all those who have reverence for the word of the Lord, to read it, and to impress it diligently upon their memory, if they wish to have, first, a sum of Christian doctrine, and secondly, a way to benefit greatly from reading the old as well as the new Testament. When they have done this they will recognize, by experience, that I have not wanted to abuse words. If anyone is unable to understand all the contents, he should not therefore despair, but he should read on, hoping that one passage will give him a more familiar explication of another. Above all, he should have recourse to the Scripture in order to consider the testimonies I take from it.[158]

---

[158] OS 3.7.15–8.27. "A fin que les Lecteurs puissent mieux faire leur proffit de ce present livre, ie leur veux bien monstrer en brief, l'utilité qu'ilz auront a en prendre. Car, en ce faisant, ie leur monstreray le but, auquel ils devront tendre et diriger leur intention, en le lisant. Combien que la saincte Escriture contienne une doctrine parfaicte, a laquelle on ne peut rien adiouster: comme en icelle nostre Seigneur a voulu desployer les Thresors infiniz de sa Sapience: toutesfois une personne, qui n'y sera pas fort exercitée, a bon mestier de quelque conduicte et addresse, pour sçavoir ce quelle y doibt cercher: a fin de ne s'esgarer point cà et là, mais de tenir une certaine voye, pour attaindre tousiours a la fin, ou le Sainct Esprit l'appelle. Pourtant l'office de ceux qui ont receu plus ample lumiere de Dieu que les autres, est, de subvenir aux simples en cest endroict: et quasi leur prester la main, pour les conduire et les ayder a trouver la somme de ce que Dieu nous a voulu enseigner en sa parolle. Or cela ne se peut mieux faire par Escritures, qu'en traictant les matieres principales et de consequence, lesquelles sont comprinses en la Philosophie Chrestienne. Car celuy qui en aura l'intelligence, sera preparé a proffiter en l'eschole de Dieu en un iour, plus qu'un autre en trois mois: d'autant qu'il sçait a peu pres, ou il doibt rapporter une chascune sentence: et ha sa reigle pour compasser tout ce qui luy est presenté. Voyant donc que cestoit une chose tant necessaire, que d'ayder en ceste façon ceux qui desirent d'estre instruictz en la doctrine de salut, ie me suis efforcé, selon la faculté que le Seigneur m'a donnée, de m'employer a ce faire: et a ceste fin i'ay composé ce present livre. Et premierement l'ay mis en latin: a ce qu'il peust servir a toutes gens d'estude, de quelque nation qu'ilz feussent: puis apres desirant de communiquer ce qui en pouoit venir de fruict a nostre Nation Françoise: l'ay aussi translaté en nostre langue. Ie n'ose pas en rendre trop grand tesmoignange, et declairer combien la lecture en pourra estre proffitable, de peur qu'il ne semble que ie prise trop mon ouvrage: toutesfois ie puis bien promettre cela, que ce pourra estre comme une clef et ouverture, pour donner acces a tous enfans de Dieu, a bien et droictement entendre l'Escriture saincte. Parquoy si doresenavant nostre Seigneur me donne le moyen et opportunité de faire quelques commentaires: ie useray de la plus grande brievetéqu'il me sera possible: pource qu'il ne sera pas besoing de faire longues digressions, veu quei'ay icy desduict, au long, quasi tous les articles qui appartiennent a la Chrestiente. Et puis qu'il nous fault recongnoistre, toute verité et saine doctrine procedder de Dieu: i'oseray hardiment protester, en simplicité, ce que ie pense de cest œuvre, le recongnoissant estre de Dieu, plus que mien. comme, a la verité, la louenge luy en doibt estre rendue. C'est que i'exhorte tous ceux qui ont reverence a la parolle du Seigneur, de le lire, et imprimer diligemment en memoire, s'ilz veulent, premierement auoir une somme de la doctrine Chrestienne: puis une entrée a bien proffiter en la lecture tant du vieil que du nouveau Testament. Quand ilz auront cela faict: ilz congnoistront, par experience, que ie ne les ayu point voulu abuser de parolles. Si quelqu'un ne peut comprendre tout le contenu, il ne fault pas qu'il se desespere pourtant: mais qu'il marche tousiours oultre, esperant qu'un passage luy donnera plus familierement exposition de l'autre. Sur toutes choses, il fauldra auoir en recommandation, de recourir a l'Escriture, pour considerer les tesmoignages que i'en allegue."

To interpret the mind of the author of scripture, one must have Christian doctrine well in hand.[159] That this seems to set up a circular procedure cannot be denied, nor would Calvin wish it to be. Rather, he sees doctrine and scripture continually modifying each other, creating one of the more significant hermeneutical circles of which he is continually conscious. Scripture is not laid out systematically, although it contains perfection, that is, it contains everything necessary for it to perform its task, which is to reveal God and God's will for humans. God had good reasons for having the scriptures be such, and although Calvin occasionally commented upon them, he was rarely concerned with the reasons that believers have received the scripture in its present form. He was far more concerned with the practical issue of the possibility of either not seeking the correct thing in the scripture, or for wandering too much.[160]

It is an item of no little interest that the first concern that Calvin states, that people need a guide to understand how they are to understand scripture if they are not very experience in it, is specifically a hermeneutical concern, and involves the issue of the preconception (*Vorgriff*).[161] Obviously, the preconception is something we grasp in advance, some kind of fore-conception.[162] This fore-conception, or particular privileged way of conceiving the meaning of the text, has been stated as a necessity for the process of understanding by modern hermeneutical theorists. Calvin goes just as far, and seems to make it a necessity for finding the right meaning.

Calvin's second concern, that a person ought "to know what he ought to look for in it, so that he will not wander here and there, but will hold to a sure path, in order that he might attain the goal to which the Holy Spirit calls him,"[163] is more practically cast. Even if one, through wandering about in the fields of the Lord, as it were,

---

[159] Richard Muller has pointed out that "What Calvin intended to teach was the church's doctrine, not his own doctrine." *The Unaccommodated Calvin: Studies in the Foundation of a Theological Tradition* (Oxford: Oxford University Press, 2000), 7. Though this insight almost begs for more discussion, alone it represents a significant instruction that the reader of Calvin needs to understand. Calvin believed, more or less, that it was possible and necessary to grasp the outline of the Church's teaching, prior to and as a help in interpreting the scripture.

[160] *Argument du Present Livre*, OS 3.7.23–25.

[161] *Argument du Present Livre*, OS 3.7.23–25.

[162] See Heidegger, 191.

[163] *Argument du Present Livre*, OS 3.7.23–25. "a fin de ne s'esgarer point cà et là, mais de tenir une certaine voye, pour attaindre tousiours a la fin, ou le Sainct Esprit l'appelle."

might eventually stumble upon the correct goal, that is hardly a commendation of such a method. Rather, the directed reader follows the path of doctrine, knowing what his goal is, and strengthening his march toward that goal by constantly fortifying the strength of the goal by confirming it in scripture, and applying it in life.

Calvin's over-arching theological enterprise revolved around two poles. The first is the *Institutes*, a summary of Christian doctrine and guide to the scriptures. The second was the collection of specific efforts at explication of the Bible, sermons, lectures, and commentaries. The two poles were indivisibly connected. Although the commentaries are far less known by the modern audience, that does not change the fact that Calvin saw these two poles as mutually supportive, and neither is envisioned as a complete opus, to be taken alone. The perfect doctrine is within scripture, and it is the effort of the *Institutes* and commentaries to unfold that doctrine. Finally, both poles are standing under the judgment of scripture, as Calvin makes clear when he beseeches his reader, "Above all, I must urge him to have recourse to Scripture in order to weigh the testimonies that I adduce from it."[164] Calvin never permitted his hermeneutical project to become a tradition on par with scripture, but rather it was intended to form the way into scripture, and always to be measured against the constant testimony of the scriptures.

2. *From Part to Whole, Three Times*

Calvin also drew out the hermeneutical circles inherent within the study of scripture, that of the part of a particular book to its whole; the relationship of the specific book to the corpus of that scriptural author; and placing the particular passage within the context of the whole of scripture. He did this constantly, and skillfully, drawing upon a prodigious memory, and, after the Romans commentary of 1540, upon his previously published commentaries. A demonstration of this tendency in each of its manifestations will help to clarify the meaning, and then it will be more profitable to comment upon the meaning lying behind the use of this technique.

Calvin always believed that each book of the scripture represented a coherent effort at expression by its author. Thus, he presents an

---

[164] *Argument du Present Livre*, OS 3.8.25–27. "sur toutes choses, il fauldra auoir en recommandation, de recourir a l'Escriture, pour considerer les tesmoignages que i'en allegue."

"*Argumentum*" at the beginning of each commentary, to which he will relate architectonic comments throughout the commentary proper.[165] This *Argumentum* presents a re-construction of the circumstances of the writing of the book, both the circumstances which provoked the writing of the particular book,[166] and an overall sense of its general meaning.[167] Further, Calvin presented the necessary knowledge of the origi-

---

[165] Of course, this was a commonplace of medieval and Reformation exegesis.

[166] Comm. I Corinthians, Argumentum, CO 49.297–298. "Again, because Corinth was ruled by vices that many commercial cities are troubled with, luxury, pride, vanity, pleasures, insatiable covetousness, ambition; just so those vices had invaded also the church, so that discipline had greatly declined. Further, there was already a falling off from the pure teaching, so that one of the fundamentals of the faith, the resurrection of the dead, was being spoken of in doubt." "Rursum quum regnarent Corinthi vitia, quibus laborare ut plurimum mercatoriae urbes solent, luxuria, fastus, vanitas, delitiae, inexplebilis habendi cupiditas, ambitio: sic in ecclesiam quoque ipsam invaserant, ut valde collapsa esset disciplina. Quin etiam doctrinae puritas concidere iam coeperat, ut praecipuum religionis caput, resurrection mortuorum in dubium vocaretur." Comm. II Corinthians, Argumentum, Ad Corinthios 5.13–15. "Now his goal in writing can be understood, that it was to perfect what he had already begun, so that he would find all in good order when he arrived." "Nunc quem in finem scribendo respexerit, tenemus: nempe ut quod iam coeperat, perficeret, quo omnia bene constituta inveniret suo adventu." Comm. Galatians, Argumentum, Ad Galatas, 6.2–14. "In Paul's day they were under the sovereignty of Rome. He had faithfully established them in the pure Gospel, but false apostles had entered in his absence and corrupted the true seed by false and defective dogmas. Indeed, they taught that the observance of ceremonies was still necessary. This might seem a thing of small importance. But Paul struggles for it as a fundamental head of the Christian faith. Not without merit does he do so, for it is no small evil to suffocate the clarity of the Gospel, to lay a snare for consciences and to take away the distinction between the old and new testaments. He saw that these errors were connected to an impious and pernicious opinion on the meriting of righteousness. And this is why he fights so earnestly. When we have been reminded what gravity and seriousness are held in this dispute, we must study it with even greater emphasis." "Tempore Pauli sub Romanorum ditione erant. Porro quum pure ac fideliter eos instituisset in Euangelio, supervenerant eo absente pseudoapostoli, qui verum semen falsis et vitiosis dogmatibus corruperant. Docebant enim necessariam esse adhuc observationem caeremoniarum. Videri poterat res levis momenti in speciem. At Paulus tanquam de primario Christianae fidei capite dimicat. Neque immerito. Non enim leve malum est suffocari Euangelii claritatem, laqueum iniici conscientiis, tolli discrimen Veteris et Novi testamenti. Videbat praeterea his erroribus coniunctam quoque esse impiam et perniciosam opinionem promerendae iustitiae. Haec causa est, cur tanta vehementia et contentione depugnet. Nos quoque admoniti, quam gravis et seria disputatio hic tractetur, eo plus attentionis afferamus ad legendum."

[167] Comm. Romans, Argumentum, Ad Romanos, 5.18–19. "Then he enters on the principal question of the whole Epistle, that we are justified by faith." "Atque ita ingreditur principalem totius epistolae quaestionem, Fide nos justificari." Comm. Ephesians, Argumentum, Ad Ephesios, 151.10–11. "The first three chapters are principally occupied in commending the grace of God." "Primis autem tribus capitibus praecipue versatur in commendatione gratiae Dei." Comm. Colossians, Argumentum, Ad

nal recipients of the material. The importance of audience and context should be clear. Not only would this have been completely harmonious with the dictates of humanist method, it also maintains a particular strand of Christian biblical interpretive method. Augustine, in considering the things which are necessary for a correct interpretation of the scripture, saw that among the pagan arts history was to be maintained through necessity.[168] Hugh of St. Victor saw an understanding of the arts as essential to the correct explication of Holy Writ. Even someone as leery of the arts as Bernard of Clairvaux constantly makes allusions within his sermons which require a knowledge of the context and character of his audience to understand.[169] Calvin was continuing a basic Christian understanding of the interpretive art when he placed such a high value upon knowing the whole context of a particular passage.

However, Calvin used this knowledge to reconstruct the settings of the writings of books of scripture. In his arguments, he would lay out the history of the writing of a particular book which he was about to explain. Then, throughout the exposition, Calvin doggedly maintains that reconstruction as the framework to which understanding must be attached. Further, Calvin used this hermeneutic pre-knowledge to nuance the understanding of particular dilemmas within scripture. Calvin depends upon his knowledge of the audience, people with itching ears, such as the Corinthians, to help to understand why particular commands are given, or why commands are given in a particular form.

Calvin read Paul's work in much the same way. By seeing Paul's adherence to "nature" as a situatedness within a particular historical context with particular conventions, Calvin allowed a difference to exist between some of Paul's sayings and the mind of the Holy Spirit. Literally, in Paul's writings there are two levels, the trans-historical, and

---

Colossenses, 384.8–10. "This, therefore, is the principal goal at which he aims, that all things are taught in Christ, and that he alone should be satisfactory and more than sufficient for the Colossians." "Hic ergo scopus est praecipuus, ad quem tendit, ut in Christo omnia esse doceat, ideoque ipsum unum satis superque debere esse Colossensibus."

[168] On Christian Doctrine, 74. De Doctrina Christiana, II.xxxix.58. Augustine went on to wish that someone would write an encyclopedia giving explanations of the meanings of all the unfamiliar terms and places in the scriptures.

[169] Bernard of Clairvaux, Sermons on the Song of Songs. Mark S. Burrows has pointed out in his "'To Taste with the Heart:' Allegory, Poetics, and the Deep Reading of Scripture," Interpretation 56 (2002): 168–180, that Bernard invites his community to engage with the whole of their selves in receiving the nourishment of scripture.

the conventional. Frequently, there is significant overlap.[170] The only way to ascertain the difference is to turn to a knowledge of the context and audience.

These arguments, insofar as they exercise a hegemonic function upon the interpretation of the text, and are drawn from a close reading of the text, are themselves instances of specific passages and the whole book forming a hermeneutical circle. But even in the first commentary, that upon Romans, in which Calvin's *Argumentum* is somewhat differently styled, sufficient anticipations of this style appear through the body of the text.[171] For instance, Calvin explains Romans 1.12 through the use of the same word in Romans 12.3.[172] In another instance, at Romans 3.18, Calvin refers his reader back to a previously made argument in Romans 1.26, about the catalog of human vices which may be found among the human race severally.[173] In Romans 9.4 and 9.6, Calvin refers back to the distinction he has found in Paul's letter at Romans 3.3.[174] Finally, Calvin will also use the part to differentiate from a separate part, explaining Romans 14.8 through the use of Romans 6.11, and differentiating between "to live toward the Lord," and "being made alive by the Lord's Spirit.".[175]

Calvin immediately broadened this usage of part/whole within a book, to the next level, that of part/whole within the Pauline corpus.[176] He attempted to distinguish specific usages of particular concepts by recourse to Paul's other letters. Thus, Calvin cites I Thess. 4.7 to

---

[170] The Corinthians and their itching ears (*pruriebant aures*) are a case in point—see Comm. I Corinthians 3.11, CO 49.353.

[171] Calvin presents the letter to the Romans much more as a theological treatise to be explained, than a historical document to be re-constructed. This perhaps has to do with its character as the key to scripture, or perhaps is an acknowledgement that Paul does not know these people, and thus that the whole of the teaching is far more universally cast than the epistles to churches Paul had founded or previously visited.

[172] Comm. Romans 1.12, Ad Romanos 22.86.

[173] Comm. Romans 3.18, Ad Romanos 64.45–46.

[174] Comm. Romans 9.4 and Romans 9.6, Ad Romanos 195.44 and 199.60.

[175] Comm. Romans 14.8, Ad Romanos 296.77. "Domino vivere," and "eius Spiritu vegetari."

[176] This has been noted by Helmut Feld, in his "Hermeneutische Voraussetzungen und Theologische Leitideen der Johannes-Interpretation J. Calvins." *Calvin's Books: Festschrift dedicated to Peter De Klerk on the occasion of his seventieth birthday*, edited by Wilhelm H. Neuser (Heerenveen: J.J. Groen en Zoon, 1997), 105–116. Feld argues that Calvin comes to his understanding of II Corinthians through reference to Ephesians 1.4. Further, Feld sees Calvin depending upon John 3.16, leading to an even broader interpretive circle.

explain Rom. 1.7,[177] Eph. 4.13 to illustrate Rom. 1.12,[178] and I Thess 5.3 to clarify Rom. 1.17.[179] Calvin can even go so far as to delineate within the Pauline corpus between usages of the same word. This is the case in I Corinthians 10.29, when he distinguishes between the narrow use of conscience (*conscientiam*) in that passage, and the broader uses in Romans 13.5 and I Timothy 1.5.[180]

Not surprisingly, Calvin also broadened beyond the range of the Pauline corpus to explain the meaning of Paul.[181] This should not be surprising, given Calvin's understanding of the dual authorship of the scriptures. Unless the Holy Spirit should be confused, or actually varied in its message, the different parts of the scripture should be able to be used rather cavalierly to understand difficult portions. Thus, we see Calvin using John's gospel to explain Rom. 1.4;[182] dealing with a possible objection from Acts when considering Rom. 1.5;[183] explaining from Heb. 13.15 that the substance of Rom. 1.8 is that the thanksgiving for the gift of faith should be given through Christ;[184] and explicating the grace of being able to call upon God as "my God," in Rom. 1.8 through the testimony of Jer. 30.22![185]

In each of the part-whole hermeneutical "sub-circles" that Calvin used, the rationales for using it are completely in character with his other theological and hermeneutical concerns. The first circle, that of the intra-book circle, is only a logical corollary to a humanist attempting to understand the mind's argument behind the rhetoric of a particular book. The second circle is somewhat more complex, but remains much the same. The complexity is added through the addition of the Holy Spirit's authorship, but this is not as significant for Calvin as it has been for later readers. The third circle, that of the part/whole of the

---

[177] Comm. Romans 1.7, Ad Romanos 17.15–16.

[178] Comm. Romans 1.12, Ad Romanos 22.92.

[179] Comm. Romans 1.17, Ad Romanos 27.52–53.

[180] Comm. I Corinthians 10.29, CO 49.470.

[181] Calvin also frequently will use Pauline material to explicate other parts of scripture. For a helpful analysis of some examples of this, see Barbara Pitkin's *What Pure Eyes Could See: Calvin's Doctrine of Faith in Its Exegetical Context* (Oxford: Oxford University Press, 1999), 82–83, where Pitkin notes that Calvin's consideration of faith in James is framed by his pre-existing stance, taken from Paul.

[182] Comm. Romans 1.4, Ad Romanos 15.42.

[183] Comm. Romans 1.5, Ad Romanos 16.88–89.

[184] Comm. Romans 1.8, Ad Romanos 19.73–74. Calvin generally did not hold for Paul's authorship of Hebrews.

[185] Comm. Romans 1.8, Ad Romanos 19.77. Calvin has little or no scruple about moving from New to Old Testament.

whole of scripture, points to Calvin's idea that the scripture contains one message, and has one application. The one message of scripture is the triune God, and its one application is the edification of believers. Thus, it only makes sense that a long document would be able to interpret itself by juxtaposition of more and less clear passages.[186]

3. *From Scripture to Audience*

Finally, Calvin employed what is possibly his most daring hermeneutical circle, that of the text, and the receiving community. This never falls into a reader-response nihilism, but far more resembles a paradigm of application. Calvin mentions the *applicatione* of a testimony in his comments upon Rom. 11.11, although in the negative.[187] However, that negative does not change the fact that Calvin makes it clear through his comment that the whole point of reading a commentary is so that the testimonies of the scripture may be applied in the life of the Christian or Christian community. Further, Calvin holds out the basic premise that through the design of God, no one has the full possession of the best interpretation of the contents of the scripture.[188] Add to this the fact that Calvin turns his own interpretation over to the court of the decision of the reader,[189] and the conclusion, though startling, is clear. Calvin held that the *communis sensus* was essential to finding the meaning of the scriptures.[190] Through the interplay of the minds of believers struggling to understand the doctrine of salvation, and sharing that edifying doctrine, the body of Christ is edified, and the fullest meaning of the scripture is more nearly approximated.

But to what audience did this word refer? Can the audience of Calvin's writings be seen to be a dispersed community of scholars, those

---

[186] Though Alexandre Ganoczy and Stefan Scheld criticize Felicity Edwards' work for her conclusion that Calvin takes over Luther's prominent principle of "sacra scriptura sui ipsius interpres," without being able to give adequate examples of this, there can be no doubt that Calvin did refer to the scripture to understand the scripture. See their *Die Hermeneutik Calvins*, 3–4.

[187] Comm. Romans 11.11, Ad Romanos 248.105.

[188] Comm. Romans Dedicatory Epistle, Ad Romanos 3.107–110.

[189] Comm. Romans 10.14, Ad Romanos 231.44. "but each must form his considered opinion." "sit salvum cuique iudicium."

[190] Calvin was clear that preachers must stand "under" the Word of God—Jean-Marc Berthoud calls their role wholly that of the "servant of the Word of God." Berthoud, "La formation des pasteurs et la predication de Calvin." *La revue reformee* 49 (1998): 19–44.

whom Calvin may have known in his scholarly days at Paris? Or is it a trans-historical community, the Church through the ages, with whom Calvin is conversing about the scripture?[191] Or is it as simple as the congregation(s) of the city of Geneva?[192] Although all three options mentioned here have some reason to be called "the" audience, the greatest weight will be given by Calvin to the congregation in Geneva, the artisans, bourgeoisie, merchants and day laborers to whose life he attempted to apply the messages of the scripture.[193] The interplay of the realities of this community and the meaning of God's word was the constant immediate horizon for the living of the Christian life.[194]

Edification

The final principle which Calvin brings to the understanding of the scripture, a grounding pillar so deep that it will break forth in several ways throughout his thought, is that the scripture exists for the edification of the Church. Again and again, the language of *aedificatio*, or edification, directs Calvin's searching of the scripture. The purpose of

---

[191] Ganoczy and Scheld argue this when they state that "Unsere Untersuchung wird verdeutlichen, daß sich Calvin sehr wohl darum bemüht, die Auslegung im Sinne der 'analogia fidei' durchzuführen, wobei das Apostolicum, nach dessen Grundstruktur in überraschender Weise sein Argument des Epheserbriefcommentars aufgebaut ist, eine maßgebliche Rolle spielt." *Die Hermeneutik Calvins*, 4.

[192] In considering a sermon on Matthew 28.1–10, Olivier Millet has noted that Calvin's loci (lieux) method can mold his rhetorical method, at times so strongly as to "provoque des distorsions dans las laecture du texte biblique," I will consider Millet in the next chapter especially, but note his point here to demonstrate his sense of Calvin's theological method engaging his rhetorical style. See Olivier Millet, "Sermon sur la Resurrection: quelques remarques sur l'homiletique de Calvin." *Societe de l'Histoire du Protestantisme Francais* 134 (1988): 683–692.

[193] See my article "*Ecclesia, Legenda atque Intelligenda Scriptura*: The Church as Discerning Community in Calvin's Hermeneutic." *Calvin Theological Journal*, 36 (2001): 270–289. Francis M. Higman has pointed out that prior to the Reformation, there were tracts designed for the education of the laity. However, these were based on morality, rather than doctrine. He sums up "One point is clear: it is taken as axiomatic that the basic teaching of the Church for the benefit of the laity consists in understanding the fundamental liturgical texts: the Lord's Prayer, the Creed, the Ave Maria, and the Ten Commandments." "Theology for the Layman in the French Reformation 1520–1550." *The Library* 9 (1987): 108.

[194] An excellent example of this phenomenon is given by Wilhelmus T.H. Moehn, in his consideration of the necessary communal setting of Calvin's Acts sermons. See his *God Calls Us to His Service: The Relation Between God and His Audience in Calvin's Sermons on Acts* (Geneve: Droz, 2001).

doctrine is the edification of the Church. The sacraments unite and
build us up into the body of Christ. The very purpose of the scripture
is not simply revelation, but a revelation which edifies and moves the
body of believers into piety.[195] *Aedificatio*, however, is both a hermeneutical principle, and a principle of theological coherence for Calvin. As
such, it deserves a later treatment.

Example of Hermeneutic Process

Can an example of the process of hermeneutical reasoning that we
are claiming be given? Yes. Calvin's work of interpretation towards a
church order provides sufficient warrant. The consideration of Calvin's
interpretation of Romans 12.8 offers an excellent instance of hermeneutical reasoning.[196] In Romans 12.8, Calvin finds the warrant for a "double diaconate."

> *He who gives abundantly, let him do it in simplicity.* We see clearly from these
> latter parts that this is a demonstration of what is the legitimate use of
> God's gifts. By speaking of "givers" (Per μεταδιδοῦντας), he does not
> understand those who give their own things, but the Deacons who pre-
> side over the distribution of the public property of the Church. However,
> by speaking of the ones who show mercy (ἐλεοῦντας), he means wid-
> ows and other ministers who were appointed to give care to the sick,
> according to the custom of the ancient Church. There are two different
> functions, that of providing what is necessary for the poor, and that of
> handling the work of attending to them. Concerning the former task, he
> designates simplicity, by which without fraud or personal consideration
> they are to administer faithfully their commission. From the latter he
> wants them to work with a display of cheerfulness, so that they will not,
> as so often happens, detract from the charity which they give by thir ren-
> der by their morose attitude. As nothing affords more consolation to the

---

[195] On the definition of piety, see Sou-Young Lee's "Calvin's Understanding of
Pietas," in *Calvinus Sincerioris Religionis Vindex*, edited by Wilhelm Neuser and Brian Armstrong (Kirksville, MO: Sixteenth Century Journal Publishers, 1997), 322–339. The
main difficulty with Lee's work is his effort to draw *pietas* into a horizontal, as well
as a vertical dimension. (234–237) Perhaps the relative brevity of that portion of his
argument demonstrates that the material to support such a view is not easy to find in
Calvin's thought.

[196] I choose this text, rather than others, because of the scholarly disagreement over
it, summarized in Elsie A. McKee's article, "Calvin's Exegesis of Romans 12:8–Social,
Accidental, or Theological," *Calvin Theological Journal* 23 (1988): 6–18. McKee's article
provides an extraordinary opportunity to consider the wider scholarly reception of her
thesis, and by extension, our own.

sick or to anyone otherwise distressed than the sight of helpers eagerly and readily disposed to afford him help, so if the poor observes a glum countenance on those who help him, he will take it as an affront.[197]

Calvin sets out here a differentiated diaconate, split into those who care for the poor, and those who care for those who are ill.[198] The question that illustrates our thesis is why does he do so?[199] Is the answer that Calvin found this situation when he arrived in Geneva in 1536, and sought for a textual warrant for keeping it so?[200] That is certainly a plausible explanation, and one which tends to draw social historians.[201] These scholars point out that no such statement is to be found in the 1536 *Institutes*, and reason that Calvin has been influenced by a useful division which he finds already present when he arrives in Geneva, after the first edition of the *Institutes*, but before his Romans commentary. Robert Kingdon has written:

> What happened within the years between 1536 and 1539 to give Calvin a new conception of the diaconate? I do not find any really definitive answer to this question. But the answer that first suggests itself to me is that Calvin witnessed the successful operation of a double diaconate

---

[197] Comm. Romans, 12.8, Ad Romanos, 271.81–272.94. "*Qui largitur, in simplicitate*. Ex istis posterioribus membris clare perspicimus, hic nobis demonstrari quis sit legitimus donorum Dei usus. Per μεταδιδοῦντας, de quibus hic loquitur, non eos intelligit qui largiuntur de suo: sed Diaconos qui publicis Ecclesiae facultatibus dispensandis praesunt. Per ἐλεοῦντας autem, viduas et alios ministros qui curandis aegrotis, secundum veteris Ecclesiae morem, praeficicbantur. Sunt enim functiones duae diversae, [erogare] pauperibus necessaria, et [suam illis tractandis operam impendere. Caeterum prioribus] assignat simplicitatem qua sine fraude aut personarum acceptione, fideliter sibi commissa administrent: ab his obsequia vult exhiberi cum hilaritate, ne morositate sua (quod evenire plerumque solet) gratiam officiis detrahant. Ut enim aegrum vel alio quovis modo afflictum nihil magis solatur quam ubi videt alacres ac promptos ad opem sibi ferendam animos: ita si tristitiam cernat in eorum vultu a quibus iuvatur, id in contumeliam suam accipiet." The material within the brackets is from the later editions of the Romans commentary.

[198] McKee has also examined Calvin's interpretation of I Timothy 5.17–18 on this issue in her "Les Anciens et l'Interpretation de 1 Tm 5, 17 chez Calvin: Une Curiosite dans l'Histoire de l'Exegese." *Revue de Theologie et de Philosophie* 120, (1988): 411–417.

[199] That this is a controverted point is well known. For a review of the opinions see McKee, "Calvin's Exegesis of Romans 12:8–Social, Accidental, or Theological?" 6–11.

[200] McKee, "Calvin's Exegesis of Romans 12:8–Social, Accidental, or Theological?" 7.

[201] See J.K.S. Reid, "Diakonia in the thought of Calvin," in *Service in Christ: Essays Presented to Karl Barth on His 80th Birthday*, ed. J.I. McCord and T.H.L. Parker, (London: Epworth Publishing, 1966), 101–109; and Robert Kingdon, "Calvin's Ideas about the Diaconate: Social or Theological in Origin?" in *Piety, Politics, and Power: Reformation Studies in Honor of George Wolfgang Forell*, ed. C. Lindberg, (Kirksville, MO: Sixteenth Century Journal Publishers, 1984), 167–180. McKee surveys others, 7.

for two years in the city of Geneva. He became personally acquainted with the hospitaliers who managed the General Hospital and with the procurators who supervised its operations. ... It seems to me probable that Calvin was impressed with this institution for the discharge of the Christian obligation to care for the poor, that he searched Scriptures for warrant for it, and that he found the warrant he was seeking in Romans 12:8.[202]

In addition to the social explanation, intellectual historians have weighed in, generally seeing the interpretation of Romans 12 as either a consequence of a rigorist approach to the plural office theory, or as an outgrowth of Martin Bucer's influence over Calvin.[203] Again, these seem plausible, Bucer's influence on Calvin is well-known, and the Reformed emphasis on the plural offices of ministry is a commonplace, supported by Calvin's own four-fold division of ministry into the offices of doctor, pastor, elder and deacon.

The difficulty with these theses is that they tend to represent Calvin as a blank slate, uopn which others wrote. Calvin's own persona and mind disappear. The solution which McKee offers saves Calvin from that fate, and illustrates our position rather well.

I believe that the most convincing explanation for Calvin's gradual development of the twofold diaconate and his curious use of Romans 12:8 lies in his own exegetical and theological methods and presuppositions. What happened between the Latin *Institutes* of 1539 and the edition of 1543 was the writing of the commentary on Romans. In explaining Romans, Calvin had to deal not only with Romans 12:8 but also with Romans 16:1–2, the pericope that calls a woman, Phoebe, *diaconos*. A commentator who took all of Scripture seriously and believed that it revealed a unified church order could not ignore Phoebe's title, particularly in view of the fact that other texts established the diaconate as a permanent ecclesiastical office.[204]

Here, the use of Calvin's hermeneutical presupposition of the single voice of scripture explains his choice of a heretofore unfamiliar interpretive option. One can also see that the model of hermeneutical circles drawn above allows for the acceptance of some of the material from the social historians, but as correlative, rather than as explicative. That is to say, Calvin's hermeneutical circle of the scripture and its audience, instantiated in the church of Geneva, allowed him to learn from that

---

[202] Kingdon, "Calvin's Ideas about the Diaconate," 178.
[203] McKee surveys these positions, 9.
[204] McKee, "Calvin's Exegesis of Romans 12:8–Social, Accidental, or Theological?" 16.

example of the division of the diaconate, and incorporate this into a hermeneutic presupposition already present in the 1536 *Institutes*, that of the agreement of scripture with itself.[205]

Conclusion

Calvin's hermeneutical positions cannot be understood without acknowledging his anti-speculative and hierarchically guarded epistemology, and his turn to the authority of the scriptures. Following those insights, Calvin sets the whole of the interpretive project within the divine-human dynamic, most especially represented in his principle of accommodation. Further, Calvin allows for and even demands a unity of interpretation by his understanding of the unity of the divine message to humanity, represented by his unity of the two testaments, a unity of substance, but not of clarity. Then, Calvin is able to set out interpretation's goal as describing the mind of the author, but that mind is a dual divine and human mind, and frequently the more important to describe is the divine mind. Finally, Calvin assumes a set of hermeneutical circles, which are the only way to enter into the scriptures. Overarching all of these goals is Calvin's central belief in the usefulness, the edifying nature, of scripture and true doctrine drawn from it.

It is now possible to address the queston of *how* to consider Calvin's thought and his approach to scripture. Calvin wrote that it was almost the interpeter's "only responsibility to make accessible the mind of the writer."[206] Although that does not seem ideologically cast, what Calvin does not identify, because it is so engrained in him that it does not need saying, are his hermeneutical presuppositions. Here, twenty-first century readers must take care to consider not only what Calvin says, but also what remains unsaid. The Enlightenment critique of prejudice or presupposition, which seems supportable on the basis of Calvin's declaration to Grynaeus, is wholly foreign to Calvin's practice. He identifies controls on what one finds in the scripture such as that one must

---

[205] Admittedly, my solution will not finally answer the question of social vs. theological, but it points toward McKee's direction, which is as much as can be expected in seeking explanations at such a distance.

[206] Comm. Romans, Dedicatory epistle. Ad Romanos, 1.9–10. "Et sane quum hoc sit prope unicum illius officii, mentem scriptoris, quem explicandum sumpsit, patefacere."

first understand the mind of the Holy Spirit. Further, that scripture is meant for the edification of the believing community, and is properly intended for its use. In no wise is the interpretation of the scripture to be approached through contextual means alone, for context is a tool that is to be applied by the appropriately trained exegete: a training that for Calvin included doctrine. A modern objection that this approach to the scripture involves an importation of doctrine into the province of biblical studies becomes entirely anachronistic when levelled against the sixteenth century. Calvin's interpretive effort retains its coherency because of the interplay of his hermeneutical principles and his exegetical practices. However, the hermeneutic necessarily stands prior to the exegetical, aiming at a particular goal, knowing and being united with Christ. If this order is not preserved, the critic of Calvin's interpretation will simply see his biblical work as a series of moves constructed to reach a pre-conceived outcome. That question must wait for the fourth chapter. In the next chapter, we turn to examining how Calvin's exegetical practices or rules help to fill out these hermeneutical principles.

The divine-human dynamic that is characteristic of all of Calvin's theology is present in his hermeneutics, as might be expected. But the place of that divine-human interaction is necessarily and always the Church. Both as the institution with thousands of years of history, and as the gathered body of believers, Calvin drives the interpretive project into this horizon. Here is where the fusion of horizons takes place, here is where the mystical gaining of God's truth occurs. Thus, there is within Calvin's hermeneutic principles the classical pattern of procession and return. The truth to be found within the explicative process is that which nourishes the community toward its final end in the divine person who gave that truth originally.

CHAPTER THREE

EXEGETICAL PRACTICES

For Calvin, the point of scripture is to prepare the believer for the true worship of God and union with Christ. It reveals all that is necessary for salvation, but not as a set of perfect words.[1] Therefore, it must be interpreted. Calvin's understanding of biblical exegesis reveals his deepest convictions about the nature of scripture. Our intention to discern those convictions brings us immediately in contact with the much-disputed question of his humanism.[2] Recent scholarship, such as the work of Olivier Millet and Peter Opitz reminds us that a consensus on this topic remains elusive.[3] No one doubts the influence of Renais-

---

[1] OS 3.60.17–18. ICR I.vi.1. "It was not unsuccessful, then, that he added the light of his word so as to become known for salvation." "Itaque non frustra verbi sui lumen addidit, quo innotesceret in salutem."

[2] We must be careful about going too far with Calvin's humanism. Though his exegetical methods owe much to the humanist influences, his theological conclusions frequently differ radically from those of other Renaissance thinkers. Charles Trinkaus has pointed out that in his handling of a closely related set of "Renaissance problems," including epistemology, man and the universe, providence and free will, Calvin completely abandoned "any hope for the spiritual or moral regeneration of mankind by its own efforts." It seems then that in some sense, Calvin assumed some of the characteristics of the scholarship of the Renaissance, without accepting some of the substance of its basic positions. See Trinkaus, "Renaissance Problems in Calvin's Theology," 317–340 in *The Scope of Renaissance Humanism* (Ann Arbor: University of Michigan Press, 1983), esp. 332–333. Standing over against Trinkaus' position is Donald Williams' work, that denies Renaissance humanism had a particular definable set of theses or doctrines, but rather is set apart by a "strong interest in the classical writers from a standpoint of grammar and rhetoric." (68) If this position is taken, then Calvin can be seen as more of a humanist scholar, although he still will temper the conclusions grammar and rhetoric will lead him to for the purpose of edification. See Donald T. Williams, "John Calvin: Humanist and Reformer," *Trinity Journal* 5 (1976):67–78.

Williams' position is supported by James Michael Weiss' claim that "humanists before and during the Reformation did *not*–this point requires considerable emphasis in the face of perennial misunderstanding–they did *not* share philosophical or theological positions on human nature, revelation, justification, sacraments, free will, or the other questions that generated Reformation controversy." "Humanism," II.264–272 in *Oxford Encyclopedia of the Reformation*, in 4 volumes, edited by Hans J. Hillerbrand, et al. (Oxford: Oxford University Press, 1996), 265.

[3] Millet's work, which presents Calvin's theological method as being rhetorical, stakes out one pole in this discussion. Peter Opitz agrees, at least so far as the impact

sance humanism on Calvin's exegesis, but the extent of that influence is debatable.[4] As we shall see in our discussion of Calvin's exegesis of Paul's letters, humanism alone is not sufficient to explain his understanding of the texts. This point has been made by Alexandre Ganoczy and Stefan Scheld, who have suggested other influences in addition to humanism, such as Faber Stapulensis' understanding of the relationships between truth and scripture and spirit and the letter, and his use of the literal meaning of scripture.[5]

Certainly, Calvin's style of interpretation and many of his exegetical practices were in broad accord with the humanistic scholarship popular in some circles during his day. Two possible explanations, which are not mutually exclusive, include Calvin's own training at Bourges and Paris,[6] and his desire to speak with a voice that would be heard among the learned men and women.[7] However, there is still a further issue to consider. Did Calvin use humanistic exegesis as a tool, occasionally

---

of humanism, especially in the formation of Calvin's more mature thought, beginning with the 1539 *Institutes*. "Er stellt deshalb seine Institutio in den intellektuellen—das heißt für ihn selbstverständlich humanistischen—Kontext seiner Zeit und expliziert gleich zu Beginn den von ihm vertretenen spezifischen Zusammenhang von Gotteserkenntnis und Selbsterkenntnis aufgrund seiner Wort-Gottes-Theologie, aber in Auseinandersetzung mit einem humanistischen Grundgedanken." *Calvins Theologische Hermeneutik* (Neukirchen-Vluyn: Neukirchener, 1994), 187.

[4] Scholars have also wondered whether too much weight is being given to the impact of sixteenth-century humanism. David Willis, in his "Rhetoric and Responsibility in Calvin's Theology," *The Context of Contemporary Theology*, edited by Alexander J. McKelway and E. David Willis (Atlanta: John Knox Press, 1974), noted that one of the rhetorical traditions that inspired Calvin was a Christian one, namely Augustine, especially in *De Doctrina Christiana*. Further, D.F. Wright has pointed out in the context of a study of Calvin's use of accommodation that a too-great dependence on the explanatory powers of humanistic rhetoric can lead scholars astray from Calvin's actual usage. He offers a "modest corrective" to the "fashionable recent tendency to explain too much of Calvin in terms of the rhetorical tradition." "Calvin's Accommodating God," *Calvinus Sincerioris Religionis Vindex*, edited by Wilhelm Neuser and Brian Armstrong (Kirksville, MO: Sixteenth Century Journal Publishers, 1997), 16.

[5] *Die Hermeneutik Calvins*, 47.

[6] Shuger states that "Law is the characteristic discipline of the late Renaissance, in much the same way that logic is the characteristic discipline of the Middle Ages: it leaves its mark on other fields of inquiry. Law was of course a specialized field but it was also part of the erudite *encyclios paideia*." *The Renaissance Bible: Scholarship, Sacrifice, and Subjectivity* (Berkeley: University of California Press, 1994), 52.

[7] This is Serene Jones' position in her *Calvin and the Rhetoric of Piety*, Columbia Series in Reformed Theology (Louisville: Westminster John Knox Press, 1995), chapter 2. The "community of humanistically minded scholars and aristocrats" are her third audience. (53).

rejecting the directions it would lead, or rather does the practice of humanistic exegesis become an actual hermeneutical principle driving Calvin's thought? In this case, the research clearly shows that Calvin had a prior, and to him, higher goal than following out the dictates of humanistic interpretive models.[8] We see this most clearly when he made textual emendations based on readings that contain fuller teaching or doctrine.[9] For Calvin, New Testament study was not about the setting out of a perfect text, but rather a service to the forming of the Christian body into Christ. When interpretation ceases to do this, it fails to be a Christian use of the possession of the Church, the scriptures.[10]

---

[8] Jerry H. Bentley points this out, negatively, when he claims that "The Reformation created a new and not always healthy environment for philological studies on the New Testament. Theology came often to dominate philology in the later sixteenth century. Too much doctrine was invested in certain passages of scripture to allow full rein to critical philologists, who might undermine cherished interpretations. Limiting this study to pre-Reformation scholarship will enable us to avoid many problems introduced into New Testament study by scholars' prior theological commitments, and to concentrate attention instead on a purer philological tradition in New Testament studies." *Humanists and Holy Writ*, 13. Also, we must temper T.II.L. Parker's optimism about Calvin's "remarkable fidelity to the document he is explaining." "Calvin's Commentary on Hebrews," 135–140 in *Church, Word, and Spirit: Historical and Theological Essays in Honor of Geoffrey W. Bromiley*, edited by James E. Bradley and Richard A. Muller (Grand Rapids: Eerdmans, 1987), 140. Parker's comment leads toward a Protestant orthodoxy of seeing the Reformers as those who "really followed" where God's Word led. This thesis must be set aside, in favor of the Reformers in general and Calvin in particular setting out a particular framework for textual meaning.

[9] Comm. Philippians 1.21, Ad Philippenses 309.18–25.

[10] At this point, it would seem that I have left Calvin open to the charge of eisegesis. I do not believe so, Calvin was a careful textual critic, though not so thorough-going as Erasmus. I am not saying that he denigrated the text, or would have changed it to suit his purposes. What I am saying is that his hermeneutical principles of the purpose of the scriptures took priority over his textual and philological work. I assume this would be Bentley's point in his charge concerning the ways that theology dominated philology in the Reformation.

However, it seems that Bentley's point is rather too confident in the purity of the scholarship of his philologists. His own research demonstrates that the editors of the Complutensian Polyglot were quite wary about moving too far from established readings of the Vulgate, even when their notes establish that the stronger textual evidence supported the change (91–111). Yet he does not criticize them, but characterizes them "an extremely conservative scholarly circle." (110)

Bentley wishes to see the work of Valla, the Complutensian Polyglot editors and Erasmus within the history of scholarship (192), and to demonstrate that here is a fountainhead of modern New Testament scholarship (218–219). In the case of the beginning

A related difficulty arises when we turn to Calvin's reading and use of the church fathers.[11] Here the distinction between hermeneutics and exegesis is important, for although Calvin frequently differed with the patristic authorities in the *manner of handling* the scripture, he remained in broad agreement with them on the appropriate *meaning* of the scripture. Exegetical differences have too often been allowed to obscure hermeneutical similarities, which are far more significant. This will become evident in the Pauline commentaries, which we shall examine according to Calvin's principal exegetical tools: paraphrase, contextual interpretation, scripture's self-interpretation, tradition's possibilities, the stance of humility, simplicity's sake, and the goal of fuller meaning.

---

of the use of sophisticated tools, such as the use of the *lectio dificilior*, he is certainly correct. However, Bentley also seems to argue that the humanists managed to avoid prior theological commitments, and to dedicate themselves to a purer philological enterprise. This is naïve. Bentley himself notes that Erasmus had the goals of "personal transformation, social reform, and religious renewal" standing behind his technical scholarship on the New Testament (124). That sounds suspiciously like a hermeneutical set of presuppositions. Further, scholars such as John Payne, in his "Erasmus on Romans 9:6–24" 119–135 in *The Bible in the 16th Century*, edited by David Steinmetz (Durham: Duke University Press, 1990); Thomas Torrance, in his "The Hermeneutics of Erasmus," 48–76 in *Probing the Reformed Tradition: Historical Studies in Honor of Edward A. Dowey, Jr.*, edited by Elsie Anne McKee and Brian G. Armstrong (Louisville: Westminster John Knox Press, 1989); and Manfred Hoffman in his *Rhetoric and Theology: The Hermeneutic of Erasmus* (Toronto: University of Toronto Press, 1994), have all found positive hermeneutic stances in Erasmus. To see the humanists as free from prejudice, able to make the New Testament an "object of detached literary, historical, and philological analysis" (217), is to misread them, and to make them both more and less than they were.

So far as the issue of Calvin and humanism goes, the points I wish to make are simply these. First, although Calvin used humanistic tools, they remained at the level of tools. Second, in going a different way from the humanists who were not Reformers, Calvin is not sliding backwards on the evolutionary scale of scholarship, rather he is taking a different road, that which is more hermeneutically cast.

[11] David Steinmetz insightfully points out in his "Divided by a Common Past: The Reshaping of the Christian Exegetical Tradition in the Sixteenth Century." *The Journal of Medieval and Early Modern Studies* 27 (1997): 245–264, that "It is not the case that there was a unified Catholic approach to biblical studies in the sixteenth century dominated by traditional Catholic biblical scholars, deeply suspicious of humanism (a plodding *via exegetica antiqua*), that was challenged by a unifed Protestant approach, inspired by humanism and promoted by newly hatched Protestant dissenters (an innovative *via exegetica moderna*)."

Paraphrase

One of Calvin's favorite techniques for explicating a text, particularly a text in which the meaning is not immediately clear, was the use of the paraphrase.[12] Calvin introduced paraphrastic interjections with cues such as "as if to say," (*acsi diceret*),[13] or "in this sense," (*hoc sensu*).[14] These cues signal to the reader Calvin's attempts to restate Paul's mind and purpose. In commenting upon Romans 1.22, Calvin writes "Paul preserves this principle, that anyone, if he is alienated from God's worship, is not so unless by his own fault, as though he said, 'Because they exalted themselves proudly, God has made them foolish by his just vengeance.'"[15] Again, in commenting on Romans 2.1, he writes "Therefore he takes away their excuse, because they knew the judgment of God, and nevertheless they transgressed the law, as though he said, 'Although you do not approve the vices of others, and seem to be a punisher of faults and an enemy to them; because, however, you are not immune to them, if you will consider yourselves, you are not able to proffer any defense for yourselves.'"[16]

The use of paraphrase in Calvin's exegesis is intriguing.[17] The purpose was to re-state rather than to move directly into doctrinal formulation. Yet, as a skilled rhetorician, Calvin surely knew that no two formulations are exactly the same. In re-stating a biblical text something

---

[12] That this is a common humanist tool for interpreting scripture hardly needs to be asserted, Erasmus' paraphrases were properly famous.

[13] Comm. Philippians 3.3, Ad Philippenses 349.2. To paraphrase: This cue can be translated as "that is to say," or "as if he said," or even "to paraphrase."

[14] Comm. Romans 3.2, Ad Romanos 55.27.

[15] Comm. Romans 1.22, Ad Romanos 31.106–108. "Nam principium illud retinet Paulus, Neminem, nisi propria culpa, a Dei cultu esse alienum. acsi diceret, Quoniam superbe se extulerunt, iusta Dei ultione fuerunt infatuati."

[16] Comm. Romans 2.1, Ad Romanos 37.12–16 "Ideo enim inexcusabiles facit, quia et ipsi Dei iudicium norunt, Legem nihilominus transgrediuntur: acsi diceret, Tametsi non consentis aliorum vitiis, imo videris ex professo hostis ac vindex vitiorum: quia tamen ab illis non es immunis, si te vere consideras, non potes obtendere ullam defensionem."

[17] Olivier Millet has considered this as a form of "variation" in Calvin's style. He notes two forms, the shorter and the longer than the original. "La paraphrase qui reprend une second fois l'idée peut être plus brève (interpretatio), ou plus longue ('paraphrase' á proprement parler)." *Calvin et la dynamique de la parole: Etude de rhétorique réformée* (Paris: Librairie Honoré Champion, 1992), 734.

must be weighted differently from the original, or there is no clarification. Does that subtle re-weighting or re-placing of emphasis represent the first step in doctrinal understanding and application? Yes and no. The evidence seems to point toward Calvin using this technique to open (*patefacere*) the mind of the author, and thus to clarify original meanings and flow of conversations.[18]

Examples of this habit, or exegetical practice, could be cited to the point of tedium: for example, in the Romans commentary alone Calvin uses the device in 2.1 (three times), 3.2, 3.3, 5.2, 5.18, 8.17, and 11.13.[19] Paraphrase can also be found in the I Thessalonians commentary, at 4.15,[20] and in the II Thessalonians commentary at 2.13,[21] in the Galatians commentary at 2.4,[22] in the Ephesians commentary at 1.20,[23] in

---

[18] A different theory has been offered by Richard Gamble who suggests that Calvin is adopting the style of the Biblical authors in his "Exposition and Method in Calvin," *Westminster Theological Journal* 49 (1987): 153–165. However, it seems a simpler explanation to assume that these are paraphrastic explanations, much like Erasmus' sets of paraphrases. A more fruitful avenue of research might be to examine whether Calvin was influenced by Erasmus in this regard. For instance, we considered above a paraphrase of Calvin's on Romans 1.22. Calvin writes, "Paul maintains this principle, that if a man is estranged from the worship of God, it is his own fault, as though he said, 'Because they have exalted themselves in pride, they have been made foolish by the righteous vengeance of God.'" Erasmus, on this same passage, writes "But they have become puffed up by the vapour of empty glory and, in their vanity, have been deceived by their own cogitations. Their foolish hearts have been darkened by a cloud of arrogance. And they have become foolish and unlearned because they boasted that they were wise and learned." Erasmus, *Paraphrases on Romans and Galatians*, edited by Robert D. Sider, translated and annotated by John B. Payne, Albert Rabil, and Warren S. Smith, CWE 42 (Toronto: University of Toronto Press, 1984), 18. The differences are immediate and obvious. Calvin attributes the action of making foolish to God, Erasmus, to the foolish people. Here is a case in point where Calvin is turning humanist tools to his own work, rather than feeling obliged to accept their conclusions.

[19] Romans *2.1*, Ad Romanos 37.12–13; *3.2*, Ad Romanos 55.27; *3.3*, Ad Romanos 56.62; *5.2*, Ad Romanos 103.41; *5.18*, Ad Romanos 117.96; *8.17*, Ad Romanos 172.51; and *11.13*, Ad Romanos 249.32.

[20] Comm. I Thessalonians 4.15, CO 52.166. This is an un-introduced instance, where Calvin supplies no rhetorical cues.

[21] Comm. II Thessalonians 2.13, CO 52.205.

[22] Comm. Galatians 2.4, Ad Galatas 34.5.

[23] Comm. Ephesians 1.20, Ad Ephesios 173.2.

the Philippians commentary at 2.15,[24] and in the Colossians commentary at 2.5.[25] These are merely select examples.

Rather than simply enumerating examples, we need to investigate their purpose. Calvin made varied and distinct use of paraphrase, not merely to re-state or clarify the apostle but also to provide further elucidation. At Romans 3.5, for instance, he uses it to fill in the missing material about the mindset of Paul's opponents. He records the "thoughts" of the antagonists,

> Even though this was a digression from the main point, it was necessary for the apostle to insert this material, so he would not seem to give the wicked an opportunity to speak evilly, that he knew they would take. For since they were looking out for an opportunity of defaming the Gospel, they had in David's testimony the means available to support their slander. 'If God seeks nothing other than to glorify men, why does he blame them when they fail, since by their failure they glorify him? Certainly, his being offended is unjust, if the cause of his becoming angered comes from that by which he is glorified.[26]

This allows a clarification of Paul's argument, as the reader "sees" how the opponents of the apostle were thinking, a disposition with which, according to Calvin, Paul had become painfully familiar, and which he was able to counteract in his argument. Further, this particular passage demonstrates how Calvin begins his paraphrase with little warning outside of the signs noted above. He then proceeds to a new line of thought.

A more common form is Calvin's habit, seen in that same verse, to paraphrase Paul to explicate better the mind of the apostle. "The word

---

[24] Comm. Philippians 2.15, Ad Philippenses 335.19–23. "He wants believers to be like lamps, which shine in the darkness of the world. It is as though he said, 'unbelievers, it is true, are children of the night, and there is nothing in the world except darkness. But God has illuminated you in this faith, in order that the purity of your life might shine forth in that darkness, so that His grace may appear more brightly.'" "Vult fideles instar lampadum esse, quae in mundi tenebris luceant. Acsi diceret: sunt quidem infideles filii noctis, et in mundo nihil est praeter tenebras. Sed in hunc fidem illuminavit vos Deus, ut refulgeat vitae vestra puritas in his tenebris, quo illustrior appareat sua gratia."

[25] Comm. Colossians 2.5, Ad Colossenses 420.30.

[26] Comm. Romans 3.5, Ad Romanos 59.38–46. "Quanquam extra causam principalem est digressio: necesse tamen Apostolo fuit eam interserere: ne malignis ansam maledicendi, quam ultro sciebat ab illis captari, praebuisse ipse videretur. Nam quum imminerent ad omnem occasionem diffamandi Euangelii, habebant in Davidis testimonio quod arriperent ad stuendam calumniam, Si nihil aliud quaerit Deus, quam ab hominibus glorificari: cur in eos adimadvertit ubi delinquunt, quum delinquendo eum glorificent? Iniuste certe offenditur si causam irascendi ex eo accipit quod glorificatur."

wrath, that is used here for judgment, refers to punishment, as if he had said, 'Is God unjust, in punishing those sins by which his righteousness is exemplified?'"[27] Of course, both examples are expansions of Paul's rhetoric and mind, as Calvin knows. This is *Paul's* account of his enemies, and Paul's answer to them. Thus, these first two forms of the paraphrase are two different species of a single genus.

I shall term this first usage of the paraphrase device the doctrinal, because Calvin's use of restatement carries within it a tendency towards his doctrine. Further, it represents an effort to get at the writer's intention behind the text, and to clarify the rhetoric and logic of the human author. Here, Calvin fulfills his own dictum for the understanding of texts, that of grasping the intention of the author.[28] But that is only one end to which Calvin employs this tool.

The second usage is the textual use, for it is employed when Calvin seeks to clarify the textual meaning in question. When expounding Romans 2.8, for example, Calvin runs into a text that he feels does not supply sufficient material to ensure that the reader will arrive at the intended meaning. He explains:

> The speech is a little confused. First, it is torn away from its course. The line of argument demands that the second part of the comparison should correspond to the first, like this. 'The Lord will give eternal life to those who by perserverance in good works seek glory, honor, and immortality; to the contentious and disobedient, eternal death.' The completion should then be supplied, 'Glory, honor, and incorruption have been set aside for the former, for the latter however, there has been wrath and affliction set aside.'[29]

The purpose of this form of paraphrase is not the author's meaning as it is concealed by a difficult metaphor, but to re-construct the meaning that has been obscured by clumsy style, or imperfect grammar. This is illustrated by Calvin's defensive excursus on the importance of the

---

[27] Comm. Romans 3.5, Ad Romanos 59.57–59. "**Irae** vocabulum, quod pro iudicio usurpatur, hic transfertur ad poenam: acsi dixisset, An iniustus est Deus qui scelera ulciscitur, quae iustitiam eius illustrant?"

[28] Comm. Romans, Dedicatory epistle.

[29] Comm. Romans 2.8, Ad Romanos 42.68–75. "Aliquantum confusa est oratio. Primum, ob abscissum tenorem: filum enim dictionis requirebat, ut secundum collationis membrum priori cohaereret, in hunc modum, Dominus iis, qui per boni operis perseverantiam, gloriam, honorem et immortalitatem quaerunt, redditurus est vitam aeternam: contentiosis autem et immorigeris, aeternam mortem. Tum subnecteretur illatio, paratam illis quidem esse gloriam et honorem et incorruptionem: his autem, repositam esse iram et afflictionem."

rough style of the apostolic writings.[30] Though Calvin defends Paul vigorously, he nevertheless finds the literary style to be made from rough words (*contemptibili verborum*). The paraphrase, therefore, is necessary to prevent mis-understanding caused by grammar and style. Here, one finds Calvin of two clearly conflicting minds. On the one hand, he can defend the rudeness of scripture's eloquence, and the necessity of that barbarity.[31] On the other, the (over?)barbarity of Paul's words and styling hinders understanding.[32] One wonders whether Calvin would have been so charitable about the sense of the passage being undisturbed had he found such rhetoric in an opponent's work. The whole case points again to Calvin's aim at a hermeneutical pre-understanding that will control signification in difficult passages.

This textual use of paraphrase to clarify grammatical points is also common for Calvin, and can be noted at Philippians 2.6, where he uses a paraphrase of Paul's wording to introduce his translation choice of the subjunctive.[33] A similar passage can be found in his comment upon Colossians 2.5, where Calvin comments upon the causative use of the conjunctive in both Latin and Greek.[34] This use of paraphrase is far less oriented toward doctrinal understanding, and more toward simple elucidation.

---

[30] Comm. Romans 2.8, Ad Romanos 42.77 79. "The sense, however, of this speech is hardly upset, we should be content this in apostolic writings. From other writers, eloquence is to be learned, here under the poverty of humble words, spiritual wisdom is to be sought." "Sensum tamen orationis id minime turbat quo in scriptis Apostolicis contenti sumus. Ex aliis enim discenda est eloquentia: hic sub contemptibili verborum humilitate, spiritualis sapientia quaerenda est."

[31] See Calvin's comment upon I Corinthians 1.17.

[32] Millet's concern about the acceptance of a biblical eloquence is aptly pointed out here. See his *Calvin et la dynamique de la parole: Etude de rhétorique réformée* (Paris: Librairie Honoré Champion, 1992), 185–256. Millet begins by stating "L'existence d'une rhetorique biblique, qui relève des catégories de la rhétorique classique, mai qui differe de cell-ci par son inspiation et ses intentions, est un fait acquis dans la pensée chrétienne depuis saint Augustin. Calvin prend place à cet égard dans une tradition ravivée par les méthodes humanistes d'analyse des textes bibliques."

[33] Comm. Philippians 2.6, Ad Philippenses 321 2–6. "For when he says, 'he would not have regarded,' it is as though he had said, 'He knew, indeed, that it was lawful and right for him,' in order that we that we should know that his submission was voluntary, not one of necessity. Prior to this it has been translated in the indicative, 'he regarded', but the context requires the subjunctive." "Nam quod dicit: non fuisset arbitratus, perinde valet, acsi dixisset: Sciebat quidem id sibi licere fasque esse, ut sciamus voluntariam fuisse submissionem, non necessitatis. Hactenus transtulerunt in modo indicativo: arbitratus est. Verum contextus requirit modum subiunctivum."

[34] Comm. Colossians 2.5, Ad Colossenses 420.28–32. "'Rejoicing,' he says, 'and seeing;' that is, 'because I see.' Because the conjunction means the causative, as is

I am noting two distinct usages of the paraphrastic tool in Calvin's commenting style. The latter generally may be described as an effort to clarify a textual point, or to simplify a stylistic manner foreign to sixteenth-century ears. It is helpful to remember that Calvin was working with a rather a more fluid text than that available to modern scholars. The critical resources available to him were primitive by modern standards, and the possibilities for an exhaustive search of a wide number of textual sources generally impossible. Further, the argument about the intentional corruption of the text of scripture always hovered in the background for biblical textual critics. This charge was leveled against the Jews concerning the Old Testament, against Jerome and Rome in the case of the Vulgate, against Erasmus concerning the new learning, and against the Reformers by Rome in the case of many of their textual emendations.

Because of this background, the clarification of ambiguous grammar or style within the sacred text was not in the early sixteenth century an exercise without theological or polemical overtones.[35] This clarification paraphrase was a tool of understanding of the meaning of the biblical text. Calvin did not attempt in this textual paraphrase to win a polemical point. Rather, he considered this a necessary step for explicating the text; the essential step to ensure that his audience would understand the sense of the work.[36]

The doctrinal use of the paraphrase must be considered a first step towards creedal formulation. This is demonstrated by a return to a

---

customary in Latin and Greek. Just as if he said, 'Go on as you have begun, for I know that you have always held to the right course; because distance is not an obstacle to me seeing you with the eyes of my mind.'" "›Gaudens‹, inquit, ›et videns‹, hoc est: quia video. Copula enim particulam causalem valet, quod Latinis et Graecis est usitatum. Perinde est, acsi diceret: Pergite, qua coepistis; scio enim vos hactenus tenuisse rectum cursum, quoniam non obstat loci distantia, quominus vos oculis mentis aspiciam."

[35] Though to consider that this exercise is ever without theological and polemical overtones seems rather ignorant of both the complexity of arriving at a "text" of scripture, and the debates that still occur over the correct readings of scripture.

[36] See however Richard C. Gamble, in the position that he takes in his "*Brevitas et Facilitas*: Toward an Understanding of Calvin's Hermeneutic," *Westminster Theological Journal* 47 (1985): 1–17. Gamble concludes that "Calvin, in rejecting frivolous rhetoric, regards the simplicity of the Bible and attempts to imitate that style as his own." (15) Though there is much truth here, and though Calvin does follow a paradigm of simplicity, this stance ignores the basic fact that Calvin thought he frequently had to paraphrase the biblical text so that they could be understood. The "ultimate presupposition of this hermeneutic—the clear brevity of the Scriptures," is too great a claim to support on the basis of the evidence.

previous example, Calvin's comment upon Romans 1.22. Calvin writes "Paul maintains this principle, that if a man is estranged from the worship of God, it is his own fault, as though he said, 'Because they have exalted themselves in pride, they have been made foolish by the righteous vengeance of God.'"[37] Calvin's own supplied text for this passage is "Professing themselves to be wise, they became fools.", which certainly does not contain the explicit mention of pride, the agency through that the people become foolish, or that this is a "righteous vengeance."[38] One cannot deny that Calvin has moved somewhat beyond the words of the page to supply extra meaning, and that this addition is aimed at his preferred doctrinal ends.

We can now see in Calvin's exegetical use of paraphrase two distinct purposes. On the one hand, it is a teaching and clarifying tool, an effort at finding a manner of expressing a message that will be most useful to the hearer. Like a teacher who is constantly seeking new metaphors and new ways of illustrating her points to her classes, so Calvin attempts to re-state the message of hazy or unclear passages to represent those truths with different images. This does not seem to be an intentional interpretation of the text, but rather a sort of transposition of the textual melodies so as to allow them to speak more clearly for themselves. On the other hand, Calvin's doctrinal use of this tool clearly reflects the hermeneutical-doctrinal presuppositions from his hermeneutical principles. In these instances, Calvin uses the paraphrase to demonstrate how a passage is to be understood. In this case, Calvin is already halfway back to his doctrinal framework, the rubric under which the messages of the scripture should be considered.

---

[37] Comm. Romans 1.22, Ad Romanos 31.106–108. "Nam principium illud retinet Paulus, Neminem, nisi propria culpa, a Dei cultu esse alienum. acsi diceret, Quoniam superbe se extulerunt, iusta Dei ultione fuerunt infatuati."

[38] Comm. Romans 1.22, Ad Romanos 28.79. "Quum se putarent sapientes, stulti facti sunt:"

Contextual Interpretation

Consciousness of particular context is another hallmark of Calvin's exegetical rules.[39] He frequently turns to the context for choosing the meaning of a passage, the meaning of a particular word, or the flow of the argument.[40] In fact, his *Argumenta* act as contextual guides for the setting of each epistle, detailing the provenance of the texts, from where they were written, and their place in the ministry of the writer, if such information could be determined and is helpful for understanding the book.[41] To demonstrate, I quote one of his shortest, the Argumentum of his II Thessalonians commentary.

> The notion that this epistle was sent from Rome, as the Greek manuscripts commonly assert, seems improbable to me, for Paul would have made some mention of his imprisonment, just as he usually does in the other epistles. Also, around the beginning of the third chapter he implies that he is in danger from unreasonable and evil men. We may gather from this that he wrote the epistle in the course of his journey when he was going to Jerusalem. From an early date it was commonly held by Latin writers that the epistle was written at Athens. The occasion, however, of his writing was to prevent the Thessalonians from thinking that they were neglected because he had not visited them on the hurried journey which he was making elsewhere. In the first chapter, Paul exhorts them to patience. In the second chapter, a vain and fabulous opinion, that the coming of Christ was imminent had become popular, his argument disproves it. This is because first there must come dissension in the church, and a great part of the world must turn from God treacherously;

---

[39] Again, it will not come as a surprise that this was a hallmark of humanistic exegesis in general. Erasmus advised that to understanding the meaning of scripture, we must find out "what is said, by whom, to whom, with what words, at what time, at what occasion, and what precedes and what follows." *Ratio Vera Theologiae*, 195:1–198:32, quoted in Manfred Hoffmann, *Rhetoric and Theology: The Hermeneutic of Erasmus*, (Toronto: University of Toronto Press, 1994), 33.

[40] Alexandre Ganoczy and Stefan Scheld have considered several points that I have placed under this rubric in their section on Textkritik. See *Die Hermeneutik Calvins: Geistesgeschichtliche Voraussetzungen und Grundzüge* (Wiesbaden: Franz Steiner Verlag GMBH, 1983), esp. 136–169. Myung-Jin Ahn, in "Calvin's Attitude toward the fathers and Medieval Interpretation from the Perspective of the Principles of Brevitas et Facilitas," *Calvin in Asian Churches*, vol. 1, edited by Sou-Young Lee (Seoul: Korea Calvin Society, 2002), 65–89, frequently notes the importance of this tool, without making explicit the relation of this to *brevitas* or *facilitas*.

[41] Ganoczy and Scheld, *Die Hermeneutik Calvins*, claim that "Dabei geht es ihm vor allem darum, das, was der Autor in einer bestrimmten Situation sagen wollte und was das Gesagte unter den konkreten geschichtlichen Umständen bedeutete, klarzumachen." (145).

indeed, Antichrist must reign in the temple of God. In the third chapter, after having commended himself to their prayers and briefly encouraging them to constancy, he orders them to correct severely those who lead an idle life at the expense of others. If they do not obey these warnings they are, he teaches they are to be excommunicated.[42]

Here one can see the way that Calvin uses his *Argumentum* to set out some of the contextual beacons by which his comments will be guided. Paul is not in prison, but is busy, hence the soothing of worries of neglect. Further, Paul must address certain matters of belief, because he will not soon be there to preach and teach on those matters. The function of the *Argumentum* is to set a framework through which his reader can more easily enter into the text's shifts, and more easily remember the important issues with which the text will deal. It is helpful to remember that the commentaries are written for the learned, for those who will be preaching, though learned laypeople are never far from Calvin's mind during the writing of his Pauline commentaries. The *argumenta* serve as mnemonic devices intended to bring to mind quickly the most crucial points in the text for the pastor as he prepares to teach or preach.

Calvin's use of contextual clues to select particular meanings and readings is not unique. In fact, it represents one of his areas of the closest proximity to the humanist approach to texts. Calvin employs this mechanism in his commentaries in three distinct ways. His first use is the "argument use," which considers the context of the argument's flow. Elucidating II Corinthians 1.20, Calvin uses this variety of the contextual tool to argue for a particular reading, noting that the Greek manuscripts disagree, offering two variants. After choosing the "Quare et per ipsum sit amen."[43] reading, he offers his reasoning.

---

[42] Comm. II Thessalonians, CO 52.185–186. *Argumentum* (complete) "Hanc epistolam Roma esse missam, ut vulgo habent Graeci codices, mihi non est probabile: nam de suis vinculis aliquid attigisset, sicuti in aliis solet. Deinde circa initium tertii capitis sibi instare periculum significat ab hominibus importunis: unde coniici potest, quum Hierosolymam tenderet, ex itinere scripsisse. Et iam olim Athenis fuisse sculptam, passim receptum fuit apud Latinos. Haec autem scribendi causa fuit: ne se neglectos putarent Thessalonicenses, quod alio festinans Paulus ad eos non venisset. Primo capite hortatur eos ad patientiam. Secundo, vanam et fabulosam opinionem, quae de propinquo Christi adventu sparsa invaluerat, hoc argumento refellit, quia prius oporteat fieri discessionem in ecclesia, et bonam orbis partem perfide a Deo deficere: imo Antichristum regnare in templo Dei. Tertio capite, postquam se precibus eorum commendavit, et breviter animavit ad constantiam, severe corrigi iubet eos qui otiose ex alieno vivunt. Quod si non obtemperent monitionibus, excommunicandos esse docet."

[43] Comm. II Corinthians 1.20, Secundam ad Corinthios 30.28–31.1. "**Wherefore**

I confess that the other reading is more usually chosen. However, it is
flat, and I have no doubt in preferring that which contains fuller teaching
and is more aptly suited to the context. For Paul is admonishing the
Corinthians of their duty that to respond with their amen after they have
been taught in the simple truth of God.[44]

In concentrating upon the flow of argument and rhetoric, Calvin moves
away from an atomistic view of scripture. Calvin shuns the glorification
of the Word, with the concomitant understanding that every word must
have a specific reason for its inclusion, which was common among the
early Church writers. To consider this under the rubric of interpretation, for Calvin the unit of meaning is the argument, with the sentence
or phrase standing as important sub-units.[45]

Calvin employs the "argument use" instrument frequently throughout his commentaries.[46] Writing on Colossians 2.13, he considers two
different interpretations, and decides the case contextually. "I favor
the former interpretation, because it corresponds better with the context."[47] Examining the meaning of I Thessalonians 2.7, he records that

---

also through Him is the amen. Here the Greek manuscripts are not in agreement.
Some have them joined together together in one, 'All the promises of God that exist
are through him and through him amen to the glory of God through us.' The other
reading, which I have followed, is more expedient and contains a fuller meaning."
"*Quare et per ipsum sit amen.* Hic etiam Graeca exemplaria non consentiunt. Quaedam
enim habent uno contextu: ›Quotquot sunt Dei promissiones, per ipsum sunt etiam, et
per ipsum amen, Dei ad gloriam per nos.‹ Verum diversa lectio, quam sequutus sum,
magis est expedita et sensum pleniorem continet."

[44] Comm. II Corinthians 1.20, Secundam ad Corinthios 31.7–11. "Diversa lectio
fateor magis est usitata. Sed quia frigida est, hanc praeferre non dubitavi, quae pleniorem doctrinam continet; deinde ad contextum longe est aptior. Officii enim Corinthios admonet Paulus, ut suum amen respondeant, postquam in simplici Dei veritate
fuerunt edocti."

[45] Likewise with Erasmus, who claimed that "The best reader of the divine books
looks for the understanding of the words from what is said." *Ratio Vera Theologiae*,
284:28–285:35, quoted in Manfred Hoffmann, *Rhetoric and Theology: The Hermeneutic of
Erasmus* (Toronto: University of Toronto Press, 1994), 37.

[46] Though it is outside the scope of our study, we may note that Calvin attempted
to take this same level of cultural-linguistic sophistication into his interpretation of
the Old Testament as well. Max Engammare has established that though Calvin was
not familiar with rabbinical Hebrew, his biblical Hebrew was sufficient to give good
translations of the Hebrew—"Quant à l'hébreu biblique, il est indéniable que Calvin
le connaisait relativement bien. La majorité des traductions données au début d'un
sermon sont tout à fait fidéles." "Joannes Calvinus Trium Linguarum Peritus? La
Question de L'Hebreu." *Bibliotheque d'Humanisme et Renaissance: Travaux et Documents*. 58
(1996): 58.

[47] Comm. Colossians 2.13, Ad Colossenses 429.13–24. "Hence we know that all the
ungodly, however they may seem to themselves to be actually living and flourishing, are,

"τὸ Βαρὺ" has two possible significations. But he immediately clarifies that "But the context requires that το Βαρυ should be taken to mean *authority*."[48] Again, when resolving the apparent contradiction between I Corinthians 11.3 and Galatians 3.28, Calvin does so almost wholly by depending upon the context of the passages. In the Galatians passage, where the difference between male and female is abolished, Calvin believes that it is the "spiritual kingdom of Christ" that is the object of the discussion. "I respond that the solution depends on the circumstances of the two passages. When Paul negates the difference between man and woman, he is speaking about the spiritual kingdom of Christ, where no respect is shown for persons, and they are not taken into consideration, for it has nothing to do with the body, nothing to do with the external societal human relationships, but is wholly about the spirit."[49] On the other hand, when Paul maintains a distinction between men and women in this chapter of the first epistle to the church at Corinth, Calvin allows that Paul has left civil order basically intact, concluding "He does not at the same time confuse the civil order and also leaves alone the distinctions and honors, because it is impossible to be without these in this life in community. But in this place he discusses with external points of honor and decorum, and these are part of ecclesias-

---

nevertheless, spiritually dead. In this way the passage will correspond with the second chapter of Ephesians, where it is said, 'Remember that in the past when you were Gentiles, and were called uncircumcision by that Circumcision which is made with hands in the flesh, at that time you were without Christ, alienated from the nation of Israel, and strangers to the promises'. Taking it metaphorically, this would be an allusion to natural uncircumcision, but Paul would here be speaking of the stubbornness of the human heart against God and of a nature defiled by wicked affections. I favor the former interpretation, because it corresponds better with the context." "Unde sequitur impios omnes, dum sibi maxime vivi et florentes videntur esse, tamen spiritualiter mortuos. Hoc modo conveniret hic locus cum secundo capite Ephesios, ubi dicitur: Memineritis, quod aliquando, quum essetis Gentes, vocatique praeputium ab ea Circuncisione, quae manu fit in carne, illo tempore eratis absque Christo, alienati a politia Israel et hospites promissionum. In translatione esset quidem allusio ad naturale praeputium, sed tamen Paulus hic loqueretur de contumacia cordis humani adversus Deum et natura pravis affectibus inquinata. Ego priorem expositionem magis amplector, quia melius quadrat contextui."

[48] Comm. I Thessalonians 2.7, CO 52.148. "sed contextus postulat, ut τὸ Βαρὺ pro autoritate sumatur."

[49] Comm. I Corinthians 11.3, CO 49.474. "Respondeo, solutionem pendere ex locorum circumstantia. Quum mulierem a viro differre negat, tractat de spirituali Christi regno, ubi personae non aestimantur, nec in rationem veniunt: nihil enim ad corpus, nihil ad externam hominum societatem, sed totum in spiritu situm est."

tical polity."[50] Calvin explicitly states that his solution "depends upon
the circumstances of that place" (*pendere ex locorum circumstantia*). Without
a full knowledge of the contexts and issues at stake, Paul appears to
contradict himself. Only through context can the meaning that resolves
this difficulty be found.

The second way that Calvin exercises the contextual tool is the
"authorial use." Time and again, the situation of the writer, whether
in jail, as occasionally is the case for Paul, or bereaved, as one sees
in David in the Psalms commentary, becomes an exegetical key. For
instance, in explicating Philippians 1.12 ff, Calvin's thoughts turn continually to Paul's incarceration.[51] Again, when considering the Psalm 7,
Calvin cannot resist supplying the information that David is speaking
about Saul in the second verse. "But as the wicked cruelty of the king,
like a firebrand, had kindled against him, though an innocent person,
the hatred of the whole people, he had good reason also for turning his
pen particularly against him."[52] Calvin can even go so far as to see Paul
prevaricating for a good pastoral reason.[53]

There is a third use of context for Calvin, the "vocabulary use",
where the knowledge of the stylistic choices and glossary peculiar to

---

[50] Comm. I Corinthians 11.3, CO 49.474. "Neque tamen civilem ordinem interea
confundit, aut honorum distinctiones, quibus non potest carere communis haec vita.
Hic vero disputat de externa honestate atque decoro, quae pars est politiae ecclesias-
ticae."

[51] Comm. Philippians 1.12 ff, Ad Philippenses 304.7–9. "It may have occurred that
the Philippians were somewhat discouraged by the persecution of their Apostle." "Id
accidere Philippensibus poterat, ut Apostoli sui persequutione nonnihil deiicerentur."

[52] Comm. Psalms 7.2, CO 31.79. "Sed quia impia regis crudelitas, instar facis, contra
hominem innoxium totius populi odia inflammabat, merito etiam peculiariter in ipsum
stylum convertit."

[53] Comm. I Thessalonians 4.15. CO 52.166. "By speaking in the first person he
makes himself among the number of those who will live until the last day. He wanted
to stir up the Thessalonians to wait for it, and to hold all the believers in suspense,
so that they would not promise themselves some particular time. Granted, he knew by
a particular revelation that Christ would come at a somewhat later time; however it
was still necessary that this common doctrine should be handed on to the church, in
order that believers might be ready at all hours. In the meantime, this was necessary
to cut off the opportunity taken by many for indulging curiosity, as he will later do
at greater length." "Quod autem in prima persona loquens, se quasi unum facit ex
eorum numero, qui usque ad diem extremum victuri sunt: eo vult Thessalonicenses in
exspectationem erigere, adeoque pios omnes tenere suspensos, ne sibi tempus aliquod
promittant. Nam ut demus ipsum ex peculiari revelatione scivisse venturum aliquanto
serius Christum: hanc tamen ecclesiae communem doctrinam tradi oportuit, ut fideles
omnibus horis parati essent. Interea simul ansam curiositati multorum praecidi oportuit, quod prolixius deninde faciet."

each writer provides more insight. Thus, commenting upon Colossians 1.27, Calvin writes that "Indeed, 'riches' to Paul signifies 'greatness,' as is well known."[54] Again, writing upon the term "*diaconis*,"[55] Calvin argues that his choice of the referent as "*oeconomos*" is correct, since that is Paul's more frequent usage.[56] Perhaps the most striking instance of Calvin's employment of this tool comes only a few pages later, when Calvin denies an interpretation vigorously. "Some understand the love of the Philippians is directed at the Philippians themselves, as the people say, 'Your reverence', 'Your paternity.' But this is absurd. For no such instance occurs in Paul, nor had such foolishness come about."[57] The significance of this instance as evidence for a particular exegetical strategy cannot be denied. Calvin rejects the possibility of a particular idea being within the text both because of the lack of another corroborating example within the Pauline corpus, and because the idea at issue had not yet come into vogue. Calvin uses a similar familiarity with Paul's style to conclude that the Epistle to the Laodiceans cannot be from Paul's hand.[58]

---

[54] Comm. Colossians, 1.27, Ad Colossenses 415.6–7. "Divitiae enim amplitudinem significant Paulo, ut notum est."

[55] The consideration of the diaconate was a loaded question in the first half of the 16th century. For a survey of the exegetical positions, see Elsie Anne McKee, *John Calvin on the Diaconate and Liturgical Almsgiving* (Genève: Librairie Droz, 1984).

[56] Comm. Philippians 1.1, Ad Philippenses 296.11–15. "This term may be taken in two ways: either for ministers to and curators of the poor, or for elders, who were appointed for the maintenance of morals. As, however, it is more usual in Paul in the former sense, I understand it to mean stewards, who superintended the distributing and receiving of alms." "Potest bifariam accipi hoc nomen: vel pro ministris et curatoribus pauperum, vel pro senioribus, qui constituebantur ad mores regendos. Sed quoniam usitatius est in priore sensu apud Paulum, potius intelligo oeconomos, qui distribuendis eleemosynis et recipiendis praeerant."

[57] Comm. Philippians 1.9, Ad Philippenses 301.23–27. "Quod nonnulli charitatem Philippensium accipiunt pro ipsis Philippensibus, qualiter vulgo barbari loqui solent: ›Vestra reverentia‹, ›Vestra paternitas‹, absurdum est. Neque enim tale exemplum extat in Paulo, necdum in consuetudinem venerant tales ineptiae."

[58] Comm. Colossians 4.16, Ad Colossenses 464.2–5. "However there was an exceedingly crass imposture when some good-for-nothing person, I do not know who, used this pretext with audacity to forge, a work that is so weak, that nothing can be conceived more foreign to Paul's spirit." "Impostura autem nimis crassa fuit, quod nebulo nescioquis hoc praetextu epistolam supponere ausus est adeo insulsam, ut nihil a Pauli spiritu magis alienum fingi queat." Calvin may have been familiar with this idea from his contact with Lefèvre, who counted the epistle to the Laodiceans among the authentic writings of Paul. For more on Lefèvre, see Jerry Bentley's *Humanists and Holy Writ: New Testament Scholarship in the Renaissance* (Princeton: Princeton University Press, 1983), 10–11.

The "vocabulary use" of context in Calvin must be linked to the humanistic influences, both in his training, and in his mature reading.[59] These methods of Calvin are frequently noted in the literature as common tools of humanist scholars of the early sixteenth century.[60] His own training in textual reading had been influenced by some of the acknowledged masters, such as Alciati.[61] Further, Calvin was unafraid to borrow from humanist scholars, occasionally without citation. This is certainly the case in Calvin's comment about the Epistle to the Laodiceans. Erasmus had dismissed the possibility of this being from the pen of Paul at exactly the same verse, Colossians 4.16, in his *Annotations*.[62] Contrary to Calvin's claim that he does not know who (*nescioquis*), he certainly does know the fellow—Faber Stapulensis.[63]

The fourth function of the contextual tool was the "cultural," where Calvin considered the world out of which the biblical text was generated, giving ample attention to Hebraicisms, Greek and its idioms, and the society in which the human author and his audience were situated.[64]

The first of these required a knowledge of Hebrew that has not always been granted to Calvin.[65] Frequently, Calvin used his knowledge of Hebrew language and culture to penetrate further into the text, or even to correct the interpretation or translation of other scholars. Such was the case in his critique of Erasmus' translation and interpretation of I Thessalonians 2.13.[66]

---

[59] Basil Hall has stated that "Calvin's method derives ultimately from Valla, through Erasmus, in the succinct grammatical explanation of the text, but he is unlike Erasmus in avoiding all needless reference to learned authors and occasional allegorizing. He was concerned for edification as well as instruction." Hall, "Calvin and Biblical Humanism," *Proceedings of the Huguenot Society of London* 20 (1960): 195–209.

[60] See Jerry H. Bentley's *Humanists and Holy Writ: New Testament Scholarship in the Renaissance* (Princeton: Princeton University Press, 1983), esp. chapters 4 and 5.

[61] Quirinus Breen, *John Calvin: A Study in French Humanism*, 2nd ed. (New York: Archon Books, 1968), 44–52.

[62] Bentley, *Humanists and Holy Writ*, 178.

[63] The veiled reference would be another example of humanist style.

[64] By noting four particular uses of context in his commentary, I am not suggesting that I have exhausted the possibilities.

[65] Richard Simon, the 17th century French Catholic went so far as to say that Calvin only knew the characters of the Hebrew Alphabet. Of course, this would denigrate not only Calvin's understanding of the Old Testament, but also the skills of his Hebrew teachers—either Francois Vatable or Simon Grynaeus and Wolfgang Capito. See W. McKane's "Calvin as an Old Testament Commentator," *Nederduitse Gereformeerde Teologiese Tydskrif* 25 (1984): 250–259.

[66] Comm. I Thessalonians 2.13, CO 52.152. "Erasmus has gone astray, taking the phrase to mean 'the word of the hearing of God,' as if Paul meant that God had been

Calvin's use of Greek hardly needs to be defended. His command of Greek was not seriously contested by other scholars of his day, and his commentaries on the New Testament are filled with references to the insights that can be gleaned from the original language.[67] A few examples should suffice for this point. Calvin makes use of Greek or early Greco-roman culture to settle points at I Thessalonians 3.1,[68] II Thessalonians 2.6,[69] Philippians 1.27,[70] and Ephesians 5.4.[71] Beyond this,

---

disclosed. Later he changed this to 'the word by which you learned God,' this was because he did not notice that it was a Hebrew idiom." "Male Erasmus, qui vertis sermonem auditus Dei: ac si Deum intelligeret Paulus patefactum. Postea mutavit, sermonem quo Deum discebatis. Non enim ab eo animadversa fuit hebraica phrasis."

[67] T.H.L. Parker considers it as "an irrefragable principle that his commentaries on the New Testament were interpretations and expositions of the Greek text and not of his own or another's Latin version." *Ioannis Calvini Opera Exegetica, Commentarius in Epistolam ad Hebraeos*, edited by T.H.L. Parker (Geneva: Droz, 1996), xxiii.

[68] Comm. I Thessalonians 3.1, CO 52.156. "The word ευδοκησαμεν, which denotes an eager mindset, means the same thing." "Eodem pertinet verbum ευδοκησαμεν, quod promptam animi inclinationem designat."

[69] Comm. II Thessalonians 2.6, CO 52.200. "Το κατεχον here properly signifies an impediment, or cause of delay." "Το κατεχον proprie impedimentum, vel causam morae hoc loco significat."

[70] Comm. Philippians 1.27, Ad Philippenses 313.30–314.5. "The expression Paul used in Greek is ambiguous. The old interpreter (the Vulgate) interpreted it *collaborantes fidei* (laboring together with the faith). Erasmus has *adiuvantes fidem* (helping the faith), as if they gave help to the faith to the best of their strength. But since the dative in Greek is put for the ablative of instrumentality because that language has no ablative, I do not doubt that this is the sense of the Apostle: 'Let the faith of the Gospel draw you together, more especially as it is a common armor against the same enemy.' In this manner the particle σὺν, which others refer to faith, I refer to the Philippians, and this is better, if I am not mistaken." "Loquutio, qua Graece usus est Paulus, ambiqua est. Quare vetus interpres vertit: ›collaborantes fidei‹, Erasmus: ›adiuvantes fidem‹, quasi fidei opem ipsi pro virili adferrent. Sed quum dativus apud Graecos ponatur pro ablativo instrumenti, propterea quod ablativo caret lingua illa, non dubito, quin sit hic sensus Apostoli: Coniungat vos Euangelii fides, praesertim quum illa vobis sit communis armatura adversus eundem hostem. Hoc modo particulam συν, quam alii ad fidem referunt, ego refero ad Philippenses, et melius, nisi fallor."

[71] Comm. Ephesians 5.4, Ad Ephesios 255.25–256.2. "Others prefer 'giving of thanks'. I am pleased with Jerome's interpretation. For Paul had to set something general in opposition to our words with those vices. For if he had said, 'While they delight in frivolous or abusive talk, you must give thanks to God,' it would have been too restricted. The Greek word εὐχαριστία admits of our translating it 'grace.' Therefore the meaning will be, 'All our words ought to be filled with true sweetness and grace, so that we mingle the useful with the sweet.'" "Alii malunt gratiarum actionem. Mihi placet Hieronymi interpretatio. Debuit enim Paulus superioribus vitiis generale aliquid opponere, quod in sermonibus nostris eluceat. Nam si dixisset: Interea dum illi frivolis nugis et scurrilitate se oblectant, vos agite gratias Deo, fuisset imis restrictum. Patitur

he is familiar enough with the Greek to style himself an occasional text critic. This is the path he takes at Ephesians 5.9,[72] and 5.14.[73]

More intriguing than Calvin's use of Greek grammar and philology was his recourse to the contextual nature of discourse, and especially to the context of the human author and audience. Calvin realized that Paul was a first-century thinker who was conditioned by the cultures in which he moved and taught. There is even a slight condescension towards Paul for making the mistake of universalizing what was truly only a convention.

> He again proposes nature as the teacher of what is proper. Now, what he means by 'natural' is was accepted by common consent and usage at that time, at least among the Greeks. For it was not always considered a disgrace for men to have long hair. The histories relate that formerly, that is in the first ages, men wore long hair in every country. The poets therefore called the ancients "unshorn." It was not until a later time in Rome that they began to use barbers, around the time of Africanus the Elder. And at the time when Paul was writing this, in Gaul and Germany they did not yet use the practice of cutting hair. Yes, and moreover, it would have been a disgraceful thing for men, just as much as for women, to have their hair shaved or cut. But since in Greece they did not consider it very manly to have long hair, so that they called those with it effeminate, Paul at that time accepts that the custom is conformed to nature.[74]

---

autem Graecum vocabulum εὐχαριστία, ut nos gratiam vertamus. Sensus autem erit sermones nostros vera suavitate et gratia perfusos esse debere. Quod fiet, si miscebimus utile dulci."

[72] Comm. Ephesians 5.9, Ad Ephesios 258.26–27. "It is surprising that the word 'Spirit' should have crept into many Greek codices, since 'the fruit of the light' fits in better." "Mirum autem, unde in multos Graecos codices obrepserit nomen ›Spiritus‹,quum magis congruat: Fructus autem lucis sunt;".

[73] Comm. Ephesians 5.14, Ad Ephesios 262.7–9. "Where some codices for επιφαυσει, read instead εφαψεται, that is, 'he shall touch'; it is an evident error." "Quod aliqui codices pro επιφαυσει legunt εφαψεται, hoc est: ›continget‹, manifestus est error."

[74] Comm. I Corinthians 11.14, CO 49.478. "Iterum naturam illis decori magistram proponit. Quod autem omnium consensu et consuetudine receptum tunc erat, et quidem apud Graecos, vocat naturale: nam viris non semper fuit coma dedecori. Olim ubique viros fuisse comatos, hoc est, primis saeculis, referunt historiae. Unde et poetae vocare solent intonsos veteres trito epitheto. Sero tonsoribus Romae uti coeperunt, circa aetatem Aphricani superioris. Et quo tempore scribebat haec Paulus, nondum in Galliis et Germania invaluerat tondendi usus. Quin potius deforme fuisset non minus viris quam mulieribus, radi aut tonderi: sed quoniam in Graecia parum virile erat alere comam, ut tales quasi effeminati notarentur: morem iam confirmatum pro natura habet."

A close reading of this passage demonstrates several interesting points. First, Calvin is not actually defending Paul, as he normally chooses to do. He is explaining how Paul could write something and accredit it to nature when so clearly it was not an issue of nature, but rather of convention. Secondly, Calvin demonstrates a full recognition of the fallibility of the human author of scripture.[75] The explanation is wholly historical/contextual, rather than an effort to confirm the truth of Paul's position. Thirdly, Calvin wants at least some of his readers to follow him on that journey of discovery of Paul's fallibility. Otherwise, the long discourse on the history of hair makes no sense. This might be one of the most significant points yet made about Calvin's exegetical practice. Although he is at pains to defend the human authors of the scriptures where they are making doctrinal points, he is not averse to allowing them to be seen as human, and therefore fallible, when issues of *adiaphora* or inconsequential detail are at stake.

For Calvin, however, the rule of context was a strong canon, but not a supreme principle. He could suggest the overruling of context on the basis of the usefulness of the less-supported message. This seems to be the case in his comment upon II Corinthians 11.20.

> There are three possible meanings here. He might be ironically re-proaching the Corinthians, because they could bear nothing on account of their delicacy; he might be charging them with negligence that they surrendered themselves to such a shameless servitude to the false apostles; or he might be referring, as if he were another person, to charges made against him without any justification, as if he had usurped a right of tyrannical domination over them. The second sense has the support of Chrysostom, Ambrose and Augustine and is commonly accepted. This one does suit the context best. However, to me the third interpretation is just as good. Indeed we see how time and again he was slandered by the evil, as though he were a domineering tyrant—which he certainly was not. As the other meaning is more received, however, I have no objection that it should be accepted.[76]

Here, Calvin has already stated that the second option is that which best fits the context (*optime congruit contextui*). However, he values the message of the third, perhaps because of the troubles he himself was

---

[75] Again, the usefulness of the two-fold author is seen.

[76] Comm. II Corinthians 11.20, Secundam ad Corinthios 184.19–185.4. "Triplex potest esse sensus: vel quod ironice Corinthios perstringat, quia nihil ferre queant, ut solent delicati; vel quod socordiae eos insimulet, quod pseudoapostolis se in puden-dam servitutem addixissent; vel quod referat quasi in aliena persona, quod odiose de ipso praedicabatur, acsi tyrannicum imperium sibi adversus eos usurparet. Secundus

having with the Genevans during the time of writing it in late 1546.[77] In any case, after establishing that one meaning best fits the context, Calvin proffers another, and allows his reader to choose the more suitable. However, the phrase "I have no objection" (*non repugno*), is hardly a ringing endorsement. This is a rather unique case, but demonstrates again that for Calvin, the use of context was a tool that helped to reach a goal rather than a law that could not be knowingly violated.

John Calvin made full use of contextual interpretation, and in doing so demonstrated his allegiance to humanistic ideals concerning the interpretation of texts. This tool, however, was balanced by the use of paraphrase, as well as others. Occasionally, Calvin can be seen to override the fruit of contextual reading, but in general, it is one of his most precious means of grasping the mind of the writer, and for denying atomistic exegesis that would concentrate upon individual words in isolation from one another.

Scripture Interprets Scripture

As with the other Reformers, Calvin held to the principle that scripture interprets scripture. Though this statement might seem to attack my point of the importance of hermeneutic and exegetical structures, any reader of even the English translations of Calvin's New Testament commentaries will find Calvin constantly clarifying his point on one passage of scripture through the use of another. Calvin used Johannine material to clarify Paul.[78] As noted in the section on Calvin's hermeneutics, Calvin's license to do this stems from the unity of the message of the scriptures, founded upon the unity of their author. But when Calvin uses this as a tool it is with different purposes in mind.[79] Since Calvin's

---

sensus Chrysostomo, Ambrosio, Augustino placet, adeoque communiter receptus est. Equidem optime congruit contextui. Quanquam mihi tertius non minus arridet. Videmus enim, ut passim a malevolis traductus fuerit, quasi impotenter dominaretur. A quo tamen longissime aberat. Sed quoniam alter ille est receptior, non repugno, quin valeat."

[77] For an excellent detailed history of Calvin's trials with the Genevans, see William Naphy's *Calvin and the Consolidation of the Genevan Reformation* (Manchester: Manchester University Press, 1994).

[78] Comm. Galatians 1.4, Ad Galatas 15.19 ff.

[79] To expand the field of quotations upon which this research is based, I avoid repeating notice of the citations given in the hermeneutical section on part to whole, chapter 2, which would, of course, also be appropriate.

habit is so clear from cursory glances at either the English or Latin text, it will be more useful to examine a few instances of his usage at depth, rather than to pile up citations.

One use of Calvin's habit of allowing scripture to interpret scripture is the filling out of an implied meaning in the text, by reference to another text that is more direct in its sense. Thus, Calvin will turn from a cloaked meaning, or doctrinal consequence that is not fully clear, to a more lucid statement of that position in another portion of the scripture. One instance of this comes in Calvin's comment upon Colossians 1.20, when he interprets "those above the earth, and in heaven" (*Tam super terram, quam in caelis*). After noting that this *could* reasonably mean all created being, Calvin interprets it traditionally as referring only to men and angels (*homines et Angeli*). The problem, of course, is with angels. Humans need a pacificator, but do the angels?

Calvin's answer is yes. First, the angels need to be set at final peace with God, since as created being they are still able to fall. Secondly, Calvin avers that their obedience is not perfect. They do not fully satisfy God in every respect. Here, Calvin supplies a text from Job 4.18, that "*In Angelis suis reperiet iniquitatem.*" Calvin immediately notes that this cannot be referred to the Devil, since that is too obvious. Rather, for Calvin, the message from the two passages together is clear. "We must, therefore, resolve that there is not in the angels so much righteousness as would suffice for full union with God. They have, therefore, need of a peace-maker, through whose grace they may wholly cleave to God."[80]

---

[80] Comm. Colossians 1.20, Ad Colossenses 403.2–404.8. "As to angels, however, that is a question that is not easily solved. ... Between God and angels the issue is very different. Because there was there no revolt, no sin and consequently no separation. However, there are two causes for the Angels to need to be set at peace with God. Since they are creatures, they are not out of danger of falling, unless they are confirmed by the grace of Christ. Indeed, it is not a little thing for the perpetuity of peace with God to have a fixed status in righteousness, which no longer fears fall or revolt. Further, in that very obedience which they do give to God, they do not have such total perfection so as to satisfy God wholly in every part and without pardon. And this, without doubt, is the sense of that statement in the Book of Job, 'He will find iniquity in his angels'. For if it is expounded of the devil, so what? But the Spirit pronounces there that the greatest purity is soiled, if seen in the light of the righteousness of God. We must, therefore, lay it down that the angels do not have so much righteousness as would suffice for full union with God. They have, therefore, need of a peace-maker, through whose grace they may wholly be joined to God." "De Angelis autem quaestio non facilis ad explicandum ... Inter deum et Angelos longe diversa ratio. Illic enim nulla defectio, nullum peccatum, ideoque nullum divortium. Sed tamen duabus de causis Angelos quoque oportuit cum

Obviously, Calvin is solving a problem in a New Testament text by reference to a passage from the Old Testament, demonstrating that the unity of testaments does, in some manner, work both ways, and that at times the passage of greater intelligibility might be found in the older witness.

Another use of Calvin's interpretation through scripture is to refer back to the wider usage of the term, or concept. An instance of this can be seen in his comment on Colossians 1.26. Calvin interprets the hidden mystery (*mysterium reconditum*) as the gospel. However, this is not completely clear from the text. To demonstrate the veracity of his approach, Calvin turns to other passages. He writes "Here he calls it [the gospel] a sublime secret which was hidden from ages and generations, that is, from the beginning of the world, through all the many revolving ages. However, that he is speaking of the gospel, is clear from Rom. 16.25, Eph. 3.9, and similar passages."[81]

Though one is familiar more with Luther's ideal of scripture interpreting scripture, this instrument is widely used by the magisterial Reformers, and Calvin's usage is neither surprising, nor particularly innovative.[82] However, it is one of the tools he has in his workshop as he approaches the scripture to ascertain what message God wishes believers to hear.

Deo pacificari. Nam quum creaturae sint, extra lapsus periculum non erant, nisi Christi gratia fuissent confirmati. Hoc autem non parvum est momentum ad pacis cum Deo perpetuitatem: fixum habere statum in iustitia, ne casum aut defectionem amplius timeat. Deinde in hac ipsa obedientia, quam praestant Deo, non est tam exquisita perfectio, ut Deo omni ex parte et citra veniam satisfaciat. Atque huc proculdubio spectat sententia ista ex libro Iob: ›In Angelis suis reperiet iniquitatem.‹ Nam si de diabolo exponitur, quid magnum? Pronuntiat autem illic Spiritus summam puritatem sordere, si ad Dei iustitiam exigatur. Constituendum igitur non esse tantum in Angelis iustitiae, quod ad plenam cum Deo coniunctionem sufficiat. Itaque pacificatore opus habent, per cuius gratiam penitus Deo adhaereant."

[81] Comm. Colossians 1.26, Ad Colossenses 413.23–26. "Hic vocat sublime arcanum, quod incognitum fuerit seculis et generationibus, hoc est ab initio mundi per tot aetatum circuitus. Quod autem de Euangelio loquatur, apparet ex cap. 16,25 epistolae ad Roma., ad Ephesios cap. 3,9 et similibus."

[82] Luther's dicta about interpreting scripture by scripture can be supported in various places from his works. I quote his reply to Erasmus from *De Servo Arbitrio*. *Luther: On the Bondage of the Will*, LCC 27, (Philadelphia: Westminster Press, 1969), 110–111. WA 606–609. "I admit, of course, that there are many texts in the Scriptures that are obscure and abstruse, not because of the majesty of their subject matter, but because of our ignorance of their vocabulary and grammar; but these texts in no way hinder a knowledge of the subject matter of Scripture. ... The subject matter of the Scriptures, therefore, is all quite accessible, even though some texts are still obscure owing to our

Tradition's Possibilities

Perhaps one of the most astonishing features of Calvin's commentaries is his constant reference to the Church's traditions, both doctrinal and exegetical.[83] Those readers who have been too swayed by the term *sola scriptura* either must ignore Calvin's actual custom, or soon are disabused of this too-facile mnemonic.[84] Calvin is fully aware that he is working as a theologian and exegete of the Church, an institution with fourteen centuries of history.[85] This is a necessity for the Genevan

---

ignorance of their terms. Truly it is stupid and impious, when we know that the subject matter of Scripture has all been placed in the clearest light, to call it obscure on account of a few obscure words. If the words are obscure in one place, yet they are plain in another; and it is one and the same theme, published quite openly to the whole world, which in the Scriptures is sometimes expressed in plain words, and sometimes lies as yet hidden in obscure words. Now, when the thing signified is in the light, it does not matter if this or that sign of it is in darkness, since many other signs of the same thing are meanwhile in the light. Who will say that a public fountain is not in the light because those who are in a narrow side street do not see it, whereas all who are in the marketplace do see it?" Interestingly, Luther turns immediately away from the words of scripture to the subject matter. Although he perhaps displays an unwarranted confidence in being able through further study to clarify all issues, basically Luther makes a hermeneutical move of addressing unclear words by clear meanings. It may be that a study of Luther's hermeneutics and exegesis would be more fruitful following this avenue, than to multiply the accounts of his exegetical tools, especially as Luther's career spans widely divergent exegetical practices. See Alexandre Ganoczy and Stefan Scheld, *Die Hermeneutik Calvins*, Einleitung.

[83] John Thompson notes that the idea of the rejection of tradition is a too-common fallacy about the Reformation's exegesis. "Although the exegesis of the Reformation era has often been characterized as having shaken off traditional views in favor of the unadorned Word of God, the reality is rather different. Sixteenth-century commentators were constantly in conversation with their patristic, medieval, and rabbinic predecessors, and many of these traditional views survive, albeit often in new forms." John Thompson, *Writing the Wrongs: Women of the Old Testament among Biblical Commentators from Philo through the Reformation* (Oxford: Oxford University Press, 2001), 69. That thread is still available, see Cottret's comments upon Calvin's rejection of received interpretations, Bernard Cottret, *Calvin: A Biography*, 308.

[84] Calvin is not alone among the Reformers in taking this stance. Heinrich Bullinger, to give only one instance, can go so far as to state "In so far as the Holy Fathers have not digressed from this kind of interpretation, I have not only recited them as interpreters of the Scriptures but have venerated them as elected tools of God." Quoted in Fritz Büsser, "Bullinger as Calvin's Model in Biblical Exposition: An Examination of Calvin's Preface to the Epistle to the Romans," 64–95 in *In Honor of John Calvin, 1509–1564*, edited by E.J. Furcha (Montreal: Faculty of Religious Studies, McGill University, 1987), 74.

[85] Though this was not as striking a characteristic of the humanistic exegesis of Calvin's day, it was still a common pattern. Erasmus suggests working with commentaries of the ancient interpreters, and advises Origen, Basil, Nazianzen, Athanasius,

Reformer if he truly believed himself to be reforming, and not merely innovating. Thus, he frequently gives the opinions and positions that come from the strands of tradition,[86] and then either offers one of his own, or decides among the several presented.[87] Further, he regularly lauds positions that have the patina of antiquity, and denigrates faddish newness.[88]

Calvin demonstrated this habit throughout his commentaries.[89] It was a practice that reflected a deep appreciation for the Church's tradition across time and was integral to his exegesis, from his very first effort at biblical commentary.[90] Occasionally, he takes this custom too far, at least for the purpose of brief elucidation. For instance, in commenting upon II Corinthians 4.6, Calvin provides four different inter-

---

Cyril, Chrysostom, Jerome, Ambrose, Hilary and Augustine. *Ratio Vera Theologiae*, 295:1–297:5, quoted in Manfred Hoffmann, *Rhetoric and Theology: The Hermeneutic of Erasmus*, (Toronto: University of Toronto Press, 1994), 38. This raises the question of access to the older sources. Karlfried Froehlich, in his "The Fate of the *Glossa Ordinaria* in the Sixteenth Century." *Die Patristik in der Bibelexegese des 16. Jahrhunderts*, edited by David C. Steinmetz (Wiesbaden: Harrassowitz Verlag, 1999), 19–47, has noted that Erasmus himself had access to and probably uncritically quoted printed versions of the *Glossa ordinaria*. However, though Froehlich is able to demonstrate varying levels of dependence upon the *Glossa* in the work of Reformers such as Bucer and Bullinger, this is impossible at this time in Calvin's work. "For Calvin and the Geneva theologians after his death, the *Glossa ordinaria* had ceased to play a role, *any* role as an accepted source of patristic exegetical material, or even as a source in its own right." (37).

[86] W. McKane goes too far in opining that Calvin's "... animus against Catholic exegesis is more powerful than that that operates against Jewish exegesis ..." Calvin frequently mines the Church's tradition in search of useful ore. W. McKane, "Calvin as an Old Testament Commentator." *Nederduitse Gereformeerde Teologiese Tydskrif* 25 (1984): 251.

[87] Olivier Millet notes Calvin's admirable knowledge of the Fathers and his sense that they are the first source of ideas of theological and historical argumentation for the Church. *Calvin et la dynamique de la parole: Etude de rhétorique réformée* (Paris: Librairie Honoré Champion, 1992), 168.

[88] An example can be seen in Calvin's comments upon Romans 7, where he makes clear that he is following the "corrected" view of the later Augustine on the divided self. See David C. Steinmetz, *Calvin in Context* (Oxford: Oxford University Press, 1995), 110–121.

[89] This is not simply a position of humility, but an effort to grasp the tradition of the Church. For an example of this, see Elsie McKee's "Les Anciens et l'Interpretation de 1 Tm 5, 17 chez Calvin: Une Curiosite dans l'Histoire de l'Exegese." *Revue de Theologie et de Philosophie* 120, (1988): 411–417, which points out the way in which Calvin's interpretation does draw upon the two-fold elder that is a common theme in the prior exegetical tradition.

[90] See his Romans commentary, where he begins by considering Paul's name, immediately deliberating on the possibilities offered up by various patristic commentators.

pretive options.[91] His offering of prior interpretive traditions can be seen both in his more famous disdain toward the opinions of others and in his less-frequently noted humility before the text. The contemptuous Calvin is more familiar, it is true. One example should suffice. In considering Philippians 2.9, Calvin mentions the tradition of interpreting this passage as a basis for the doctrine of merit.[92] But he does so only to deny that possibility in the strongest terms. "Who cannot see that it is at the instigation of Satan that they claim that the principle fruit is in Christ himself, that he thought of himself before thinking on our account, that he merited glory for himself before salvation for us?"[93]

However, the more humble Calvin appears in the above-mentioned comment upon II Corinthians 4.6. Calvin offers four interpretations. He provides his own opinion in concurrence with Chrysostom, which is the fourth, but also commends Ambrose's different solution, and allows the reader to use his own judgment.[94] And occasionally, Calvin strikes

---

[91] Comm. II Corinthians 4.6, Secundam ad Corinthios 74.23.

[92] Comm. Philippians 2.9, Ad Philippenses 324.7–9. "This passage has given occasion to the sophists, or rather they have seized it, to say that Christ merited first for Himself, and then for others." "Hic locus occasionem dedit sophistis, vel ipsi potius eam arripuerunt, ut dicerent Christum primo sibi meritum esse, deinde aliis."

[93] Comm. Philippians 2.9, Ad Philippenses 325.3–6. "Quis ergo negct istos Satanae instinctu contra reclamare: praecipuum esse fructum in ipso Christo, ipsum priorem sui quam nostri rationem habuisse, sibi ante gloriam esse promeritum quam nobis salutem?" It might be worth noting here that Calvin follows a position very close to that of Scotus, that the reason for this salvation vehicle, i.e., the cross, is simply and only God's will. David Steinmetz has pointed out that at times, specifically in Romans 8, Calvin only considers the fathers in order to quarrel with them. He makes this point in order to assert that Calvin "treats the Fathers as partners in conversation rather than as authorities in the medieval sense of the term." *Calvin in Context* (Oxford: Oxford University Press, 1995), 137.

[94] Comm. II Corinthians 4.6, Secundam ad Corinthios 74.23–75.12. "I see that it is possible to explain this passage in four different ways. First, God has commanded light to shine from the darkness, that is, by the ministry of humans who according to their nature are darkness, he has brought the light of his gospel to the world. Second, God in the place of the Law which was obscured in shadows, has caused the light of the Gospel, so has brought light out of darkness. The people who like of clever arguments could easily accept such explanations. However, anyone who inspects this thing more closely will know that these do not express the Apostle's meaning. The third follows, which is that of Ambrose. When all was covered in darkness, God kindled the light of his Gospel. Humans were sunk in the darkness of ignorance when suddenly God shone forth to them by his Gospel. The fourth explanation is Chrysostom's, who thinks that Paul makes an allusion here to the creation of the world, in this way. God, who by His Word created light, as if out of darkness, has now spiritually illuminated us when we were buried in darkness. This anagogy between light that is visible and corporeal and light that is spiritual has more grace and

the middle ground, offering various opinions, choosing between those offered, but not forcing the reader to make the same choice.[95] This latter option can be seen in his commentary upon I Thessalonians 1.3. Calvin writes:

> "Through the work of faith" I take this as the effect of faith. This effect can be explained in two ways, either passively or actively. It may mean that faith was in itself a notable illustration of the power and efficacy of the Holy Spirit, because it (the spirit) worked powerfully in exciting faith, or because faith later produced its fruit outwardly. I believe that the effect is in the root of faith instead of in its fruits. It is as if he said, a rare power of faith has shown itself powerfully in you.[96]

Without doubt Calvin wishes his reader to follow his interpretation. However, the very placing of the other option within the commentary, as well as the fact that it is not denigrated, leaves that second option

---

there is nothing forced in it. The preceding interpretation is not badly put. Everyone may use his own judgment." "Video hunc locum quadrifariam posse exponi. Primo sic: Deus iussit lucem e tenebris splendescere, id est hominum ministerio, qui suapte natura tenebrae sunt, lucem Euangelii sui mundo protulit. Secundo sic: Deus in locum Legis, quae obscuris umbris erat involuta, fecit Euangelii lucem succedere, atque ita e tenebris lucem eduxit. Qui argutias amant, facile istas expositiones admitterent. Sed qui propius rem inspexerit, agnoscet non congruere menti Apostoli. Sequitur tertia, quae est Ambrosii: Quum omnia tenebris operta essent, Deus lumen Euangelii sui accendit. Demersi enim erant homines in ignorantiae tenebris, quum illis subito Deus per Euangelium affulsit. Quarta est Chrsysostomi, qui putat allusisse Paulum ad mundi creationem, hoc modo: Deus, qui verbo suo lucem creavit quasi ex tenebris erutam, idem nunc spiritualiter nos illuminavit, quum essemus in tenebris sepulti. Haec anagoge lucis visibilis et corporeae ad spiritualem plus habet gratiae et in ea nihil est coactum. Proxima tamen non male quadrat. Fruatur quisque suo iudicio."

[95] Johannes van Oort's claim that Calvin cites patristic authors in order to refute their well-known opinions which disagree with his own lacks nuance. At times, Calvin does that, at other times he does quite the opposite. The present analysis demonstrates the reasons for Calvin's transformative reception, and that his doctrinal preference for Augustine did not blind him to the occasional shortcomings of the African doctor's exegetical efforts. Van Oort, "John Calvin and the Church Fathers," *The Reception of the Church Fathers in the West: From the Carolingians to the Maurists*, 2 vols., edited by Irena Backus (Leiden: Brill, 1997), 675, 677. Oort's conclusions are seconded by Myung-Jin Ahn, in "Calvin's Attitude toward the fathers and Medieval Interpretation from the Perspective of the Principles of Brevitas et Facilitas," *Calvin in Asian Churches*, vol. 1, edited by Sou-Young Lee (Seoul: Korea Calvin Society, 2002), 65–89.

[96] Comm. I Thessalonians 1.3, CO 52.140–141. "*Opus fidei*. Accipio pro effectu. Sed hic effectus duplici modo potest exponi, passive et active: vel quod fides in se illustre virtutis et efficaciae spiritus sancti specimen fuerit, quod potenter operatus sit in ea excitanda: vel quod ipsa fructus deinde suos extra protulerit. Ego effectum in ipsa potius fidei radice quam in fructibus constituo: ac si diceret, rara vis fidei potenter in vobis se exseruit."

very much open. Further, Calvin does not rhetorically stress his desire for his position, calling it only an "opinion."

Calvin is aware of the unitary nature of the Christian exegetical tradition, and occasionally can be seen critiquing it.[97] He can be a termagant when dismissing the foolishness of whomever set the various chapter and verse divisions when he believed they disrupt the understanding of the argument. This is the case, for instance, in his criticism of the division between the fourth and fifth chapters of Ephesians.[98] Further, he can sometimes wonder aloud why insufficient attention has been paid to a particular text or question raised by that text within the tradition. Such is the case when Calvin (the lawyer) considers Paul's prohibition against law-suits from I Corinthians 6.7.[99]

Bluntly put, Calvin follows tradition whenever possible.[100] When explaining I Corinthians 3.11, Calvin concludes that Paul is the master who with his preaching builds on the foundation of the Church that is Christ alone (*in Christo rite fundatos fuisse Corinthios praedicatione Pauli*).[101] This gives Calvin the opportunity for a short digression upon tradition.

> The summary is this, that the church must always be founded on Christ alone. Paul had carried out his role in this function among the Corinthians so faithfully that nothing could be found lacking in his ministry. Therefore all those who come after him cannot serve the Lord well, nor be heard as ministers for Christ, unless by studying to make their doctrine like his, and to retain the foundation which he set down. From this we can learn that those people are not faithful workers for the edification of the church, but instead are its dissipators, when they succeed true

---

[97] Sometimes, Calvin's critiques assume too much that is hardly in evidence for a general audience. Parker points this out in his "Calvin the Exegete: Change and Development." *Calvinus Ecclesiae Doctor.* International Congress on Calvin Research, edited by Wilhelm Neuser (Kampen: J.H. Kok, 1980), 37.

[98] Comm. Ephesians 5.1, Ad Ephesios 253.13–14. "Here we see that the division of chapters is particularly bad, as it has separated sentences which are closely related." "Ita videmus in distinctione capitum male discerptas fuisse sententias, quae inter se prorsus cohaerent."

[99] Comm. I Corinthians 6.7, CO 49.391. "It is extraordinary that this question has not been more assiduously discussed by ecclesiastical writers. Augustine has worked more diligently than the others, and approaches nearer the scope. But even his work is not free from obscurity, though he does teach truth." "Mirum est hanc quaestionem non fuisse exactius discussam a scriptoribus ecclesiasticis. Augustinus plus diligentiae impendit quam reliqui, et propius ad scopum accessit. Sed est ipse quoque nonnihil obscurus, utcunque verum doceat."

[100] Discussing Calvin's understanding of tradition necessarily raises the question of his understanding of history. I will consider that especially in chapters 5 & 6.

[101] Comm. I Corinthians 3.11, CO 49.353.

ministers and do not work to accommodate their own doctrine and follow after what has begun well, so as to make clear that they are not starting something new. For what is more destructive than confusing believers well grounded in pure doctrine, with a new kind of teaching, so that they vacillate about the foundation uncertainly?[102]

If it seems somewhat surprising to see Calvin effectively holding to a "tradition" for Christian doctrine, we must remember the controls he places upon that tradition, both explicitly and implicitly. The explicit control is clear—the foundation of this tradition is Christ. Moreover, Calvin equates the teaching of Christ with the apostolic teaching about Christ. Paul is a perfectly faithful interpreter, nothing more could be desired from his ministry. This tradition must be followed by ministers who come later; they are to subject themselves to it as to a rule and a goal. Only by maintaining that first foundation can they hope to maintain the Church. If they do not follow that origin, it is, in Calvin's eyes, as if they are a later generation of builders who without regard for the original blueprints attach un-supported flying buttresses to the edifice, causing it to overbalance away from its true foundation.

This rather odd definition of tradition is born out in Calvin's comment upon I Corinthians 11.2. Paul's use of παραδόσεις (traditions) gives Calvin the opportunity to clarify the proper authority of tradition. Calvin notes that something must be said to those in Rome about their use of this passage to defend a doctrine of traditions that depends in part on oral authoritative traditions, an idea with which he cannot agree. After some invective, Calvin begins to delineate his position.

> Now, I do not deny that some of the traditions of the apostles were not written down, but I do not concede that these were elements of doctrine, nor were they things necessary for salvation. What were they? Those things pertaining to order and polity. We know that each church is free to set up the form of polity that is useful for it, and is to its advantage, because the Lord has given no certain prescriptions about this. Thus,

---

[102] Comm. I Corinthians 3.11, CO 49.353–354. "Summa est, ecclesiam nonnisi in solo Christo fundatam esse oportere: Paulum his partibus ita fideliter perfunctum fuisse apud Corinthios, ut nihil desiderari possit in eius ministerio: proinde quicunque succedent, non aliter posse bona fide servire Domino, nec audiendos esse pro Christi ministris, nisi illius doctrinae suam coaptare studeant, ac retineant fundamentum quod posuit. Hinc colligimus, non esse fideles operarios ad aedificandam ecclesiam, sed potius eius dissipatores, qui dum succedunt veris ministris non se accomodare student eorum doctrinae, ac persequi quod bene inchoatum est, adeo ut prorsus appareat, nihil eos novi operis aggredi. Quid enim perniciosius quam fideles probe institutos in pura doctrina turbare novo genere docendi, ut fundamenti incerti vacillent?"

Paul who first founded the church at Corinth, gave form to it by pious and honest institutions, in order that things would be done decently and in order, as is set forth in chapter 14.[103]

Calvin does allow some traditional oral authority, but not actually a truly authoritative oral tradition. Only those points that he will elsewhere define as *adiaphora* are left in this category. The polity of the individual church, set by circumstance and the bounds of good sense, is the example provided. He specifically denies that any point of doctrine, that is the teaching that must be believed in order to foster the Christian life, lies completely within the oral tradition. The more significant points are protected in the scriptures and are, therefore, open to the interpretation of the whole body of Christ.

Nevertheless, Calvin's exegetical practice regularly includes the setting before his audience the exegetical traditions of the Church, which were either to be accepted or critiqued. He believed that the important terms in a given passage had a history shaped by the Church's struggle with that text; a struggle revealed in the interpretations of the fathers and later commentators. Though Calvin speaks disparagingly of "traditions", he was consciously in coversation with a living discourse on the meaning of the scriptural text.

The Stance of Humility

It may seem odd to those familiar with Calvin's polemic and vitriol to read that one of his rules for the proper way to address oneself to the scriptures is a posture of modesty.[104] Beyond the fact that this claim is supportable, it also makes another excellent argument for

---

[103] Comm. I Corinthians 11.2, CO 49.473. "Ego autem non nego quin aliquae fuerint apostolorum traditiones non scriptae: sed non concedo fuisse doctrinae partes, nec de rebus ad salutem necessariis. Quid igitur? quae pertinerent ad ordinem et politiam. Scimus enim unicuique ecclesiae liberum esse, politiae formam instituere sibi aptam et utilem: quia Dominus nihil certi praescripserit. Ita Paulus ecclesiae Corinthiacae primus fundator, institutis quoque piis et honestis eam formaverat, ut decenter et ordine illic agerentur omnia: sicuti praecipiet cap. 14."

[104] This was completely in character with much of the humanist scholarship of the day. Erasmus states that the new theologian approaching scripture must have a heart filled with simplicity, innocence, and humility of faith, the singleness of love, and an eagerness to learn. *Ratio Vera Theologiae*, 178:19–180:9, quoted in Manfred Hoffmann, *Rhetoric and Theology: The Hermeneutic of Erasmus* (Toronto: University of Toronto Press, 1994), 32. However, so far as the totality of the humanist habit of humility goes, Lucien

further study in Calvin's exegetical writings.[105] Moreover, this stance is completely harmonious with some of the statements Calvin makes in his letter to Grynaeus. Calvin includes in that letter the declaration that "God has never given such a great benefit to his servants that each possessed a full and perfect understanding of every part of their subject. Without a doubt his purpose here was in order that first we should be kept in humility, and second that we should be constrained to be in communication with our brothers."[106] From the beginning of his more strictly exegetical works, Calvin believed that not only would no one exegete have complete and perfect understanding of the scriptures, but that God had ordained difference to cultivate humility among those who would take up the task of interpretation. Calvin sees this as the proper way for a teacher to maintain his own progress.[107]

Further, just as Calvin's engaged in a conversation with the great commentators of the Church's history, so too was he thoroughly familiar with the exegetical models open to him through the work of later masters and of his contemporaries.[108] In beginning his commentary on the epistle to the Romans, Calvin is mindful especially of Melanchthon, Bullinger, and Bucer, and praises each in turn. He then feels it necessary to justify his own commentary, mentioning that he hopes that in this choice he will not be seen as envious.[109]

Febvre's work throws much of that from the realm of sincerity into the domain of style. See his *The Problem of Unbelief in the Sixteenth Century: The Religion of Rabelais*, translated by Beatrice Gottlieb (Cambridge: Harvard University Press, 1982), 18–21.

[105] In fact, Bernard Cottret has written that "The first requirement of a preacher was humility." Bernard Cottret, *Calvin: A Biography*, 295.

[106] Comm. Romans, Dedicatory epistle, Ad Romanos 3.107–110. "Nunquam enim tanto beneficio servos suos dignatus est Deus, ut singuli plena perfectaque omni ex parte intelligentia praediti essent. nec dubium quin eo consilio, ut nos in humilitate primum, deinde communicationis fraternae studio retineret."

[107] Comm. I Corinthians 14.31–32, see below for discussion. Just as certainly, Calvin kept before all pastors the task of continual reading of the scriptures, without which teaching and exhortation were impossible. See his comments on I Timothy 4.13. Cottret has noted that the sacred eloquence was distinguished from the common by the dignity of the subject. Bernard Cottret, *Calvin: A Biography*, 294.

[108] In a section entitled "Agreeing to Differ," J.L.M. Haire has noted Calvin's ability to allow some questions to remain un-resolved, and his willingness to follow other commentators at times. See his "John Calvin as an Expositor." *Irish Biblical Studies* 4 (1982): 2–16.

[109] Comm. Romans, Dedicatory epistle, Ad Romanos 2.68–69. "In addition, I had hoped that by using a different kind of writing I would not be accused of envy, which was my primary fear." "Ad haec, sperabam fore ut in diverso scribendi genere nulla aemulationis invidia premerer, quae mihi in primis timenda erat."

Calvin's own humility was an undercurrent running through his commentaries. This is evident not only in his constant anthropological attacks on the status of sinners, but also in his own approach. For instance, when considering Galatians 4.25, Calvin at first strikes a pugnacious tone toward some of the patristic exegetes, calling Jerome's position futile, and he lumps Chrysostom's interpretation with that of Jerome, declaring his philosophizing to be no less childish.[110] But later on that same page, Calvin admits alterations in own position, that he has learned from the same Chrysostom he critiqued. "But why does he compare the present Jerusalem with Mount Sinai? Although I was once of the opposite opinion, I now agree with Chrysostom and Ambrose, who expound it of the earthly Jerusalem, and indeed that it had then degenerated into a servile doctrine and worship."[111] What Calvin takes away from Chrysostom with one hand, he gives back with the other. He admits that his own position has changed, for the better, because of his following the older tradition.

This is not an isolated incident of humility.[112] Discussing the sacraments in his commentary upon I Corinthians 10, Calvin notes that his own position is not so strong that he would wish to use it as the basis of a quarrel, rather, he professes his unwillingness to cavil on the basis of what seems obvious to him. "However, I do not want to dispute with anyone about this; I am simply stating what seems to me to be the case."[113] In that same commentary, when reflecting on 13.8, Calvin acknowledges that the statement that "love never ends" has been used to fortify the doctrine of the intercession of the saints on behalf of those still on earth. Calvin's language in the following debate is full of questioning. Though he does not hold, and does not wish his readers to hold the position in question, he cannot refute it with scriptural evidence. Thus, we find the extraordinary rhetoric, for Calvin, of permission to speculate. "If we may speculate about the status of the dead, it seems a more probable conjecture that the blessed dead do not know what hap-

---

[110] Comm. Galatians 4.25, Ad Galatas 109.12–14, "futilis", "nec minus puerile Chrysostomi commentum philosophantis".

[111] Comm. Galatians, 4.25, Ad Galatas 110.2–6. "Verum cur praesentem Ierusalem componit cum monte Sina? Tametsi aliquando fui in contraria opinione, assentior tamen Chrysostomo et Ambrosio, qui de terrena Ierusalem exponunt, et quidem ut tunc ad servilem doctrinam et cultum degeneraverat."

[112] Similar language can be found in Calvin's comment upon I Corinthians 15.29. See below.

[113] Comm. I Corinthians 10.3, CO 49.454. "Quamquam nolim de hac re cum quoquam litigare: tantum ostendo quid mihi videatur."

pens here, than that they are conscious of what our necessities are."[114] Finally, Calvin concludes that he must leave this question undecided (*relinquo in medio*), because there is not sufficient scriptural testimony to decide the point (*nullo scripturae testimonio suffultum esse*).[115] Calvin does occasionally mention the changes in his positions, conceding that his own progress is evidence that his precociousness is evidence of fallability.[116] In a similar manner, he will occasionally state his own opinion (*meo iudicio*) when two possible pious interpretations are possible, making clear that his opinion is not a demand of doctrine, but rather a learned preference.[117]

This stance of humility before the scripture, and before his fellow exegetes, was not always Calvin's disposition. Far too frequently, the reader finds Calvin venting his spleen rather forcefully, though generally skillfully. However, humility was Calvin's ideal, one that he set out not only for others, but also for himself. Considering I Corinthians 14.31–32, Calvin turns again and again to a type of authority that is unafraid of receiving criticism. Teachers must be learners, and no one is to be above criticism, since the Holy Spirit blows where it wills.[118]

---

[114] Comm. I Corinthians 13.8, CO 49.512. "Si divinare de mortuorum statu licet: verisimilior est coniectura, nescire sanctos mortuos quid hic agatur, quam eos esse conscios nostrarum necessitatum."

[115] Comm. I Corinthians 13.8, CO 49.512. "Truly, more than enough has been said, for the very point the papists argue I leave undetermined, so that I may not raise any contention about something that does not deserve it. It was important to notice, in passing, how little support is given them from this place, in which they think they find such a strong apparatus. Let it be enough for us, that it has no support from any testimony of scripture, and that, consequently, it is maintained by them rashly and carelessly." "Verum iam plus satis est: id enim ipsum, pro quo depugnant papistae, relinquo in medio: ne de re supervacua contentiones moveam. Operae pretium tamen fuit obiter attingere quam parum illis suffragetur hic locus, in quo se habere putant tam validam machinam. Nobis satis sit, quod asserunt, nullo scripturae testimonio suffultum esse: proinde temere et inconsiderate ab illis asseri." Obviously, Calvin is saying that the Papist's point is unsupported. However, his own argument implies that no scriptural warrant exists on either side, so it is safe and prudent to leave the issue undecided, as opposed to those who make a strong assertion, and so are *"temere et inconsiderate."*

[116] Comm. Galatians 4.25, I Corinthians 15.29.

[117] Comm. Colossians 1.18, Ad Colossenses 400.21 ff.

[118] Comm. I Corinthians 14.31, CO 49.530. "For no one will ever be a good teacher, who does not show himself to be teachable, as no one will ever be found is perfect alone by himself, having so great a perfection of doctrine, that he cannot benefit from listening to others. Therefore, let all those who accept the office of teaching accept this principle, that they should take their turns as students, they should not be annoyed at having to do so, whenever others are given the opportunity of building up the church." "Nemo enim unquam bonus erit doctor, qui non se docilem exhibeat

The Genevan Reformer finds in Paul's language in Romans 9 a rule of humility (*regulam humilitatis*) that does not only apply to their direct interactions with the divine being, but also to all human contact with God's chosen forms of revelation.[119] Calvin sets out the archetype of humility in his comments upon Ephesians 4.1. He not only argues that humility is the necessary for the Church's unity, but places it first among virtues.[120] Here, we see Calvin's characteristic care for the order of teaching (*ordo docendi*), when he states in his final comment in the section that "it will be useless to order patience unless we make men's

---

sitque semper ad discendum paratus. Siquidem nemo unquam reperietur qui ita unus abundet perfectione doctrinae, quin alios audiendo proficiat. Sic ergo docendi munus obeant omnes, ne detrectent aut moleste ferant esse discipuli vicissim, quoties aliis datum fuerit unde ecclesia aedificetur."

[119] Comm. Romans 9.20, Ad Romanos 211.94–98. "There are some, too, who believe that God is opened to great disgrace if such power is credited to him. But in their delicacy, are they better theologians than Paul, who has set this as a rule of humility of believers, in order that they should respect the power of God and not evaluate it by their own judgmen." "Sunt etiam qui Deum magno probro exponi causantur si tale ei defertur arbitrium. Quasi vero cum suo fastidio meliores sint Theologi, quam Paulus qui hanc statuit humilitatis regulam fidelibus, ut Dei potentiam suspiciant, non autem aestiment e suo iudicio."

[120] Comm. Ephesians 4.1–2, Ad Ephesios 219.21–220.3. "When he descends to the particulars, he gives humility first. The reason is, because he was about to speak of unity. However the first step, to reach that is humility. This again produces meekness, which renders us patient. And by keeping with our brethren we retain that unity which would otherwise be broken a hundred times a day. Let us remember, therefore, the principle thing in cultivating brotherly kindness, is humility. Where do impudence, pride, and insult towards brothers come from? Where do quarrels, taunts, and reproaches come from, besides every one loving himself too much, and pleasing himself too much? Whoever puts aside arrogance and pleasing himself, will become meek and easy. Therefore whoever is endued with such moderation will choose to be ignorant of and tolerate many things in the brothers. Let us note this order and context, because it will be useless to order patience unless we make men's spirits meek and correct their ferocity, useless to preach on meekness, unless we have begun with humility." "Quum ad species descendit, primum locum dat humilitati. Ratio est, quia de unitate verba facturus erat. Primus autem gradus, quo ad eam pervenitur, est humilitas. Haec enim mansuetudinem ex se parit, quae nos deinde reddit patientes. Fratres autem nostros sustinendo retinemus unitatem, quae alioqui centies quotidie abrumperetur. Meminerimus ergo principium colendae fraternae benevolentiae esse humilitatem. Unde enim protervia, fastus, contumeliae adversus fratres? Unde rixae, unde insultationes et probra, nisi quia se quisque nimis amat et nimis sibi placet? Ergo qui arrogantiam deposuit et sibi desiit placere, mansuetus erit et facilis. Tali porro moderatione quisquis erit praeditus, multa fratribus ignoscet, multa tolerabit. Quare notandus est hic ordo et contextus, quia de patientia inutiliter quis praecipiet, nisi mansuefecerit animos et ferociam correxerit, frustra de mansuetudine concionabitur, nisi ab humilitate sumpserit exordium."

spirits meek and correct their ferocity, useless to preach on meekness, unless we have begun with humility." This was a sign that the Reformer believed humility to be an excellent virtue to instill in others, and in himself.

Calvin's critics might answer that Calvin felt that this virtue of humility was best left for others, that his role in humility would best be that of a teacher. Such readers should consider Calvin's return to the ideal of humility in his commentary on Philippians. Treating Philippians 2.4, Calvin lauds humility, and demands that all esteem others more highly than themselves.[121] Then he asks, somewhat rhetorically but perhaps also somewhat autobiographically, how a truly superior person can highly esteem those who are truly below him? Calvin answers:

> But it is asked, how is it possible that one who really is superior to others can suppose those to be above him whom he knows to be far beneath him? I answer that this wholly depends on the right estimate of God's gifts and our own infirmities. For however anyone may have outstanding endowments, he should consider that they have not been given to him that he might be self-complacent, that he might exalt himself or even venerate himself. Let him instead work at correcting and detecting his faults, and he will have great material for humility. In others, on the other hand, he will regard with honor whatever they have of excellence, and will in love bury their faults. Whoever grasps this rule, will have no difficulty in preferring others before himself. ... Therefore is possible that a pious man, even though aware that he is superior, may still hold others in greater esteem.[122]

Here is the familiar Calvin, with one eye upon God, and the other firmly upon humanity. However, this is also a glimpse of the unfamiliar Calvin, a window on the inner man who was so notorious for maintaining his distance. Calvin always spoke of how his motivation for writing the commentaries, and in fact many of his works, was the necessity

---

[121] Comm. Philippians 2.4, Ad Philippenses 318.17–18. "He defines true humility in this way: when each considers himself less than others." "Definit autem quae sit vera humilitas: dum scilicet quisque se aliis postponit."

[122] Comm. Philippians 2.4, Ad Philippenses 318.24–319.5. "Se quaeritur, qui fieri possit, ut qui re ipsa excellit prae aliis, existimet eos praestantiores, quos procul a se distare novit. Respondeo hoc totum a recta aestimatione donorum Dei et nostrarum infirmitatum pendere. Nam utcunque praeclaris dotibus quis polleat, reputare debet non in hoc sibi esse collatas, ut sibi placeat, se efferat, vel etiam habeat in pretio. Rursum se exerceat excutiendis et agnoscendis suis vitiis, et habebit largam humilitatis materiam. In aliis contra, quicquid est virtutum, honore prosequetur, vitia charitate sepeliet. Hanc regulam qui tenebit, non difficulter alios sibi praeferet. ... Fieri ergo poterit, ut pio homini, licet praestantiorem se noverit, potior tamen sit aliorum ratio."

placed upon him by friends and Church leaders. But a further sub-
sidiary motivation is not ruled out. When the reader sees these long
excursions into the character of Paul, or how even the superior man
must be continually finding his own faults, and excavating the excel-
lences of others as a remedy to his soul, as well as a gift to the Church,
can we not see a self-conscious Calvin? Part of the lure of Calvin's
writing is his own ability to penetrate deeply into the human psyche,
to plumb the depths of both its fears and its joys. Certainly he did
not need recourse to Luther's *Tischreden* to gain some experience of the
human interior journey. In Calvin, the reader comes upon a man who
had an intimate acquaintance with the daily struggles of the conscience
with inordinate desires; who at the same time had no intention of turning his life into his own object of study, and lived in no small fear of
becoming an idol.

Although seeing Calvin as a man torn between two poles has become popular, the problem with that portrayal is not its complexity, but
its simplicity.[123] To freeze portions of a particular human's history and
output and divide that accumulation into a dualistic scheme may not be
too mean-spirited, but rather too elementary to grasp both the subtlety
and the grossness of a truly remarkable mind. The striking point is
not that there might be two Calvins, but that any analyst removed
by more than four centuries should reduce the number of faces, or
personae, to two.[124] The irascible Calvin is also the weeping Calvin,
crying to Farel of the loss of his companion for life. The thundering
Calvin of the sermons is also the awestruck Calvin, nearly rendered
speechless by the power and glory of God. The lawyer Calvin, writing
practical laws and good codes for Geneva was also the slightly mystical
Calvin, proclaiming the wonder of the ways that God ravishes the
faithful. Moreover, each and every Calvin is constantly there, denying
the possibility of the grasp of the hagiographer, the polemicist, the
critic, and even the biographer. For better or worse, the Calvin who
could deny that the Roman Church had anything in it that deserved
more than contempt is also the same Calvin who cannot approach
the scriptures for either his own salvation or that of his congregation
without a prayer for the assistance of the Holy Spirit, and a turning
toward the exegetical tradition of that very Roman Church. Calvin's

---

[123] William Bouwsma's *John Calvin: A Sixteenth Century Portrait* (Oxford: Oxford University Press, 1988), most clearly presents this portrait.
[124] Bouwsma calls his effort a linking of two portraits, 9.

humility before the scriptures marks a certain effect of his piety, both personal and corporate, which finds its full significance only within the context of his whole theological complex.

Simplicity's Sake

Another rule of Calvin's about the interpretation of scripture is that the meaning is to be simple, or straightforward (*germanus*).[125] The extraction of meaning from the text must be clear, not forced, and simple.[126] Throughout Calvin's commentaries, this remains a constant refrain, and a somewhat continuous critique of the patristic and medieval exegetical traditions.[127] Calvin steadfastly argued against twisting (*torquere*) the sense of a particular text in order to reach a desired interpretation.[128] This is true even in those cases where the desired interpretation

---

[125] Richard C. Gamble has argued that a key to Calvin's hermeneutics is that Calvin critiques the humanistic rhetoric of his day by choosing a style reflective of the "Bible's own method of exposition." While my own analysis does not support Gamble's stressing this fact so strongly, there is little doubt that he is correct in his grasp of Calvin's goal. See his "*Brevitas et Facilitas*: Toward an Understanding of Calvin's Hermeneutic." *Westminster Theological Journal* 47 (1985): 1–17; and "Exposition and Method in Calvin." *Westminster Theological Journal* 49 (1987): 153–165. Basil Hall seems to be on a similar track in his delineation between "biblical humanists" and humanists. "Calvin and Biblical Humanism." *Proceeding of the Huguenot Society of London* 20 (1960): 195–209.

[126] Erasmus provides a similar rule in his rejection of (over)sophistication in his *Enchiridion*. Torrance states his rule. "Because the teaching of Christ that we hear in the scriptures is essentially simple and unsophisticated, we must bring to the reading of the text the simple and bright eye, the purity of heart and faith of which the gospel speaks; that is to say, we must govern our life by the rule and pattern of the love of Christ if we are to hear what he has to teach us, letting him always occupy the central point in all our relations with him and with others. This means that we have to renounce the sophistications that we are tempted to bring to the text, for they can only corrupt our understanding of it–they derive either from false dialectics or form false affections, in which we seek to wrest form the scripture to serve our own ambition and to bolster up our own aims. Erasmus admits that the teaching of the scriptures in this way is a perilous undertaking, for it cuts across so many interests and concerns to which others have given themselves, and rouses their hostility." "The Hermeneutics of Erasmus.," 57–58.

[127] Marvin Anderson points this out in his "John Calvin: Biblical Preacher(1539–1564)." *Scottish Journal of Theology*,42, (1989): 167–181, noting three different types of orators whom Calvin attacks. These are those who conceal the truth, those who use too extravagant a language and too little fidelity to the meaning, and those sophists who turn away from simplicity.

[128] One of Calvin's favorite whipping boys for this is Augustine, who is balanced by the fine example of Chrysostom. Olivier Millet writes "Nous avons d'ailleurs vu qu'il

represents an orthodox point of doctrine. The foundation of orthodoxy is not sufficient warrant, for Calvin, to depart from the plain sense (*sensus germanus*).[129]

This tendency is generally available throughout Calvin's commentaries. In his commentary upon I Corinthians, Calvin explicitly returns to this theme on least four separate occasions. Commenting upon I Corinthians 6.18, he mentions the interpretation that some give for "his own body" refers these words to those who are united to Christ. Although the value of such a position seems obvious, Calvin rejects it as "argumentative rather than sound."[130] Discussing the advice of Paul on the avoidance of women in I Corinthians 7.1, Calvin takes Jerome to task for extracting too much from Paul's words, and thus turning advice about what is advantageous into a precept about what states are best for the Christian. The student of context even supplies a possible reason for Jerome's mistake![131]

---

reproche à saint Augustin sa 'prolixité', évidemment opposée à sa propre briéveté. Mais cela ne veut pas dire que Calvin n'a pas trouvé chez les Pères des modèles d'éloquence. ... Enfin, si notre auteur a pu de fait trouver dans la littérature patristique des formes d'expression et de style, cet intérêt littéraire, tel que nous pouvons le saisir chez Calvin, relève principalement des attitudes et des stratégies de l'orateur: nous rencontrerons Tertullien pour l'apologète, Augustin pour le 'défenseur infatigable de la foi', et nous allons ici nous intéresser à Chrysostome comme théologien vulgarisateur et prédicateur, car c'est notamment à travers Chrysostome que Calvin réfléchit sur la mission et les formes du '*munus docendi*.'" *Calvin et la dynamique de la parole: Etude de rhétorique réformée* (Paris: Librairie Honoré Champion, 1992), 169.

[129] The modern reader of Calvin's commentaries must be careful here. When Calvin writes of the plain sense of scripture, it is a very easy step to understand him as saying "the literal sense" in a modern sense of that term. David Steinmetz is quite right to note "... the fact that for Calvin as for Origen the meaning of the Bible could not be collapsed into a bare historical account of the activities of ancient Semites." "Calvin and the Irrepressible Spirit." *Ex Auditu* 12 (1996): 103.

[130] Comm. I Corinthians 6.18, CO 49.399. "argutum magis quam solidum."

[131] Comm. I Corinthians 7.1, CO 49.401. "Further, it is important to note what he means by the word 'good', when he says that it is good to keep away from marriage, so that we may avoid the conclusion, which is the opposite of what is intended, that the marriage connection is therefore bad. That is what happened in the case of Jerome, not so much because of ignorance, at least that is my view, but more through the fervor of controversy. For although that famous man possessed outstanding virtues, he labored under one signal defect, that in disputing he became very intemperate and abrupt and was not always concerned with respecting the truth. Thus his [Jerome's] inference here is, 'It is good not to touch a woman, therefore it is wrong to touch her.' Paul truly does not use 'good' in that signification here, so that it is opposed to what is evil or full of vice. Instead he only shows what is expedient in view of all the troubles, annoyances and responsibilities, which come to those who are married. Further, we must always pay attention to the modification which he adds. Therefore Paul's words

When Calvin reaches the eleventh verse of the tenth chapter, he
again opts for a straightforward interpretation and translation of τέλη—
ends, rather than the less common "mysteries," although he notes that
"mysteries" would fit quite well. The force of the exegetical tradition,
combined with the straightforward character of the "ends" translation
compels Calvin's choice.[132] Finally, when Calvin explicates I Corinthians 15.29, he demonstrates both his distaste for interpretations which
are not sound, and his own exegetical and doctrinal progress. He
writes:

> Now let us search out the meaning. At one time I thought that Paul was
> pointing out the universal goal of baptism here, because the utility of
> baptism is not wholly contained in this life. But after that, when I gave
> more careful consideration to the words, I saw that Paul is dealing with
> one specific issue. For he is not speaking of everyone when he says, "what
> will they do who are baptized?" Moreover I do not like interpretations
> which are argumentative rather than solid. What then? I say that the
> people who are baptized for dead are those who are thought of as dead
> already, and who have given up all hope of life. And so the preposition
> υπερ will have the meaning of the Latin *pro*, as we say *habere pro derelicto*,
> to regard as abandoned. That meaning is not forced.[133]

---

mean no more than this, that it is indeed expedient and suitable for a man not to be
bound to a wife, so long as he is able to do without one." "Porro notandum est quid
per nomen boni intelligat, quum pronuntiat bonum esse abstinere a coniugio: ne ex
adverso ratiocinemur, malum igitur esse coniugii vinculum, quod Hieronymo accidit,
non tam ignorantia (ut ego quidem sentio) quam contentionis fervore. Nam quum
polleret eximiis virtutibus vir ille: insigni etiam vitio laboravit, quod in disputando
magna intemperie abreptus non semper quid verum esset respexit. Ille ergo sic colligit,
bonum est non tangere mulierem, ergo malum est tangere. Verum Paulus non accipit
hic bonum in ea significatione, ut malo aut vitioso opponitur: sed tantum ostendit quid
expediat propter tot molestias, taedia, sollicitudines, quae coniugatos manent. Deinde
spectanda est semper moderatio quam subnectit. Nihil ergo aliud potest elici ex Pauli
verbis quam expedire quidem et commodum esse homini, non alligari uxori, si modo
carere possit."

[132] Comm. I Corinthians 10.11, CO 49.461. "'Goals' (τελη) sometimes means mysteries, and that meaning is not without some support in this verse. However I follow the
received interpretation, for it is simpler." "Τέλη aliquando sunt mysteria: quae significatio non male fortassis huic loco quadraret: sequor tamen receptam lectionem, quia
simplicior est."

[133] Comm. I Corinthians 15.29, CO 49.551. "Nunc sensum quaeramus. Aliquando
putavi universalem baptismi finem designatum hic fuisse a Paulo: neque enim baptismi
utilitas hac vita continetur: sed quum postea accuratius verba expenderem, animadverti
Paulum hic aliquid speciale attingere. Non enim de omnibus loquitur, quum dicit, quid
facient qui baptizantur? Deinde non amo argutas interpretationes, quae non perinde
sint solidae. Quid ergo? Baptizari pro mortuis dico, qui iam mortui censeantur, et qui

Through a more careful concentration upon the words, Calvin adopts a meaning that is less witty, but more solid, and perhaps an interpretation which could be more easily followed by a less talented reader or audience.[134]

This exegetical rule of Calvin's is by no means restricted to the I Corinthians commentary. In the II Corinthians commentary, Calvin defends his interpretation of 1.11, noting that "In this interpretation nothing is forced."[135] Considering 1.17, he notes that he knows of other possibilities, fit for those who enjoy playing with arguments. "I see what response is possible, if one likes to play with cleverness." Calvin's reply is brief and cutting. "But I like nothing that is not solid."[136] Over the interpretation of 2.5, Calvin chides Ambrose, writing, "But that is more clever than strong."[137] Again, when differing from the Vulgate in his text of 6.13, Calvin defends his own rendering. "The Vulgate [old interpreter], because it did not follow Paul's mind, has added the participle 'having', (*habentes*), which is not the meaning Paul expressed. However, in our exposition, which is also that of Chrysostom, there is nothing forced."[138]

Calvin's opinions on the necessity of simplicity and straightforwardness in exegesis and interpretation did not change, but rather inten-

---

de vita omnino desperaverint. Atque ita particula υπερ valebit latinum pro: ut quum dicimus, habere pro derelicto. Quae significatio non est coacta."

[134] This tendency of Calvin's must be nuanced. Certainly, he is attempting to replace outlandish allegorizing with the straightforward sense of scripture. However, Calvin does not succeed totally in setting forth a literal exegesis, if that was ever his aim. David Steinmetz writes "Calvin ridiculed Origen and set out to extirpate allegorical interpretations of the Bible. He discovered that the nature of the book he sought to interpret did not allow the abolition of allegory, but only the pruning of its excesses. Allegory and typology (or what the late medieval interpreters called the literal-prophetic sense of the Bible) found a home in Calvin's exegesis alongside his literal-historical interpretations." "Calvin and the Irrepressible Spirit." *Ex Auditu* 12 (1996): 105.

[135] Comm. II Corinthians 1.11, Secundam ad Corinthios 19.18. "In hoc sensu nihil est coactum."

[136] Comm. II Corinthians 1.17, Secundam ad Corinthios 27.13–14. "Video, quid responderi queat, si libeat argutiis ludere. Sed nihil amo nisi solidum."

[137] Comm. II Corinthians 2.5, Secundam ad Corinthios 38.5–7. "Sed illud est argutum magis quam firmum."

[138] Comm. II Corinthians 6.13, Secundam ad Corinthios 114.12–15. "Vetus interpres, quia non assequebatur Pauli mentem, addito participio ›habentes‹, suum magis quam Pauli sensum expressit. In nostra autem expositione (quae etiam Chrysostomi est) nihil est coactum." One can see here Calvin using three of his tools, the simple sense, context of Paul's mind, and tradition's possibility offered by Chrysostom, to arrive at his text and his interpretation.

sified over the years. In the Galatians group of commentaries, first published in 1548, this is again a recurrent theme.[139] Analyzing Galatians 1.15, Calvin remarks that although some have placed too much into the word 'separated' (*segregationis*), this is a mark of their reasoning too subtly. Further, he implies that the practice of reasoning thusly is always erroneous and inappropriate. He asserts that "Some have philosophized too subtly and therefore erroneously and immoderately on the word 'separated.'"[140] It is in the Galatians commentary, at perhaps the most famous text in the history of the study of Christian exegesis and allegory, Galatians 4.24, (even though he writes about it in v. 22), that Calvin takes the opportunity to speak against this subtle reasoning and interpreting.

> But he writes that these things are ἀλληγορούμενα. Origen, and many others along with him, have seized this occasion of twisting Scripture in various ways away from the genuine sense. For they concluded that the literal sense is too bare and poor and that beneath the bark of the letter there are deeper mysteries which cannot be extracted but by hammering out allegories. And it was easy for them to do that, for the world always has and always will prefer speculations which seem ingenious, to solid doctrine. Because of such approval excess increased more and more, so that he who played this game of handing Scripture not only was allowed to escape with impunity but even was given the highest tribute. For many ages no man was considered to be ingenius unless he cleverly transfigured with subtlety the sacred Word of God. This was undoubtedly a trick of Satan to impair the authority of Scripture and take away any true advantage from reading it. This profane use God punished with a just judgment when he suffered the pure meaning to be buried under false glosses. Scripture, they say, is productive and thus bears multiple senses. I acknowledge that Scripture is the most rich and inexhaustible fount of all wisdom. But I deny that its productivity consists in the various meanings which anyone may fasten to it at his pleasure. Let us know then, that the true meaning of Scripture is the natural and simple one, and let us embrace and hold it resolutely. Let us not merely neglect as doubtful, but boldly set aside as deadly corruptions, those pretended expositions which lead us away from the literal sense.[141]

---

[139] Calvin treated Galatians, Ephesians, Philippians and Colossians as a group, and never published these commentaries other than as a group. This group was published as the second commentary to come from the press of Jean Gerard in Geneva, Calvin having left his old printer, Wendelin Rihelius in Strasbourg.

[140] Comm. Galatians 1.15, Ad Galatas 26.21–23. "Porro quod nonnulli subtilius philosophantur in vocabulo segregationis, id abs re et intempestive faciunt." Calvin is here slighting one of his favorite exegetes, Chrysostom.

[141] Comm. Galatians 4.22, Ad Galatas 106.10–107.6. "Caeterum quia scribit haec

Allegory is to be eschewed because it represents an effort to set aside the authority of scripture, and to impair the "advantage of reading it." Further, although Calvin admits that scripture is inexhaustible, he does not truly accept the concept of several layers of meaning.[142] Rather, he is like a critic who believes that the central meaning of the text can be established by a properly prepared exegete. Calvin will allow, obviously, for metaphor and simile.[143] But his view of the task of scripture does not easily permit multiple meanings without rather stringent circumscriptions. The task of scripture is the revelation of doctrine, and that doctrine most particularly designed for the edification of the community of believers. The multiplication of meanings would most likely obfuscate that purpose, so is generally denied.

How does Calvin then deal with Paul's use of the term "allegory"? He states that Paul is using the term imprecisely, and cites Chrysostom as his authority for this view.[144] The passage is not the presentation of an allegory, but rather, Calvin states, an "anagoge". The context of

---

esse ἀλληγορούμενα, inde occasionem arripuit Origenes, et cum eo permulti alii, Scripturae a genuino sensu huc illuc torquendae. Sic enim colligebant literalem sensum nimis humilem esse et abiectum. Latere igitur sub literae cortice altiora mysteria, quae non aliter erui possent quam allegorias cudendo. Atque id non difficulter obtinuit. Nam speculationes, quae speciem argutiae prae se ferunt, semper mundus praetulit solidae doctrinae et praeferet. Tali approbatione crevit magis ac magis licentia, ut in tractandis Scripturis ludere non modo impune permissum fuerit, sed etiam summae laudi tributum. Neminem siquidem multis seculis ingeniosum putarunt, nisi qui subtiliter transfigurare sacrosanctum Dei verbum sciret ac auderet. Hoc proculdubio Satanae commentum fuit ad elevandam Scripturae authoritatem et verum ex lectione illius tollendum usum. Quam profanationem ultus est Deus iusto iudicio, quum adulterinis glossis passus est puram intelligentiam obrui. Scriptura, inquiunt, foecunda est, ideoque multiplices sensus parit. Ego Scripturam uberrimum et inexhaustum omnis sapientiae fontem esse fateor. Sed eius foecunditatem in variis sensibbus nego consistere, quos quisque sua libidine affingat. Sciamus ergo eum esse verum Scripturae sensum, qui germanus est ac simplex, eumque amplectamur et mordicus teneamus. Fictitias expositiones, quae a literali sensu abducunt, non modo negligamus tanquam dubias, sed fortiter repudiemus tanquam exitiales corruptelas."

[142] Richard Muller and John Thompson see the usages of the Reformation as expanding the literal sense so as to include the other three senses of the *quadriga* within them. Richard Muller and John L. Thompson, "The Significance of Precritical Exegesis: Retrospect and Prospect," *Biblical Interpretation in the Era of the Reformation*, edited by Richard A. Muller and John L. Thompson (Grand Rapids: Eerdmans, 1996), 335–345.

[143] In the material immediately following, Calvin allows for Moses to use figurative language, in this case anagoge.

[144] Comm. Galatians 4.22, Ad Galatas 107.20–21. "And certainly Chrysostom acknowledges that in the word allegory is the meaning of catechresin. That is most true." "Et certe Chrysostomus in vocabulo allegoriae fatetur esse catechresin. Quod verissimum est."

Calvin's statement clarifies that his use of this term is rather narrow,
including mainly metaphor and typology.

> And an *anagoge* of this sort is not alien to the genuine and literal meaning,
> when a comparison was drawn between the Church and the family of
> Abraham. Indeed as the house of Abraham was then the true Church,
> it is hardly to be doubted that the principal and most memorable events
> that occurred in it are all types for us. Just as therefore there was an
> allegory in circumcision, in sacrifices, in the whole Levitical priesthood,
> as there is today in our sacraments, so I say that there was also in the
> house of Abraham. But this does make a retreat from the literal sense.[145]

Typology, the pre-figuring in the Old Testament of more revealed
events and persons and realities in the New Testament, is allowed
by Calvin. The problems inherent in this position have been noted
by scholars,[146] but some have been misled into thinking that Calvin
actually did use an allegorical exegetical method by the standards of
the patristic and medieval exegetes.[147]

Turning again to the issue of simplicity, Calvin extolls the genuine
meaning,[148] and sets aside subtle philosophizing.[149] In Colossians 1.24,

---

[145] Comm. Galatians, 4.22, Ad Galatas 107.10–18. "Neque vero aliena est a genuino literae sensu eiusmodi anagoge, quum a familia Abrahae similitudo ducitur ad
Ecclesiam. Quemadmodum enim Abrahae domus tunc fuit vera Ecclesia, ita minime
dubium est, quin praecipui et prae aliis memorabiles eventus, qui in ea contigerunt,
nobis totidem sint typi. Sicut ergo in circuncisione, in sacrificiis, in toto sacerdotio
Levitico allegoria fuit, sicuti hodie est in nostris sacramentis, ita etiam in domo Abrahae
fuisse dico. Sed id non facit, ut a literali sensu recedatur."

[146] S.H. Russell, "Calvin and the Messianic Interpretation of the Psalms," *Scottish
Journal of Theology* 21 (1968): 37–47. Russell's critique mainly stems from a historical-
critical stance, and his effort to see whether Calvin's theology can still be of use within
that context.

[147] I disagree here with Robert H. Ayers' article, "The View of Medieval Biblical
Exegesis in Calvin's Institutes," *Perspectives in Religious Studies* 7 (1980): 188–193, and its
implication of Calvin's idea of exegesis in his commentaries. Ayers' article provides such
a broad notion of "allegory" that any exegete may be seen to be using it. However, in
doing so, he fails to take the medieval and Reformation settings into account. The best
setting out of the medieval consideration of allegory remains that of Henri de Lubac,
Exégèse médiévale: les quatre sens de l'Écriture (Paris: Aubier, 1959–1964).

[148] Comm. Galatians 6.5, Ad Galatas 140.26. "genuina mens."

[149] Comm. Philippians 2.9, Ad Philippenses 326.1–10. "I know that some philosophize with subtlety on the name 'Jesus', that it was derived from the ineffable name
Jehovah. But in the reasons, however, which they allege, I find no solidity. I have no
pleasure in inane cleverness, and it is dangerous to play around in such an important
issue. Besides, who does not see that it is forced, and that it is anything but a genuine
exposition, when Paul speaks of Christ's whole majesty, to restrict his meaning to two
syllables? This is as if any one were to investigate the basis of the word 'Alexander', in
order to find there the greatness of the name that Alexander acquired for himself. Their

he offers a short summary of the place of simplicity in explanation: "What could be clearer, less forced, or simpler? The explanation is that Paul is happy in his persecution because he considers, as he writes elsewhere, that we must carry about in our body the mortification of Christ, so that his life may be manifested in us all."[150] Clarity, non-forcing or twisting, and simplicity are the three marks that Calvin notes here. In a sense, these sum up the substance of his exegetical rule concerning simplicity.

Part of this rule for the need of simplicity was Calvin's esteem of brevity and clarity. The terms come from the Calvin's letter to Grynaeus, the dedication to the Romans commentary.[151] Calvin sought to make himself clear, perhaps at the expense of the highest Latin style. Further, Calvin's own reform of French syntax represented a giant leap forward in making the text comprehensible to readers.[152] His style was aimed at a wide audience, which included both the finest scholars and

---

cleverness, therefore, is insubstantial, and the invention is foreign to Paul's mind." "Scio quosdam subtiliter philosophari in nomine Iesu, quasi a nomine ineffabili Iehovah sit deductum. Sed in rationibus, quas allegant, nihil solidi reperio. Ego autem inanibus argutiis non oblector, et periculosum est in re tanta ludere. Praeterea quis non videt coactam esse et nihil minus quam genuinam expositionem, quum Paulus loquatur de tota Christi maiestate, restringere eius sententiam ad duas syllabas? Perinde acsi quis elementa in dictione ›Alexander‹ excutiat, ut magnitudinem inveniat nominis, quod sibi peperit Alexander. Illorum igitur argutia parum firma, commentum vero alienum a mente Pauli."

[150] Comm. Colossians 1.24, Ad Colossenses 411.9–12. "Quid hac expositione clarius minusque coactum et magis simplex? Paulum ideo in persequutione laetum esse quia reputet, quod alibi scribit: circunferendam esse mortificationem Christi in corpore nostro, ut vita eius manifestetur in nobis."

[151] Alexandre Ganoczy and Stefan Scheld consider this in *Die Hermeneutik Calvins: Geistesgeschichtliche Voraussetzungen und Grundzüge* (Wiesbaden: Franz Steiner Verlag GMBH, 1983), 111–126. Richard Gamble has offered "*Brevitas et Facilitas*: Toward an Understanding of Calvin's Hermeneutic." *Westminster Theological Journal* 47 (1985): 1–17.

[152] See Francis M. Higman, "The Reformation and the French Language." *Esprit Createur* Winter (1976): 20–36. Higman states that the French Reformation in general and Calvin in particular, had an incommensurate impact upon the formation of the modern French language. He asserts of Calvin's style "The triumph, one might say, of the short sentence." Likewise, in "Linearity in Calvin's Thought." *Lire et Découvrir: La circulation des idées au temp de la Réforme* (Geneve: Librairie Droz, 1998), 391–402, Higman claims that "To put it at its simplest, Calvin invented the short sentence. Instead of trying to roll the whole argument along at the same time, he makes one point, then proceeds to the next one, then to the next, and so on. Whereas most sentences written in the sixteenth century (in a debate context) have eight, twelve, fifteen subordinate clauses, Calvin's rarely have more than three. Calvin's prose is not the steamroller but the cutting edge: not the broad front, but the *line*. *Linearity* is the primary feature of Calvin's language." (397).

those who simply thirst to know more of Christian doctrine, simple laypeople. I do not argue that Calvin's interpretation was always a portrait of austerity. In fact, he could spend enormous effort on the interpretation of biblical metaphors.[153] However, in the main, it is fair to say that Calvin's ideal of simplicity is a rule of exegetical and rhetorical practice that guides his choice of expression.

But why? Although this particular question may take this investigation too far at this stage, it must be at least provisionally answered as a summation. The reason that Calvin denied the more clever, more subtle, more twisting interpretations was his emphasis on the recipient of those interpretations. For Calvin, the audience, which ultimately must be a Christian congregation, must always be kept in view. The doctor of the Church, through the pastors of the Church, must feed the members of the Church with edifying food. Any moment of forgetfulness of this central concern is perilous. The congregants may not be able to read Greek or Hebrew, they may not be able to quote the great minds of the early or medieval Church, they may not be able to construct truly original or innovative syntheses, but at least some of them could read, and that number swelled during the sixteenth century. The scriptures were placed in their hands, and they were commanded to read and hear them. Their understanding was the standard for clarity.[154] In other words, the laity were not to become professional theologians, formulating felicitous doctrinal statements, but, crucially, they should be able to understand that the doctrines they heard were clearly grounded in the scriptures. Thus, the pastors whom Calvin was directly instructing through his commentary must be intelligible to the congregational members, so as to guide them in their devotions, in their edifying reading of the scriptures, and in their formation in the school of God (*schola Dei*).

---

[153] Jane Dempsey Douglass has noted this in her "Calvin's Use of Metaphorical Language for God: God as Enemy and God as Mother." *Princeton Seminary Bulletin* 8 (1987): 19–32.

[154] Olivier Millet speaks of Calvin's desire for the "vulgarisation" of Christian doctrine as a reason for the Reformer's being drawn to Chrysostom. *Calvin et la dynamique de la parole: Etude de rhétorique réformée* (Paris: Librairie Honoré Champion, 1992), 170–176.

Exegesis' Goal—Fuller Meaning

The final exegetical tool for Calvin appears simultaneously obvious and mysterious. In the first place, what other goal could exegesis have than the full meaning? Secondly, one might ask, what level of fuller meaning can an exegete provide once he has disavowed allegory? That is to say, how can there be more or less full meanings drawn from the plain sense of the text? Not infrequently the reader finds Calvin stating a preference on account of its "fuller meaning".[155] For example, in II Corinthians 4.4, he asserts that "There is some doubt whether 'the gospel of the glory of Christ' stands for 'the glory of the gospel,' according to the Hebrew idiom, or rather 'the Gospel in which Christ's glory shines'. This second reading, because it is fuller, is preferable."[156] Or, in Philippians 1.21, Calvin commends a reading of the text because it is less forced, more in agreement with the preceding material, and contains a fuller doctrine (*pleniorem continet doctrinam*).[157] Again, in Philippians

---

[155] T.H.L. Parker has stated that "Textual criticism is always a delicate art. The criticism of Calvin's New Testament text presents special problems, for we are dealing with a translator who more than once states his preference for a literal translation but who will give a free rendering when he thinks that it better expresses the sense of the passage, a translator, moreover, who is not scrupulous to make his running heads (that is, the few words of the text which preface individual comments) consistent with his own translation of with his comments." "Calvin the Exegete: Change and Development." *Calvinus Ecclesiae Doctor*. International Congress on Calvin Research, edited by Wilhelm Neuser (Kampen: J.H. Kok, 1980), 36. Obviously, even though Parker usually finds Calvin to be generally correct, even his benign judgment cannot deny Calvin's eccentricities with the text.

[156] Comm. II Corinthians 4.4, Secundum ad Corinthios 73.7–10. "Dubium est, an Euangelium gloriae Christi posuerit pro glorioso Euangelio, secundum phrasin Hebraicam, an vero pro Euangelio, in quo lucebat Christi gloria. Hoc secundum, quia est plenius, magis amplector."

[157] Comm. Philippians 1.21, Ad Philippenses 309.18–25. "Interpreters have up until now, in my opinion, given a wrong translation and exposition to this passage, for they make this distinction, that Christ was life to Paul, and death was gain. But I make Christ the subject in both clauses, so that he is declared to be gain to him both in life and in death; for it is common in Greek to leave the word πρός to be understood. Besides that this meaning is less forced, it also agrees better with the previous statement, and contains a more complete doctrine." "Hactenus hunc locum, meo iudicio, male verterunt et exposuerunt interpretes. Sic enim distingunt: quod Christus fuerit Paulo vita, et mors lucrum. Ego autem Christum in utroque membro orationis facio subiectum: ut tam in vita quam in morte lucrum esse praedicetur. Graecis enim vulgare est subaudire particulam πρός. Praeterquam autem quod hic sensus minus est coactus, etiam melius cohaeret cum proxima sententia et pleniorem continet doctrinam."

3.9, Calvin defends his departure from the text of others by this device, contending that "In this way, the sense will be more full and the doctrine more complete."[158]

What are we to make of Calvin's intention? First, we must note that it is a text critical tool. In each of the cited cases, Calvin used the goal of the fuller meaning, or more complete doctrine, to direct his choice of supplying the πρός, or of accepting a reading against the Hebrew idiom, or of translating a verb as a deponent, rather than a true passive. Calvin demonstrates full knowledge that translation is a step of interpretation.[159] The use of this tool in Calvin's exegetical scheme was to present a solid base for interpretation shaped by his core idea of scripture's purpose. That purpose is the imparting of doctrine leading to Christ. Scripture is important not in itself, not for the inspiration of the human authors who wrote it, nor for the amazing antiquity that it carries, but as the vehicle of doctrine intended by the Lord for humans. Its capacity to amaze, to strike dumb, to frustrate, to charm, and to enchant, are always functions of its meaning, not of its sheer beauty, nor of its perfect style.[160] Thus, scripture's amazing and inexhaustible characteristics are functions of its purpose, the handing down of meaning. That this meaning will be understood and applied in particular human communities is a fact of which the Genevan Reformer was well aware. But that is part of the source of that inexhaustible quality—the continual bringing into contact of the divine doctrines, and stubborn and diverse human communities.

---

[158] Comm. Philippians 3.9, Ad Philippenses 355.23–26. "For, in this manner, the sense will be fuller, and the doctrine richer. Paul renounced everything that he had, that he might recover it in Christ; and this corresponds better with the word 'gain', for it means that it was no trivial or ordinary gain, because Christ contains all things in himself." "Nam hoc modo plenior erit sensus et uberior doctrina: Paulum renuntiasse omnibus, quae habebat, ut recuperaret in Christo, idque melius verbo lucrifaciendi respondet, quia significat non exiguum illud aut vulgare esse lucrum, quum in se Christus omnia contineat."

[159] Comm. Philippians 1.21, Ad Philippenses 309.18–19. "Interpreters have up until now, in my opinion, given a wrong translation and exposition to this passage;" "Hactenus hunc locum, meo iudicio, male verterunt et exposuerunt interpretes." Calvin closely links "verterunt"—translation, and "exposuerunt,"—exposition, deeming that the one causes the other.

[160] See Comm. I Corinthians. This represents another instance in which Calvin agrees with Augustine.

Conclusion

Having considered Calvin's exegetical tools, as well as his hermeneutical principles, it is now possible to comment on their relationship. Calvin's exegetical practices tend to clarify and reify his hermeneutical principles in specific instances. Further, each rule can be correlated to a portion of his hermeneutic grounding. Thus, his use of paraphrase aids the reader in understanding the author. His use of contextual interpretation allows the mind of the author to speak in specific instances, and avoids difficulties between passages, permitting the voice of the scripture to remain unified. When he uses scripture to illuminate other passages of scripture, he dwells within the hermeneutical circle of part and whole, either of book, author, or complete Bible. When he reaches for the tradition, he is using the hermeneutical circle of doctrine and scripture. The stance of humility brings his own person, as well as any other teacher, before the desk of the one Master, firmly placing him as a learner ready to be edified. Simplicity clarifies the necessity of the move from scripture to audience. Finally, the exegetical/critical goal of the fuller meaning instantiates the interpretation's goal.

Thus, although Calvin's exegetical practices *tend* to incarnate specific instances of his hermeneutic principles, the more revealing moments are those where his hermeneutic over-rules the humanistic impulses of his exegetical practice. It is at these points that Calvin revealed himself to be answering a call prior to that of his methodology. Therefore, the question of his use of paraphrase, and his shift from explication to doctrine can be considered under this rubric.

As we noted above, Calvin's first use of paraphrase cannot be considered merely an explicative effort, but moves directly towards the formulation of doctrine. This has been illustrated in his comments upon Romans 1.22, where Calvin supplies those things left out of the biblical text to sharpen his own theological positions. Thus, paraphrase is intended to offer what Paul "should have said". Insofar as the intellectual attempt to understand a text goes, this must be considered a failing. That is to say, if the issue before us is the history of scholarship, Calvin could be faulted here.[161]

This brings us to the conclusion that Calvin's own self-understanding as biblical exegete has little to do with pure scholarship. Rather, schol-

---

[161] See Bentley, 13.

arship was to be in the service of the Church's search for God's truth. In that case, the interpretive excesses involved in Calvin's paraphrase were part of a pedagogical enterprise aimed at the edification of the Church. Seen thus, the supplying of paraphrase is more understandable. However, it still does not become a strength, but rather a weakness in his efforts at interpretation. Calvin himself was noted and decried as a Judaizer for denying the pious impulses that led other interpreters to twist textual meanings in an effort to find too much support for Christian doctrines in certain Old Testament texts.[162] Yet, in his overzealous use of paraphrase Calvin leaves himself open to the same charge.

Could Calvin have used other exegetical practices or devices given his hermeneutical principles? For Calvin the answer is affirmative, for the exegetical practices must always be subordinate to the hermeneutics. This subordination allows a certain amount of freedom from predictability. This may seem counterintuitive, as I have been arguing for the priority and a certain hegemony of the hermeneutical over the exegetical. However, that hegemony is result-oriented. The consequence of an exegetical practice can be rejected by a prior commitment to a hermeneutical position. The choice of particular exegetical instruments, however, remains far more free.

Calvin could have used a limited allegory scheme, a heavier dependence upon text criticism, or a topical (*loci communes*) method. Each is found within the exegetical writings of the other magisterial Reformers. He could not, however, have consciously chosen practices that would have worked against his communicative desires. That is the most important concept to grasp in this discussion. Though the instrumental character of exegetical rules allows the interpreter to choose or reject them consciously, the goal is always the communication of the text to particular audiences. Calvin's audiences—the people of the Church, theological candidates, and the humanistic community—defined his exegesis. The exegetical practices are set out for the instrumental purposes of explication, and explication to particular audiences. Seen in this light, they are somewhat more independent of the hegemony of hermeneutical principles. I argue that while hermeneutics must have priority over exegesis the relationship remains reciprocal.[163] This is

---

[162] See David L. Puckett's *John Calvin's Exegesis of the Old Testament*, Columbia Series in Reformed Theology (Louisville: Westminster John Knox Press, 1995), introduction for a short survey of these instances.

[163] Here I argue somewhat with David C. Steinmetz, who wrote that "At any event,

because of the invisible nature of hermeneutics behind the structure of theological reality. This comes out in those moments when exegetical paths are foreclosed by Calvin's hermeneutical stance.

Thus Calvin was neither a man of the medieval age, occasionally anticipating the truth and freedom of the Renaissance (or Enlightenment!), nor was he a renaissance man retaining sporadic, embarassing artifacts of the medieval world in his interpretive thought. He was a biblical interpreter with an inherently conservative doctrinal hermeneutic supplied by Augustinianism.[164] His exegetical rules, however, were strictly humanistic and patristic. The father who embodied his ideal of exegesis was not Augustine, Ambrose, or Bernard, but that Antiochene model, Chrysostom.

Calvin's interpretive model, as that of earlier Augustinians, was teleologically shaped. This interacts with both his wider theological project and his practical pastoral concerns. Calvin saw the interpretive endeavor moving toward the purpose (*scopus*) of scripture, Christ.[165] Further, it is Christ, who defines the nature and substance of the Church in the key model of the Church as the body of Christ, who is central to Calvin's ideal of preaching, the life of the believing community, and the sense of the Church.

It was Calvin's understanding of the Church, both as the contemporary congregation and as the historical body stretching back to Abraham, that defined his approach to the reception of the earlier authorities. Calvin could adopt a broadly Augustinian doctrinal position while

---

it is essential not to overestimate the importance of hermeneutics or underestimate the importance of prior exegesis. In my judgment what has already been written on a passage of Scripture is far more important that exercises more influence on subsequent exegesis than the hermeneutical theory of any would-be interpreter." "Divided by a Common Past: The Reshaping of the Christian Exegetical Tradition in the Sixteenth Century," *The Journal of Medieval and Early Modern Studies* 27 (1997): 250.

[164] I am not arguing that Calvin was a perfect student of Augustine's. However much Calvin knew of the Augustinian corpus, and that amount increases over his career, I am not arguing textual dependence. However, the young Calvin's thought was formed by a variety of Augustinians. See Alexandre Ganoczy, *The Young Calvin*, translated by David Foxgrover and Wade Provo (Philadelphia: Westminster Press, 1987), 133–158.

[165] Again, Calvin could have received this emphasis from the humanists, such as Erasmus. Manfred Hoffmann writes that "Beyond good literature, however, language has been raised to its highest power by the final and unique inverbation of Christ as God's word in Scripture. … Scripture possesses the highest authority and therefore also the supreme power of persuasion and transformation. This is so because its author is God and its *scopus* is Christ." Manfred Hoffmann, *Rhetoric and Theology: The Hermeneutic of Erasmus* (Toronto: University of Toronto Press, 1994), 213.

avoiding, and even harshly criticizing, the exegetical methodology that
supports it. Briefly stated, Calvin denied the validity of some of the traditional exegetical practices, while accepting a strand of thought represented in a broad patristic and medieval consensus on the hermeneutical principles.

CHAPTER FOUR

SCOPUS SCRIPTURAE, INTERPRETATION'S AIM

Calvin argues that the end, or *scopus* (σκοπός), of scripture is Christ.[1] This position was by no means unique in the sixteenth century, and for Calvin it must be seen in terms of his Trinitarian thought.[2] The interpretation of scripture creates the possibility for hearers to know Christ and his benefits. It is this position that both bound Calvin to the Augustinian hermeneutical/doctrinal tradition and enabled him to loose himself from some of its exegetical practices.

---

[1] Wilhelm Niesel writes that "Since the end, the fulfilling of the law, calling us to the fear of God is Jesus Christ and the theme of the gospel inviting us to trust is also Jesus Christ, the aim of all our attention to the Bible should be the recognition of Jesus Christ." *The Theology of Calvin*, translated by Harold Knight (Philadelphia: Westminster Press, 1956), 27. Ganoczy and Scheld pronounce that "Die ganze Schrift durchzieht nähmlich im Grunde nur ein einziger Skopus bzw. Sinn: Jesus Christus." Alexandre Ganoczy and Stefan Scheld, *Die Hermeneutik Calvins: Geistesgeschichtliche Voraussetzungen und Grundzüge*, (Wiesbaden: Franz Steiner Verlag GMBH, 1983), 97. I. John Hesselink asserts that "As Calvin emphasized over and over again, Christ is the heart and soul, the life and spirit, the purpose, end, and fulfillment of the Law. Therefore, if the Law—and the Bible as a whole is interpreted in siolation from him, it is grossly misunderstood and perverted. (*Inst.* II.7.1, 2)." (80) "John Calvin on the Law and Christian Freedom." *Ex Auditu* 11 (1995): 77–89. Bernard Cottret states of the 1559 version of the *Institutes*, "Christ is henceforth at the heart of the system." Bernard Cottret, *Calvin: A Biography*, 310.

[2] On Christ as scopus, see Erasmus, especially. Thomas Torrance's "The Hermeneutics of Erasmus," 48–76 in *Probing the Reformed Tradition: Historical Studies in Honor of Edward A. Dowey, Jr.*, edited by Elsie Anne McKee and Brian G. Armstrong, (Louisville: Westminster John Knox Press, 1989), 62; and Manfred Hoffmann, *Rhetoric and Theology: The Hermeneutic of Erasmus* (Toronto: University of Toronto Press, 1994), 10, 13, 213. Alexandre Ganoczy has written of Christ as the core of scripture in Calvin's hermeneutic, beautifully summing up by writing that "Kurzum, Calvin hält an der Korrelation von Weg und Ziel, Vorbereitung und Erfüllung, Präfiguration und Wirklichkeit fest, drain liegt ein Grundzug seiner heilsgeschichtlichen Bibelauslegung. Das 'Herzstück' ist undenkbar ohne den 'Rest' und der 'Rest' ist unverständlich ohne das 'Herzstück.'" "Hermeneutische Korrelationen bei Calvin." *Reformatio Ecclesiae. Beitrage zu Kirchlichen Reformbemuhungen von der Alten Kirche bis zur Neuzeit. Festgabe fur Erwin Iserloh*, hrsg. von Remigius Baumer (Zurich: Schoningh, 1980), 617.

Scripture's Scopus—*Jesus Christ*

Christ as the *scopus scripturae* is not straightforward, for when we begin to consider the various implications that Calvin drew from this sixteenth-century humanist commonplace a confusing variety of emphases are revealed.[3] Employing a dense cluster of images and metaphors, Calvin places Christ as the end of scripture, the end of the gospel, the model of Christian action, and as the end of the Christian life. Calvin interweaves these roles of Christ to emphasize his point that Christ alone is the object of Christian faith. We shall examine his practice with the heuristic framework of Christ as the end of scripture, as the end of the Christian life, and as the end of Christian teaching.

Christ as the End of Scripture

In his earliest commentary, Calvin writes, "This is a sign which teaches that the whole Gospel is contained in Christ. To move even a step from Christ means to take oneself away from the Gospel."[4] This position, that Christ is the goal of scripture, remained fundamental to Calvin's thought, and he continued to sharpen his understanding of this idea throughout his commentaries. He expressed it openly, but it is also to be found implicitly in his theological turn to grace. When Calvin states that "*fidei nihil proponi praeter meram gratiam,*" one might see that the reception of grace is through faith, but the possibility of finding the

---

[3] Comm. John 5.39, *Ioannis Calvini Opera Exegetica, In Evangelium Secundum Johannem Commentarius Pars Prior*, edited by Helmut Feld, (Geneva: Droz, 1997), 180.11–18. "Again, we are taught in this passage that the knowledge of Christ must be sought from the Scriptures. Those who imagine what they like about Christ will ultimately have nothing but a shadowy ghost in His place. First then, we must hold that Christ cannot be properly known from anywhere but the Scriptures. And if that is so, it follows that the Scriptures should be read with the aim of finding Christ in them. Whoever turns aside from this object, even though he wears himself out all his life in learning, will never reach the knowledge of the truth." "Caeterum docemur hoc loco ex Scripturis petendam esse Christi notitiam. Nam qui de Christo imaginantur, quod ipsis libuit, tandem nonnisi umbratile spectrum eius loco habebunt. Primo igitur tendndum est non aliunde quam ex Scripturis Christum rite cognosci. Quod si ita est, sequitur hoc animo legendas esse Scripturas, ut illic inveniamus Christum. Quisquis ab hoc scopo deflectet, utcunque discendo se fatiget tota vita, nunquam ad scientiam veritatis perveniet."

[4] Comm. Romans 1.3, *Ad Romanos* 13.89–91. "Insignis locus, quo docemur totum Euangelium in Christo contineri: ut quisquis a Christo pedem unum dimoverit, ab Euangelio se subducat."

source of that grace in God the Father is not precluded.[5] But Calvin denied that God is anything other than the progenitor of grace, making Christ the true and only source of that grace. The function of faith, therefore, is the reception of Christ.[6] Faith is God's gift, but received in Christ.

Calvin states explicitly that just as Christ is the end of the law, so too he is the end of the whole of scripture. Commenting upon the veil of Moses in II Corinthians 3.16, Calvin writes:

> Since Christ is the end of the Law, to which it should to be referred, it was turned away when the Jews excluded Christ from it. Therefore just as they wander off the beaten track in reading the Law, so the Law itself becomes twisted to them and like a labyrinth, until it is referred to its own end, which is Christ. Therefore if the Jews seek Christ in the Law, the truth of God will be disclosed clearly to them. So long as they want to be wise outside of Christ, they will wander in darkness and never grasp the true sense of the Law. What, moreover, is said of the Law applies to the whole of Scripture, for certainly when it is not directed to Christ, its one goal, it is twisted and perverted.[7]

It is not surprising to find Calvin commenting that the loss of the end, or referent, of the law causes blind wandering. We are reminded of his hermeneutical approach to the scriptures, and of his concern about scripture becoming a labyrinth.

---

[5] Comm. Romans 4.16, Ad Romanos 92.27–29. "The apostle first demonstrates that nothing but pure grace is put before faith. The object of faith is pure grace. And this is its object, to speak plainly." "Hic primo ostendit Apostolus, fidei nihil proponi praeter meram gratiam: et hoc esse eius obiectum, ut vulgo loquuntur."

[6] Comm. Romans 5.15, Ad Romanos 114.15–19. "Grace, properly, is in God, and it is the effect of grace which is in us. Moreover, he says that it was by one man, Christ, because the Father has made him the fountain, from whose plenty all may drink. And he teaches us that not even a drop of life can be found outside Christ, nor is there any other remedy for our want and defect than that which he transfers to us from his own abundance." "gratia enim proprie in Deo, est effectus gratiae in nobis. Ipsam autem dicit fuisse unius hominis Christi, quia Pater eum constituit fontem, ex cuius plenitudine omnes hauriant. Atque ita docet, ne guttam quidem vitae extra Christum posse reperiri: nec aliud esse inopiae nostrae et defectus remedium, quam si ipse ex sua abundantia in nos transfundat."

[7] Comm. II Corinthians 3.16, Secundam ad Corinthios 62.17–64.2. "Nam quum eius finis sit Christus, ad quem referri debuerat, alio transversa fuit, quum inde Christum excluserunt Iudaei. Itaque sicuti in Lege per devia vagantur, ita et Lex ipsis involuta est instar labyrinthi, donec ad suum finem referatur, qui est Christus. Christum igitur si in Lege quaerunt Iudaei, perspicua illis Dei veritas patefiet. Quandiu sapere volent extra Christum, in tenebris errabunt, nec pervenient unquam ad verum Legis sensum. Quod autem de Lege dicitur, ad totam Scripturam patet: nempe ubi ad Christum non dirigitur tanquam ad unicum scopum, perperam torqueri ac perverti."

Calvin offered no more forceful or lucid summation of Christ as the sum of the Gospel than in his comment on Colossians 1.23.

> After this he notes the relationship between faith and the Gospel, when he says that the Colossians will be settled in the faith only if they do not fall away from the hope of the Gospel, that is, the hope which shines forth on us through the Gospel. For where the Gospel is, there is the hope of eternal salvation. But we must remember that the sum of all things is contained in Christ. Therefore he commands them to flee from all doctrines which lead away from Christ, in order that human minds are occupied elsewhere.[8]

The gospel for Calvin is **not** co-equal with the scriptures.[9] The gospel is the revelation of Christ, **found** in the scriptures.

This approach offers more than the mere resolution of a noted problem in Calvin's theology. First, it allows Calvin to conceive of the Bible as a container of the message of Christ, rather than "the message of Christ." It avoids bibliolatry, as well as a too-simple hermeneutic, that

---

[8] Comm. Colossians 1.23, Ad Colossenses 407.16–22. "Postea etiam relationem notat, quae fidei est cum Euangelio, quum dicit tunc fore stabiles in fide Colossenses, si non labefactentur a spe Euangelii, hoc est: quae per Euangelium nobis affulget. Nam ubi Euangelium, illis spes est salutis aeternae. Sed meminerimus summam omnium in Christo contineri. Ideo hic fugere doctrinas omnes praecipit, quae a Christo abducunt, ut alibi occupentur hominum mentes."

[9] See chapter 1. Dowey, *The Knowledge of God in Calvin's Theology*, 89–117, notes this, and attempts to discern the difference through a negative process, of attempting to find even a single instance of Calvin's stating that a particular portion of scripture is not the gospel. Failing to do so, he concludes that this is an instance of Calvin's inconsistency. However, it may be that a positive process might yield more fruit. Instead of attempting to find where Calvin states that the scripture is not the gospel, why not suggest that the gospel is the revelation of Jesus Christ, which is more or less contained in particular passages of scripture? For instance, on this model, Philippians 2 contains a strong presentation of the gospel; John 3 yields a compelling version of the gospel; and Ephesians 2 offers the same gospel, through a different metaphor. Each reveals Christ, yet under different aspects.

Dowey's difficulty seems to come from an effort to answer the question of Calvin's inspiration theory without recourse to the hypothesis of the two-fold author. Thus, he states that "To Calvin the theologian an error in Scripture is unthinkable." 104. Perhaps Calvin will not state flatly that there are errors in scripture. But he does, at least twice in the Pauline commentaries, note instances in which Paul's language is not strictly true. First, in I Corinthians 11.14, Calvin notes that Paul labels a custom to be an issue of nature. For a legal scholar, this was an issue of great significance. Understood properly, Calvin is stating that the apostle occasionally could not distinguish between convention and natural law. Second, in I Thessalonians 4.15, Calvin makes it clear that he believes Paul is telling a pastorally useful lie, which he knows to be untrue. The idea of Calvin as a strict verbal inspirationist simply cannot stand up against these texts.

prevents the exegete from understanding how the scriptures, as canon, are God's words to the people of God in different ages. Secondly, this idea grants Calvin the room to see the scriptures as alive, and avoids tying the hands of the Lord with a posterior necessity. Isaiah 43.19 now can be read into a trans-historical event horizon allowing the living God to speak and deal with the chosen people as best fits the particular situation.

For Calvin, Christ is the goal of the scripture, but more importantly, he is the goal of the gospel. The gospel is offered through the scriptures. Therefore, if there is a degree of imprecision in calling Christ the end of scripture, it is a useful imprecision. For the gospel is the purpose of the gift and creation of the scriptures.[10]

Christ as the End of the Christian Life

Calvin's theology transforms that goal of scripture into the goal of the Christian life, both individually and corporately. This life is neither mere knowledge of the facts of Jesus' life nor an assent to the proposition that it is only through Christ's grace that the believer is saved. It has more the character of a journey. The believer moves toward the goal of scripture when he is being engrafted into Christ through the mortification of the flesh, the death of the "old man", and the regeneration as an immediate consequence of justification. Calvin's comment upon Ephesians 4.20 makes this clear: "The doctrine of Christ instructs us to reject our natural qualities. One has learned nothing of Christ, if one's life differs little from that of unbelievers. Indeed the knowledge of Christ cannot be separated from the mortification of the flesh."[11]

---

[10] David Steinmetz has written that the hermeneutical principle of the nature of the Bible as Christian scripture leads to the following realization. "The Bible was not written primarily to inform us about the dietary customs of ancient Semitic tribes in the Mediterranean basin or the social organization of the late Roman world, though a good deal of useful information about both of those subjects can be culled from it. The Bible as Christian scripture (that is, the Hebrew Bible joined ot the NT rather than to the Talmud) exists to serve as an instrument of the Holy Spirit to reconcile men and women to God through Jesus Christ in the community of the Church. Unless the Bible achieves that goal in the community of the Church, it does not realize its own true nature." "Calvin and the Irrepressible Spirit." *Ex Auditu* 12 (1996): 105.

[11] Comm. Ephesians 4.20, Ad Ephesios 243.9–12. "At Christi doctrina de ingenii nostri abnegatione praecipit. Nihil ergo de Christo didicit, qui nihil vita ab infidelibus differt. Neque enim a mortificatione carnis separari potest Christi cognitio."

Believers are to lay aside the old life, and put on Christ, assuming a wholly new life.[12]

Christ is both the goal and goad of Christianity. Christ's return is the motivation to charity.

> From this we may gain a brief definition of true Christianity. It is an earnest faith, full of strength, in order that it will spare no labor when neighbors need help, but instead all the pious will occupy themselves strenuously in the duties of love, and spend their efforts on these. Intent on the hope of the manifestation of Christ they are to despise all other things, and armed with patience, they overcome both long tedium and all the temptations of the world.[13]

Christians are moved by the hope of furtherance in Christ to the works of true followers of Christ. Through these actions they increasingly assume the life of Christ.[14]

Christ is the sole channel through which God's benefits flow.[15] Calvin likens him to a fountain. It may be that the actual source of the sweet water is a hidden underground aquifer, but the only source available to humans, and the only place through which they may seek the water is the artesian spring that is Christ.

For Calvin, the metaphor of the mirror offers various ways to explain the relationship between Jesus Christ and God the Father.[16] However, that same metaphor works as a means for Christians to find in Jesus

---

[12] Comm. Ephesians 4.22, Ad Ephesios 243.29–30. "Beginning with the first, he enjoins us to put down, or put off, the old man." "A priore itaque parte incipit iubens deponere aut exuere hominem veterem."

[13] Comm. I Thessalonians 1.3, CO 52.141. "Hinc colligenda est brevis christianismi veri definitio: ut seria sit ac vigoris plena fides: ut nullis laboribus parcatur dum iuvandi sunt proximi, sed in officiis caritatis strenue se occupent pii omnes, studiaque sua impendant: ut in spem manifestationis Christi intenti, reliqua omnia despiciant: et patientia armati, tam longi temporis taedium, quam omnes mundi tentationes superent."

[14] I. John Hesselink comments upon the effects of the union of the Head with the Body. "What he experiences, we experience. In faith-union with Christ we too have ascended and begin to enjoy the heavenly life and inheritance." *Calvin's First Catechism*, Columbia Series in Reformed Theology, (Louisville: Westminster John Knox Press, 1997), 126. I would hesitate to use Hesselink's "faith-union" term, which might tend to point away from a "real" union, which is simply the essence of Calvin's doctrine of engrafting, and of the mystical union with Christ. That is effected by faith, but it actual.

[15] Comm. II Corinthians 3.4, Secundam ad Corinthios 52.9–11. "He adds 'through Christ', which is his custom. This is because he is the channel through which all God's benefits flow to us." "Addit ›per Christum‹, suo more. Quod hic veluti canalis est, per quem ad nos omnia Dei beneficia fluunt."

[16] For an overview of the importance of the metaphor of the mirror for Calvin's understanding of anthropology, see Brian Gerrish's "The Mirror of God's Goodness:

what they are themselves to become. For while Christians may now be utterly burdened with of the cares of this world, the victory has already been won, it has taken life within them. Therefore, Calvin explains

> Only Christ, therefore, is the mirror in which we are able to contemplate that which the infirmity of the cross obscures in us. When our souls are roused to trust in righteousness, salvation, and glory, let us learn to turn them to Christ. Indeed, we are still under the power of death. But he, raised from the dead by heavenly power, has the dominion over life. We labor under the bondage of sin, and, surrounded by endless miseries, we fight a hard warfare. He, sitting at the right hand of the Father, exercises the highest government in heaven and earth, and triumphs gloriously over the enemies whom he has beaten and vanquished. We lie here contemptible and lowly, but the name which angels and men revere, and devils and wicked men dread, has been given to him. We are oppressed here by the poverty of all our gifts, but he has been appointed by the Father to be the sole arbiter and dispenser of all things. For these reasons, it is to our good to transfer our thoughts to Christ, that in him, as in a mirror, we may see the glorious treasures of Divine grace, and the immeasurable greatness of that power which has not yet been manifested in ourselves.[17]

Calvin uses the language of the mirror (*speculum*) once again, but here it is transformed. Rather than reflecting that which is, the mirror "pre-flects" that which will be, and that which is not yet (*nondum*). The contemplation of Christ, achieved only by the believer whose mind has been roused to trust in righteousness and salvation, reveals the very goal toward which he travels. Christ's benefits are there to be grasped, to be grown into, as the believer becomes ever more fully engrafted into Christ.

A Key Metaphor in Calvin's View of Man," in *Readings in Calvin's Theology*, edited by Donald K. McKim, (Grand Rapids, MI: Baker Book House, 1984), 107–122.

[17] Comm. Ephesians 1.20, Ad Ephesios 173.11–25. "Solus itaque Christus speculum est, in quo contemplari liceat, quod in nobis propter crucis infirmitatem subobscurum est. Ita quum fiducia iustitiae, salutis et gloriae erigendi sunt animi, discamus eos ad Christum convertere. Nos enim adhuc mortis subiacemus imperio. Ille caelesti poten tia excitatus a mortuis vitae dominium habet. Nos sub peccati servitute laboramus et infinitis miseriis circundati militamus duram militiam. Ille ad dexteram Patris sedens summam in caelo et terra gubernationem obtinet et divictis subactisque hostibus mag-nificum triumphum agit. Nos hic contempti et ignobiles iacemus. Illi datem est nomen, quod Angeli et homines revereantur, diaboli etiam et impii reformident. Nos hic dono-rum omnium inopia premimur. Ille omnium arbiter ac dispensator constitutus est a Patre. His de causis operaepretium est sensus nostros in Christum transferre, ut in eo, quasi in speculo, gloriosos divinae gratiae thesauros et immensam virtutis magni-tudinem cernamus, quae nondum in nobis sunt conspicua."

This message of regeneration in the Pauline commentaries is also the message of the *Institutes*. In the *Institutes*, Calvin sets out the overarching themes for his discussion of the Christian life. Those themes are mortification and vivification, and Calvin deliberates upon their proper meaning. He states "It means, the desire to live in a pious and saintly way, a desire arising from rebirth; as if it were said that man dies to himself so that he may begin to live to God."[18] The dying in order to live, coupled with the holy desire, is the key to Calvin's conception of self-denial. The self that is being denied is a false self. This self which is dying lived in the world of exile as a native. The self which is dead was a counterfeit, a golem. It seemed to live, but it was not the true life, the life Creator intended. Again and again, Calvin stresses that believers belong not to themselves, but to God. In faith believers are to be transformed to the life in the Spirit, and not conformed to the life of smoke. (Romans 12.2) In the life that we live to God, the devotion which arises from this rebirth takes on the form of desire. The re-born pilgrim (*viator*), wants to live the life pleasing to God; the good and holy intentions are not mere by-products, but a necessary components of the Christian life.

Further, the life of the Christian, or the life of faith, is necessarily the life of love. Calvin contends that mortification can only take place when humans fulfill the duties of love. These duties are neither empty nor attempts at moral perfection. They are shaped by true mortification undertaken in love. "Therefore we will have this mortification in us only if we fulfill the duties of love. However, the one who simply performs all the duties of love does not fulfill them, even if that one neglects nothing. One must fulfill them from a sincere feeling of love."[19] Believers have died to themselves so that Christ's love could live in them.

Perhaps Calvin's most beautiful statement of this dynamic of the new life is found in his consideration of how even in the storms of this earthly life faith is able to grasp the union with Christ.

> Indeed, he [Paul] teaches that the damnation which we have merited has been swallowed up by the salvation in Christ. And to confirm this he uses the same reason I have used, that Christ is not outside us (*non extra nos est*),

---

[18] OS 4.58.4–6. ICR, III.iii.3. "quum potius sancte pieque vivendi studium significet, quod oritur ex renascentia: quasi diceretur hominem sibi mori ut Deo vivere incipat."

[19] OS 4.157.23–27. ICR, III.vii.7. "Haec ergo mortificatio tum demum habebit in nobis locum, si charitatis numeros impleamus. Ille autem implet non qui omnibus charitatis officiis solummodo defungitur, etiamsi nullum praetermittat: sed qui ex syncero amoris affectu id facit."

but dwells within us. Not only does he cleave to us by an indivisible bond of fellowship, but with a wonderful communion, day by day, he grows more and more into one body with us, until he becomes completely one with us. Yet I do not deny what I said above: that certain interruptions of faith occasionally occur, according as its weakness is violently twisted back and forth. Thus in the thick darkness of temptations its light is suffocated. Yet whatever happens, it does not desist from its earnest quest for God.[20]

Christ grows daily more into one body (*unum corpus*) with believers; human inconstancy is exchanged for his stability, mortal sin is traded for his righteousness, and earthly failings are replaced by divine attainments. Certainly believers stumble and waver, but faith reminds Christians that, on account of God's fidelity, they cannot fail.

Calvin explains how the message of the gospel and the learning of Christ is an area in which believers can continually progress. Arguing with Erasmus concerning the intended audience of II Corinthians 3.18, Calvin writes

> At the same time he notes both the force of the revelation and our daily progress in it. He uses this similitude to make three points. First, that we need not fear obscurity when we approach the Gospel. This is because in it God clearly shows us his face. Second, that this should not be a dead contemplation, but we through it should be transformed into the image of God. Third, neither of these things happens all at once, but by a continual progress we increase both in the knowledge of God and in conformity to his image. … Note that the goal of the Gospel is that the image of God, which has been covered over by sin, is repaired in us, and that this restoration is progressive and goes on during our whole life, because God makes his glory shine in us little by little.[21]

---

[20] OS 4.35.4–15. ICR, III.ii.24. "Docet enim, eam quam a nobis meremur damnationem, Christi salute absorptam esse: atque ad id confirmandum, ea quam attuli ratione utitur: quia Christus non extra nos est, sed in nobis habitat: nec solum individuo societatis nexu nobis adhaeret, sed mirabili quadam communione in unum corpus nobiscum coalescit in dies magis ac magis, donec unum penitus nobiscum fiat. Neque tamen inficior, quod nuper dixi, quasdam interdum interruptiones fidei contingere, prout eius imbecillitas inter violentos impetus huc vel illuc flectitur. Ita in densa caligine tentationum suffocatur eius lumen. Quicquid tamen accidit, a quaerendi Dei studio non desistit."

[21] Comm. II Corinthians 3.18, Secundam ad Corinthios 66.8–16, 20–24. "Verum simul et vim revelationis notat et quotidianum profectum. Nam ob haec tria similitudine ista usus est: non esse, quod obscuritatem vereamur, quum accedimus ad Euangelium. Illic enim Deus faciem suam nobis conspicuam exhibet. Deinde non decere, ut haec sit mortua contemplatio, sed nos per eam transformari in Dei imaginem. Tertio, non impleri utrunque uno momento in nobis, sed crescendum esse continuo successu tam in notitia quam conformitate imaginis Dei. … Nota hunc esse finem Euangelii, ut

Christ as the goal of Christians contains both individual and corporate meanings. Each believer on the journey toward God (*viator*) progresses daily, but God also draws the collective closer together into a single reality. Commenting upon I Corinthians 1.9, in translating κοινω-νίας Calvin prefers to offer "*communionem*" instead of the Vulgate's "*societatem*," or Erasmus' "*consortium*." He elaborates "For this is the goal of the gospel, that should be ours, and that we be ingrafted into his body. But where the father gives him to us as a possession, he also communicates himself to us in him, and because of this we truly participate in every good."[22] The "*communio*" then is not the "*communio sanctorum*," but rather the "*communio corpus Christi*."[23] Christ then pulls believers together into a true communion of members in a single body.

Christians are called to become knowledgeable about Christ, but, for Calvin, this knowledge is not an intellectual accomplishment with either little affective consequence or small effect in the believer's actions. For Calvin, the knowledge of Christ is a fountain which pours forth true belief that both takes over the inner person and activates that person toward Christian action.[24] Believers are called to put on Christ, both through the discipline of self-denial, and the bearing of afflictions that point us toward meditation on the goal of this life. Calvin calls these internal and external mortification.[25]

Dei imago, quae inducta fuerat per peccatum, reparetur in nobis, atque huius instaurationis progressionem tota vita esse continuam, quia paulatim gloriam in nobis suam illustrat Deus."

[22] Comm. I Corinthians 1.9, CO 49.313. "Nam hic finis est evangelii, ut Christus noster fiat, ac nos in eius corpus inseramur. Ubi autem illum nobis possidendum donat pater, se quoque ipsum nobis in eo communicat: hinc vero manat bonorum omnium participatio."

[23] Dennis Tamburello sees Calvin as placing the unio mystica most in the sacraments, and could have gone even further in his analysis. Calvin's theology of the Lord's Supper makes it the most conspicuous place of communal engrafting into Christ. See Tamburello's *Union with Christ: John Calvin and the Mysticism of St. Bernard*, Columbia Series in Reformed Theology, (Louisville, KY: Westminster John Knox Press, 1994), esp. 97–107.

[24] Cf. OS 3.53.10–14. ICR I.v.9. "And this especially is to be observed, we are summoned to a knowledge of God: not one which is content with empty speculation and merely flies in the brain, but that which will be solid and fruitful if we rightly understand it, and if it takes root in the heart." "Atque hic rursus observandum est, invitari nos ad Dei notitiam, non quae inani speculatione contenta in cerebro tantum volitet, sed quae solida futura sit et fructuosa si rite percipiatur a nobis, radicemque agat in corde."

[25] Comm. II Corinthians 4.10, Secundam ad Corinthios 77.36–78.3. "The word 'mortification' has a different meaning here than in many other places in Scripture. For it often means self-abnegation, when we renounce the lusts of the flesh and are

Calvin reminds his audience that the grace of Christ is a constant admonition to maintain contact with Christ. In commenting upon Galatians 1.4, he states

> From the beginning, he commends the grace of Christ, in order to recall the Galatians to him and to retain them in him. For if they had grasped the significance of this benefit of redemption they would never have lapsed into alien observances. Whoever rightly knows Christ holds him tightly, embraces him with both arms, is completely taken up with him and desires nothing beyond him. Therefore the best remedy for purging our minds of any kind of error or superstition is to keep in remembrance what Christ is to us and what he has brought to us.[26]

Christ is for believers the sole redeeming source, and the gift that he has brought is the grace to be received as sons and daughters of God, allowing redeemed sinners to have a merciful Father, rather than a righteous judge in God.

Commenting upon Galatians 2.19, Calvin writes that the purpose of dying with Christ is that one might live to God.

> When he states that he had been crucified with Christ, he is explaining how we, who are dead to the law, live to God. Engrafted into the death of Christ, we absorb a secret strength (*arcanam vim*) from it, as the shoot does from the root. Again, Christ has affixed the autograph of the Law, which was contrary to us, to his cross. Therefore, crucified with him to all the Law's curse and guilt, we are freed. Whoever tries to set this liberation aside, makes the cross of Christ void. But let us remember that we are delivered from the yoke of the Law only when we are joined into one with Christ, just as the shoot draws its sap from the root only by coalescing into one nature.[27]

---

renewed into obedience to God. Here it means those afflictions that make us meditate on the end of this present life. To teach more gracefully we may call the former meaning internal mortification and the latter external." "Mortificationis verbum aliter hic capitur quam multis Scripturae locis. Significat enim saepe abnegationem nostri, dum renuntiamus concupiscentiis carnis et renovamur in obedientiam Dei: hic autem afflictiones, quibus exercemur ad meditandum praesentis vitae interitum. Docendi gratia prior illa vocetur interior mortificatio, haec vero externa."

[26] Comm. Galatians 1.4, Ad Galatas 14.32–15.3. "Commendat hic ab initio Christi gratiam, ut ad eum Galatas revocet atque in ipso retineat. Nam si digne reputassent hoc redemptionis beneficium, nunquam ad alienas observationes delapsi fuissent. Qui enim Christum rite novit, eum mordicus apprehendit et amplectitur utroque brachio. In eo totus occupatur, nihil praeter ipsum desiderat. Itaque hoc quoque optimum remedium est, quo purgemus mentes quovis genere errorum ac superstitionum: reducere in memoriam, quid nobis sit Christus et quid nobis attulerit."

[27] Comm. Galatians 2.19, Ad Galatas 54.32–55.9. "Se vero dicens cum Christo crucifixum esse modum exprimit, qualiter Legi mortui Deo vivamus, quum scilicet

The theme of engrafting into Christ is presented clearly here. The living into Christ is plainly exhibited in the botanical metaphor. Calvin uses one verb, *haurio*, to consider both the drawing of life from the Christ and the drawing of nutrition from the root by the shoot. The point of the Christian life is Christ, both knowing him and living through him. Christians live through Christ in two ways, regarding justification and regarding regeneration (*regenerationem* and *iustitiae acceptionem.*)[28] The point of the gospel, therefore, is the message of Christ.

The gospel is wholly concerned with salvation. Inspired by Ephesians 1.13, Calvin states that Paul makes the gospel the word of truth, and the instrument of salvation. It is the guide to human life, the place of safe abiding. Against this safety, Calvin sets the experience of the world, wherein people wander through winding paths, believing that they have found truth in vain imaginations.[29] But since salvation is only through Christ, how could their end be other than the saving knowledge of Christ?

Life itself is defined by Calvin as the union of the soul with God. But that union comes only through being engrafted into Christ. This is the

---

insiti in mortem Christi arcanam inde vim, tanquam surculus a radice, haurimus. Porro Christus chirographum Legis, quod erat nobis contrarium, cruci suae affixit. Ergo cum ipso crucifixi ab omni Legis maledictione et reatu liberamur. Qui hanc liberationem irritam facere conatur, evacuat Christi crucem. Sed meminerimus non aliter nos solvi a iugo Legis, quam dum efficimur unum cum Christo. Quemadmodum surculus non aliter humorem a radice trahit, quam si in unam naturam coalescat."

[28] Comm. Galatians 2.20, Ad Galatas 55.17–24. "Christ lives in us in two ways. The one life is that by his Spirit governing us and directing all our actions. The other is that he gives us participation in his righteousness, in order that, when we can do nothing of ourselves, in him we are accepted by God. The first pertains to regeneration, the second to the free acceptance of righteousness, and this is how the passage should be understood. If someone wishes to take it of both, I willingly agree." "Porro vivit Christus in nobis dupliciter. Una vita est, quum nos Spiritu suo gubernat atque actiones nostras omnes dirigit; altera, quod participatione suae iustitiae nos donat, ut quando in nobis non possumus, in ipso accepti simus Deo. Prior ad regenerationem pertinet, secunda ad gratuitam iustitiae acceptionem, de qua hunc locum intelligere licebit, quanquam si quis de utraque accipere malit, libentius amplectar."

[29] Comm. Ephesians 1.13, Ad Ephesios 165.23–166.15. "He employs two epithets for the Gospel, 'the word of truth', and the 'instrument of the Ephesians salvation'. Both should be observed diligently. For since nothing is more earnestly attempted by Satan than to imbue our minds either with doubt or contempt of the Gospel, Paul furnishes us with two shields, by which we may repel both temptations. Therefore against all doubt we should oppose this testimony, that the Gospel is not only certainly true, which cannot deceive, but is called, κατ' ἐξοχὴν, the word of truth, as if there were no truth outside of it. Therefore if we are ever solicited to despise or dislike it, let us remember that its power and efficacy lie in bringing us salvation. In the same way elsewhere

thrust of his interpretation of Ephesians 2.1, when he claims that "the union of our soul with God is the true and only life; and that outside Christ we are inwardly dead, because sin reigns in us, and it is the cause of death."[30]

Calvin represents this new life in both internal and external metaphors. The external speaks of "putting on the new life", "putting on Christ", or "shedding the old man". As Calvin notes, both in the Romans and Ephesians commentaries, this is a garment metaphor, which matches nicely the imputation model of acceptance of grace so frequently tied to Reformed theology. But the external is not the complete story. Calvin also speaks of the living by the Spirit of Christ. This new spirit is a new internal informing principle.[31] Here, Calvin moves not toward that which is outer, but turns toward the interior image of God. This image, which permitted the reflection of God's righteousness (*quasi speculo repraesentaret*), has been wiped out (*deleta est*) through sin.[32] Its

---

he teaches that it is the power of God to salvation for believers. But here he portrays more. He reminds the Ephesians that having been made partakers of salvation, they had learned this by experience. Therefore these people are miserable who through wandering in many paths fatigue themselves, as the world frequently does, neglecting the Gospel, and pleasing themselves with erratic fables. They learn so long and never reach the knowledge of the truth or find life. But blessed are they who embraced the Gospel and constantly remain in it! This, without a doubt, is truth and life."

"Duplici autem epitheto Euangelium ornat, quod sit sermo veritatis et quod Ephesiis fuerit salutis instrumentum. Haec duo epitheta diligenter observanda sunt. Nam quum nihil magis moliatur Satan, quam ut vel contemptu Euangelii vel dubitatione mentes nostras imbuat, duobus clypeis nos hic Paulus munit, quibus utranque tentationem propulsemus. Ergo adversus omnes dubitationes discamus hoc testimonium opponere: Euangelium non modo certam esse veritatem, quae fallere nequit, sed κατ᾽ εξοχην vocari sermonem veritatis, quasi extra ipsum nulla esset proprie veritas. Deinde ne quo unquam vel contemptu vel taedio solicitemur, occurrat, quae sit eius vis et effectus, hoc est, quod salutem nobis afferat. Quemadmodem alibi docet esse Dei potentiam in salutem credentibus. Quanquam hic plus exprimit. Significat enim experimento hoc perceptum fuisse ab Ephesiis, quia salutis facti fuerint compotes. Miseri igitur, qui per multas ambages vagando se fatigant, sicuti mundus ex magna parte Euangelio posthabito se erraticis commentis oblectat, quia diu discendo nunquam ad scientiam veritatis perveniunt, nec vitam reperiunt. Beati autem, qui Euangelium amplexi in eo constanter manent, quum indubia sit veritas et vita."

[30] Comm. Ephesians 2.1, Ad Ephesios 178.8–10. "coniunctionem animae nostrae cum Deo veram esse et unicam eius vitam, ac proinde extra Christum nos esse penitus mortuos, quia regnat in nobis peccatum, mortis materia."

[31] Comm. Ephesians 4.23, Ad Ephesios 244.24–245.7.

[32] Comm. Ephesians 4.24, Ad Ephesos 245.13–21. "Adam was at first created in the image of God, so that he might represent, as in a mirror, the righteousness of God. But because that image has been destroyed through sin, it must now be restored in Christ. The regeneration of the godly is indeed, as is said in II Cor. 3.18, [Calvin

restoration, accomplished by Christ alone, is a far more powerful grace
and is humanity's proper end. Thus it is imperitive that the faithful be
led to Christ in scripture.

Can Calvin actually be saying such a terrible thing, that the *imago Dei*
in which humanity was created has utterly been destroyed? Certainly
this is not a small question. But neither is it a simple matter in Calvin's
theology. This point has been clearly articulated by Torrance, who
has written that "The notion of the divine image in Calvin's theology
has far greater significance than its modest entrance [*in the Institutes*]
suggests; for the way in which Calvin interprets it opens up, better than
anything else, the heart of his understanding of man and his place in
the world."[33] Further, Calvin refuses to sanction an exegetical escape
from the problem through the positing of a distinction between image
"*imagine*" and likeness "*similitudine*."[34] Calvin knows of this device, but
considers it ridiculous.[35]

---

refers to his commentary upon that passage] nothing else than the reformation of the
image of God in them. But there is a far more rich and powerful grace of God in this
second creation than in the first. Yet Scripture only notes that our highest perfection
consists in our conformity and similitude to God." "Nam et initio creatus fuit Adam
ad imaginem Dei, ut iustitiam Dei quasi in speculo repraesentaret. Sed quoniam imago
illa deleta est per peccatum, ideo nunc in Christo instaurari oportet. Nec sane aliud
est regeneratio piorum quam reformatio imaginis Dei in illis, quemadmodum 2. Ad
Corinth. 3,18 dictum est. Quanque longe uberior est ac potentior Dei gratia in hac
secunda creatione, quam prima fuerit. Sed hoc tantum respicit Scriptura, quod summa
nostra perfectio sit conformitas et similitudo, quae nobis est cum Deo."

[33] Thomas Torrance, *Calvin's Doctrine of Man*, (London: Lutterworth Press, 1949), 52.

[34] Although this is exactly how one of Calvin's favorite Augustinians, Bernard of
Clairvaux, attacks the problem. See his *De Gratia et Libero Arbitrio*, ix.28, MPL 182.1016.
See Luke Anderson's "The *Imago Dei* Theme in John Calvin and Bernard of Clairvaux," in *Calvinus Sacrae Scripturae Professor*, International Congress on Calvin Research,
edited by Wilhelm Neuser, (Grand Rapids: Eerdmans, 1994), 178–198, for a consideration of this theme in the two theologians' work.

[35] OS 3.178.1–16. ICR I.xv.3. "Also, there is a not insignificant dispute over 'image'
and 'likeness'. Interpreters seek a difference between these two words without cause,
because 'likeness' has been added by way of explanation. First, we know that repetitions
were common in Hebrew, in which they often give two words for one thing. Second,
there is no ambiguity in the thing itself, simply man is called God's image because he
is similar to God. Accordingly, those who philosophize more subtly over these terms
appear to be ridiculous: they apply Zelem, that is, image, standing in the substance
of the soul, and Demuth, that is, likeness, in its qualities, or some other explanation.
God determined to create man in his image, to clarify the obscure saying, by way of
explanation repeats it in this phrase, 'to his likeness,' as if he were saying that he was
going to make man, in whom he would represent himself as in an image, by means
of engraved marks of likeness. Therefore Moses, a little after, reciting the same thing,
repeats 'image of God' twice, while omitting any mention of 'likeness.'" "Disputatio

Yet Calvin is also capable of speaking more positively of God's image in humanity. For example, when exhorting his audience to the works of charity, Calvin immediately looks to the "*imago Dei*" still present in all as a motivating force. "The Lord commands all universally to do good. Yet the great part of them are most unworthy if estimated according to their own merit. But here scripture helps in the best way when it teaches that we are not to respect what men merit of themselves but to consider upon the image of God in them, to which we owe all honor and love."[36] In that same place, Calvin addresses the most troubling issue, the command to love those who hate us. Once again, he argues that the image of God still shines forth in the enemies too strongly to be denied, driving Christians, contrary to their natural human instincts, to love that other nature in their enemies.

> Assuredly there is only one way to reach that which is not merely difficult but against human nature: that is to love those who hate us, to repay evil with good, to return blessings for reproaches. This way is that we remember not to consider men's evil intention but to look upon the image of God in them, which cancels and effaces their transgressions, and with its beauty and dignity entices us to love and embrace them.[37]

Does Calvin then simply put forth a confused welter of images that sometimes refute his own position? Although some have argued exactly

---

etiam non parva est de imagine, et similitudine, dum interpretes differentiam quae nulla est, inter duas istas voces quaerunt: nisi quod similitudo vice expositionis addita est. Primo scimus Hebraeis tritas esse repetitiones quibus rem unam bis explicant; deinde in re ipsa nulla est ambiguitas quin Dei imago nominetur homo, quia Deo similis est. Unde ridiculos esse apparet qui subtilius philosophantur in nominibus illis, sive Zelem, hoc est imaginem, statuant in substantia animae, et Demuth, hoc est similitudinem, in qualitatibus sive aliud diversum afferant; quia ubi Deus hominem creare decrevit in imagine sua, quod erat obscurius, exegetice repetit hac particula, Ad similitudinem; quasi diceret se hominem facturum, in quo seipsum velut in imagine repraesentaret, propter insculptas similitudinis notas. Itaque Moses paulo post idem recitans, imaginem Dei bis ponit, omissa similitudinis mentione."

As an aside, it is instructive to see how many of the practices of Calvin's exegetical practice in his commentaries are transferred into the *Institutes*. His arguing from Hebrew idiom, his disdain for philosophizing, and his argument from the following scripture are all features which were noted in the third chapter.

[36] OS 4.156.29–34. ICR III.vii.6. "Omnibus in universum benefacere Dominus praecipit, quorum magna pars indignissimi sunt, si proprio merito aestimentur: sed hic optima ratione subvenit Scriptura, quum docet non esse respiciendum quid ex seipsis mereantur homines, sed imaginem Dei in cunctis considerandam, cui nihil non et honoris et dilectionis debeamus."

[37] OS 4.157.15–22. ICR III.vii.6. "Hac profecto una via pervenitur ad id quod humanae naturae prorsus adversum est, nedum difficile: ut diligamus eos qui nos odio

that point,[38] a better alternative is offered by a perspectival approach.[39] Calvin offers a contrast between what humans are in themselves, and what they are in view of God's desire for the goal of creation. In and of themselves, they are entirely corrupt, and the image of God is destroyed in them (*imago Dei deleta est*). However, in view of the original purpose of creation, and the humanity which still separates the race from the rest of God's creatures, human beings are to be viewed as created in God's image.[40] Thus, humanity's truest possibility, the re-formation of the created truth in the image of Christ, remains achievable.[41]

This goal of Christ is not a wholly explainable process, nor fully an act of intellection. For those to whom Calvin is a cold logician or more properly a determined rhetorician demonstrating a simple path of particular steps toward a Christian life, Calvin's comment upon the familiar marriage text from Ephesians 5.29–30 must come as a shock. Calvin's rhetoric here has a peculiar beauty.

> He proceeds to establish the rights of marriage on Christ and the Church; for a more powerful example could not have been adduced. And first he speaks of the unique love of a husband for his wife as exemplified by Christ; and an instance of that unity which belongs to a marriage is declared to exist between himself and the Church. This is a remarkable passage on the mystical communication which we have with Christ. He says that we are members of him, of his flesh, and of his bones. First, this is not hyperbole, but the simple truth. Secondly, he does not simply mean that Christ partook of our nature, but wants to express something deeper (and emphatically) καὶ ἐμφατικώτερον. He refers to Moses' words in Genesis chapter 2.24. What does it mean then?

---

habent, beneficiis mala pensemus, probris benedictiones referamus: si meminerimus non hominum malitiam reputandam esse, sed inspiciendam in illis Dei imaginem: quae inductis ac obliteratis eorum delictis, ad eos amandos amplexandosque sua pulchritudine ac dignitate nos alliciat."

[38] Especially Richard Stauffer. See his *Dieu, la creation et providence dans la predication de Calvin*, (Berne: Peter Lang, 1978), 201.

[39] The perspectival approach to Calvin's anthropology is the contribution of Mary Potter Engel, in her *John Calvin's Perspectival Anthropology*, American Academy of Religion Series, no. 52, edited by Susan Thistlethwaite, (Atlanta: Scholars Press, 1988).

[40] I. John Hesselink, *Calvin's First Catechism*, Columbia Series in Reformed Theology, (Louisville: Westminster John Knox Press, 1997), 67. See Hesselink's book, 62–68, for an excellent discussion of this issue.

[41] Luke Anderson points out that the true basis in Calvin's theology for the understanding of the imago dei is the renovated image, drawn from the New Testament. "The *Imago Dei* Theme in John Calvin and Bernard of Clairvaux," 180.

When Eve was formed out of the substance of her husband Adam, and thus was a part of him, so, if we are to be true members of Christ, we coalesce into one body by the communication of his substance. Therefore, Paul describes our union with Christ, a symbol and pledge of which is given to us in the holy Supper.[42]

Thus, Calvin's exegesis points absolutely to a mystical happening that pulls the believer's substance toward Christ.

This engrafting into Christ is the entrance of the believer into the kingdom of God. Certainly, Calvin recognized that the reality of that entrance is, in some manner, delayed. He likens it to an inheritance, secured against a later date.[43] Though the enjoyment of those riches is not yet the heir's to possess, there is no doubt that the inheritance is his. Accordingly the correct interpretation of Philippians 3.12, where the opposite seems to be said, becomes significant for Calvin. The text states that Paul has not yet attained, in this pre-state, the goal that he desires. Calvin's answer to this is that Paul has not yet arrived "At sharing completely in Christ's sufferings, in order to have a full taste of the power of the resurrection and know him perfectly."[44] However, that does not deny the possibility of progress, nor does it signify that Paul was unable to complete the tasks which God had laid upon him. Rather, although he had "... acquired enough to be sufficient for

---

[42] Comm. Ephesians 5.29–30, Ad Ephesios 271.20–272.10. "Pergit coniugii iura in Christo et Ecclesia sancire, quia hoc exemplo nihil habebat efficacius. Et primo quidem quod de singulari viri erga uxorem amore praecepit, Christum praestitisse docet. Deinde illius, quam in coniugio posuerat, unitatis specimen in ipso et Ecclesia extare testatur. Et est locus insignis de mystica communicatione, quam habemus cum Christo. Dicit nos esse eius membra, ex carne et ossibus. Primum, non est hyperbolica loquutio, sed simplex. Deinde non tantum significat Christum esse naturae nostrae participem, sed altius quiddam exprimere voluit καὶ ἐμφατικώτερον. Refert enim Mosis verba, Geneseos capite 2,24. Quis ergo erit sensus? Quemadmodum Heva ex Adae mariti sui substantia formata est, ut esset quasi pars illius, ita nos, ut simus vera Christi membra, substantiae eius communicare et hoc communicatione nos coalescere in unum corpus. Denique eam nostri cum Christo unionem hic Paulus describit, cuius in sacra Coena symbolum et pignus nobis datur."

[43] Comm. Philippians 3.12, Ad Philippenses 359.11–12. "in order that the inheritance is certain, but we do not yet enjoy the possession of it." "... ut certa quidem sit haereditas, nondum tamen eius possessione fruamur."

[44] Comm. Philippians 3.12, Ad Philippenses 359.16–18. "Nempe ut in solidum communicet Christi passionibus, ut perfectum habeat gustum potentiae resurrectionis, ut ipsum plane cognoscat."

executing the task committed to him.",[45] that never-ending progress in this life is the lot of those who would come to know Christ, since the subject matter is so difficult.[46]

This new life in Christ grants two gifts, justification and regeneration. Calvin concludes

> The second principal part of our salvation is newness of life. For principally in these two things consist the total benefit of redemption, remission of sins and spiritual regeneration (Jer 31.33). What he has already said was a great thing, that righteousness has been acquired for us by the death of Christ, so that, our sins being abolished, we are acceptable to God. Now, however, he teaches that there is in addition to this another benefit equally great, that is the gift of the holy Spirit, by which we are reformed to the image of God. And this is a passage worthy of note, that free righteousness is not conferred to us in Christ without our being at the same time regenerated by the Spirit to the obedience of righteousness; as he teaches us elsewhere that Christ is made to us righteousness and sanctification. The former we obtain by free acceptance, and the latter is a gift of the holy Spirit, when we are made new men. However there is an inseparable connection between both.[47]

---

[45] Comm. Philippians 3.12, Ad Philippenses 359.21–22. "... quia tantum comprehenderat, quantum ad exequendum munus sibi commissum sufficeret."

[46] Comm. Philippians 3.12, Ad Philippenses 359.18–20. "He admonishes, therefore, by his own example that we must progress, and that the knowledge of Christ is so difficult, that even those who only strive for it, are nevertheless not perfect, as long as they live." "Proficiendum igitur exemplo suo admonet, ac rem tantae molis esse Christi cognitionem, ut qui in ea sola elaborant, nunquam tamen perfecti sint, quandiu vivunt."

[47] Comm. Colossians 1.22, Ad Colossenses 406.17–29. "Secunda pars praecipua salutis nostra, vitae novitas scilicet. Nam his duobus membris praecipue constat totum redemptionis beneficium: peccatorum remissione et regeneratione spirituali, Ierem. 31,33. Hoc iam quod dixit, magnum erat: acquisitam nobis esse iustitiam morte Christi, ut abolitis peccatis Deo grati simus. Sed nunc aliud accedere aeque praeclarum docet: nempe Spiritus sancti donationem, qua reformamur ad imaginem Dei. Et locus est observatione dignus, non conferri nobis gratuitam iustitiam in Christo, quin Spiritu etiam regeneremur in obedientiam iustitiae; quemadmodum alibi docet Christum nobis factum esse iustitiam et sanctificationem. Illud consequimur acceptatione gratuita, hoc autem dono Spiritus sancti, dum novi homines efficimur. Utriusque autem individuus est nexus."

Christ as the End of Christian Teaching

Finally, for Calvin, Christ as the end of scripture means that Christ is also the end of Christian teaching.[48] Here, most clearly, Calvin allows all the senses of *telos* or *scopus* to emerge. Christ is the aim of Christian teaching, its final measure, its stopping point beyond which no teacher can go, and the final period which brings prophecy to an end. Calvin calls the learning of Christ the fundamental teaching, the one teaching which Christian teachers are forbidden to overthrow.[49] This is because Christ is the one foundation of the Church.[50] Calvin interprets Paul to mean that Christ is sufficient for all of the Church's life, both for the life of regeneration and charity; and for the life of righteousness and redemption. Further, those who do not use the substance of Christ, tear out the heart of God's truth.[51] As Calvin states, the Church is built up only on Christ for its life and glory.[52] The point of the scriptures, the message of salvation, cannot be found anywhere outside of Christ.

---

[48] The reader is reminded of Calvin's comment on Christ's prophetic office. OS 3.473.19–24, 474.15–18. ICR II.xv.2. "On the other hand, it is to be noted that he received anointing, not only for himself for the part of teaching, but for his whole body that the power of the Spirit might be present in the continuing preaching of the gospel. This however, remains fixed: the perfect doctrine he has brought has imposed an end upon all prophecies. ... And the prophetic dignity is held in Christ, that we know that in the sum of doctrine as he has given it to us includes all parts of perfect wisdom." "Atque hic rursus notandum est, non sibi modo untionem accepisse, ut fungeretur docendi partibus: sed toti suo corpori, ut in continua Evangelii praedicatione virtus Spiritus respondeat. Interea manet illud fixum, hac quam attulit perfectione doctrinae finem impositum fuisse omnibus prophetiis: ... Atque huc tendit prophetica dignitas in Christo, ut sciamus in summa doctrinae quam tradidit, inclusos esse omnes perfectae sapientiae numeros."

[49] Comm. I Corinthians 3.11, CO 49.354. "doctrina fundamentalis".

[50] Comm. I Corinthians 3.11, CO 49.354. "Christus enim unicum est ecclesiae fundamentum:".

[51] Comm. I Corinthians 3.11, CO 49.354. "Indeed, Christ is the one foundation of the Church, but there are many who put forward the name of Christ as an excuse, and drag out the universal truth of God by the roots." "Christus enim unicum est ecclesiae fundamentum: at multi sunt, qui nomen Christi quum obtendunt, radicitus evellunt universam Dei veritatem."

[52] Comm. I Corinthians 3.11, CO 49.354. "It is to be seen therefore in what way the Church is properly built up on Christ; that he alone is set up for righteousness, redemption, sanctification, wisdom, satisfaction, cleansing, in short for life and glory." "Videndum est igitur quomodo rite super Christum aedificetur ecclesia: nempe si ipse solus statuitur pro iustitia, redemptione, sanctificatione, sapientia, satisfactione, purgatione, vita denique et gloria."

> Now, if Christ is not truly known, and is only called the name of redeemer, while at the same time righteousness, sanctification and salvation are sought elsewhere, he is cast out from the foundation, and imitation stones are substituted in his place. ... For since Christ is the foundation of the Church, because he is the one cause of salvation and eternal life, because in him we know God the father, because we have the fountain of all our goods in him, if he is not known truly as such, he ceases to be the foundation.[53]

The amount of teaching Calvin squeezes into this passage is itself a tribute to his own forceful brevity. Christ is the fount of salvation; Christ is the source of true Christian knowledge of God the Father. Christ is the source of Christian blessings, both temporal and eternal; Christ is the sum of Christian teaching. There is no Christian teaching apart from the knowledge of Christ.[54]

Again, in explicating II Corinthians 1.19, Calvin finds Paul summing up the whole gospel in the knowledge of Christ.

> In these words he shows that all his teaching consisted of the simple knowledge of Christ only, just as in that the whole Gospel is truly contained. Thus those who teach anything but Christ wander into the wilderness, however much they may pride themselves on their show of wisdom. For he is the end of the Law and so the head, sum and perfection of all spiritual doctrine.[55]

Further, if one of the aims of Christians is salvation, then the true knowledge of Christ is paramount. The only way to the benevolence

---

[53] Comm. I Corinthians 3.11, CO 49.354. "Quod si Christus utcunque agnoscitur et vocatur nomine redemptor, interim alibi quaeritur iustitia, sanctificatio et salus: depellitur a fundamento, et adulterini lapides in eius locum subrogantur: ... Nam quum ideo sit fundamentum ecclesiae Christus, quia unica est causa salutis et vitae aeternae, quia in eo Deum patrem cognoscimus, quia in ipso habemus bonorum omnium fontem: nisi talis agnoscitur, iam fundamentum esse desinit."

[54] Comm. I Corinthians 3.11, CO 49.354. "To sum up, Paul does not oppose any kind of teaching in contrast to knowledge of Christ; but there is a comparison between him and the other ministers." "Denique non opponit Paulus Christi notitiae ullam doctrinae speciem, sed potius relatio est inter ipsum et reliquos ministros."

[55] Comm. II Corinthians 1.19, Secundam ad Corinthios 28.32–29.4. "Caeterum his verbis significat totam suam doctrinam simplici unius Christi cognitione fuisse comprehensam, sicuti revera totum Euangelium in ea continetur. Itaque vagantur extra oleas, qui aliud quam unicum Christum docent, quacunque alioqui sapientiae ostentatione turgeant. Nam ut est finis Legis, ita caput, summa, complementum denique omnis spiritualis doctrinae."

of the Father is through the clothing of Christ.[56] Only when believers are in Christ do they find a graciously inclined Father in the Lord.[57]

As noted above, Christians are called to become knowledgeable about Christ. It is necessary to set out that for Calvin, doctrine does not have an academic aridity about it. Clearly and necessarily, doctrine for Calvin is the lived understanding which forces both horizontal and vertical action. Doctrine is part of faith. On the other hand, it is never an issue of intellectual assent to a set of propositions. This is the meaning of the term "lived understanding". If one truly believes in the Christ, and understands that belief, one is compelled to act in accordance with that knowledge. This is part of what it means to be engrafted into Christ and receiving the Holy Spirit. The portion of lived understanding which informs life is continually progressing. Thus, the Christian life is a kind of adolescence that is never finished, but still progresses.[58]

This view of Christian doctrine was central to Calvin's explication of Paul's claim in Galatians 3.1, "Who was before your eyes," Calvin writes, "Therefore he says that his teaching was so clear that it was not actually bare doctrine, but was more truly the living and express image of Christ. Therefore they had a knowledge that could bring

---

[56] See Randall Zachman's *The Assurance of Faith: Conscience in the Theology of Martin Luther and John Calvin*, (Minneapolis: Fortress Press, 1993), esp. ch. 12, for a consideration of how Calvin does (and does not), use the righteousness of Christ to clothe the sinner so that she might find a loving Father, rather than a harsh Judge.

[57] Comm. II Corinthians 1.19, Secundam ad Corinthios 29.29–31. "This is a memorable statement and one of the main precepts of our faith. Moreover, it depends upon another principle, that it is only in Christ that God the Father is favorable toward us." "Sententia memorabilis et unum ex praecipuis fidei nostrae capitibus. Pendet autem ex alio principio, quod nonnisi in Christo propitius est nobis Deus Pater."

[58] Comm. Ephesians 4.14, Ad Ephesios 234.22–29. "But those are truly founded in the doctrine of Christ, who although not yet perfect, have so much prudence and strength as to know what is best, and proceed steadily in the right course. Thus the life of believers, which is marked by desire and progress toward their appointed state, is like adolescence. When therefore I said that in this life we are never men, this ought not to be taken to the other extreme, as they say, as if there were no progress beyond childhood. After we are born in Christ, we ought to grow, so as not to be children in understanding." "Qui autem vere fundati sunt in Christi doctrina, tametsi nondum perfecti sint, habent tamen tantum prudentiae et roboris, ut sciant deligere, quid sit optimum, et constanter pergant in recto cursu. Ita fidelium vita, quae assiduo profectu ad statum suum gradum aspirat, adulescentiae similis est. Quod ergo dixi nunquam in hac vita nos esse viros, non debet trahi ad alterum extremum, quod vocant, acsi non fieret progressus extra pueritiam. Nam postquam Christo nati sumus, debemus adolescere, ita ut non simus intelligentia pueri."

before them his appearance."[59] Paul's doctrine sets forth, with all the skill of the most accomplished rhetorician, the crucified Christ. To do so, his preaching must have been accompanied by the power of the Spirit.[60] The Galatians have no need for anything further, because no mechanical propositional teaching was proposed to them. Instead, the living doctrine of Christ (*viva doctrina Christi*) has been placed before them.

Further, Calvin makes it abundantly clear that the opposite of preaching unadorned doctrine (*nuda doctrina*) is the task of **all** preachers. He advises

> Let those who wish rightly to discharge the ministry of the Gospel, learn not only to speak and proclaim but also to penetrate into consciences, in order that so that people may feel Christ crucified and that his blood may drip. When the Church has such painters as these it no longer needs wood and stone, that is, dead imitations, it no longer requires any pictures. And certainly images and pictures were first allowed into Christian temples when, partly the pastors had transformed into mere shadows, partly when they gave a few words from the pulpit so coldly and perfunctorily that the power and efficacy of the ministry were wholly extinguished.[61]

Calvin's ideal preacher penetrates past mere intellectual assent to the imagination.[62] The blood of Christ is **seen** to flow in a Christian church where the Word is rightly preached. The believer's conscience accuses

---

[59] Comm. Galatians 3.1, Ad Galatas 59.27–30. "Dicit igitur tantam fuisse doctrinae suae perspicuitatem, ut non tam fuerit nuda doctrina quam viva et expressa imago Christi. Eam igitur habuerant notitiam, quae aspectui conferri posset."

[60] Comm. Galatians 3.1, Ad Galatas 60.16–18. "Such a representation would not have been possible by eloquence or techniques of rhetoric, unless that efficacy of the Spirit been present, of which he spoke in both the epistles to the Corinthians." "Talis repraesentatio nulla eloquentia, nullis rhetorum coloribus fieri potest, nisi adsit illa Spiritus efficacia, de qua dictum fuit in utraque ad Corinthios." On the theme of the Holy Spirit making preaching efficacious, see also Comm. Ephesians 1.13; and ICR II.xv.2.

[61] Comm. Galatians 3.1, Ad Galatas 60.18–61.5. "Itaque qui rite Euangelii ministerio defungi volent, discant non tantum loqui et declamare, sed etiam penetrare in conscientias, ut illis Christus crucifixus sentiatur et sanguis eius stillet. Ubi tales Ecclesia pictores habet, minime amplius indiget ligneis et lapideis, hoc est mortuis simulachris; minime picturas ullas requirit. Et certe tunc primum simulachris et picturis apertae fuerunt templorum fores apud Christianos, quum partim obmutuissent Pastores essentque mera idola, partim ita frigide et perfunctorie pro suggestu pauca verba facerent, ut penitus extincta esset vis et efficacia ministerii."

[62] It may be noted that Calvin's historical reconstruction seems also a task of imagination. For a review of the relationship between early Christian art and theology, see Robin Jensen's *Understanding Early Christian Art* (London: Routledge, 2000).

and convicts him, forcing him to confession and contrition. This is a "*viva doctrina*" that stirs up hearts and causes actions. The importance of pedagogy suddenly springs to life, breaking the boundaries of the too-easy definition of Reformed faith as being intellectual or "head-centered." Teaching is persuasion to action based on an understanding which commands assent from head, heart, and hands.

If in Christ Calvin finds the end of the scriptures, of the Christian life, and of Christian teaching, he also finds in Christ the goal and terminus of faith. This is the subject of our next section, a consideration of the doctrine of faith, and its reception of Christ, and the Trinity.

Christ and Faith's Reception

Christ is not a way-station on the Christian journey. He is, rather, the reason for the journey, the point through which humans are given access to the re-pristination of the image of God. Christ is available through the gospel, but finally, Christ's gospel may be understood only through faith.[63] Christ defines the journey of the pilgrim (*viator*), the *terminus ad quem*, the point beyond which one may not go, nor wish to go.

> For the apostle wanted to explain what is the nature of true faith, and when it exists; that is, when the Son of God is known. For to him alone faith ought to look, on him depend, in him to rest and terminate. If it tries to go farther, it will disappear, for it will no longer be faith, but a delusion. Let us remember that true faith is so contained in Christ, that it neither knows, nor desires to know, anything beyond him.[64]

The chief symmetry of the temple of faith is unity, followed by progress or increase.[65] One might turn this toward increase in knowledge or

---

[63] Comm. Colossians 2.2, Ad Colossenses 419.4–6. "Let us learn from this that the Gospel can be understood by faith alone, not by reason, nor by the perspicacity of the human understanding, because otherwise it is a thing that is hidden from us." "Verum hinc discamus sola fide, non ratione, nec perspicacia humanae mentis Euangelium posse capi, quia alioqui res est a nobis abscondita."

[64] Comm. Ephesians 4.13, Ad Ephesios 233.33–234.4. "Voluit enim Apostolus exponere, quaenam sit vera fides et ubi consistat: nempe quum Filius Dei cognoscitur. Nam in ipsum solum respicere debet fides, ab illo pendere, in illo quiescere et concludi. Ultra si tendat, evanescet, neque amplius erit fides, sed fallacia. Meminerimus ergo veram fidem ita in Christo contineri, ut praeter eum nihil sciat adeoque nec scire appetat."

[65] Comm. Ephesians 2.20, Ad Ephesios 199.3–4. "But the principle symmetry consists in unity of faith. After that follows progress or increase. For those who are not

obedience to the Church, broadly defined.[66] But Calvin immediately
follows that statement with its clarifying opposite. "For those who are
not united in faith and love, in order that they might advance in Christ,
have a profane edifice, which has nothing in common with the temple
of God"[67] The end of the Christian's journey must always be found in
and through Christ.

But what is this faith? Calvin's definition comes from the *Institutes*.

> Now we shall possess a complete definition of faith if we say that it
> is a firm and certain knowledge of the divine benevolence toward us,
> founded upon the truth of the graciously given promise in Christ,
> through the holy Spirit revealed to our minds and sealed upon our
> hearts.[68]

The faith that Calvin holds out is a trinitarian faith, grounded in the
truth of Christ's promise, grasping the divine benevolence, and sealed
in us through the interior action of the Holy Spirit. Here, the believer
finds both the divine economy offered in the scriptures, and the truth
of experience. The definition of faith itself is a Christian primer, or
perhaps a Christian paradigm, reminding in contemplation the benefits
of knowing God, and how access to God is gained.

For Calvin, Christ defines the proper goal or scope of faith (*proprium
fidei scopum*).[69] Christ is the goal at which faith aims, the message which

---

united in faith and love, in order that they might advance in Christ, have a profane
edifice, which has nothing in common with the temple of God." "Sed praecipua sym-
metria in fidei unitate consistit. Deinde sequitur profectus vel incrementum. Quicunque
non ita sunt fide et charitate uniti, ut in Christo proficiant, profanam habent aedificationem, cui nihil est cum templo Dei commune."

[66] Brian Gerrish notes that "In content, *fides* and *pietas* are identical insofar as both
denote the right human response to the paternal goodwill of God. They differ in that
fides is directed to the assurance of God's goodwill in Christ. *Pietas*, true religion, and
its restoration as *fides*–this is the actual theme of Calvin's *pietatis summa*." "From Calvin
to Schleiermacher: The Theme and Shape of Christian Dogmatics," in *Continuing the
Reformation: Essays on Modern Religious Thought*, (Chicago: University of Chicago Press,
1993), 188.

[67] Comm. Ephesians 2.21, Ad Ephesios 199.4–6. "Quicunque non ita sunt fide et
charitate uniti, ut in Christo proficiant, profanam habent aedificationem, cui nihil est
cum templo Dei commune."

[68] OS 4.16.31–35. ICR III.ii.7. "Nunc iusta fidei definitio nobis constabit si dicamus
esse divinae erga nos benevolentiae firmam certamque cognitionem, quae gratuitae
in Christo promissionis veritate fundata, per Spiritum sanctum et revelatur mentibus
nostris et cordibus obsignatur."

[69] Comm. Colossians 1.4, Ad Colossenses 389.14–15. "He says faith in Christ, in
order that we always remember that Christ is the proper goal of faith." "Fidem in
Christo dicit, ut semper meminerimus proprium fidei scopum esse Christum."

faith receives. Faith aims at Christ as an archer at a target. Grasping
who Christ truly is saves the believer from the traps laid in human
doctrines. Considering Colossians 1.12, Calvin warns that "For this
was the one remedy for the Colossians against all the traps, by which
the false apostles sought to grasp them, properly to hold what Christ
was. For how does it happen that we are driven around with so many
doctrines, but because the power of Christ is not perceived by us? For
Christ alone makes all other things suddenly disappear."[70] This is a
vital text for two reasons. First, Calvin makes an obvious disparaging
remark about "doctrines," without taking the care to set that term off
by some adjective, such as "human," or "false." There is a hint here
that even the best doctrines are mere paths to Christ and not ends in
themselves.

Secondly, Calvin argues that Christ's appearance drives everything
away; all doctrines fail before the presence of Christ. When the believer
knows Christ, the doctrines are like childhood grammar mnemonics
which are no longer useful, and are frequently forgotten in favor of
the truth that they served to signify. Christ is the goal of scripture,
and Christ is the goal of Christian doctrine. When Christ is gained,
both doctrine and scripture fall away, much like hope will fail when
the believer sees Christ face to face. This fact leads to an interesting
observation about the nature of theology, and how Calvin's theology
coheres.

Calvin's Theological Center

Since the publication in 1922 of Hermann Bauke's *Die Probleme der Theologie Calvins*, scholars have wrestled with his principal thesis that there
is no central doctrine in Calvin's theology.[71] In slaying the dragon of the
Schweizer and Baur thesis that predestination is the center, Bauke gave
Calvin scholarship an inestimable gift. However, since that date, many

---

[70] Comm. Colossians 1.12, Ad Colossenses 395.11–16. "Hoc enim unicum erat remedium Colossensibus adversus omnes insidias, quibus eos tentabant pseudoapostoli:
probe tenere, quid esset Christus. Unde enim fit, ut circumferamur tot variis doctrinis,
nisi quia nobis non est perspecta Christi virtus? Solus enim Christus facit, ut subito alia
omnia evanescant."

[71] Hermann Bauke, *Die Probleme der Theologie Calvins*, (Leipzig:Hinrichs'schen, 1922),
20. Bauke replaces the central doctrine idea with three formal principles, which are
rationalism, *complexio oppositorum*, and biblicism.

scholars have either cited Bauke to refute him, or to justify their own acceptance of his theory.[72] Those who would disagree with Bauke have suggested various centers for Calvin's theology, including Christology, the doctrine of faith, and even the sacramental word.[73] Those more congenial to his argument have demonstrated an even greater aversion to seeing system, or even avoidance of self-contradiction, in Calvin's thought.[74]

Given the mountain of material set forth on both sides of this problem, why should we attend to this conversation? First, because tracing the opposition between Calvin's Augustinian doctrine and his non-allegorical exegetical model offer a clear window on this problem. Secondly, the debate is central to our contention that Calvin cannot be thought of as an exegetical theologian, though perhaps he may be titled a hermeneutical theologian. Finally the question of a central doctrine in Calvin's theology cannot be separated from his interpretive and pastoral concerns, where our contention is that the edification of the Church was primary.[75]

Calvin's organization of his mature theology was tied to the pastoral function. The difference between the *Institutes* of 1536 and the edition of 1539 was the reality of the Church. In 1536, when Calvin first published the *Institutes*, it was as a handbook of the religion for the learned reader, resembling some of the projects of Erasmus. This was sensible, Calvin had spent the previous years of his life in learned and university societies–his readers were people like Cop, the Duchemins,

---

[72] See Mary Potter Engel's *John Calvin's Perspectival Anthropology*, American Academy of Religion Series, no. 52, edited by Susan Thistlethwaite, (Atlanta: Scholars Press, 1988), ix–xi, for a thumbnail sketch of these impulses.

[73] Christology is Wilhelm Niesel's contribution, see his *The Theology of Calvin*, translated by Harold Knight, (Philadelphia: Westminster Press, 1956); the doctrine of faith is Peter Brunner's, see his *Vom Glauben bei Calvin*, (Tübingen: Mohr, 1925); Brian Gerrish has argued for Calvin's coherence through a concentration on the sacramental nature of the Word, see his *Grace and Gratitude: The Eucharistic Theology of John Calvin* (Philadelphia: Fortress Press, 1993).

[74] See John Leith, "Calvin's Theological Method and the Ambiguities in his Theology," in Reformation Studies, ed. F.H. Littell, (Richmond: John Knox, 1962); and H. Jackson Forstman, *Word and Spirit: Calvin's Doctrine of Biblical Authority*, (Stanford, CA: Stanford University Press, 1962).

[75] Alexandre Ganoczy and Stefan Scheld wrote "Unter den reformatorischen Theologen des 16. Jahrhunderts hat diesen Sachverhalt vielleicht keiner so klar durchschaut wie Johannes Calvin. Seine Auslegung will kirchlich sein, sowohl was deren Voraussetzungen als auch was deren Zwech und Ziel angeht." *Die Hermeneutik Calvins: Geistesgeschichtliche Voraussetzungen und Grundzüge*, 89.

and Cordier. By 1539, on the other hand, Calvin had learned the painful lessons of the pastorate. He had had a miserably disappointing stint in Geneva, and was already the pastor of his second congregation, in Strasbourg, where he was mentored by an experienced and talented pastor, Martin Bucer.

Most of all, Calvin has realized that an Erasmean program of gentle reform through moral reform and scripture reading was insufficient to restore the Church. Thus, the *Institutes* of 1539 was no longer the Christian's handbook of six chapters, but moves decisively into its new direction, that of being a textbook for ministers, gaining eleven chapters in the process. Beyond the added material, certain critical changes to the text signal this change of focus. The alteration to the doctrine of faith provides an example. It is illustrative of the point of pastoral concern that Calvin's first definition of faith presented in 1536 barely resembled his 1559 definition. The 1536 definition, in comparison, was not only shorter, but answers fewer of the concerns that his later, Trinitarian definition is specifically crafted to satisfy. In 1536, the young Calvin, a humanist scholar who had never been burdened with the care of a church, publishes in Basel this definition of "faith": "And thus this true faith–which can at last be called 'Christian'—is nothing else than a firm conviction of mind whereby we determine with ourselves that God's truth is so certain, that it is incapable of not accomplishing what it has pledged to do by his holy Word [Rom. 10:11]."[76] The re-enforcement of the economic Trinity does not appear. More importantly, though, this doctrine of faith is a much simpler knowledge of God's truth, with no consideration of the terror that the believer sometimes feels. There is also no acknowledgment that faith consists of the knowledge of God's benevolence towards us. Calvin arrived at his Trinitarian definition of faith as an effort to represent the presentation of the whole God in salvation, and as pastoral counsel. Both the constant interpretation of the scriptures; and the long experience of the pastoral task, or more correctly speaking, the care and cure of souls, had changed Calvin's understanding of what sense of "*fides*" it was most important to define. By 1539, Calvin had seen the necessity of placing a whole new order in place, and education, both of a preaching clergy, and of a critical and scripture-reading laity, will be a central ingredient in that order.[77]

---

[76] John Calvin, *Institutes of the Christian Religion: 1536 Edition*, translated and annotated by Ford Lewis Battles, (Grand Rapids: Eerdmans Publishing Co., 1975), p. 43.

[77] Cornelius Augustijn notes the change in his work on Calvin's Strasbourg period.

Further, it is not insignificant that the reformer of Geneva employs only two permanent orders of clergy, both of whom have significant roles to play in the formation of the Church. Calvin allowed that doctors and pastors or ministers are permanent, rather than temporary, orders of ministry.[78] Moreover, the tasks of the pastor and the doctor overlap considerably. Pastors are committed to the care of a particular congregation, while doctors have the instruction of pastors and the whole Church as their particular bailiwick.[79]

Calvin gives a model of useful doctrine in his Timothy commentary, in which he sees the purpose of doctrine as the edification of the Church. Once again we see his theological enterprise was not the unfolding of the consequences of a particular central doctrine, but the

He writes "I am trying in my wording to do justice to the tension to which the man was exposed. The totally different world, till then unknown to him, with which he became acquainted in the German free city, in the empire, and in German Protestant churches, the figures of Capito, Bucer, and the German theologians, especially Melanchthon: these all broadened his horizons, influenced this theology, and—even more important—sharpened his awareness that the gospel is embedded in a particular social situation and does not remain unaffected by it." "Calvin in Strasbourg," in *Calvinus Sacrae Scripturae Professor*, International Congress on Calvin Research, edited by Wilhelm Neuser, (Grand Rapids: Eerdmans, 1994), 168. Augustijn is pointing out both Calvin's life education, and his grasp of the situated character of the gospel.

[78] Comm. Ephesians 4.11, Ad Ephesios 231.6–11. "As well, it should be noted that among these offices which Paul enumerates, only the last two are perpetual. For God adorned his Church with Apostles, Evangelists and Prophets, only for a time. This is excepting where religion has collapsed, then he raises up Evangelists outside of order, who are to recall to light the pure doctrine to its lost position. Without Pastors and Doctors, however, there can be no government of the Church." "Notandum praeterea est ex officiis, quae hic enumerat Paulus, postrema tantum duo perpetuo esse. Nam Deus Apostolis, Euangelistis et Prophetis Ecclesiam suam nonnisi ad tempus ornavit, nisi quia ubi collapsa est religio, Euangelistas extra ordinem excitat, qui puram doctrinam postliminio in lucem revocent. Sine Pastoribus autem et Doctoribus nullum potest esse Ecclesiae regimen."

[79] Comm. Ephesians 4.11, Ad Ephesios 230.18–231.5. "Therefore, Pastors in my judgment, are those with the care of a particular flock. I have no objection to their receiving the name of Doctors, if we recognize that there is another kind of Doctor, who superintends both the formation of Pastors and the instruction of the whole Church. Sometimes he can be a pastor who is also a doctor, but the duties are different." "Pastores ergo sunt, meo iudicio, quibus certi gregis cura commissa est. Quibus Doctorum nomen attribui non displicet, modo interim sciamus alterum esse Doctorum genus, qui tam formandis Pastoribus quam erudiendae toti Ecclesiae praesunt. Non quin idem interdum Pastor esse queat, qui Doctor est, sed quia facultates sunt diversae." My attention was first drawn to this distinction in Calvin's thought by Darlene Flaming, especially in her paper, "True Imitations: Calvin's Use of the Apostolic Example," given at the Sixteenth Century Studies Conference, 26 October 1996, in St. Louis, Missouri.

setting out of the necessities for the upbuilding of the Church. Here, the pedagogical model is especially significant. The familiar words concerning the right order of teaching (*ordo recte docendi*), ring in the ears of those who study Calvin's theology.[80] This concern for edifying education itself became a theological principle. That is to say, Calvin seems to make the theological move of accommodation that asserts that there can be no unedifying doctrine, and further, no edifying doctrine which cannot be pedagogically presented in a sound manner.[81]

A final set of benefits come from this ideal of seeing Calvin as a pastoral theologian. These benefits are heuristic in nature. By this means one is able to defend the rationality of Calvin's theological project without having to seek the non-existent center of his theology.[82] Instead of attempting an architectural analysis, of finding which metaphors or principles act as the main structural support beams in Calvin's theology, the effort to see Calvin's theology as the *edificatio ecclesia* provides direction for all of these theses to be considered alongside one another rather than in competition.[83] This permits perspectivalism,[84] rhetorical analysis,[85] the turn to Christology,[86] a central metaphor of union with Christ,[87] and even the denial of a single architectural principle

---

[80] OS 3, 33.38–34.3. ICR I.i.3. "Yet, even though the knowledge of God and of ourselves is so mutually connected, the order of right teaching demands that we discuss the former first, then we will descend afterward to proceed to the latter." "Utcunque tamen Dei nostrique notitia mutuo inter se nexu sint colligatae, ordo recte docendi postulat ut de illa priore disseramus loco, tum ad hanc tractandam postea descendamus."

[81] Here, I disagree with Brian Gerrish's implication of a division between pedagogy and theology. Criticizing Calvin's Catechism and its contrast between Baptism and the Lord's Supper, Gerrish writes "Pedagogically the contrast may well be effective. But in theology nothing is quite so simple, and the image of divine parenthood is not going to see us through all the intricacies." *Grace and Gratitude: The Eucharistic Theology of John Calvin*, (Philadelphia: Fortress Press, 1993), 125. For Calvin, there can be no doctrine which does not edify and cannot be taught soundly.

[82] Bauke, 20.

[83] Having said that, I am extremely taken with Francis M. Higman's ideal of Calvin's linearity as the model. Though Higman notes that on a road each stage is necessary, he also points out that the goal of a road is its destination. See his "Linearity in Calvin's Thought." *Lire et Découvrir: La circulation des idées au temp de la Réforme* (Geneve: Librairie Droz, 1998), 391–402.

[84] Engel, 1.

[85] Jones, 6.

[86] Niesel, 246–250.

[87] Charles Partee, "Calvin's Central Dogma Again." *Sixteenth Century Journal* 18 (1987):191–199, suggests this as an organizing principle. Dennis Tamburello suggests much the same in his later *Union with Christ: John Calvin and the Mysticism of St. Bernard,*

greater room to work, and it obviates the need for the constant bow-
ing in Bauke's direction, whether in approval or rejection. While these
approaches to the coherence of Calvin's work are significant, our position demands that the Church be central to any analysis of Calvin's
thought, and it permits Calvin to stand again as a doctor and pastor in
the Church.

Doctrina et Communitas

Two terms, "*doctrina*" and "*communitas*," or doctrine and community,
have been used throughout this chapter. But perhaps now, the interaction of the fields of meaning that these two produce can be seen more
clearly. Certainly, *doctrina* has to do with Christian teaching, or formation. But it has to do with a wider forming of life, the intellectual **and**
integral learning, the lived knowledge which Calvin seeks as the regeneration into the *communio Christi*.[88] The students in the *schola Dei* may be
individuals, but they are always being formed into a wider commonwealth. Moreover, *communitas*, though a term signifying a plural reality, drives relentlessly toward a perfect union. The dynamic relationship between these two foci can then be considered under two topics:
preaching and the textual community, and discipline as the formation
of Christ's body.

Preaching and the Textual Community

For Calvin, the greatest part of the task of the pastor is preaching.[89]
He carefully sets out the office of pastor, delineating it from that of
the doctor. He asserts the difference most clearly in his comments on
Ephesians 4.11.

Columbia Series in Reformed Theology, (Louisville, KY: Westminster John Knox Press,
1994), but without apparent reference to Partee's article.

[88] Bucer influenced Calvin in seeing communion as the central notion which tied
together three levels of union in the Christian society. These are union with Christ,
union with the saints, and the living communion of a society. For more on this, see
Willem van't Spijker, "Bucer's influence on Calvin: church and community," 32–44
in *Martin Bucer: Reforming Church and Community*, edited by D.F. Wright, (Cambridge:
Cambridge University Press, 1994), 33–34.

[89] T.H.L. Parker especially makes this point. See his *Calvin's Preaching* (Louisville:
Westminster John Knox Press, 1992).

> Paul speaks indiscriminately of Pastors and Doctors as if they are one and the same order. I do not deny that the name Doctor does, to some extent, belong to all Pastors. But this reason does not move me to confound two offices, which I see to differ from each other. Of course the duty of all Pastors is to teach, but there is a particular gift of interpreting Scripture, in order that sound doctrine may be retained. And it is possible for someone to be a Doctor who is not qualified to preach.

> Therefore, Pastors in my judgment, are those with the care of a particular flock. I have no objection to their receiving the name of Doctors, if we recognize that there is another kind of Doctor, who superintends both the formation of Pastors and the instruction of the whole Church. Sometimes he can be a pastor who is also a doctor, but the duties are different.[90]

The interpretation of this passage is made somewhat tricky by the two sentences beginning *"Tametsi enim,"* and ending *"non erit appositus."* All pastors are to teach. But is the peculiar gift of interpreting scripture, so that sound doctrine for the catholic Church may be maintained, also given to the pastors, or rather to the doctors, some of whom may not be fitted for preaching? Calvin's Latin does not give a definitive answer, though the smoother system of reference is genus, first species, second species. In that scheme, since the second clause is given as a gift of pastors through the removal of it from the sphere of doctors, the sense would most likely be that the first clause is given to doctors. Thus, the statement would read "Though all teaching officers must teach, a particular gift of interpreting scripture for the maintenance of pure doctrine is given to doctors, while the gift of preaching must be held by all pastors."

However, a stronger evidence for this reading of an ambiguous passage can be mustered. In Calvin's *Draft Ecclesiastical Ordinances* of 1541, the two offices of pastor and doctor are set out. For pastors, "Their office is to proclaim the Word of God, to instruct, admonish, exhort

---

[90] Comm. Ephesians 4.11, Ad Ephesios 230.12–231.5. "Paulum de Pastoribus et Doctoribus promiscue loqui, acsi unus idemque esset ordo. Neque etiam nego Doctoris nomen in omnes Pastores aliquatenus competere. Verum ratio illa me non movet, ut duo haec confundam, quae video inter se differre. Tametsi enim omnium Pastorum est docere, peculiare tamen est donum interpretandae Scripturae, ut dogmatum sanitas retineatur. Et Doctor aliquis esse poterit, qui tamen concionando non erit appositus. Pastores ergo sunt, meo iudicio, quibus certi gregis cura commissa est. Quibus Doctorum nomen attribui non displicet, modo interim sciamus alterum esse Doctorum genus, qui tam formandis Pastoribus quam erudiendae toti Ecclesiae praesunt. Non quin idem interdum Pastor esse queat, qui Doctor est, sed quia facultates sunt diversae."

and censure, both in public and private, to administer the sacraments
and to enjoin brotherly corrections along with the elders and colleagues."[91] Doctors, on the other hand, are giving the authoritative
teaching office.

> The office proper to doctors is the instruction of the faithful in true
> doctrine, in order that the purity of the gospel be not corrupted either
> by ignorance or by evil opinions. As things are disposed today, we always
> include under this title aids and instructions for maintaining the doctrine
> of God and defending the church from injury by the fault of pastors and
> ministers. So to use a more intelligible word, we will call this the order of
> the schools. The degree nearest to the minister and most closely joined
> to the government of the Church is the lecturer in theology, of which it
> will be good to have one in Old Testament and one in New Testament.[92]

Here, it is clearly declared that pastors are to preach, admonish, administer the sacraments, and engage in the discipline of the corporate body.
Doctors are to instruct all the faithful in true doctrine. Further, the link
to the Ephesians passage is strengthened in the attention to scripture.
Where in Ephesians Calvin had stated "the particular gift of interpreting scripture" is given to doctors, in the *Ecclesiastical Ordinances*, he sets
out that there should be two doctors, one for each Testament. Calvin
permits no division between theology and scripture.

But what then of the ministry of the pastors, those proclaimers of
God's Word? This task is nothing else than the edification of Christ's
body, the binding together of the believers into a perfect body. Calvin
sees Paul laying out the model of the building up of the body through
preaching.

> In place of what he had said, 'the constitution of the saints', he now
> puts, 'the edification of the body of Christ,' but with the same sense.
> Our true soundness and perfection consists in our being united into

---

[91] Calvin, *Projet d'Ordonnances Ecclesiastiques, Septembre et Octobre 1541*, CO 10.17. "...
leur office est dannoncer la parole de dieu pour endoctriner, admonester, exhorter et
reprendre tant en publiq comme en particulier, administrer les sacremens et faire les
corrections fraternelles avec les anciens et comys."

[92] *Projet d'Ordonnances Ecclesiastiques, Septembre et Octobre 1541*, CO 10.22. *Draft Ecclesiastical Ordinances*, 62–63. "Loffice propre de docteurs est denseigner les fidelles en saine
doctrine, affin que la purete de levangile ne soit corrompue ou par jgnorance ou par
maulvaises opinions. Toutesfous selon que les choses sont auiourdhuy disposees nous
compregnons en ce tiltre les aydes et jnstructions pour conserver la doctrine de dieu et
faire que lesglise ne soit desolee par faulte de pasteurs et ministres, ainsi pour user dun
mot plus jntelligible nous appellerons lordre des escolles.

Le degre plus prochain au ministere et plus conioinct au gouvernement de lesglise
est la lecture de thelogie, don't jl sera bon quil y en ait au vieil et nouveau testament."

the body of Christ. He could not have commended the ministry of the Word with greater honor than by attributing this effect to it. What is more excellent than to form the Church of Christ, in order that it may be established in its right and perfect soundness? But this work, so admirable and divine, the Apostle here declares to be accomplished by the external ministry of the Word. From this, the insanity of those who neglect this means and still hope to become perfect in Christ is plain. Such are the fanatics, who invent secret revelations of the Spirit for themselves, and the proud, who think that for them the private reading of the Scriptures is enough, and that they have no need of the common ministry of the Church. For if the Church is built up by Christ alone, it is certainly his to prescribe the grounds by which it shall be built. But Paul clearly testifies that there is no other way, according to the command of Christ, for us to be rightly united or perfected than by the outward preaching, when we allow ourselves to be ruled and taught by men. This is a universal rule, which covers both the highest and the lowest. The Church is the common mother of all the godly, which bears, nourishes, and governs in the Lord both kings and commoners; and this is done by the ministry. Those who neglect or despise this order want to be wiser than Christ.[93]

Christ has ordered that the edification of the Church will happen through the preaching of the Word. This is not an inherent quality of preaching, but the will of the Lord. Finally, the high place of preaching in Calvin's theology comes down to the fact that the Lord has willed that faith comes from hearing (*ex auditu*). Preaching and teaching should not be considered different tasks, but rather two forms of the same task.

---

[93] Comm. Ephesians 4.12, Ad Ephesios 232.13–233.4. "Pro eo, quod dixerat: ›constitutionem sanctorum‹, mox subiungit: ›aedificationem corporis Christi‹, eodem sensu. Nam illa est legitima nostra integritas et perfectio, si coalescamus omnes in unum Christi corpus. Non potuit honorificentius Verbi ministerium commendare, quam dum hunc illi effectum tribuit. Quid enim praestantius quam constitui Christi Ecclesiam, ut iusta sua et perfecta integritate constet? Atqui tam praeclarum opus et divinum externo Verbi ministerio perfici Apostolus hic praedicat. Unde eos insanire palam est, qui praeterito hoc medio se in Christo perfectos fore sperant. Cuiusmodi sunt fanatici, qui arcanas Spiritus revelationes sibi fingunt et superbi, qui privatam Scripturae lectionem sufficere sibi putant, ut nihil indigeant communi Ecclesiae ministerio. Nam si Ecclesiae aedificatio a solo Christo est, ipsius etiam sane est praescribere, quam aedificatio rationem esse velit. Paulus autem aperte hic testatur non alio modo, secundum Christi praescriptum, rite coagmentari nos et perfici quam per externam praedicationem, dum per homines patimur nos regi ad doceri. Haec universalis est regula, quae tam ad summos quam ad infirmos extenditur. Et certe Ecclesia communis est piorum omnium mater, quae tam reges quam plebeios gignit in Domino, nutrit et gubernat. Quod fit ministerio. Proinde supra Christum sapere volunt, qui hunc ordinem vel negligunt vel contemnunt."

But can this work? Can we not take up a stance of skepticism, and wonder about the flattery of Reformed preaching?[94] Could the laity "get it?" An important point which cannot be forgotten is that Calvin, especially in the early portions of his career at Geneva, was not preaching to Calvinists but to Catholics, those whose religious formation had centered on the mass, which was inherently visual. Calvin radically re-shaped this to a worship form in which the central act, preaching, was aural.[95] Those who critiqued this change had good reason to do so.

What is the nature of the community, this *communitas*, which we have called a "textual community?" First, by claiming it as a textual community, we are by no means suggesting universal literacy. "The question of oral versus written tradition need not be framed in inflexible terms. What was essential for a textual community, whether large or small, was simply a text, an interpreter, and a public. The text did not have to be written; oral record, memory, and reperformance sufficed."[96] Rather, the claim is made that the community is formed around understandings of a text or texts. This interpretation has a powerful community-forming effect. "Through the text, or, more accurately, through the interpretation of it, individuals who previously had little else in common were united around common goals. Similar social origins comprised a sufficient, but not necessary, condition of participation. The essential bond was forged by means of belief; its cement was faith in the reality of belonging. And these in turn were by-products of a general agreement on the meaning of a text."[97]

The claim we are making about Calvin's public, the community he was consciously attempting to form, is that it was bound together by a decidedly hermeneutical project, the interpretation of certain key texts.[98] Of course, the Bible held pride of place among these. But others

---

[94] Euan Cameron, *The European Reformation*, (Oxford: Oxford University Press, 1991), 311.

[95] Robert M. Kingdon, "Change and Continuity in History," Plenary Address, Sixteenth Century Studies Conference, 25 October 1997, Atlanta.

[96] Brian Stock, "Medieval Literacy, Linguistic Theory, and Social Organization," 30–51 in *Listening for the Text: On the Uses of the Past*, (Philadelphia: University of Pennsylvania Press, 1990), 37.

[97] Stock, "Medieval Literacy, Linguistic Theory, and Social Organization," 37.

[98] This interpretation, though centered in the community, is bolstered by the appeal to the trans-historical community, through the appeal to earlier authorities. Thus, Calvin's appeals to Bernard of Clairvaux's reforming efforts throughout Book IV of the *Institutes* are not only polemical, but also for the forming of the consciousness of the

were also in the central consciousness, and perhaps brought more readily to hand. These would include the catechism, the Decalogue, and the Lord's Prayer. These were powerful texts, to both literate and illiterate, and were to be learned by memory.[99]

What evidence can we actually bring to bear to conclude that the community was being formed through its embrace of a central set of texts, and the interpretation of them? First, there is Calvin's harping on the ideal of the Church as a *schola dei*, or *schola Christi*. Whether for good or for ill, we miss a salient point about Calvin's young life if we neglect to relate it to school. Calvin lived in the academic environment, and curriculum is about what is being read. We can see this at several points in his work, but a particularly strong example comes from his commentary on Ephesians 4.17. Remarking on how the knowledge of Christ must change the life of believers, Calvin writes "That those who have been taught in the school of Christ and enlightened by the doctrine of salvation, should follow vanity and differ in nothing from the unbelievers and the blind on whom no light of truth has ever shown, would be totally absurd."[100] This passage perfectly illustrates the school quality of Calvin's ideal community, and its nature of formation, rather than simple intellectual knowledge.

Further, we have the testimony of Conrad Badius about Calvin's own preaching. Explaining Calvin's desire not to publish his sermons, Badius wrote that Calvin "... preached simply and nakedly to accommodate the coarseness of the people, without elaborate apparatus or arrangement."[101] Whether that was the only reason that Calvin did not wish to publish those sermons we cannot know. But we do have this testimony that Calvin obviously accommodated his own erudition for the formation of a lay community.

Secondly, we may note that although this was Calvin's project, he was not alone in it. One of Calvin's printers, Robert Estienne, pub-

---

present community. See W. Stanford Reid, "Bernard of Clairvaux in the Thought of John Calvin," *Westminster Theological Journal* 41 (1978):127–145, 131.

[99] Robert Kingdon, "Calvin's and the Genevans' Efforts to Control Hate," unpublished paper given at The Ninth Colloquium on Calvin Studies, 31 January 1998, Davidson, North Carolina. Kingdon relates that these were to be learned in catechetical classes, by repetition of short phrases, until perfection was achieved.

[100] Comm. Ephesians 4.17, Ad Ephesios 238.19–22. "Nam eos, qui edocti sunt in Christi schola et salutis doctrina sunt illuminati, vanitatem sectari et nihil differre ab infidelibus et caecis, quibus nulla unquam affulsit lux veritatis, nimis absurdum est."

[101] Quoted in Bernard Cottret, *Calvin: A Biography*, 292.

lished a "*Nova Glossa Ordinaria*" in 1553.[102] Estienne was one of the
scholar-printers who had fled from Paris to Geneva to pursue his trade
without fear of persecution.[103] In his preface, Estienne makes it clear
that his desire in printing this new continuous commentary was to
replace the old *glossa ordinaria*. To do so, he began by printing a new
edition of the Vulgate. However, his edition included a "new version",
the Zürich Protestant Latin version of Leo Jud, which infuriated the
Paris theologians.[104]

Estienne eventually concluded that the freedom of conscience was
not available to him in Paris, and went to Geneva. Here, he found
himself being instructed in piety and in the right understanding of the
scriptures. The story is best recounted in his own preface.

> Here among the beasts I encountered men who proclaim God's good-
> ness as worthy of love and celebration and preach both his grace and
> his mercy in their fullness, serving as Christ's ambassadors in his name.
> They so present him to their brethren and set forth his portrait, as it
> were, before their eyes that the image and face of the Son of God, pre-
> viously unknown to me but now so splendidly depicted,[105] and the new
> lineaments and teaching of the gospel instilled in me the greatest amaze-
> ment and astonishment. For I reckoned that I had hitherto made such
> progress in the knowledge of Jesus Christ that I judged myself capable of
> being their teacher, whereas the outcome was quite different—the oppo-
> site of what I supposed. ...
>
> Once I had removed myself far enough from those lowland wolves
> which pollute the minds of everyone with their flatulence, and began
> to experience among these mountains instruction in Christian piety and
> religion which comprises God's Word and his sacraments, I consulted the
> Scriptures to ascertain whether the teaching I was hearing agreed with

---

[102] David F. Wright, "Robert Estienne's *Nova Glossa Ordinaria*. A Protestant Quest for
a Standard Bible Commentary," 40–54 in *Calvin: Erbe und Auftrag: Festschrift für Wilhelm
Heinrich Neuser zum 65. Geburtstag*, edited by Willem van Spijker, (Kampen: Kok Pharos
Publishing House, 1991), 41.

[103] Estienne states that "I betook myself to the mountains, amid whose peaks savage
and wild beasts have their haunts, but I found among those mountains more humanity,
genuineness and godliness than among the theologians, and greater recognition and
gratitude to their Creator than among those who, in innocent sheep's clothing, mali-
ciously seduce people from the true fear of God and prevent creatures having access to
their Creator through Jesus Christ." Wright, "Robert Estienne's *Nova Glossa Ordinaria*,"
45.

[104] Wright, "Robert Estienne's *Nova Glossa Ordinaria*," 44.

[105] Note the parallel between the language of depiction in Estienne's preface and in
Calvin's commentary on Galatians 3.1. Comm. Galatians 3.1, Ad Galatas 60.18–61.5.

them. Since our mind is wicked and perverse, I expected to find some divergence and some noticeable omissions.

But—God be praised!—I found the greatest possible consistency, agreement and concord.[106]

Of course, there is the difficulty of accepting Estienne's preface at face value. He testifies that he was basically ignorant of the gospel, some scholars have disputed this, and the requisite knowledge to oversee a version of the scripture threatening to the Paris masters was not insignificant.[107] However, let us direct our attention to the patterns that he draws. First, although in the hinterlands, Estienne encountered preaching of Christ so strong that he is turned from a teacher into a student. This preaching brings amazement and astonishment, and calls upon him for action. His response is to read the scriptures to affirm the content of the preaching.

Already, we have a model, given by Estienne's preface, of the action of a member of the textual community in Geneva. The text being interpreted is the Bible, the interpretation is strong and vivid. But Estienne's response is not automatic obedience, but rather a move of verification. He avoids the easy belief (*levis credulitas*), that Calvin bids against, and sees for himself whether he should grant authority. When he finds the preaching in accord with scripture, he accepts this community, and his place in it. Indeed, he represents his next move, that of finishing the *Nova Glossa*, as a response to Christ's goodness, and service to God.[108] He declares that "This knowledge of God's perfect kindness, so necessary for salvation, can be found only in the Holy Scriptures, and in their purest and truest understanding, which is best provided by the most faithful expositions of their interpreters." To complete his work, then, he chose to draw "interpretations not only from the old doctors of the church but also from those who in our present age daily preach Jesus Christ purely and sincerely without corruption."[109] From the Reformers, Estienne included expositions of Bucer, Osiander and Bullinger in the Latin edition, and added Calvin in the French edition of 1554.[110]

---

[106] Wright, "Robert Estienne's *Nova Glossa Ordinaria*," 45–46.

[107] Wright points to E. Armstrong's contention in *Robert Estienne Royal Printer*, (Appleford, 1986), 263.

[108] Wright, "Robert Estienne's *Nova Glossa Ordinaria*," 46.

[109] Wright, "Robert Estienne's *Nova Glossa Ordinaria*," 46.

[110] Wright, "Robert Estienne's *Nova Glossa Ordinaria*," 41–42.

Thus, Estienne's project gives our study two invaluable pieces of information. First, Estienne's preface provides a contemporary illustration of the textual community in Geneva. Secondly, the fact of Estienne's publishing the *Nova Glossa Ordinaria* in Latin and French stands as strong evidence that both those learned in Latin and those who could only handle the French language were willing to purchase instruments to help in their own understanding of the scriptures.

Further evidence for our thesis can be provided. Though we shall turn to this more clearly in the next section, recent research into the Consistory records during Calvin's day are shedding light on this topic.[111] During the Bolsec controversy and its aftermath, the Consistory of Geneva questioned several citizens of Geneva over their holding a position on predestination which was considered too sympathetic to Bolsec.[112] Although this might be considered a piece of negative evidence, it supports the conclusion of a textual community fully engaged in the business of considering the meaning of the scriptures for the life of the body. Though most of those questioned by the Consistory were working people, they felt comfortable making some judgments on doctrinal matters, based on scriptural knowledge. "These common artisans clearly did not follow the theological nuances of the debate over predestination, and tended to defer to the clergy for judgments on issues of this sort. But they nevertheless had absorbed some theological principles. They were all persuaded that any theological debate must be resolved by appeal to Holy Scripture. They had adopted that basic guideline of the Protestant Reformation. If they were persuaded of the

---

[111] This project, by a team of scholars under the direction of Robert M. Kingdon, has already shown enormous promise for understanding the reception of Reformed teaching among the people of Geneva. Kingdon writes that a systematic exposition of the records of this body rescues it from the distortions that have come from concentrating upon a very few spectacular cases. "Our knowledge of the operations of the Consistory has been distorted considerably by the concentration of past historians on a few spectacular cases of people who protested vehemently and were punished severely. They give the impression that the Consistory was a kind of inquisitorial court. But protests were in fact the exception. The Consistory was closer to an obligatory counseling service than to a court. This power to admonish and reconcile was the only power that everyone from the beginning agreed the Consistory possessed." Kingdon, "A New View of Calvin in the Light of the Registers of the Geneva Consistory," 21–34 in *Calvinus Sincerioris Religionis Vindex*, edited by Wilhelm Neuser and Brian Armstrong, (Kirksville, MO: Sixteenth Century Journal Publishers, 1997), 23.

[112] Robert Kingdon, "Popular Reactions to the Debate between Bolsec and Calvin." 138–145 in *Calvin: Erbe und Auftrag: Festschrift für Wilhelm Heinrich Neuser zum 65. Geburtstag*, edited by Willem van Spijker, (Kampen: Kok Pharos Publishing House, 1991), 140–143.

truth of Bolsec's position, it was because they had become convinced that he was interpreting Scripture with even more authority than their own Genevan ministers."[113]

Further, this constant relationship with these central texts resulted not only in noetic and intellectual effects, but also in effects of piety. All considerations of God through the scriptures require a response, the correct response, which is pious worship.[114]

Discipline as the Forming in Christ's Body

We may now turn to the conscious forming of the corporate body, done as an outgrowth of the community's consciousness of its struggle with these foundational texts. Did this make a difference? Further, can it be demonstrated that the members of the body took into their own consciences these messages, rather than being coerced by a vengeful clergy? To put it another way, is Genevan discipline a result of persuasion of God's truth, or evidence for the theory that Calvin was a religious dictator?

Once again the new research on the Consistory records is helpful. Here we find the story of a woman called before the Consistory on a charge of malice. When directed to recite the Lord's Prayer, she does so, but changes the phrase "as we forgive our debtors." Immediately, the pastors catch her editorial work, and ask her reason. She states that someone has sinned against her, and that she cannot forgive them.[115] Obviously, the pastors wished that she were able to practice a greater charity, yet her unwillingness provides a concrete clue that she had rightly understood the force of the clause about forgiveness. Further, she had internalized it to the point of refusing to state it in its original form, so as to keep herself from lying.

Those brought before the Consistory were not there, generally, for an ecclesiastical whipping. In point of fact, the Consistory could not order any corporal punishment, its greatest threat was excommunication.[116] Normally, the intention was spiritual healing, which was attempted

---

[113] Kingdon, "Popular Reactions," 145.

[114] Carlos M.N. Eire, "'True Piety Begets True Confession': Calvin's Attack on Idolatry," 247–276 in *John Calvin and the Church*, edited by Timothy George, (Louisville: Westminster John Knox Press, 1991), 253.

[115] Robert Kingdon, "Calvin's and the Genevans' Efforts to Control Hate."

[116] Kingdon, "A New View of Calvin in the Light of the Registers of the Geneva Consistory," 23.

through a process of hearing the complaint, deciding the facts of the matter, and the administration of a "remonstrance," or "admonition."[117] This was a semi-private affair, with only the members of the Consistory and parties to the case being present. Further, the process generally ended with the acceptance of this admonition. That is to say, "If the party summoned accepted this scolding in a good spirit, displaying true repentance without protest or complaint, the matter was concluded."[118]

Biblical doctrine was frequently the motivating factor in the reconciling work. Often, the records note that the remonstrances contained biblical references.[119] Calvin is noted, in the case of a woman accused of defending the practice of adultery, as ministering with "beautiful admonitions taken from the Holy Scriptures."[120] One conclusion of those working on the Consistory records is that "a very real determinant of Calvin's power in Geneva is found in his use of the Bible. He clearly knew the Bible very well. He could produce on-the-spot quotations from the Word of God that seemed to his listeners to be particularly appropriate for whatever topic was under discussion. He was also skillful in defending his use of those quotations, persuading his listeners that he really understood their meaning better than anyone in the audience."[121] This is a key text for the support of our contention of a textual community, and for Calvin's interpretive power! The community is bound together by this text and its interpretation, and acknowledges Calvin as a particularly astute interpreter.

Finally, we must point out the aim of the Consistory process. It was not a method of punishment. Not only did the Consistory not have corporal power, but its work was frequently done after the accused

---

[117] Kingdon, "A New View of Calvin in the Light of the Registers of the Geneva Consistory," 22.

[118] Kingdon, "A New View of Calvin in the Light of the Registers of the Geneva Consistory," 23. Kingdon goes on to clarify that "If the case involved several people (for example some sort of public quarrel) within a family, among business partners, or between neighbors, the scolding might be followed by a formal reconciliation. In serious cases this reconciliation would itself become a kind of public ceremony. These scoldings and reconciliations brought most cases to an end."

[119] Kingdon, "A New View of Calvin in the Light of the Registers of the Geneva Consistory," 24.

[120] Kingdon, "A New View of Calvin in the Light of the Registers of the Geneva Consistory," 24.

[121] Kingdon, "A New View of Calvin in the Light of the Registers of the Geneva Consistory," 24.

had already served a sentence for the offence, imposed by the civil authorities.[122] Instead of serving a punitive function, the work of the Consistory was for the healing and wholeness of the Body of Christ. "The remonstrance seems to have carried with it an act of public forgiving, and it signaled the formal integration of the accused back into the Christian community."[123] This model is fully in accordance with Calvin's own earliest hopes for the organization of a Christian society. In the *Articles concerning the Organization of the Church and of Worship at Geneva* of 1537, Calvin stated the need for a consistory-type process, and clearly set out that its action would be for the healing discipline of the body.

> We have deliberately required of you to be pleased to ordain and elect certain persons of good life and witness from among the faithful, perse-vering and not easily corrupted, who should be dispersed and distributed in all the quarters of the city, having oversight of the life and government of each of them; and if they see any vice worthy of note to find fault with in any person, that they communicate about it with some of the ministers, to admonish whoever it is that is at fault and to exhort him in brotherly fashion to amendment. If it be found that such remonstrances have no result, he must be advised that his obstinacy will be reported to the Church. And then if he recognize his error, how great is the profit of this discipline![124]

The formation into Christ's body, so frequently seen in the sacraments, has now been more widely distributed into the power of the word. Through teaching, preaching, and discipline, all of which are based on the application of scripture, Calvin envisioned a Christian society, where the regeneration of the individuals into the engrafting together into Christ is the earthly move toward a heavenly home.

---

[122] Kingdon, "A New View of Calvin in the Light of the Registers of the Geneva Consistory," 25–27.

[123] Kingdon, "A New View of Calvin in the Light of the Registers of the Geneva Consistory," 27.

[124] Calvin, *Articles Concernant L'Organisation de l'Eglise et du Culte a Genève, Proposés au Con-seil par les Ministres le 16. Janvier 1537.* CO 10.10. "Et pour ce faire nous avons délibéré requerir de vous que vostre playsir soyt ordonner et eslire certaynes personnes de bone vie et de bon tesmoignage entre tous les fideles, pareillement de bonne constance et que ne soyent poent ayses a corrumpre, lesquelz estans departis et distribues en tous les quartiers de la ville, ayant loil sus la vie et gouuernement dung chascun et sil voyent quelque notable vice a reprendre en quelque personne, quil en communiquent auecq quelcung des ministres pour admonester quicunque sera celluy lequel sera en faulte et lexorter fraternellement de se corriger. Et si on veoyt que telles remonstrances ne profi-tent rien, le aduertir que on signiffiera a lesglise son obstination. Et lors sil se recognoyt, voyla desja vng grand prouffit de ceste discipline."

Conclusion

Through this chapter we have seen how Calvin combines his hermeneutical principles and exegetical practices to aim at the goal of the
scriptures, Christ. This feeds directly into his overarching theological
paradigm of the edification of the Church into Christ, accomplished
through persuasive education. This is his horizon, the definite vision
of the goal of Christian teaching, Christian formation, and Christian
truth.

Calvin saw Christ at the center of the Christian experience. This is
not to take a position on the question of Calvin as a Christo-centric,
theo-centric, or Spirit-centered theologian.[125] Rather, it is a recognition of Christ's centrality to the mediation between believers and God.
Thus, Christ is the end of the scriptures, Christ defines Christian teaching, Christ models Christian life. Christ offers, through the mystical
union of believers into himself, the new possibility which is the essence
of Christianity, which is found in the Church, which is his body.

This whole dynamic defines the activity of theology. This remains
constant, and is trans-historically valid. However, the historical circumstances in which this task is performed change. Thus, to use scholastic
language, the substance of the theological enterprise is the edification
of the Church into the Body of Christ. The accidents of what is necessary and pedagogically useful in various circumstances are necessarily
changing. Therefore, the theme of theology as edification remains constant, from the patristic age to the Reformation, and by implication, to
today.

---

[125] This is a false distinction, which only appears in secondary literature about
Calvin's theology, and never in Calvin's thought itself. For Calvin, the whole Trinity
is constantly working together, and though he speaks of the tasks of particular persons,
his theology, as a coherent complex, does not bear too great dependence upon any
member. I. John Hesselink notes this in *Calvin's First Catechism*, Columbia Series in
Reformed Theology (Louisville: Westminster John Knox Press, 1997), 118. See also
Stephen Edmondson's emphasis on the unified activity of the Trinity in his discussion of
doctrine of Christ. *Calvin's Christology* (Cambridge: Cambridge University Press, 2004),
119–149.

CHAPTER FIVE

TRADITION RECEIVED THROUGH FIRE

If any one's work is burned, he suffers loss, however he will be saved; yet as through fire. (I Corinthians 3.15)[1]

However, he will be saved Paul speaks, clearly, of those who aways retain the foundation, but mix hay with gold, straw with silver, and wood with precious stones. That is to say that they build on Christ, but because of following the weakness of the flesh they give way to something human, or through ignorance they turn aside to some extent from the exact purity of the word of God. Many of the saints were like that, Cyprian, Ambrose, Augustine and others. You can also add, if you like, from those more recent, Gregory and Bernard, and others like them, whose purpose it was to build on Christ, but who, however, often turned away from the right method of building (*aedificandi*).[2]

This citation from and comment upon I Corinthians 3.15 is programmatic for Calvin's effort at retrieving the patristic and medieval doctrinal and exegetical traditions.[3] Although he believed in the efforts of the Fathers to interpret the scriptures, and wishes to accept the mantle of their orthodoxy, he saw that there are problems inherent in their biblical exegesis, and occasionally in the teaching they draw from their exegesis.[4] Although Calvin was clear on the necessity of contact with

---

[1] Comm I Corinthians 3.15, CO 49.353. "si cuius opus arserit, iacturam faciet: ipse autem salvus fiet, sic tamen tanquam per ignem."

[2] Comm. I Corinthians 3.15, CO 49, 357. "*Ipse autem salvus fiet, etc.* Paulum de iis loqui constat, qui retento semper fundamento foenum auro, stipulam argento, lignum lapidibus pretiosis admiscent: nempe qui in Christo aedificant, sed propter carnis imbecillitatem patiuntur aliquid humanum, aut per ignorantiam nonnihil ab exacta verbi Dei puritate deflectunt. Quales etiam fuerunt multi ex sanctis, Cyprianus, Ambrosius, Augustinus, et similes: adde etiam si libet, ex recentioribus, Gregorium et Bernardum, aliosque eius notae, qui, quum haberent hoc propositum ut in Christo aedificarent, a recta tamen aedificandi ratione saepe aberrarunt."

[3] I differ here from Anthony N.S. Lane. In his "Calvin's Sources of Saint Bernard," *Archiv für Reformationsgeschichte* 67 (1976):253–283, Lane comments that this exegesis was simply "following a well-established Reformation tradition." (273) I believe that Calvin goes further than that; even if this is a commonplace in other Reformers, Calvin uses it as a model for the reception of tradition.

[4] Irena Backus has noted Calvin's desire to grasp the orthodoxy of the fathers even when not following their teachings in her *Historical method and confessional identity in the era of the Reformation, 1378–1615* (Leiden: Brill, 2003).

the teaching of the Church through the ages, the only legitimate connection was through the teaching of the same gospel message as derived from the chosen method of God's revelation, the scriptures of the Old and New Testaments.[5] This teaching will in every age be the teaching of, or forming in, the Christian religion.[6]

An examination of both Calvin's parallel treatment of I Corinthians 3.15 in the *Institutes* and of his high view of the piety of the patristic authors supports this view. When he considers this text in the course of his denial of purgatory, for which it was a proof-text, he offers another interpretation harmonious with that of the commentary.

> First, we see that the Apostle used a metaphor when he called the doctrines devised by men "wood, hay, and stubble." The reason for this is clear, that just as wood when put on fire is destroyed and lost, the same will happen to those things when they come to be tested. Now everyone knows that such a trial comes from the Spirit of God. Therefore, to follow the thread of his metaphor and put the parts in their proper relationships to one another, he calls the trial of the Holy Spirit "fire." For, just as silver and gold, the nearer they are brought to the fire, give stronger proof they are genuine and pure, in the same way the more carefully the truth of the Lord is tested in a spiritual examination, the more completely its authority is confirmed. As "hay, wood, and stubble" are set on fire, they are suddenly consumed, in the same way, the inventions of men, not grounded in the word of the Lord, cannot bear testing by the Holy Spirit, but immediately fall and perish. In short, if invented doctrines are compared to "wood, hay, and stubble" because like "wood, hay, and stubble" they are burned in the fire and

---

[5] In 1980, David Steinmetz published his celebrated article, "The Superiority of Pre-Critical Exegesis," *Theology Today* 27 (1980): 27–38. In that work, Steinmetz argued for the truth of the "pre-critical" exegesis, as measured against the aims of the historical-critical method. That work has been consciously followed and updated in Richard Muller and John L. Thompson's "The Significance of Precritical Exegesis: Retrospect and Prospect." *Biblical Interpretation in the Era of the Reformation*, edited by Richard A. Muller and John L. Thompson (Grand Rapids: Eerdmans, 1996), 335–345. In this work, the difference in emphases between pre-critical and historical-critical is considered, without too great a denigration of either, although certainly with a loss of status for historical-critical. The historical-critical method attempts to proffer a method which will ensure truth and lack of prejudice. Muller and Thompson suggest that this approach denies the very fact that the intended recipient of these biblical texts are a determining factor in the correct interpretation of them.

[6] In pointing to the fathers as appropriate conversation partners, and only noting a few medievals who tend towards patristic models of theology and exegesis, Calvin is again echoing a humanist theme. Erasmus directed his students to study the oldest doctors and expositors. Torrance, "The Hermeneutics of Erasmus," 58. However, Erasmus also directed the students to pay closest attention to those who departed furthest from the letter of scripture. Here, Calvin would violently disagree!

destroyed, though the actual destruction is only completed by the Spirit of the Lord, the Spirit is that fire by which they will be tested. This test Paul calls "the day of the Lord" using the common saying of Scripture. Indeed it is called "the day of the Lord" whenever he reveals his presence to men in any way; indeed, his face shines most, when his truth gleams forth. Now we have proved that Paul means by "the fire" nothing but the testing by the Holy Spirit. But how are those saved through that fire who suffer the loss of their works? This will not be difficult to understand if we consider what kind of men he is speaking of. For he is referring to those architects of the Church who, keeping a lawful foundation, build upon it with unsuitable materials. That is, those who do not fall away from the principal and necessary doctrines of the faith go astray in less important and less dangerous matters, mixing their own invention with the word of God. Such, I say, must suffer the loss of their work by the destruction of their fictions. They themselves, however, are saved, yet so as by fire; that is, not that their ignorance and delusions are approved by the Lord, but they are purified from them by the grace and power of the Holy Spirit.[7]

The Holy Spirit cleanses and purifies the work of the theologians in order that they might be saved. Likewise, future generations, though

---

[7] OS 4.142.10–143.10. ICR III.v.9. "Principio, videmus Apostolum metaphora usum esse, quum doctrinas hominum capite excogitatas, lignum, foenum, et stipulam vocavit. Ratio quoque metaphorae prompta est: nempe quod velut lignum, statim atque igni admotum fuerit, consumitur et deperditur, sic neque illae perdurare poterunt, quum eas examinari contigerit. Porro eiusmodi examen a Spiritu Dei proficisci neminem latet. Quo igitur filum metaphorae prosequeretur, ac partes iusta correlatione inter se aptaret, ignem appellavit examen Spiritus sancti. Perinde enim atque aurum et argentum, quo propius ad ignem admoventur, eo certiorem probitatis puritatisque probationem referunt: ita Domini veritas, quo exactius spirituali examine expenditur, eo maiorem sumit authoritatis confirmationem. Quemadmodum foenum, lignum, stipula, igni admota, corripiuntur in subitam consumptionem: ita hominum inventa, Domini verbo non stabilita, Spiritus sancti examen ferre nequeunt, quin concidant protinus et dispereant. Denique si commentitiae doctrinae, ligno, foeno, stipulae comparantur, quod instar ligni, foeni, stipulae comburantur ab igne, et corrumpantur in interitum, non autem conficiuntur aut profligantur nisi a Domini Spiritu: sequitur, Spiritum esse ignem illum a quo probabuntur; cuius probationem vocat Paulus diem Domini, vulgato Scripturae usu. Dies enim Domini esse dicitur quoties suam praesentiam hominibus aliquo modo manifestat. Tum vero potissimum facies eius lucet ubi veritas eius illucet. Iam evictum est, non alium esse ignem Paulo, quam Spiritus sancti examen. Quomodo autem per ignem illum salvi fiunt qui operis iacturam patiuntur? Idipsum intelligere non erit difficile, si consideremus de quo genere hominum loquatur. Siquidem eos Ecclesiae architectos notat qui retento legitimo fundamento, disparem materiam superstruunt: hoc est, qui non deflectentes a praecipuis et necessariis fidei capitibus, in minoribus nec ita periculosis hallucinantur, commenta sua Dei verbo admiscentes. Tales, inquam, operis iacturam facere oportet, abolitis eorum commentis: ipsi autem salvi fiunt, sed quasi per ignem, hoc est, non quod eorum ignorantia et hallucinatio coram Domino sit probabilis: sed quia Spiritus sancti gratia et virtute ab illa repurgantur."

they cannot claim the perfection of the Holy Spirit, nor have anything to do with the salvation of those who have gone before, can and must be about the work of testing the building. They must determine which pieces are firmly founded on God's word, and which will fall apart under the heat of a later age whose thought patterns and assumptions are different.

Calvin attempted a delicate task of "right dividing" in his own consideration of religion and interpretation. The solutions that he poses to this problem are ingenious, and subtle. To understand this, one must bear in mind the principle that for Calvin, teaching the precepts of religion was more important than correct scriptural interpretation.[8] Though such an assertion might make latter-day Reformed thinkers howl, the material was evident.[9]

First, to return to Calvin's prefaces to the *Institutes*, he saw his task as furthering the doctrine of piety (*pietatis doctrinam*),[10] and argued that reading scripture required being equipped with the summary of religion in all its parts (*religionis summam omnibus partibus*).[11] His comments concerning understanding the scriptures, when juxtaposed with the teachings of religion, indicate the priority of religion.

> Therefore that which we most hope for in the present life, even though it were otherwise highly hoped for, we are not to look in the present life for perpetual consensus among us on the exposition of passages of scripture. When, therefore, we depart from the views of our predecessors, we are not to be stimulated by any lust for innovation, not to be impelled by any desire to slander others, not to be aroused by any hatred, and not to be prompted by any ambition. Only necessity should force us, and we are to have no other object than that of doing good. We are to try to do the same also in expounding Scripture, but in the teachings of religion, in

---

[8] For a different solution to the same problem, see the case of Urbanus Rhegius, noted in Scott Hendrix' "The Use of Scripture in Establishing Protestantism: The Case of Urbanus Rhegius," in *The Bible in the 16th Century*, edited by David Steinmetz, (Durham: Duke University Press, 1990), 37–49.

[9] That Calvin clearly does not see a potential conflict here should give insight into how he is thinking about these categories. For Calvin, *religio* is prior to and more important than scriptural interpretation. That they could conflict is unthinkable, since both are directed from the same divine source.

[10] OS 3.5.30–6.4. "mihi quoque probe conscius sim, ipsum et angelos testes habeam, nihil ex quo officium doctoris in Ecclesia suscepi, mihi fuisse propositum quam Ecclesiae prodesse, sinceram pietatis doctrinam asserendo:". ICR, John Calvin to the Reader, 4. "It is properly clear in my own conscience, and have God and the angels to witness, that since I undertook the office of doctor in the Church, I have had no other purpose than to benefit the Church by maintaining the pure doctrine of godliness."

[11] OS 3.6.21–22.

which God has particularly desired that the minds of his people should be in agreement, we are to take less liberty. I have studied both of these, as my readers will easily grasp.[12]

Although Calvin placed extraordinary importance upon the right interpretation of scripture, he never lost sight of the goal, which is right religion. God allows less liberty with dogma than with interpretation of scripture! Here, Calvin returned to Augustine's tutelage. Although the Genevan Reformer could not make the same statement as the Bishop of Hippo that a pious interpretation wrongly reached is not incorrect, they agreed that the point of scriptural interpretation is the succoring of the Christian life.[13]

Calvin wished to affirm both the doctrine of the early Church, and particularly its Augustinian strand, and address the difficulty of paring away, for pedagogical purposes, the method of interpretation that supported that doctrine. This involved him in the task of a transformational reception; a re-setting of doctrinal teaching to meet vastly changed circumstances. He makes theses receptive moves by considering various exegetical quarrels that he picks with theologians taken from his list of the Fathers.

As demonstrated by the tables published by A.N.S. Lane, Calvin's frequent quotation of and dependence upon Augustine is undeniable.[14] However, certain understandings of Augustine's work, which have until now been left out for the sake of convenience, require further exploration.[15]

---

[12] Comm. Romans, Dedicatory Epistle to Grynaeus, Ad Romanos 3.110–4.19. "Ergo quum sperandum in praesenti vita non sit, quod maxime alioqui optandum esset, ut in locis Scripturae intelligendis perpetua sit inter nos consensio: danda est opera ut nulla novandi libidine incitati, nulla suggillandi alios cupiditate impulsi, nullo instigati odio, nulla ambitione titillati: sed sola necessitate coacti, nec aliud quaerentes quam prodesse, a superiorum sententiis discedamus: deinde ut id fiat in Scripturae expositione: in religionis autem dogmatibus, in quibus praecipue voluit Dominus consentaneas esse suorum mentes, minus sumatur libertatis. Utriusque studium mihi fuisse, facile deprehendent lectores."

[13] Augustine, Confessions, translated by Henry Chadwick, (London. Oxford University Press, 1991), Book XII, xviii, (27), pp. 259–260. See below.

[14] A.N.S. Lane lists the citations to Augustine in Calvin's 1559 Institutes, listing 478 particular citations, drawn from 50 works in the Augustinian corpus. This does not include works from Pseudo-Augustine. These are listed in Appendix II of "Calvin's Use of the Fathers and the Medievals," Calvin Theological Journal, April, 1981, 202. The indices in the pertinent volumes of CNTC list 47 specific references to Augustine in the Pauline commentaries, a number which is only exceeded by the citations to Chrysostom.

[15] This is not to say that I am going to attempt to prove the case of Augustine's use

Augustine's Interpretation

Calvin's measured distancing of himself from Augustine's interpretive practice and the Augustinian hermeneutical tradition was an attempt to reclaim the Bishop of Hippo from the "Augustinians". Approaching Augustine's exegesis can be terribly daunting because he wrote so much through his career, all of which was colored by his reception of scripture, that the sources threaten to overwhelm the effort. Calvin saw *all* of Augustine's theological works as interpretive works, and he engaged with positions taken from the breadth of the bishop's corpus. Nevertheless, a strand can be delineated, that while not exhausting Augustine's genius, does represent some of the important issues that Calvin received and rejected. Perhaps, Calvin was "an" *Augustinian*, without exhausting the range of being "Augustinian."[16]

Augustine, writing in Book XII of the *Confessions*, considers the task of biblical study, especially in the context of the Church's faith.

> In Bible study all of us are trying to find and grasp the meaning of the author we are reading, and when we believe him to be revealing truth, we do not dare to think he said anything which we either know or think to be incorrect. As long as each interpreter is endeavouring to find in the holy scriptures the meaning of the author who wrote it, what evil is it if an exegesis he gives is one shown to be true by you, light of all sincere souls, even if the author whom he is reading did not have that idea and, though he had grasped a truth, had not discerned that seen by the interpreter?[17]

----

of scripture as carefully or as exhaustively as that of Calvin. To do so would be to take on another full length study. For the sake of space, more will have to be understood on the basis of earlier studies.

[16] Eric Leland Saak notes the wide range of meaning for "Augustinian" in both the late middle ages and in modern historiography in his "The Reception of Augustine in the Later Middle Ages," *The Reception of the Church Fathers in the West: From the Carolingians to the Maurists*, 2 vols., edited by Irena Backus (Leiden: Brill, 1997), 367–373. Saak also notes that there are at least two sides of Augustinianism in the fourteenth century, that of the university and that of the non-university studia.

[17] Augustine, *Confessions*, in 3 volumes, edited by James J. O'Donnell, (Oxford: Oxford University Press, 1992), 1.174. *Confessions*. Translated by Henry Chadwick. (London: Oxford University Press, 1991), Book XII, xviii, (27), pp. 259–260. "Omnes quidem qui legimus nitimur hoc indagare atque comprehendere, quod voluit ille quem legimus, et cum eum veridicum credimus, nihil quod falsum esse vel novimus vel putamus audemus eum existimare dixisse. dum ergo quisque conatur id sentire in scripturis sanctis quod in eis sensit illi qui scripsit, quid mali est si hoc sentiat quod tu, lux omnium veridicarum mentium, ostendis verum esse, etiamsi non hoc sensit ille quem legit, cum et ille verum

This passage raises as many problems and questions as solutions. Does Augustine mean to say that any interpretation which is generally pious can be received in good conscience? Does this mean that a plethora of interpretations, which might denigrate the whole concept of a unifying message of scripture can arise? To study Augustine's interpretation further, let us consider his *De Doctrina Christiana*, in which he sets out his principles and rules for interpreting scripture. This reveals how Augustine was neither capricious nor condoned arbitrariness in Christian faith and exegesis, but offered an integrated hermeneutic of *caritas* as an overarching theme in his theology.

The problem is refined through attention to Augustine's doctrine of inspiration. Augustine held that scripture was the result of the addition of the inspiration of the Holy Spirit, whose purpose cannot be entirely known, to the work of human scribes. The result might be described as an "over-fullness" (*sensus plenior*) of meaning in scripture. Augustine could write with perfect confidence that

> However, sometimes there is not only one but perhaps two or more interpretations are understood from the same words of Scripture. And so, even if the meaning of the writer is unknown, there is no danger, provided that it is possible to show from other passages of the Scriptures that any one of them is in accord with truth... In fact, the author perhaps saw that very meaning, too, in the same words which we are anxious to interpret. And, certainly, the Spirit of God who produced these words through him also foresaw that this very meaning would occur to the reader or listener; further, He took care that it should occur to him because it also is based upon truth. For, what could God have provided more generously and more abundantly in the Holy Scriptures that the same words might be understood in several ways, which other supporting testimonies no less divine endorse?[18]

---

nec tamen hoc senserit?" Hereafter cited as *Confessions*, giving first the Chadwick and then the O'Donnell renderings.

[18] Augustine, *De Doctrina Christiana*, edited by Martin Joseph, (Turnholt: Brepols, 1962), III.xxxvii.38. *Christian Instruction*, translated by John J. Gavigan, The Fathers of the Church, vol. 2, (New York: Cima Press, 1947), III.(38).27, p. 147. Hereafter cited as *Doctrina* for the Latin and *Instruction* for the English, with book, both paragraph numbers, and page numbers. "Quando autem es eisdem scripturae uerbis non unum aliquid, sed duo uel plura sentiuntur, etiam si latet, quid senserit ille, qui scripsit, nihil periculi est, si quodlibet eorum congruere ueritati ex aliis locis sanctarum scripturarum doceri potest; ... Ille quippe auctor in eisdem uerbis, quae intellegere uolumus, et isam sententiam forsitan uidit et certe dei spiritus, qui per eum haec operatus est, etiam ipsam occursuram lecotri uel auditori sine diuitatione praeuidit, immo ut occurreret, quia et ipsa est ueritate subnixa, prouidit. Nam quid in diuinis eloquiis largius et uberis

The Holy Spirit places extra meanings under the first definition,
some of which are intentional, others not. The Bible is a collection of
doctrine, not an infallible text. Some scholars have noted the tendency
in Augustine to see the human authors of the scriptures as little more
than "mere instruments". This tendency allowed him a rather cavalier
attitude towards both textual criticism and original meanings.[19] The
Bible is a book which needs to be interpreted, then. First because of
human lack of knowledge, but also because the Spirit has placed extra
meaning there specifically in it for believers.

Certainly, Augustine's understanding of scripture differed from modern conceptions. However, if anything, this should intensify our interest
in his hermeneutic. As the literal sense, in the modern meaning of that
term, is not the highest for Augustine, and since he accepted a possibility of multiple correct interpretations of a single text, we need to grasp
his unifying principle for scriptural interpretation in order to discern
the coherence of his exegetical work.

Augustine wrote *De Doctrina Christiana* as an aid to understanding and
teaching scripture.[20] This, however, begs further questions. It suggests
that there was a need for help in these two areas, and it advances the
notion that, for Augustine, scripture was a book that, in order to be
properly interpreted, required that meaning be made of every word.
Augustine believed that scripture was like a book that both drew in the
cautious reader and defeated the proud. He could say,

> Those who read indiscreetly are deceived by numerous and varied in-
> stances of obscurity and vagueness, supposing one meaning instead of
> another. In some passages they do not find anything to surmise even

---

potuit diuinitus prouideri, quam ut eadem uerba pluribus intellegantur modis, quos alia
non minus diuina contestantia faciant adprobari?"

[19] Gerald Bonner, "Augustine as Biblical Scholar," in *The Cambridge History of the Bible*:
Vol. 1, *From the Beginnings to Jerome*, edited by P.R. Ackroyd and C.F. Evans, (London:
Cambridge University Press, 1970), 557.

[20] Doctrina, prologue, 1. Instruction, 19. "There are certain precepts for treating
the Scriptures which I think may not inconveniently be transmitted to students, so
that they may profit not only from reading the work of expositors but also in their
own explanations of the sacred writings to others. I have undertaken to explain these
rules to those able and willing to learn, if God our Lord will not deny me, in writing,
those things which He usually suggests to me in thought." "Sunt praecepta quaedam
tractandarum scripturarum, quae studiosis earum uideo non incommode posse tradi,
ut non solum legendo alios, qui diuinarum litterarum operta aperuerunt, sd etiam ipsi
aperiendo proficiant. Haec tradere institui uolentibus et ualentibus discere, si dominus
ac deus noster ea, quae de hac re cogitanti solet suggerere, etiam scribenti mihi non
deneget."

erroneously, so thoroughly do certain texts draw around them the most impenetrable obscurity. I am convinced that this whole situation was ordained by God in order to overcome pride by work and restrains from haughtiness our minds which usually disdain anything they have learned easily.[21]

The literal words of scripture were not enough for Augustine. Far from our own age of literalism, he believed that the Bible was a great classic that was by nature esoteric. Bonner writes strongly, but not incorrectly, that "for Augustine, it is not so much the words of the Bible themselves as the doctrine underlying the words which is important."[22] This conclusion is buttressed by Augustine's own claim that "The man who relies upon faith, hope, and charity and resolutely holds fast to them does not need the Scriptures, except to teach others."[23]

Scripture contains teaching of both signs and things (*rerum vel signorum*).[24] The things which it contains can be organized into three classifications. "There are some things which are to be enjoyed, others which are to be used, others which are enjoyed and used."[25] Enjoyment of a thing is a love or cleaving to something for its own sake, while use of something is the application of that thing to obtain what is desired. The two classifications should not be confused. Augustine clarifies that the things of this world are for use.[26] Therefore, "The proper object of our enjoyment, therefore, is the Father, Son, and Holy Ghost, the Same who are the Trinity, one supreme Being, accessible to all who enjoy Him, if, indeed, He is a thing and not rather the Cause of all things, or, perhaps, both Thing and Cause."[27] In explaining the differences between the two, Augustine determines that there are four kinds of

---

[21] *Doctrina*, II.vi.7. *Instruction*, p. 65. "Sed multis et multiplicibus obscuritatibus et ambiguitatibus decipiuntur, qui temere legunt, aliud pro alio sentiens, quibusdam autem locis, quid uel falso suspicentur, non inueniunt: ita obscure dicta quaedam densissimam caliginem obducunt. Quod totum prouisum esse diuinitus non dubito ad edomandam labore superbiam et intellectum a fastidio reuocandum, cui facile inuestigata plerumque uilescunt."

[22] Bonner, 547.

[23] *Doctrina*, I.xxxix.43. *Instruction*, 59. "Homo itaque fide et spe et caritate subnixus eaque inconcusse retinens non indiget scripturis nisi ad alios instruendos."

[24] *Doctrina*, I.ii.2, *Instruction*, 28.

[25] *Doctrina*, I.iii.3, *Instruction*, 29. "Res ergo aliae sunt, quibus fruendum est, aliae quibus utendum, aliae quae fruuntur et utuntur."

[26] *Doctrina*, I.iv.4, "utendum est hoc mundo," *Instruction*, 30.

[27] *Doctrina*, I.v.5, *Instruction*, 30. "Res igitur, quibus fruendum est, pater et filius et spiritus sanctus eademque trinitas, una quaedam summa res communisque omnibus fruentibus ea, si tamen res et non rerum omnium causa, si tamen et causa."

things to love. The first is God above; the second is ourselves; the third are those equal to us, or other people; and the fourth is that below us, which are our bodies.[28] The key to loving all of these things correctly is the two-fold love commandment of Christ, that "You shall love the Lord your God with all your heart, and with all your soul, and with all your mind, and you shall love your neighbor as yourself."[29] Augustine took literally the explanation that upon these two commandments rested all the law and the prophets.

In explaining this double command, Augustine claims

> He lives a just and holy life who appraises things with an unprejudiced mind. He is a person who has a well-regulated love and neither loves what he ought not, nor fails to love what he should.[30]

The well-regulated, or well-ordered love, is a significant key to Augustinian theology and his hermeneutical principle.

Scripture is occasionally unclear. Sometimes this is to entice the reader to spend more time searching out its truths, and sometimes it is to humble the proud. In either case, there must be some way to handle these obscurities. Although Augustine will later give principles and methods for the interpretation of particular passages, as well as commenting upon others, he gives his overall hermeneutical stance early in *De Doctrina Christiana*. Near the end of Book I, Augustine pronounces that "The summary of all that has been said since we began our discussion of *things* is that we are to realize that the plenitude and the end of the law and of all Sacred Scripture is the love of a thing which is to be enjoyed and the love of another thing which can enjoy that first thing with us, since there is no need for a precept that each one is to love himself."[31] That this hermeneutic contains within it a Platonic restatement of the Matthean two-fold love commandment is

[28] *Doctrina*, I.xxiii.22, "Cum ergo quattuor sint diligenda, unum quod supra nos est, alterum quod nos sumus, tertium quod iuxta nos est, quartum quod infra nos est." *Instruction*, 43.

[29] Matthew 22.37–40.

[30] *Doctrina*, I.xxvii.28, *Instruction*, 47. "Ille autem iuste et sancte uiuit, qui rerum integer aestimator est; ipse est autem, qui ordinatam habet dilectionem, ne aut diligat, quod non est diligendum, aut non diligat, quod diligendum est, aut amplius diligat, quod minus diligendum est, aut aeque diligat, quod uel minus uel amplius diligendum est, aut minus vel emplius, quod aeque diligendum est."

[31] *Doctrina*, I.xxxv.39, *Instruction*, 56. "Omnium, igitur, quae dicta sunt, ex quo de rebus tractamus, haec summa est, ut intellegatur legis et omnium diuinarum scripturarum plenitudo et finis esse dilectio rei, qua fruendum est, et rei, quae nobiscum ea re frui potest, quia, ut s quisque diigat, praecepto non opus est."

no mistake, or chance rendering. Augustine invariably holds that love, or *caritas*, is both the end of the scriptural message as well as the reason for the creation. He affirms this immediately by cautioning against interpretations which do not expose love. "Whoever, then, appears in his own opinion to have comprehended the Sacred Scriptures, or even some part of them, yet does not build up with that knowledge the two-fold love of God and his neighbor, has not yet known as he ought to know."[32] Augustine's work in the second and third books of *De Doctrina Christiana* consistently advances this theme.

Further, this same theme is in Augustine's mind when he discusses in Book XII of the *Confessions* the possibility of plural interpretations. Directly before the passage cited above, Augustine, in the context of a discussion of the interpretation of Genesis 1, states,

> Moreover, the law is good for edification if it is lawfully used, since its end is love out of a pure heart and a good conscience and unfeigned faith. Our master well knows on which two precepts he hung all the law and the prophets. My God, light of my eyes in that which is obscure, I ardently affirm these things in my confession to you. So what difficulty is it for me when these words can be interpreted in various ways, provided only that the interpretations are true?[33]

This consistency is demonstrated almost immediately in the second book. In Augustine's recitation of the seven gifts of the Holy Spirit, the bishop cannot resist the temptation to refer his student once again to his summary of the Christian life. The third step, the step of knowledge, consists of the content of the holy scriptures. And that content will contain "… nothing else except that God must be loved for His own sake, and our neighbor for the sake of God; and to love God with his whole heart, and with his whole soul, and with his whole mind, and his neighbor as himself; that is, that our entire love of our neighbor as also of ourselves is to be referred to God."[34]

---

[32] *Doctrina*, I.xxxvi.40, *Instruction*, 56. "Quisquis igitur scripturas diuinas uel quamlibet carum partem intellexise sibi uidetur, ita ut eo intellectu non aedificet istam geminam caritatem dei et proximi, nondum intellexit."

[33] *Confessions*, XII.xviii.27. *Confessions*, 259. "Ad aedificationem autem bona est lex, si quis ea legitime utatur, quia finis eius est caritas de corde puro et conscientia bona et fide non ficta; et novi magister noster in quibus duobus praeceptis totam legem prophetasque suspenderit. quae mihi ardenter confitenti, deus meus, lumen oculorum meorum in occulto, quid mihi obest, cum diversa in his verbis intellegi possint, quae tamen vera sint?"

[34] *Doctrina*, II.vii.10, *Instruction*, 67. "nihil in eis aliud inuenturus quam diligendum esse deum proper deum et proximum proper deum, illum quidem ex toto corde, ex

In the same way, after Augustine has traced the necessary knowledge and skills for the interpreter of the scriptures, he still cautions the eager new student. "When the student of divine scripture has been instructed in this manner, he should not fail to reflect upon that observation of the Apostle: Knowledge puffs up, but charity edifies."[35] The purpose to which all this effort will be channeled is the building up of charity, without which the effort is wasted.

In the third book of *De Doctrina Christiana*, Augustine continues his paean to the rule of charity. In defining his rules, or methods of interpretation, Augustine states that although the figurative meaning is to be preferred to the literal, one should not attempt to understand the literal in a figurative sense. Realizing immediately that some principle should be given to differentiate between literal and figurative passages, Augustine turns to love. "In general, that method is to understand as figurative anything in Holy Scripture which cannot in a literal sense be attributed either to an upright character or to a pure faith. Uprightness of character pertains to the love of God and of our neighbor; purity of faith, to the knowledge of God and our neighbor."[36] The converse of this statement is also true. When one is attempting to interpret a figurative expression, "… a rule like this is to be heeded; to reflect with careful consideration for a long time upon what is being read until the interpretation is drawn over to the sway of charity. If however this meaning already stands in the text, no figurative meaning is to be given."[37] This two-fold love is the basic message that is to be found in scripture.

Augustine illustrates that basic premise in his consideration of charity and its opposite, lust. "Scripture commands only charity, and censures only lust, and in that manner molds the character of men.", proclaims

---

tota anima, ex tota mente, proximum uero tamquam se ipsum, id est, ut tota proximi, sicut etiam nostri dilectio referatur in deum."

[35] *Doctrina*, II.xli.62, *Instruction*, 114. "Sed hoc modo instructus diuinarum scripturarum studiosus, cum ad eas perscrutandas accedere coeperit, illud apostolicum cogitare non cesset: Scientia inflat, caritas aedificat."

[36] *Doctrina*, III.x.14, *Instruction*, 129. "Et iste omnino modus est, ut quicquid in sermone diuino neque ad morum honestatem neque ad fidei ueritatem proprie referri potest, figuratum esse cognoscas. Morum honestas ad diligendum deum et proximum, fidei ueritas ad cognoscendum deum et proximum pertinet."

[37] *Doctrina*, III.xv.23, *Instruction*, 135. "regula huiusmodi, ut tam diu uersetur diligenti consideratione quod legitur, donec ad regnum caritatis interpretatio perducatur. Si autem hoc iam proprie sonat, nulla putetur figurata locutio."

the bishop.[38] Further, so that none are confused, that charity which Augustine praises is "a motion of the soul whose purpose is to enjoy God for His own sake and one's self and one's neighbor for the sake of God."; that which Augustine deprecates is "a motion of the soul bent upon enjoying one's self, one's neighbor, and any creature without reference to God."[39] These two messages, the commending of charity, and the condemning of lust, make up the whole of the corpus of scripture. The only differences from this rule will be of time, not of substance.

Augustine adds one more consideration which, although it will clarify his final position, does not immediately seem to participate in his construction of an integrated hermeneutic. This is his emphasis on human agency. This apparent oddity, however, is leading to Augustine's intertwining of his *caritas* hermeneutic with its proper domicile, the Church. Hence, the reader finds at the very beginning of *De Doctrina Christiana* a caution against those who would scorn human agency in spreading the gospel. "We should guard against such presumptuous and perilous snares. Instead, we should reflect that the Apostle Paul himself, even though he was thrown to the ground and instructed by the divine Voice from heaven, was nevertheless sent to a human being to receive the sacraments and be united to the Church."[40] Augustine cites other examples from scripture, such as the centurion Cornelius, the Ethiopian eunuch, and Moses listening to his father-in-law. All these demonstrate that God is willing "transmit his word to men through human means. ... Indeed, charity itself, which holds men together in a knot of unity, would not have a means of infusing souls and almost mixing them together if men could teach nothing to men."[41] Augustine

---

[38] *Doctrina*, III.x.15, *Instruction*, 130. "Non autem praecipit scriptura nisi caritatem nec culpat nisi cupiditatem et eo modo informat mores hominum."

[39] *Doctrina*, III.x.16, *Instruction*, 130. "motum animi ad fruendum deo propter ipsum et se atqu proxim propter deum", "motum animi ad fruendum se et proximo et uolibet ooropro non propter deum".

[40] *Doctrina*, prologue.6, *Instruction*, 22. "Caueamus tales temptationes superbissimas et periculosissimas magisque cogitemus et ipsum apostolum Paulum, licet diuina et caelesti uoce prostratum et instructum, ad hominem tamen missum esse, ut sacramenta perciperet atque copularetur ecclesiae."

[41] *Doctrina*, prologue.6, *Instruction*, 23. "per homines hominibus deus uerbum suum ministrare nolle uideretur. ... Deinde ipsa caritas, quae sibi homines inuicem nodo unitatis adstringit, non haberet aditum refundendorum et qusi miscendorum sibimet animorum, si homines per homines nihil discerent.transmit his word to men through human means. ... Indeed, charity itself, which holds men together in a knot of unity,

confirms this priority of the Church when he places it in the authoritative position in questions of canon.[42] The Church is the Body of Christ, the home where the scriptures rightly belonged, and the refuge where the encounter with the triune God, who is the matter, the inspirer, and the goal of the scriptures is regularly experienced through the sacramental life. It has been asserted that for Augustine, it was "within the Church that scripture is to be understood, it is by her authority that its truth is guaranteed."[43]

As far as some of the first questions are concerned, Augustine is neither capricious, nor even willing to allow any pious interpretation, regardless of the warrant of the text. He instructs that should someone understand something in the scriptures other than the author had in mind, even though that person might reach an interpretation which builds up charity, that person must be corrected. Otherwise, the neophyte interpreter will eventually run into other passages which are impossible to reconcile with his interpretation. Frustrated by this situation, he will finally allow himself to become vexed with scripture. Then, faith will be unable to accept the testimony of the scriptures, and without faith, even charity will weaken. Augustine considers this process in a penetrating analysis of the believing consciousness, and with the sure touch of the experienced teacher.

> But anyone who understands in the Scriptures something other than that intended by them is deceived, although they do not lie. However, as I

---

would not have a means of infusing souls and almost mixing them together if men could teach nothing to men."

[42] *Doctrina*, II.viii.12, *Instruction*, 69. "In the matter of canonical Scriptures he should follow the authority of the greater number of catholic Churches, among which are those which have deserved to apostolic seats and to receive epistles. He will observe this rule concerning canonical Scriptures, that he will prefer those accepted by all catholic Churches to those which some do not accept; among those which are not accepted by all, he should prefer those which are accepted by the largest number of important Churches to those held by a few minor Churches of less authority. If he discovers that some are maintained by the larger number of Churches, others by the Churches of weightiest authority, although this condition is not likely, he should hold them to be of equal value." "In canonicis autem scripturis, ecclesiarum catholicarum quam plurium auctoritatem sequatur, inter quas sane illae sint, quae apostolicas sedes habere et epistolas accipere meruerunt. Tenebit igitur hunc modum in scripturis canonicis, ut eas, quae ab omnibus accipiuntur ecclesiiis catholicis, praeponat eis, quas quidam non accipiunt; in eis uero, quae non accipiuntur ab omnibus, praeponat eas, quas plures grauioresque accipiunt, eis, quas pauciores minorisque auctoritatis ecclesiae tenent. Si autem alias inuenerit a pluribus, alias a grauioribus haberi, quamquam hoc inuenire non possit, aequalis tamen auctoritatis eas habendas puto."

[43] Bonner, 553.

began to explain, if he is deceived in an interpretation which builds up charity, which is the end of the commandments, he is deceived in the same way as a man who leaves a road by mistake but passes through a field to the same place toward which the road itself leads. But he is to be corrected and shown that it is more useful not to leave the road, lest the habit of deviating force him to take a crossroad or a perverse way. xxxvii. In asserting rashly that which the author before him did not intend, he may find many other passages which he cannot reconcile with his interpretation. If he acknowledges these to be true and certain, his first interpretation cannot be true, and under these conditions it happens, I know not why, that, loving his own interpretation, he begins to become angrier with the Scriptures than he is with himself. And if he thirsts persistently for the error, he will be overcome by it. For we walk by faith and not by sight, and faith will stagger if the authority of the Divine Scriptures wavers. Indeed, if faith staggers, charity itself languishes. And if anyone should fall from faith, it follows that he falls also from charity, for a man cannot love that which he does not believe to exist.[44]

In short, Augustine constructs a *caritas* hermeneutic as a guide because he has already ascertained that *caritas* is the basic message of the Bible. This is far different from setting a rule before knowing scripture or the love of God mediated through the Church, a rule which attempts to force scripture into a Procrustean bed.

To conclude, Augustine built a *caritas* hermeneutic which interacted with his doctrine of the Church. Viewing the Bible as a document which contains both clear and obscure passages, and as a deposit of faith which demands figurative interpretation, the Bishop of Hippo sets *caritas* as the hermeneutical principle which will arbitrate in disputes. However, this *caritas* always has two directions. The first is clear, it is the enjoyment and delight in the Trinity. This might be called the vertical axis. But there is a horizontal axis, which is just as vital, and which has

---

[44] *Doctrina*, I.xxxvi.41–xxxvii.41. *Instruction*, 59. "Sed quisquis in scripturi aliud sentit quam ille, qui scripsit, illis non mentientibus fallitur, sed tamen, ut dicere coeperam, si ea sententia fallitur, qua adificet caritatem, quae finis praeccpti est, ita falitur, ac si quisquam errore deserens uiam eo tame per agrum pergat, quo etiam uia illa perducit. Corrigendus est tamen et, quam sit utilius uiam non deserere, demonstrandum est, ne consuetudine deuiandi etiam in transuersum aut peruersum ire cogatur. xxxvii. Adserendo enim temere, quod ille non sensit, quem legiit, plerumque incurrit in alia, quae illi sententiae contexere nequeat. Quae si uera et certa esse consentit, illud non possit uerum esse, quod senserat, fitque in eo nescio quomodo, ut amando sententiam suam scripturae inciiat offensior esse quam sibi. Quod malum si serpere siuerit, euertetur ex eo. Per fidem enim ambulamus, non per speciem; titubabit autem fides, si diuinarum scripturarum uaccillat auctoritas. Porro fide titubante caritas etiam ipsa languescit. Nam si a fide quisque ceciderit, a caritate etiam necesse est cadat; non enim potest diligere, quod esse non credit."

also been commanded. This is the enjoyment of the neighbor in God. This horizontal axis is best represented by the Church.

This particular hermeneutic is more than simply a methodology, or even a principle of interpretation. *Caritas* integrates several Augustinian themes. *Caritas* is Christian life, and the Christian goal. It is both the road and the objective. The command to love is two-fold, dictating the love of God and of the neighbor. But that God is also the Christ, whose body is made up of our Christian neighbors. The love of the neighbor is rightly done through God, allowing believers to enjoy that which is not highest for the sake of the highest. For Augustine, finally, *caritas* moves the faithful (*viator*) ever onward toward the goal of delight in God, which is the end of all humanity.

Even in their most diametrically opposed statements, Calvin and Augustine betray a central concern for edification. As noted above, Calvin simply will not state that "As long as each interpreter is endeavouring to find in the holy scriptures the meaning of the author who wrote it, what evil is it if an exegesis he gives is one shown to be true by you, ... even if the author whom he is reading did not have that idea and, though he had grasped a truth, had not discerned that seen by the interpreter?" This is too great a degree of imprecision for Calvin. However, that significant difference should not allow the modern interpreter of Calvin and Augustine to be led astray from another truth, which is that the two commentators are absolutely conjoined in their idea of the purpose of the study of the scriptures as the search for edifying truth.

In considering the character of the scriptures, Calvin and Augustine are frequently so close as to seem to echo each other across the centuries. Augustine finds the idiosyncrasies of the scripture to be intentional to humble the proud and restrain the haughty. Those same concerns are in Calvin's letter to Grynaeus, where he writes that since God has so ordered it, no one can have a perfect understanding of the scripture alone, thus forcing scholars into company with each other.[45] The same battle against pride, the same encouragement to virtue through the divided and difficult character of the texts, shines as brightly in the Strasbourg study as it did in Hippo.

There are several obvious parallels between Calvin and Augustine that require further investigation. First, both agree that the study of scripture is about the receiving of knowledge.[46] Further, the humility

---

[45] Romans comm. Dedicatory epistle to Grynaeus, Ad Romanos, 3.110.
[46] The most penetrating study of the reception of knowledge in Calvin's theology

inherent in receiving the scriptures through human agency has been too frequently passed over in both theologian's writings. These musings offer grist for another mill, or at least for another day. For this study, we must demonstrate some of the parallels more explicitly. Perhaps the best method for considering the two theologian's stances toward the task of interpretation is to compare Augustine's text with specific passages from Calvin. For Augustine, that text comes from *De Doctrina Christiana*, and has already been discussed briefly.

> But anyone who understands in the Scriptures something other than that intended by them is deceived, although they do not lie. However, as I began to explain, if he is deceived in an interpretation which builds up charity, which is the end of the commandments, he is deceived in the same way as a man who leaves a road by mistake but passes through a field to the same place toward which the road itself leads. But he is to be corrected and shown that it is more useful not to leave the road, lest the habit of deviating force him to take a crossroad or a perverse way. xxxvii. In asserting rashly that which the author before him did not intend, he may find many other passages which he cannot reconcile with his interpretation. If he acknowledges these to be true and certain, his first interpretation cannot be true, and under these conditions it happens, I know not why, that, loving his own interpretation, he begins to become angrier with the Scriptures than he is with himself. And if he thirsts persistently for the error, he will be overcome by it. For we walk by faith and not by sight, and faith will stagger if the authority of the Divine Scriptures wavers. Indeed, if faith staggers, charity itself languishes. And if anyone should fall from faith, it follows that he falls also from charity, for a man cannot love that which he does not believe to exist.[47]

---

remains that of Edward A. Dowey Jr., first published in 1952. Still available in its third edition, which is not a revision, but simply adds appendices, the work does not compare Calvin's theory of the reception of knowledge of God with that of Augustine. See *The Knowledge of God in Calvin's Theology*, 3rd ed., (Grand Rapids, MI: Wm. B. Eerdmans, 1994).

[47] *Doctrina*, I.xxxvi.41-xxxvii.41. *Instruction*, 59. "Sed quisquis in scripturi aliud sentit quam ille, qui scripsit, illis non mentientibus fallitur, sed tamen, ut dicere coeperam, si ea sententia fallitur, qua adificet caritatem, quae finis praecepti est, ita falitur, ac si quisquam errore deserens uiam eo tame per agrum pergat, quo etiam uia illa perducit. Corrigendus est tamen et, quam sit utilius uiam non deserere, demonstrandum est, ne consuetudine deuiandi etiam in transuersum aut peruersum ire cogatur. xxxvii. Adserendo enim temere, quod ille non sensit, quem legiit, plerumque incurrit in alia, quae illi sententiae contexere nequeat. Quae si uera et certa esse consentit, illud non possit uerum esse, quod senserat, fitque in eo nescio quomodo, ut amando sententiam suam scripturae incipiat offensior esse quam sibi. Quod malum si serpere siuerit, euertetur ex eo. Per fidem enim ambulamus, non per speciem; titubabit autem fides, si diuinarum scripturarum uaccillat auctoritas. Porro fide titubante caritas etiam ipsa

Certain similarities are immediately apparent. First, both Augustine and Calvin are dealing here with the possibilities of misinterpretation. Though they have arrived at this issue differently, once arrived, they are quite similar. Augustine, considering the possibility of a false, though charitable interpretation, is concerned about right answers wrongly reached. He brings up the issue of reaching the destination across the field (*agrum*). Is it too far a stretch to hear Calvin echoing this when he worries about that reader who wanders here and there (*cà et là*)?[48] And Augustine's control on the vexation of the reader, the way in which this is to be avoided, is to maintain that sense intended by the scriptures, which he defines as the sense of the author. Calvin does the same thing, by maintaining the ideal of interpretation as explicating the mind of the author. Both display a pastoral and pedagogical concern for the safety of their charges, and hold that without a sure and certain guide to interpretation, the Bible offers at least a difficult, and perhaps dangerous, text to the uninitiated.

Finally, in proposing a hermeneutic which does not strictly rely upon the Church's authority, but is proven in a functional manner, while maintaining the centrality of the Church's position in interpretation, Augustine provides Calvin with a model for his own emphasis on practical edification of members of Christ's body.[49] Indeed, the key for both theologians in approaching the scriptures is a "dispositional" exegetical attitude, a certain teachableness which will allow the formation of the reader in right religion. This is the key to Calvin's insistence on correct religion—it is here where his reception of the Church's tradition is to be found most strongly.

---

languescit. Nam si a fide quisque ceciderit, a caritate etiam necesse est cadat; non enim potest diligere, quod esse non credit."

[48] Argument du Present Livre, OS 3.7.24.

[49] This is not to say that I do not recognize the impact of Augustine's other hermeneutical statements, such as the *regula fidei*. As noted, the point of this is not to say that Calvin was the wholly faithful receiver of Augustine, but rather the transformer of the orthodox religious tradition. In that effort, it is only greater proof to see Calvin ignoring Augustine's rule which is tied to an establishment which Calvin cannot support. Calvin did not permit private interpretation. However, to state the obvious, Calvin's and Augustine's ecclesiologies were significantly different, and were responses to different stimuli.

Augustine's Prodigal Heir?

We have been considering Calvin's Augustinianism, or rather his grasp of the tradition through Augustinianism, and we have noted both the "Augustinian character" of his theology and the distinctively non-Augustinian character of his exegesis. Does this suggest that Calvin was simply confused? An Augustinian with a non-Augustinian cast to his model of interpretation? Was he a sort of prodigal who returns to the ancestral home of doctrine, but has sojourned in a far country in his exegetical model? Or might a stronger conclusion be drawn, that Calvin's Augustinian character has been rather over-emphasized by recent scholarship?

Certainly, Calvin's exegetical model differs significantly from that of Augustine, and of many Augustinian exemplars. To consider the differences between Calvin and Augustine alone would take a volume as thick as Smits' tracing of Calvin's use of Augustine. The difference between Calvin's and Augustine's exegetical models can be seen most readily in considering the latter's more fanciful allegorical readings. Augustine could, in a treatise on the signification of scripture, produce such an interpretation as this famous example.

> But why is it, I ask, that if anyone says this he delights his hearers less than if he had said the same thing in expounding that place in the Canticle of Canticles where it is said of the Church, as she is being praised as a beautiful woman, "Thy teeth are as flocks of sheep, that are shorn, which come up from the washing, all with twins, and there is none barren among them?" Does one learn anything else besides that which he learns when he hears the same thought expressed in plain words without this similitude? Nevertheless, in a strange way, I contemplate the saints more pleasantly when I envisage them as the teeth of the Church cutting off men from their errors and transferring them to her body after their hardness has been softened as if by being bitten and chewed. I recognize them most pleasantly as shorn sheep having put aside the burdens of the world like so much fleece, and as ascending from the washing, which is baptism, all to create twins, which are the two precepts of love, and I see no one of them sterile of holy fruit.[50]

---

[50] *Doctrina*, II.vi.7, 35.15–36.29. "Quid est ergo, quod, si haec quisquam dicat, minus delectat audientem, quam si ad eundem sensum locum illum exponat de Canticis canticorum, ubi dictum est ecclesiae, cum tamquam pulchra quaedam femina laudaretur: *Dentes tui sicut grex detonsarum ascendens de lauacro, quae omnes geminos creant, et sterilis non est in illis?* Num aliud homo discit, quam cum illud planissimis uerbis sine similitudinis huius

Calvin could never share such a reading. However, it is possible to draw this particular line too strongly between Augustine and Calvin. Although Augustine may ask what the harm is in finding a meaning not intended by the author, he knows very well what the harm is, and so warns against making haphazardly fortuitous exegesis a constant crutch. Augustine instructs that should someone understand something in the scriptures other than what the author had in mind, even though that person might reach an interpretation which builds up charity, that person must be corrected.[51] Calvin would have no problem agreeing with this portion of Augustine's theory, although he may have scolded the bishop for creating the possibility of such an error by a too permissive exegetical scheme.

The distinction between hermeneutic principles and exegetical rules provides the most helpful vantage point for considering the problem at hand. Calvin's exegetical rules, and needs of application, differed considerably from those of Augustine. The sixteenth-century Genevan reformer molded his interpretation to fit the needs of a community very different from that of fifth-century North Africa. Nevertheless, the hermeneutical principles remain largely the same.

What are the reasons for Calvin's change of rules that give such a different look and feel to his exegesis from that of Augustine? Many can be extracted from a study of Geneva in the middle of the sixteenth century. Four general reasons suggest themselves: atheism, the issue of authority in the Reformation, implications of literacy in bourgeois culture, and Calvin's understanding of useful theology.

---

adminiculo audiret? Et tamen nescio quomodo suauius intueor sanctos, cum eos quasi dentes ecclesiae uideo praecidere ab erroribus homines atque in eius corpus emollita duritia quasi demorsos mansosque transferre. Oues etiam iucundissime agnosco detonsas oneribus saecularibus tamquam uelleribus positis et *ascendentes de lauacro*, id est de baptismate, creare *omnes geminos*, duo praecepta dilectionis, et nullam esse ab isto sancto fructu sterilem uideo."

[51] *Doctrina*, I.xxxvii.41, 58. "If he allows this error to creep in, he will be utterly destroyed by it. For we walk by faith and not by sight. Faith will totter, if the authority of the Sacred Scriptures wavers. Indeed, even charity itself grows weak, if faith totters." "Quod malum si serpere siuerit, euertetur ex eo. Per fidem enim ambulamus, non per speciem; titubabit autem fides, si diuinarum scripturarum uaccillat auctoritas. Porro fide titubante caritas etiam ipsa languescit."

Atheism

One of the first differences between Calvin and Augustine, as well and perhaps more emphatically between Calvin and some of the paradigmatic "Augustinians", was the presence of atheism. Those who would scoff at such a statement, and immediately hold up Augustine's frequent battles with various pagan opponents, should remember that those opponents, when not heterodox, were pagan, with the modern definition of that term. Augustine's opponents rarely questioned the existence of a higher being, but disagreed with Augustine on the nature and name of that being. On the other hand, modern interpreters have concluded that atheism was a significant challenge to Calvin.[52]

Atheists fell into two groups, for Calvin. The first attempted to set themselves free from God's judgment and actions in the world, though they did not deny God's existence. The second group took the next logical step, the removal of God from the conscience.[53] It is beyond the scope of this study to attempt to state with clarity those specific figures

---

[52] Serene Jones, in her *Calvin and the Rhetoric of Piety*, Columbia Series in Reformed Theology, (Louisville: Westminster John Knox Press, 1995), considers Calvin's rhetorical attack upon "atheists" as a rhetorical device, which Calvin uses to describe some humanist scholar enemies, including Agrippa, Servetus, and Rabelais. Depending heavily upon Febvre's analysis, Jones concludes that there were no atheists in the modern sense, but only those persons whose doctrine of God was so defective that Calvin found this term rhetorically useful against them. She then speculates that Calvin's own attack expands the rhetorical framework of his age, creating the possibility for true atheism. She writes "Calvin may have textually generated, in his grand rhetorical fashion, an identity that had as yet no explicit historical referent but would soon be occupied by one of modernity's most interesting characters, that very alive and popular foe known to later generations of Enlightenment theologians as the intellectual atheist." (174) This position seems historically unprovable, and highly problematic. Beyond other criticisms, it would gnaw at the heart of Jones' thesis, that Calvin is the master rhetor, drawing his audience's wills through his persuasive oratory. No master rhetor places such a timebomb in his rhetoric. Randall Zachman, in his *The Assurance of Faith: Conscience in the Theology of Martin Luther and John Calvin*, (Minneapolis: Fortress Press, 1993), has argued for a different interpretation, holding out a "functional atheism" as the referent for Calvin's atheist foes. He cites several passages in the commentaries and *Institutes* to claim that "Calvin considers the denial of God's judgment to be atheism; this makes it clear that he is less concerned with theoretical atheism than with practical atheism. Those whose impiety has reached the level of malice (*malitia*) may acknowledge the existence of some god or gods–as did the Epicureans–but by depriving God of judgment, they essentially deny God." (111) This is a far more satisfying solution to the textual evidence, which does not run afoul of the *Annalists*.

[53] Zachman, 110–112.

whom Calvin found to be in either camp,[54] but speculation about figures such as Machiavelli, writing political philosophy not grounded in God's eternal decrees,[55] Rabelais, treating the Church so harshly, and thus besmirching the true Church, and Servetus, spreading error against which he had been warned, easily spring to mind.

The presence of such opponents, and the spread of their ideas and influence, forced Calvin to make certain moves not incumbent upon Augustine. Thus, his shift toward the most highly regarded textual interpretive model among the lettered elite can be seen partly as an acceptance of the battlefield of Renaissance humanism. Calvin adopted a model of exegetical practice that attempts to maintain continuity with the important philosophical and legal texts.[56] Thus, although he does not in any way surrender the primacy of God's spirit in the interpretive process, Calvin did employ a style of writing that allowed his work to be read, and to be taken seriously, among those whose very existence he detested.

There was a parallel move in Augustine, who never completely departed from the style and genre of high classical rhetoric, nor shuns the basic philosophical constructs of his own day. The difference between the two authors, therefore, is explained by historical settings and not by theology. Separated by profoundly differing intellectual milieux, both maintained the necessity of speaking and writing in the style most intelligible to the literate elite.

Authority

A second issue between Calvin and Augustine was their conceptions of authority. Calvin could never have written that he could not have believed the gospel if the the Church had not declared it the truth.[57]

---

[54] Bernard Cottret has argued that atheists do come in two forms for Calvin, but differs, when writing about Calvin's polemics he states "Let us say that here atheism includes both those who denied God and the indifferent, who totally rejected the authority of the Bible." Bernard Cottret, *Calvin: A Biography*, 271.

[55] Quirinus Breen, *John Calvin: A Study in French Humanism*, 2nd ed., (New York: Archon Books, 1968), 80ff.

[56] Witness his work on Seneca's *De Clementia*. Ford Lewis Battles has studied this work in his "The Sources of Calvin's Seneca Commentary," in *Interpreting John Calvin*, edited by Robert Benedetto, (Grand Rapids, MI: Baker Book House, 1996), 65–89, and found keys to many of Calvin's mature tendencies, such as the way Calvin handled authorities, his style of analysis, and his ideals of education.

[57] Augustine, *Contra epistolam Manichaei quam vocant fundamenti* v (MPL 42.176; trans-

Naturally, this separated him from Augustine, but the difference can be overdrawn. While Augustine would not have recognized Calvin's ideal of authority, neither could the North African have approved the status claimed by Rome after his death. Calvin understood authority as a grant rather than a right. Authority works on the principle of reasonable judgments made about one's superior in a certain area of knowledge. For instance, laypeople frequently make decisions in areas in which they are not experts. Choosing a doctor is a good example. One makes the judgment that the doctor at a local hospital knows more about health matters, based on a reasoned assumption of his greater knowledge, testified to by various degrees and a license to practice medicine. However, it is the layperson's judgment to make, and should she receive further information upon which to act, she may change her mind. Thus, if the condition which sent her to the doctor in the first place is not alleviated, although she does not become the doctor's superior in medical knowledge, she still may well decide to grant him no further particular authority, and take her case to another doctor.

Of course, this example begs the question, "Did Calvin feel this way about the laity's judgment, especially in the interpretation of scripture?"[58] Commenting upon I Corinthians 14.32, Calvin writes

> Here is another of the reasons why it is necessary for them to take it in turns, because it will sometimes be the case that the other prophets may find fault with something in the teaching given by one of their number. It is not equitable, he writes, that anyone should be above the censure of the others. So what in fact will happen is that opportunities for speaking will sometimes come round again to somebody who was sitting in silence among the congregation. ... This means (as already noted), that nobody is exempt from the censure of others, but that all must be given a hearing, in order that the teaching may be subjected to examination.[59]

---

lated NPNF IV.131), "For my part, I should not believe the gospel except as moved by the authority of the catholic church."

[58] Cottret believes that he does. He wrote, "By exalting the condition of laymen, the Protestant Reformation reinforced the autonomy of the faithful. Calvin perceived very well that his authority itself depended primarily on knowledge and not on power, and he had to give a demonstration of it every day. Nothing guaranteed Calvin any monopoly onf interpretation." Bernard Cottret, *Calvin: A Biography*, 332.

[59] Comm. I Corinthians 14.32, CO 49.530–531. "Haec quoque una est ratio cur alternae vices sint necessariae, quia interdum accidet ut habeant alii prophetae quod reprehendant in unius doctrina. Non aequum est, inquit, quempiam esse extra aleam censurae. Ita fiet ut loquendi vices nonnunquam redeant ad aliquem ex consessu, qui tacens sedebat. ... Significat enim (sicuti iam dixi) neminem eximi aliorum censura: sed omnes hac lege audiendos, ut eorum tamen doctrina ad examen revocetur."

Calvin argued that there is no order of teacher who is above criticism by virtue of office. The alert reader might notice that Calvin here was speaking about a congregation of the prophets. The point could be made that the closest analogue within the contemporary church would either be a company of pastors, or a council of bishops. Did Calvin extend this principle of openness to criticism more widely than intra-ordination?

The answer is an emphatic, though qualified, affirmation. Calvin states that the question of discernment is incumbent upon not only the Church body, but even individual believers. "It is to be held generally, that all who exercise the office of the ministry, from the greatest to the least, are ours, so that we are free not to accept what they teach until they show that it is derived from Christ. Indeed all must be tested and obedience must be given to them only when they have shown that they are true servants of Christ."[60]

This should not be taken too far, for Calvin was hardly a Leveler. He displays a sure and certain identification with the pastor in any disputes about authority within the local church or congregation. However, that identification does not blind him to the need for the use of the mind of the community (*sensus communis*). The private arena of faith Calvin leaves to individual consciences, resting in God. But for the public sphere, that doctrine which the Church will teach, is another matter. Though it is plain that Calvin was worried about a radical threat, the necessity of an agreement among all the faithful remained a standard from which Calvin refused to retreat. That this may seem unwieldy, unworkable, or even plainly impossible in the face of human political dealings was, for Calvin, proof of God's remarkable work.

This same allowance is seen in Calvin's comments upon faith's discernment, and to whom it is given to discern. Commenting upon II Timothy 3.14, Calvin states his position.

> This passage admonishes that we should exercise the same care both to avoid false assurance in matters that are uncertain, all the teachings of humans, that the truth of God may be held with unshaken firmness. We also learn that faith should be joined together with discernment that can distinguish the words of God from human words so that we do

---

[60] Comm. I Corinthians 3.22, CO 49.361. "Caeterum hoc generaliter habendum est, quicunque ministerio funguntur, eos a summo ad infinum usque esse nostros: ut liberum nobis sit ipsorum doctrinam non amplecti, donec a Christo esse ostendant. Probandi enim sunt omnes, et tum demum praestanda illis obedientia, ubi se fideles esse Christi servos demonstraverint."

not accept blindly whatever is offered to us. Indeed, nothing is more alien to faith than an easy credulity that bids us accept everything indiscriminately no matter what its nature or source may be, for the principal foundation of faith is to know that it has its origin and authority in God.[61]

It is absolutely the duty of believers to distinguish whether or not the preached doctrine fits correctly within what they already know of faith from God's Word. Calvin puts forward the possibilities and problems of authority, which, he argues, is both to be granted and constantly judged. This notion of "granted" authority is central to Calvin's view of human interpretation of revelation. The pastor may not perform feats of interpretative acrobatics that leave behind his audiences. This is true whether he is writing or speaking either to new candidates for the ministry, or the congregation of the faithful. Subtle points of philosophizing, as well as the imaginative allegorizations of Augustine, are of little use.

Implications of Literacy

Hand in hand with the last point is the issue of Calvin's general audience, which was much more literate than those of previous Augustinian theologians.[62] This was brought about in sixteenth-century Geneva by

---

[61] Comm. II Timothy 3.14, CO 52.382. "Hic locus admonet, tam sedulo cavendam esse obstinationem in rebus minus compertis (ut sunt omnes hominum doctrinae), quam Dei veritatem inflexa constantia retinendam esse. Praeterea hinc discimus, fidei adiunctam debere esse prudentiam, quae inter Dei et hominum sermonem discernat, ne temere arripiamus quidquid proponitur in medium. Nihil enim a fide magis alienum quam levis credulitas quae promiscue quidvis et a quovis amplecti sustinet. Quia hoc praecipuum est fidei fundamentum, scire Deum sibi esse autorem."

[62] The allusion to Brian Stock's work is intentional. In the introduction to his *The Implications of Literacy: Written Language and Models of Interpretation in the Eleventh and Twelfth Centuries*, (Princeton: Princeton University Press, 1983), Stock writes "The book's principal theoretical tenets may be stated briefly as follows. Before the year 1000— an admittedly arbitrary point in time there existed both oral and written traditions in medieval culture. But throughout the eleventh and twelfth centuries an important transformation began to take place. The written did not simply supersede the oral, although that happened in large measure: a new type of interdependence also arose between the two. In other words, oral discourse effectively began to function within a universe of communications governed by texts. On many occasions actual texts were not present, but people often thought or behaved as if they were. Texts thereby emerged as a reference system both for everyday activities and for giving shape to many larger vehicles of explanation." (3)

Further, in her study of the Renaissance from the perspective of economic history,

the greater availability of more affordable books, and the wider dispersion of vulgar scriptures.[63] Calvin's audience had the possibility, which he actively encouraged, of reading the scriptures as well as commentaries and religious tracts.[64] This enabled them to compare the interpretations of their pastors with their own understandings obtained through reading and discussion.

Lisa Jardine considers the period of the Renaissance as a period of fierce pride in mercantilism and acquisitiveness (33). The buying of fine printed books must be seen as part of the acquisition of status. Thus, another reason for buying books in sixteenth century society is given, that of social status. Added to the fact that many prominent printers, including Jean Crespin, Conrad Badius, and Robert Estienne re-settled in Geneva, all of whose livelihoods depended upon selling books, and a clearer picture of the textuality of the Genevan culture becomes clear. Jardine makes it clear that a growing appetite for buying books accompanied the increasing capability for producing them. "The impact of book culture on the Renaissance depended upon the fact that the staggering escalation in book production in the course of the sixteenth century was consistently driven by commercial pressures. It was market demand as understood by the printer and his backers which determined choices of texts and strategies for distributing them." Lisa Jardine, *Worldly Goods: A New History of the Renaissance*, (New York: Doubleday, 1996), 179–180.

[63] Again, Jardine relates this issue of intellectual history to economic history. "The printed book revolutionized the transmission of knowledge, and permanently changed the attitudes of thinking Europe. Print brought with it many of the features of a book-based culture which in our everyday lives we now take entirely for granted. The scribally produced manuscript was unique (the pagination of each copy would be different); the printed book for the first time allowed two readers to discuss a passage in a work they were both reading by referring to the precise page on which it had occurred. ... The comparatively effortless production of multiple copies meant that printed books could disseminate knowledge much more rapidly, widely and accurately than their handwritten antecedents. The dramatically lower price of the printed book also made written material available for the first time to a large, less privileged readership." Jardine, 177.

[64] Francis Higman, in his *Piety and the People: Religious Printing in French, 1511–1551*, (Brookfield, VT: Ashgate Publishing, 1996), confirms the general suspicion of Calvin supplying ample French language material for those who would read. "Top of the list is quite clearly John Calvin, with 77 editions involving 46 different titles. His position as the leading writer of the French-language Reformation has never been in doubt; but his position is amply confirmed here. Some works are relatively lightweight: short treatises on relics, or on the Lord's Supper, polemics against the Paris theologians, and several extracts from his Institution. Others, however, in particular towards 1550, are substantial texts like commentaries on books of the New Testament. The range of his work is also noteworthy, from solid theology to entertaining polemics, from catechisms to liturgies. His mark is indelible–and is seen as such by the Roman Catholics in the second half of the century, during which a whole genre grows up of replies to Calvin." (5). Obviously, again, the question of sufficient literacy must be answered affirmatively—someone had to be buying these books.

This is significant for several reasons. First, this practical consequence of wider literacy probably was responsible in part for Calvin's denial of the allegorical method of interpreting scripture. That the Church had been well served by allegory for thirteen hundred years was not at stake. However, true allegory bears a certain whimsical character, and allegorical interpretation frequently has a lyrical, rather than arithmetic, relationship to the biblical text. Though Calvin frequently agreed with the doctrine produced in such a fashion, he could not, as a good pedagogue, press such a method before his congregation.

The congregation of Geneva had to hear interpretations of scripture that bore more evident relationships to the scriptural texts. The opposite would be, for Calvin, a recipe for chaos. His ideal preacher resembles a good beginning algebra teacher. When the students encounter difficulty, the steps to the solution can be laid bare before them, and they should be able to follow those steps. The allegorical interpreter, however, takes the same beginning algebra class, and uses calculus to arrive at wonderful answers, which they may sense to be correct, but cannot possibly replicate. For Calvin, the believers must have enough understanding to be able to recognize the truth of the interpretation. The believers may not, and probably cannot, generate those interpretations themselves. The purpose is that they follow the interpretation and grant it authority based on their knowledge. To demonstrate this, Calvin comments upon the task of preaching.

> This is a beautiful metaphor which accurately explains the main goal of teaching. For since we should be content with the word of God alone, what purpose is there in having daily sermons or even in the office of pastor itself? Do not all have the chance to read the scriptures for themselves? But Paul assigns to teachers (*doctoribus*) the duty of carving or dividing it, like a father dividing the bread into small pieces to distribute to his children. He advises Timothy to 'divide correctly', so when cutting the surface, like those without skill, he succeeds only in cutting the surface and leaves the interior portion and marrow untouched. But I understand what is said here to have general application to refer to a prudent distribution of the word, which is correctly regulated to the advancement of those that hear it. Others mutilate it, dismember it, some distort it, some break it in pieces, some, as I have said, keep to the outside and never come to the soul of the matter. With all these faults he contrasts a correct dividing, that is, a manner of exposition formed to edify. This is the rule by which we should judge every interpretation of scripture.[65]

---

[65] Comm. II Timothy 2.15, CO 52.367–368. "Pulchra metaphora, et quae scite

The preacher must use his skill to overcome difficulties in getting at the correct doctrine, but cannot force that correct doctrine upon the congregation from above. Rather, his task is that of the expert, of doing something that others accept to be his specific skill, but a skill and ministry which does not exceed their own by such an order of magnitude that they are unable to follow.

Thus, Calvin is able to have ministers or pastors who have a specific ministry given through the Holy Spirit, but these gifts do not separate them from the congregation so far as to put them beyond criticism by the body of believers. Rather, he sees the Church as a textual community, a community which is constantly engaged in finding its truth in God's revelation, given most clearly in the scriptures. This text is the container of the truth, rather than co-equal with it is a significant distinction, but that does not detract from the necessity of working on the meaning and implications of the central text which grants a certain objectivity to the ineffable into which all are being drawn. Calvin's vision is, therefore, one of reading and teaching, and it is small wonder that so many school metaphors and references are found in his writings.

Theology as Ædificatio

The Church's theology must be useful, it must be upbuilding, and finally, it must profit its hearers.[66] Writing on the nature of doctrine, Calvin states that this is the supreme standard for theology.

---

exprimit praecipuum docendi finem. Nam quum solo Dei verbo contentos esse nos oporteat: quorsum quotidianae conciones et ipsum quoque pastorum munus? Nonne in medio posita est scriptura? At Paulus secandi partes doctoribus assignat: ac si pater alendis filiis panem in frustra secando distribueret. Commendat autem rectam sectionem Timotheo, ne in secando cortice occupatus (ut solent inepti homines) ipsam interiorem medullam intactam relinquat. Quamquam generaliter hoc nomine prudentem verbi distributionem, et quae rite ad auditorii profectum attemperatur, intelligo. Alii enim mutilant, alii discerpunt, alii contorquent, alii disrumpunt, alii in cortice (ut dixi) haerentes non perveniunt ad ipsam animam. His omnibus vitiis opponitur recta sectio: hoc est explicandi ratio ad aedificationem formata. Est enim quasi regula ad quam exigere convenit omnem scripturae interpretationem." Leaving aside the issue that Calvin seems to mix his metaphors of cutting bread and cutting meat, I shall maintain the meat-cutting metaphor.

[66] This is not a theme peculiar to Calvin, Martin Bucer would frequently note that all that takes place in the church is subservient to her edification (*aedificatio ecclesiae*). See Willem van't Spijker, "Bucer's influence on Calvin: church and community," 32–

He judges doctrine by the fruit. Everything that does not edify should be rejected, even if it has no other fault. Further all that serves only to excite controversy should be doubly condemned. These are all these subtle questions on which ambitious men exercise their ingenuity. We must remember therefore, that this is the rule for the testing of all doctrines. Those that tend to edification may be approved, but those that give materal for fruitless controversies are to be rejected as unworthy of the church of God.[67]

Thus, Calvin needs not only a doctrine that will be helpful, but one that is, from its foundation onward, intelligible.[68] The Church is always to be upbuilt into Christ, but through understanding and correction of the human will. Here, Calvin is not out of tune with Augustine, but is fighting a phenomenon of which Augustine knew nothing—university theology. Here, one finds the greatest difference between Calvin and the scholastics. Not a doctrinal difference, not even a methodological difference, although those are both great. For Calvin, the task of theology is eminently practical. It cannot be, and never becomes, a university discipline, where various possibilities are considered in the realm of theoretical understanding. Aquinas can opine concerning *sacra doctrina* that "All the same it is more theoretical than practical, since it is mainly concerned with the divine things which are, rather than with things men do; it deals with human acts only in so far as they prepare men for that achieved knowledge of God on which their eternal bliss reposes."[69]

---

44 in *Martin Bucer: Reforming Church and Community*, edited by D.F. Wright, (Cambridge: Cambridge University Press, 1994), 39 ff.

[67] Comm. I Timothy 1.4, CO 52.252. "Aestimat a fructu doctrinam. Quaecunque enim non aedificat, repudianda est, etiamsi nihil aliud habeat vitii: quaecunque vero ad concertationes solum excitandas valet, duplici nomine damnanda est. Tales porro sunt omnes argutiae quibus ingenium suum ambitiosi homines exercent. Meminerimus ergo ad hanc regulam exigendas esse omnes doctrinas, ut ea demum probetur quae ad aedificationem facit: quae vero disceptationum materiam praebent absque fructu, respuantur tanquam ecclesia Dei indignae. Hoc examen si fuisset aliquot supra saeculis observatum, etiamsi multis erroribus contaminata fuisset religio: saltem non adeo invaluisset diabolica ista ars litigandi, quae scholasticae theologiae nomen obtinuit. Quid enim illic continetur praeter rixas, aut otiosas speculationes, unde nullus profectus redit? Proinde quo quisque in ea doctior, eo miserior iudicandus est."

[68] Here again Calvin joins a theme of Erasmus. "Theology has to do with life rather than with the syllogistic arguments of the scholastics, who quibble over contentious questions by means of dialectics and Aristotelian philosophy." Manfred Hoffmann, *Rhetoric and Theology: The Hermeneutic of Erasmus*, (Toronto: University of Toronto Press, 1994) 38.

[69] Aquinas, Summa Theologiae, Ia. I, 4. Blackfriars edition, (London: Eyre & Spottiswoode, 1958), 16. "Magis tamen est speculativea quam practica, quia principalius agit de rebus divinis quam de actibus humanis; de quibus agit secundum quod per eos

For Calvin, this is not so.[70] The shift is clearly from a priority of speculation to application, from theoretical knowledge (*episteme*) to practical knowledge (*phronesis*). It may even be that the difference is that between university and seminary, but that question has not yet been fully answered.[71]

Example from Commentary

Did Calvin truly hold to the practical ideal of theology? One of the texts that speak most succinctly to this issue is Calvin's commentary upon the two books of Timothy. Calvin's first words on the book in his Dedicatory Epistle of 1556, written to Edward, Duke of Somerset, state that the books of Timothy are wonderful for the Church.[72] Calvin's commentary upon them sheds ight upon his ideals in very practical and ecclesiastical matters. He describes the Christian life as a school of the soul, or a continual progress. Calvin sees the regenerate life as a life of progress (*profectum*).[73]

This progress is a never-ending state here on earth as believers are called to learn more in the school of God, and advance ever higher.[74]

---

ordinatur homo ad perfectam Dei cognitionem in qua beatitudo aeterna consistit."

[70] David Bagchi and David Steinmetz have pointed out that "A point which can never be made too often is that the theologians of the Reformation were not ivory-tower academics. Their principles tasks were in most cases pastoral, and we derive their theologies from utterances from the pulpit, from spiritual advice given in letters, from rushed polemical outbursts, in the midst of persecution." "The Scope of Reformation Theology," in *The Cambridge Companion to Reformation Theology* (Cambridge: Cambridge University Press, 2004), 4.

[71] See Karin Maag's *Seminary of University? The Genevan Academy and Reformed Higher Education, 1560–1620*, (Aldershot, England: Scolar Press, 1995), for the fullest treatment yet available.

[72] Comm. I and II Timothy, dedicatory epistle, CO 52.245.

[73] Comm. Ephesians 1.16, Ad Ephesios 169.20–170.4. "To thanksgiving, as is his custom, he adds prayer, in order to stimulate them to further progress. It was necessary that the Ephesians should understand that they had entered upon the right course, so they would not turn aside to some new kind of doctrine. It was also that they should know that they must proceed farther; for nothing is more dangerous than to be satisfied with what we have of spiritual benefits. However strong may be our virtues, let us always aim at further progress." "Gratiarum actioni, more suo, adiungit precationem, ut eos stimulet ad ulteriorem profectum. Nam utrunque necesse erat: ut intelligerent Ephesii rectum cursum se esse ingressos, ne ad novum doctrinae genus se reflecterent, et tamen sibi longius pergendum esse scirent. Nam spiritualium bonorum satietate nihil periculosius. Ergo quantacunque excellentia polleamus, semper accedat proficiendi studium."

[74] Comm. Ephesians 3.16, Ad Ephesios 213.21–24. "Paul wants the Ephesians to

They are propelled forward as an effect of their regeneration and like pupils advance from one grade of school to the next.[75] Unlike children, however, their schooling is never finished. The life of believers is like adolescence, not yet adulthood, and yet having left childhood behind.[76] Calvin represents the germinal presence of the indwelling of Christ in the believer, and the yet-hoped-for fulfillment.

This adolescence should lead inexorably toward two goals for Calvin: holiness, which pertains more to the first table of the law, and righteousness, which concerns the second table.[77] They are united in the regeneration of believers into the image of God.[78]

---

be strengthened, although he had already given their piety no common praise. But believers have never advanced so far as not to to need to grow more. The highest perfection of the pious in this life is an earnest desire to progress." "Optat Paulus roborari Ephesios, quibus non vulgarem pietatis laudem ante tribuerat. Sed nunquam eousque progressi sunt fideles, quin adhuc crescendum sit. Summa itaque piorum in hac vita perfectio est proficiendi studium."

[75] Comm. II Timothy 1.6, CO 52.349. "The more abundantly the grace of God was given to Timothy, all the more intent he ought to be in his desire to make daily advancement." "Quo ampliore Dei gratia praeditus erat Timotheus, eo magis illum intentum esse debere significat ad quotidiani profectus studium."

[76] Comm. Ephesians 4.14, Ad Ephesios 234.22–29. "But those are truly founded in the doctrine of Christ, who although not yet perfect, have so much prudence and strength as to know what is best, and proceed steadily in the right course. Thus the life of believers, which is marked by desire and progress toward their appointed state, is like adolescence. When therefore I said that in this life we are never men, this ought not to be taken to the other extreme, as they say, as if there were no progress beyond childhood. After we are born in Christ, we ought to grow, so as not to be children in understanding." "Qui autem vere fundati sunt in Christi doctrina, tametsi nondum perfecti sint, habent tamen tantum prudentiae et roboris, ut sciant deligere, quid sit optimum, et constanter pergant in recto cursu. Ita fidelium vita, quae assiduo profectu ad statum suum gradum aspirat, adulescentiae similis est. Quod ergo dixi nunquam in hac vita nos esse viros, non debet trahi ad alterum extremum, quod vocant, acsi non fieret progressus extra pueritiam. Nam postquam Christo nati sumus, debemus adolescere, ita ut non simus intelligentia pueri."

[77] Comm. Ephesians 4.24, Ad Ephesios 245.26–31. "If righteousness is accepted in general as uprightness, holiness will be something higher, that is the purity by which we are consecrated to God. I am rather inclined to make the distinction that holiness pertains to the first table of the Law, and righteousness to the second. Thus, it is given in the song of Zacharias, 'That we may serve in holiness and righteousness all the days of our life.'" "Iustitiam pro rectitudine si generaliter accipias, sanctitas quiddam erit altius, hoc est: puritas, qua sumus Deo consecrati. Verum non displicet ita distingui, ut sanctitas quidem ad primam Legis tabulam, iustitia autem ad secundam pertineat. Quemadmodum in Cantico Zachariae: Serviamus illi in sanctitate et iustitia omnibus diebus vitae nostrae."

[78] Comm. Ephesians 4.23–24, Ad Ephesios 244.24–245.25.

Having sketched the believer's journey, let us turn to the pastor's task. The key to understanding Calvin's overall message on the nature of the Church's doctrine in his Timothy commentary is to regard the pastoral task and the believer's school as mirrors, mutually reflective. In the same way a school teacher's task is demonstrated by the educational needs and potentials of his or her students, and the students' task is signaled by the teacher's role, so too, for Calvin do the doctrines of the pastoral ministry and the regenerate life mutually inform each other.

Calvin presents a portrait of the pastor in the Timothy commentary. The pastor is one who is the steward of the truth,[79] the teacher of the school, the foster father of the family of God.[80] The pastor's most important and basic task, which is the fount from which all the rest of his activities should flow, is the presentation of edifying doctrine.[81]

That this doctrine must be edifying is the primary consideration when considering the theological task. Calvin is so sure of this that he departs from his customary brevity to add a short treatise upon the task of theology. He makes sure that Paul supports his judgment of doctrine by its fruit.[82] Calvin's consideration of this is a vehement and even vituperative outburst. This is by no means a singular occasion of Calvin's reflection upon the importance of the theme of edification, and the evil of its opposite, useless doctrines. He returns again and again to this theme, sounding it as an organizing *leitmotif* throughout the Timothy commentary.

Calvin seems to speak about two kinds of false doctrine, though placing far greater weight upon one than the other. The first kind "… publicly struggles with the pure doctrine of the gospel,".[83] It is not Calvin's

---

[79] Comm. I Timothy 3.15, CO 52.287–288.
[80] Comm. II Timothy 2.15, CO 52.367. "But Paul assigns to teachers the duty of carving or dividing the Word, like a father dividing the bread into small pieces to feed his children." "At Paulus secandi partes doctoribus assignat; ac si pater alendis filiis panem in frustra secando distribueret."
[81] Parker presents the preacher's role as that of a teacher, depending always upon the one true Teacher. Further, the basis of Christian preaching is edification. T.H.L. Parker, *Calvin's Preaching*, (Louisville: Westminster John Knox Press, 1992), 36, 46. Consider Calvin's discussion of the ministry from Ephesians 4.11 "Teaching is the duty of all pastors; but there is a particular gift of interpreting Scripture, so that sound doctrine may be kept and a man may be a doctor who is not fitted to preach."
[82] Comm. I Timothy 1.4, CO 52.252. See quotation, earlier this chapter.
[83] Comm. I Timothy 1.3, CO 52.251. "quae palam cum pura evangelii doctrina pugnet,".

intention to conquer that particular fault, at least in this context, and he almost shrugs off this instance of false doctrine as possible, but not to the point. It is the second variety for which Calvin saves his (copious) invective. It does not have the character of open attack against true doctrine, but rather is simply non-edifying doctrine. Calvin observes that "It is indeed possible that someone professes no impious or manifest error and yet still corrupts the pious doctrine by futile boastful babbling."[84] Calvin variously calls this kind of theology "vain questions",[85] "curious disputations",[86] "useless speculations",[87] "empty doctrines",[88] "corrupting pure doctrine",[89] "quarrels and useless speculations",[90] and "curious questions".[91] Calvin is absolutely specific here that the main problem is the existence of useless speculative doctrine, which steals time from edifying teaching.[92]

Balancing Calvin's vitriol poured out upon useless theologizing is his careful delineation and acclamation for sound theology. Doctrine is to be judged by the fruit (*Aestimat a fructu doctrinam*) which it produces.[93] Good doctrine is profitable; Calvin claims that doctrine which is not, even if plausible, is useless.[94] Edifying doctrine's effects are clearly seen and are clearly positive. He summarizes

> For it will not be consistent with godliness unless it establishes us in the fear and worship of God, unless it builds up our faith, unless it trains us in patience and humility and all the duties of love. Therefore whoever does not try to teach usefully, does not teach as a teacher

---

[84] Comm. I Timothy 6.3, CO 52.323. "Fieri enim potest ut qui nullum alioqui profitetur impium vel manifestum errorem, futili tamen garrulitate se venditando, pietatis doctrinam adulteret."

[85] Comm. I Timothy Argumentum, CO 52.245. "vanis quaestionibus".

[86] Comm. I Timothy Argumentum, CO 52.245. "curiosas disputationes".

[87] Comm. I Timothy Argumentum, CO 52.247. "otiosis speculationibus".

[88] Comm. I Timothy Argumentum, CO 52.247. "inanibus doctrinis".

[89] Comm. I Timothy, 1.3, CO 52.250. "puram doctrinam adulterabant"

[90] Comm. I Timothy, 1.4, CO 52.252. "Quid enim illic continetur praeter rixas, aut otiosas speculationes, unde nullus profectus redit?"

[91] Comm. I Timothy, 1.7, CO 52.254. "quaestionibus curiosis".

[92] Brian Gerrish agrees, writing, "He [Calvin] did not object to the systematic theology of his day because it was systematic, but because it was abstract, speculative, and unedifying." *Grace and Gratitude: The Eucharistic Theology of John Calvin*, (Philadelphia: Fortress Press, 1993), 17.

[93] Comm. I Timothy 1.4, CO 52.252.

[94] Comm. I Timothy 4.6, CO 52.298. "Nam significat aliis omnibus doctrinis nihil utilitatis inesse: quantumvis sint plausibiles."

should. Whatever spectacle it may make, doctrine is neither pious nor sound unless it tends to the advancement of its hearers.[95]

Again, Calvin creates a functional criterion for judging the adequacy, or more importantly, the acceptability of the given doctrine. Only the doctrine that edifies and builds up the Body of Christ can be allowed within the Church.

Regeneration and edification act as two sides of the same coin. For the laity, Christian progress comes from the sure and certain grasp of at least some portion of the edifying doctrine presented by the pastor. On the other side of the coin, the pastor's task is the need for further up-building seen in the lives of the believers. This mutually reinforcing dynamic between pastoral practice and congregational growth allowed Calvin room to engage creatively with theological problems, such as the need for pastors and the question of pastoral authority.

The pastor's main task is edifying teaching.[96] But what is the nature of that teaching? Furthermore, was that a necessary task in an age of expanding literacy, a time of expanding availability of scriptures in vulgar languages, and given the common emphasis on personal devotion and private scripture reading? Calvin was not unaware of the possible contradictions that arose out of this mix. He chose to address these questions in his comment upon II Timothy 2.15. It is Calvin's comment upon the phrase "dividing aright the word of truth" which is of importance for this study. Calvin felt that this phrase well captured the preacher's task.[97] He extracted a tremendous amount of doctrine from a single metaphor, but we must consider what he gained from this exposition. The more radical Reformers were answered in the protest against privileged pastoral readings of scripture, yet Calvin did not grant an authoritative and definitive exegesis to all pastors by virtue of ordination to an office.

---

[95] Comm. I Timothy 6.3, CO 52.324. "Neque enim pietati consentanea erit, nisi in timore cultuque Dei nos instituat, nisi fidem nostram aedificet, nisi ad patientiam, humilitatem, omnia caritatis officia nos erudiat. Ergo quisquis utiliter docere non studet, secus docet quam oportebat: imo nec pia, nec sana est doctrina, quocunque colore fulgeat, quae ad profectum audientium non tendit."

[96] Erasmus would have agreed with Calvin's emphasis here. For him, "the *officia* of the preachers are *docere*, *delectare*, and *flectere*. Teaching is fundamental because it makes for understanding and persuasion. No one is delighted or moved by that which is neither understood nor believed." *Ecclesiastes sive de Ratione Concionandi*, 274:595–280:723, quoted in Manfred Hoffmann, *Rhetoric and Theology: The Hermeneutic of Erasmus*, (Toronto: University of Toronto Press, 1994), 47.

[97] Comm. II Timothy 2.15, CO52.367–368. See full quotation, earlier in this chapter.

The theme of edification is once again presented. But more significantly the metaphor of meat carving, when considered in conjunction with the model of believers as adolescents, gives subtle nuance to the pastoral teaching role. The message of the scriptures is not to be pureed for the tender digestive tracts of infants. On the other hand, the whole ham or roast is not to be set before the semi-mature. Rather, guidance is given that important and nutritious lessons will not be lost, nor will precious meat be thrown away with the bone.

This pattern of teaching as the correct dividing was further enhanced by Calvin's consideration of the nature of authority. The pastor has authority in the church, that is certain. But what should the nature of that authority be? How should the believers grant authority to their pastor? In his comments upon II Timothy 3.14, Calvin produces a cautionary rule about authority.

> This passage admonishes that we should exercise the same care both to avoid false assurance in matters that are uncertain, all the teachings of humans, that the truth of God may be held with unshaken firmness. We also learn that faith should be joined together with discernment that can distinguish the words of God from human words so that we do not accept blindly whatever is offered to us. Indeed, nothing is more alien to faith than an easy credulity that bids us accept everything indiscriminately no matter what its nature or source may be, for the principal foundation of faith is to know that it has its origin and authority in God.[98]

Calvin makes discrimination the task of believers. When the preacher stands before the congregation and delivers the sermon, his task, for Calvin, is to divide correctly. But the task of the believers is an active listening, a testing of the spirits, a spiritual discernment.[99] The authority

---

[98] Comm. II Timothy 3.14, CO 52.382. "Hic locus admonet, tam sedulo cavendam esse obstinationem in rebus minus compertis (ut sunt omnes hominum doctrinae), quam Dei veritatem inflexa constantia retinendam esse. Praeterea hinc discimus, fidei adiunctam debere esse prudentiam, quae inter Dei et hominum sermonem discernat, ne temere arripiamus quidquid proponitur in medium. Nihil enim a fide magis alienum quam levis credulitas quae promiscue quidvis et a quovis amplecti sustinet. Quia hoc praecipuum est fidei fundamentum, scire Deum sibi esse autorem."

[99] Though Calvin could agree broadly with Erasmus on the nature of the office of the preacher, his confidence in the hearers of preaching far outpaced that of Erasmus. Hoffmann, commenting upon the Ecclesiastes, states that "Except for a brief admonition concerning faithful hearers, Erasmus' comments on the hearers are virtually all negative. Expecting histrionics from the preachers, the impious crowd (vulgus)

accorded a preacher must always be scrutinized; the proclaimed doctrine must be received and considered in the light of what is known to
be from God.

Thus, if Calvin's use of a metaphor about dividing the meat guarded
against a theoretical degradation of the pastor's teaching task, his warning against "easy credulity" defended against the reception of teaching simply on the basis of the human messenger's standing within the
Church. The useless teachings, inventions, or wind of the Scholastics,
are to be rejected. Moreover, these useless teachings are to be rejected
by the believers, on the basis of the failure of the faith test.

Conclusion

This survey of edification in the Timothy commentary demonstrates
two points. First, the nature of the theological task is quite simply the
edification of the Church. This has enormous implications, negative
and positive, for the duties and self-understanding of the theologian.
The negative implications should be sufficiently clear: Calvin will brook
no theology which seeks to know things for the sake of knowledge.
Theology is for the upbuilding of the Church. That which does not
edify, that which is more properly speculative, simply cannot be allowed
the title of theology, or doctrine. The positive implications are less clear
from this particular exposition, but can easily be re-constructed. Since
theology is for the upbuilding of the Church, those doctrines which
can be found clearly within the scriptures, and which are useful for the
continual progress of believers must be taught.

Secondly, there is an unbreakable bond between what the modern
period has come to call the pastoral and the theological tasks. The pastor must know the congregation, and know what is necessary for the
particular congregation. Theology does not exist in a vacuum. The test
of true doctrine is whether it edifies. Doctrine which does not edify simply cannot be tolerated. Thus, the theologian must be searching constantly for the results that are the realization of the doctrine's potency.

Further, there is a mutually enlightening reflection of the teacher's
and believer's tasks. This relationship strengthens the bonds between
the pastoral and theological portions of a minister's work. The progress

---

behaves in the Christian assembly without decorum." Hoffmann, *Rhetoric and Theology:
The Hermeneutic of Erasmus*, (Toronto: University of Toronto Press, 1994), 45.

of the believers acts as a guide to the teacher, maintaining an external mark against which the teaching can be measured; the community of believers functions as the community of discourse for the discernment of truth.

Thus, three of the four concerns which led Calvin away from some of the practices of the earlier tradition are demonstrated. The nature of granted authority, and fact of wider literacy push him toward a "meat-carving" model of the pastoral preaching function. As well, theology as edifying into Christ forms Calvin's standard against which those pastoral and doctoral functions must be measured, and criticized.

Having discussed the frameworks of Calvin's transformational reception of Augustine and the other fathers, we must examine the textual evidence for Calvin's practice. To do so, I am adopting a seemingly odd device of looking specifically at the negative considerations of Augustine in Calvin's Pauline commentaries. That will bring into sharp relief the contrast between Calvin's negative view of Augustine's exegesis and his positive appreciation of the church father's doctrine.

CHAPTER SIX

RECEPTION THROUGH TRANSFORMATION

The transformational reception of the Christian exegetical tradition was the distinctive mark of Calvin's engagement with the patristic and medieval interpretive traditions. It was grounded in his conception of the Church as the classroom of the Lord (*schola Dei*) wherein scripture was the key text. It was the classroom where the congregation must, as far as possible, be trained for the Christian life.

Calvin, Transforming Augustine

With Calvin's specific references to Augustine in his Pauline commentaries, as well as citations of other patristic authorities, we will find him producing ingenious solutions to the questions of receiving the Church's traditions. He recognized his place within the stream of Church history, while seeking to re-direct that stream to water the fields of Geneva in the sixteenth century.[1] The sixteenth century context is crucial, for while the core of the Christian message remained constant, Calvin argued that its appearance was radically historically contingent.

Transformation was central to Calvin's method of receiving tradition. Granting all of Calvin's dependence upon and reverence for his doctrinal mentor, it took the Genevan Reformer no time at all in his exegetical publishing record to differ significantly from the Bishop of Hippo.[2] From his earliest published exegesis, Calvin demonstrated the

---

[1] Though I am taught by the material which the history of exegesis school puts forward, this is not actually that kind of exercise. I am not attempting to find out where all of Calvin's exegetical ideas came from, but rather how he consciously handles prior interpretive authorities.

[2] The name index to *Calvin's New Testament Commentaries*, vv. 8–12 lists forty-nine citations to Augustine in the Pauline commentaries, including Hebrews. The critical editions of Parker and Feld note two more. However, these do not change the number of negative citations. Of all the specific citations to Augustine, places where Calvin notes the bishop of Hippo by name, eleven involve issues where Calvin offers a clear critique of Augustine. That is to say, I am not considering issues where Calvin cites

kind of critique which he would direct toward Augustine's work. In
the 1540 edition of Calvin's commentary on Romans, Calvin speaks
disparagingly of Augustine's interpretation of the significance of the
name "Paul" in Romans 1.1. Calvin himself confides to the reader
that the name Paul does not carry any special significance, and that
too much time should not be spent in clarifying it. He declares that
brevity requires him to say something for those who might be interested
without becoming tedious.[3]

Calvin begins by noting those who have seen special significance
in the name Paul. He writes that some have theorized that he took
the name as a mark of his apostolic office when he converted the
proconsul Sergius.[4] Calvin concludes this was false on the basis of
Luke's testimony.[5] Then Calvin turns to those who conjecture that
the name Paul was given to Saul to mark his conversion to following
Jesus Christ, and he refers to Augustine's acceptance of this theory.
"Augustine, I imagine, approved of this hypothesis simply because it
provided him with the opportunity of some subtle argument in his
discussion."[6] Augustine had, in fact, used the opportunity to play upon
the differences between "*paulum*" and "*saule*".[7] Calvin clearly states this
in the later editions of the Romans commentary, stating that Augustine
had used this opportunity for some subtle philosophizing "... in his
discussion about the exalted Saul who had become the very small

Augustine approvingly, but an Augustine scholar might argue that Calvin is doing
violence to Augustine; this portion of the study is concerned with Calvin's self-conscious
transformations of Augustine's exegesis of the Pauline epistles, represented by those
instances where he felt it critical to name Augustine.

  [3] Comm. Romans 1.1, Ad Romanos 11.14–17.
  [4] Comm. Romans 1.1, Ad Romanos, 11.18–19.
  [5] In the 1540 edition, Calvin simply states "*a Luca ipso confutantur.*" Comm. Romans
1.1, Ad Romanos, 11, 20. In later editions, he adds that Luke's refutation of the point is
that Paul already bore the name before the conversion of Sergius.
  [6] Comm. Romans 1.1, (Ending the quotation with that portion of the translation
that fits the 1540 edition, without the later expansion.) Ad Romanos, 11.22–23. "That
Augustine was pleased with this idea, was so that he could seize the occasion for
clever philosophizing." "Quod Augustino placuisse hoc tantum nomine puto, ut argute
philosophandi occasionem arriperet."
  [7] Augustinus, *Serm. Sanct.* 42, PL 38, 605, 41–45. "Hic autem Apostolus de Saulo
Paulus, hoc est de supebo minumus: Saulus enim a Saule denominatur: paulum autem
modicum est: unde nomen suum quodam modo interpretatus, ait, 'Ego sum minimus
Apostolorum' (Id. Xv,9): ipse ergo Paulus, id est, modicus et mimimus missus ad
Gentes, praecipue ad Gentes se missum dicit." This same distinction is drawn in
Sermo CCCXV, Serm. Div. 93, PL 38, 1429, 32–42.

servant of Christ."[8] In fact, this subtle argument, or perhaps more truly this clever philosophizing, "*argute philosophandi*," breaks two of Calvin's rules of interpretation of the scriptures.[9] First, there is the problem of non-edifying theological material. Secondly, by seizing an opportunity to wax loquacious, Augustine was turning aside from the simple brevity which marks the good interpreter's work. Calvin prefers the solution offered by Origen, that Paul had two names.[10]

Although this was not a point of sincere doctrinal conflict between Calvin and Augustine, it marked a significant difference, best explained by Calvin's Renaissance contextualism opposing Augustine's conviction that each word of the scripture holds meaning. This provides an excellent example of our earlier point about principles and rules. That there was not a truly "doctrinal" difference between Calvin and Augustine comes from their unity in the principles of hermeneutics. The division is rather a contrast between how the two theologians support doctrine from scripture. In Calvin's approach, though scripture still takes a place of honor, every word does not necessarily bear edifying material. This early example from Romans provides significant marks of Calvin's ideal of exegesis, and how he was ready even to criticize his favorite authority if he senses departure from those ideals. Central to the difference between Calvin and Augustine in this case was the former's insistence on simplicity and brevity as a hallmarks of true exegesis.

This example illustrates three ways in which Calvin saw himself to be purifying the tradition. First, he believed that on the basis of other biblical evidence that Augustine was incorrect. The second point is more interesting, for Calvin attempts to maintain a division of labor between the doctrinal preparation for reading the scriptures, and the straightforward explanation of the scriptures, shorn of any ostentatious displays of philosophy or subtlety. Finally, Calvin assumes the stance of "granted" authority. As authority to interpret scripture is granted by those who are less skilled and less learned to their better-trained pastors, the product of the interpretive effort, must be understandable to the mind of lesser scholars in the school of the Lord, namely, the

---

[8] Comm. Romans 1.1, Ad Romanos 11.23–24. "dum ex superbo Saule, parvulum Christi discipulum factum disserit."

[9] Comm. Romans 1.1, Ad Romanos 11.22–23.

[10] Comm. Romans 1.1, Ad Romanos 11.24–25. "Probabilior Origenis sententia, qui binomiun fuisse indicat."

laity. The subtle word plays were not only un-edifying, but perhaps even liable to confuse a layman attempting to profit from greater study of the scriptures.

In all three purifications, or metamorphoses, Calvin transforms the received exegetical tradition. Calvin must accept transformation to maintain continuity with the religious tradition and to hold the same dispositional content as Augustine intended for his community in Calvin's own time. This was true even on small points of style and presentation.

Calvin's difference with Augustine over the explanation of Romans 3.21, however, illustrates a more fundamental rupture.

> It has not escaped me that Augustine gives a different exposition. Indeed he believes that the righteousness of God is the grace of regeneration and this grace is free, he states, because God renews us without our merit, by his Spirit. From this, however, he excludes the works of the law, that is when humans attempt to merit by themselves things of God, without self-renewal. It seems to me also important to note that some new speculative theorists proudly adduce this doctrine as though it had been revealed to them today. But the Apostle includes all works without exception, even those which the Lord produces in his own people, as the context makes plain. For certainly Abraham was regenerated and led by the Spirit of God at the time when he denies that he had been justified by works. Therefore, excluded from human justification are not only works which are morally good, as commonly termed, which are performed by the natural instinct, but also all those which even believers can possess. Again, if it is a definition of the righteousness of faith to say, 'Blessed are they whose iniquities are forgiven', there is not a dispute about different kinds of works, but the merit of works is abolished, the remission of sins alone is established as the cause of righteousness.[11]

The substance of Calvin's argument with Augustine lies in the meritorious nature of works in the process of justification. It would be easy to view this as a test case for distinguishing Calvin from Augustine,

---

[11] Comm. Romans 3.21, Ad Romanos, 68.57–71. "Neque vero me latet, Augustinum secus exponere: Iustitiam enim Dei esse putat regenerationis gratiam: et hanc gratuitam esse fatetur, quia Dominus immerentes Spiritu suo nos renovat. Ab hac autem, opera Legis excludit, hoc est quibus homines a seipsis citra renovationem conantur Deum promereri. Mihi etiam plus satis notum est, quosdam novos speculatores hoc dogma superciliose proferre, quasi hodie sibi revelatum. Sed Apostolum, omnia sine exceptione opera complecti, etiam quae Dominus in suis efficit, ex contextu planum fiet. Nam certe regeneratus erat Abraham, et Spirit Dei agebatur quo tempore iustificatum fuisse operibus negat. Ergo a iustificatione hominis non opera tantum moraliter bona (ut vulgo appellant) et quae fiunt naturae instinctu excludit, sed quaecunque etiam fideles habere possunt."

since the former in this instance shows his radical Augustinianism, a stance that goes beyond Augustine. However, to do so would ignore that Calvin does maintain a very real place in his theology for Christian progress.[12] More importantly, to indulge in questions of "how Augustinian was Calvin?" would draw this study away from its primary goal, establishing the basis for Calvin's critical reception of the exegetical and doctrinal work of Augustine and the Church.

The more useful question is not whether Calvin departed from Augustine's doctrine, but why he transformed it. The amazing instances of such departure are not those when doctrines, situated in original language and tailored to an original audience, are adapted to different circumstances. Rather, it is those when doctrines, taken as a piece of whole cloth, are sewn into a new piece of cloth and rendered an acceptable garment.

In this case, Calvin's reception of Augustine may well be pushed by a concern to refute those whom he simply terms modern flighty theorists *"novos speculatores"*. Some interpreters of Augustine were arguing that good works are ineffectual until God has renewed the individual through the Spirit (without giving Augustine credit!). However, I would ask whether Augustine in this text explicitly offers such a position.

> Here, perhaps, it may be said by that presumption of man, which is ignorant of the righteousness of God, and wishes to establish one of its own, that the apostle quite properly said, "For by the law shall no man be justified," inasmuch as the law merely shows what one ought to do, and what one ought to guard against, in order that what the law thus points out may be accomplished by the will, and so man be justified, not indeed by the power of the law, but by his free determination. But I ask your attention, O man, to what follows. "But now the righteousness of God," says he, "without the law is manifested, being witnessed by the law and the prophets." Does this then sound a light thing in deaf ears? He says, "The righteousness of God is manifested." Now this righteousness they are ignorant of, who wish to establish one of their own; they will not submit themselves to it. His words are, "The righteousness of God is manifested:" he does not say, the righteousness of man, or the righteousness of his own will, but the "righteousness of God,"—not that whereby He is Himself righteous, but that with which He endows man when He justifies the ungodly. This is witnessed by the law and the prophets; in other words, the law and the prophets each afford it testimony. The law,

---

[12] See Johan J. Steenkamp's. "A Review of the Concept of Progress in Calvin's Institutes." 69–78 in *Calvin: Erbe und Auftrag: Festschrift für Wilhelm Heinrich Neuser zum 65. Geburtstag*, edited by Willem van Spijker (Kampen: Kok Pharos Publishing House, 1991).

indeed, by issuing its commands and threats, and by justifying no man, sufficiently shows that it is by God's gift, through the help of the Spirit, that a man is justified; and the prophets, because it was what they predicted that Christ at His coming accomplished. Accordingly he advances a step further, and adds, "But righteousness of God by faith of Jesus Christ," that is by the faith wherewith one believes in Christ for just as there is not meant the faith with which Christ Himself believes, so also there is not meant the righteousness whereby God is Himself righteous. Both no doubt are ours, but yet they are called God's, and Christ's, because it is by their bounty that these gifts are bestowed upon us. The righteousness of God then is without the law, but not manifested without the law; for if it were manifested without the law, how could it be witnessed by the law? That righteousness of God, however, is without the law, which God by the Spirit of grace bestows on the believer without the help of the law,—that is, when not helped by the law. When, indeed, He by the law discovers to a man his weakness, it is in order that by faith he may flee for refuge to His mercy, and be healed.[13]

Calvin holds an interpretation of Paul that eliminates all possibility of significance for meritorious works. He criticizes Augustine for allowing the merit of works in the those who are believers. But Augustine never particularly teaches that. Rather, he does not exclude it. Actually, Calvin is presenting an interpretation of Paul's doctrine against an interpretation of that same doctrine by Augustine.

---

[13] Augustine, *De Spiritu et Littera*, PL 44, 208–209. *The Spirit and the Letter*, in Nicene and Post-Nicene Fathers, vol 5, Philip Schaff, ed., Peter Holmes, Robert Wallis and B.B. Warfield, trans. (New York: Scribner, 1886), 308–309. "Hic forte dicat illa humana praesumptio, ignorans Dei justitiam, et suam volens constituere, merito dixisse Apostolum, 'Quia ex lege nemo justificabitur': ostendit enim tantummodo lex quid faciendum, quidve cavendum sit, ut quod illa ostenderit voluntas impleat, ac sic homo justificetur, non per legis imperium, sed per liberum arbitrium. Sed, o homo, attende quod sequitur: 'Nunc autem, per Legem et Prophetas.' Parumne insonat surdis? 'Justitia,' inquit, 'Dei manifestata est.' Hanc ignorant qui suam volunt constituere: huic nolunt esse subjecti. 'Justitia,' inquit, 'Dei manifestata est': non dixit, Justitia hominis, vel justitia propriae est, sed qua induit hominem, cum justificat impium. Haec testificatur per Legem et Prophetas: huic quippe testimonium perhibent Lex et Prophetae. Lex quidem, hoc ipso, quod jubendo et minando et neminem justificando satis indicat, dono Dei justificari hominem per adjutorium spiritus: Prophetae autem, quia id quod praedixerunt, Christi implevit adventus. Nam hinc sequitur et adjungit, dicens, 'Justitia autem Dei per fidem Jesu Christi,' hoc est, per fidem qua creditur in Christum. Sicut autem ista fides Christi dicta est non qua credit Chrsitus: sic et illa justitia Dei non qua justus est Deus. Utrumque enim nostrum est; sed ideo Dei et Christi dicitur, quod ejus nobis largitate donatur. Justitia ergo Dei sini lege, non sine lege manifestata est. Quomodo enim per legem testificata, si sine lege manifestata? Sed justitia Dei sine lege est, quam Deus per spiritum gratiae credenti confert sine adjutorio legis, hoc est, non adjuto a lege. Quandoquidem per legem ostendit homini infirmitatem suam, ut ad ejus misericordiam per fidem confugiens sanaretur."

The reason for Calvin's strengthening of the anti-works stance here is clear. Calvin lived his theological life in constant argument with those who attempted to find a place for human participation in salvation. He was sensitive, perhaps oversensitve, to the possibility of that doctrine. In seeking to grasp correct religion to teach in the mid-sixteenth century, he believed that this rejection of works formed a wall which could not be breached. Accordingly he critiqued a favorite authority for leaving some room for such doctrine. This contemporary challenge shaped his reading of Augustine to an extent perhaps beyond where he might have wished to go.[14]

Another instance of difference in the Romans commentary occurs in the exposition of Abraham's infirmity in Romans 4.19. Calvin was aware that Augustine believed that the impediment to conception must have been solely on Sarah's part, as Abraham later had other children.[15] However, he uses Genesis 17 and 18 to support the opposite conclusion, that the impairment to procreation was on both of their parts.[16] Calvin does give the reason that Augustine was persuaded, since Abraham was able to sire more children after Isaac, to call him sterile would be logically incorrect. However, Calvin characterizes Augustine's objection as absurd (*absurditas*).[17]

Augustine's own reasoning does not seem so flawed as Calvin would have his readers believe. Augustine leads his listeners to a different path, contending that the reader should not take the condition of Abraham's body as a complete impediment, since he was able to sire children by

---

[14] Akira Demura argues, in his "Two Commentaries on the Epistle to the Romans: Calvin and Oecolampadius," 165–188 in *Calvinus Sincerioris Religionis Vindex*, edited by Wilhelm Neuser and Brian Armstrong, (Kirksville, MO: Sixteenth Century Journal Publishers, 1997), that Calvin is speaking against the Schoolmen of the *via moderna*. (173) Further, Demura's point that Calvin is attempting to stamp out a contemporary problem that Augustine did not face (173–174), completely supports my reconstruction of Calvin's enterprise.

[15] Comm. Romans 4.19, Ad Romanos, 95.30–96.36.

[16] It is a significant example of the style of Calvin's exegesis to consider his solution to the difficulties presented by Genesis 17 and 18. Calvin obviously reads the eighteenth chapter through the lens of the seventeenth. There, he has established that Abraham does not believe himself capable of procreation at his age. Thus, when he reaches the eighteenth chapter, and the text states that "it had ceased to be with Sarah after the manner of women," Calvin supplies the previously given knowledge, that Abraham is also unable, but Sarah even more so. The difference is one of degree, rather than quality. Both are sterile. See Calvin's commentary on Genesis, 17.15–19, 18.11–12.

[17] Comm. Romans 4.19, Ad Romanos, 95.34.

his wife Keturah after Sarah's death.[18] Rather, this statement on the condition of Abraham's body, a dead body, "*emortuum corpus*", must be seen as a comparative.[19] If Augustine's point is not absurd, however, it certainly does not fit the evidence of Genesis 17, to which Calvin grants priority. Rather, it makes common sense of the later stories of Abraham's life with Keturah. Calvin's solution hinges on a heaping up of miracles, as a proof of God's great goodness; Augustine's solution needs a bit of textual play in the scripture, which will allow him to call the "deadness" of Abraham's body a bit of hyperbole.

There is no significant doctrinal difference in this case. Neither theologian believed that this was a test case for miracles, but only a passage which necessitated some explanation. Calvin, working under a theory of scripture's sufficiency, which he believed to be frequently under attack, and attempting to demonstrate a Renaissance contextualism in an extraordinarily difficult circumstance, reacted badly to Augustine's extra-biblical solution. Augustine, writing without Calvin's particular constraints, and wishing to make better sense of Keturah's children, chose a reasonable solution. Despite their different approaches the issue does not, strictly speaking, become doctrinal, but remains in the realm of interpretation.

A paradigmatic instance of Calvin's differing exegetically with Augustine while confirming his doctrinal motive concerns Romans 5.5.[20] In this case, Calvin commended the doctrinal and pastoral goal toward which Augustine aimed. However, he did not believe that the apostle's intention supported that rendering.[21]

> He says further that the Spirit is *given*, graciously bestowed on us by the goodness of God, and not granted on account of our merits. Augustine noted this well. He was talking idly in his interpretation of the love of God. He expounded that we endure adversity with constancy, and for this reason are confirmed in hope, because having been regenerated by

---

[18] See Genesis 23–25, I Chronicles 1.32–33.

[19] Augustinus, *Quaest. in Hept.* I, XXXV, PL 34, 557–558, "Emortuum quippe corpus non ita intelligendum est, ac si omnino nullam vim generandi habere posset, si mulier juvenilis aetatis esset; sed secundum hoc emortuum, ut etiam de provectioris aetatis muliere non posset. Nam ideo de Cethura potuit, quia et juvenilis illam invenit aetatis."

[20] Comm. Romans 5.5, Ad Romanos, 106.44–54.

[21] This provides a New Testament example of what David Puckett has found in Calvin's Old Testament exegesis, of valuing the particular aim of an interpretation, notably christological interpretations, while denying the validity of those interpretations on the basis of textual reasoning. See *John Calvin's Exegesis of the Old Testament* Columbia Series in Reformed Theology (Louisville: Westminster John Knox Press, 1995), passim.

the Spirit, we love God. Though this is a pious sentiment, but it is not what Paul means. Indeed, love is not active, but is seen in a passive sense. It is certain, too, that Paul is teaching us nothing other than the true source of all love is the conviction which believers have of the love which God has for them. This is no light persuasion only with which they are tinged, but their souls are thoroughly saturated with it.[22]

Calvin draws Augustine's position from two widely separated places in his writings. The first is from *On the Spirit and the Letter* (*De Spiritu et Littera*). Here, Calvin accepts the teaching from the end of III.5, that "the good is loved, because the charity of God is diffused into our hearts, not through a free will that arises from us, but through the Holy Spirit who is given to us."[23] This teaching of Augustine's gives Calvin no particular obstacle.[24] However, when Augustine treats this text under the rubric of the virtue of patience, Calvin has far greater difficulty. It is here that Augustine writes that the process of endurance is a posterior process that confirms us in our hope, made possible because of the anterior love of God.[25] Calvin makes clear that he approves of the pious sentiment (*pia sententia*), but that it is inappropriately attached to this passage. The mind of Paul wins out. Here then is an example of Calvin placing doctrine according to the textual warrant. His intent is not to treat the text and the mind of Paul as a lifeless "other." Calvin

---

[22] Comm. Romans 5.5, Ad Romanos, 106.44–54. "Datum praeterea hunc Spiritum dicit, gratuita scilicet Dei bonitate erogatum, non autem redditum nostris meritis. Quemadmodum probe Augustinus adnotavit: qui tamen in expositione dilectionis Dei hallucinatur. exponit, nos constanter adversa tolerare, et hac ratione in spem confirmari, quia Spiritu regenerati, Deum diligamus. Pia quidem sententia, sed nihil ad Pauli mentem. Dilectio enim hic non active, sed passive capitur. et certum est, non aliud doceri a Paulo, quam hunc verum esse omnis dilectionis fontem, quod persuasi sunt fideles, a Deo se amari: nec leviter duntaxat hac persuasione tincti sunt, sed animos prorsus delibutos habent."

[23] Augustinus, *De Spiritu et Littera*, Cap. 3 (5), PL 44, 203. "Ut autem diligatur, charitas Dei diffunditur in cordibus nosris, non per arbitrum iberum quod surgit ex nobit, sed per Spiritum sanctum qui datus est nobis. (Rom. v,5)."

[24] However, one imagines that he could not have complied with Augustine's earlier statement in that same paragraph which characterized the human will as being "assisted" (*adjuvari*) to do the good. But that was not the problem at this point.

[25] Augustinus, *De Patientia*, 17, 14, PL 40, 619. "Proinde ab illo est patientia justorum, per quem diffunditur charitas eorum. Qam charitatem laudans atque commendans Apostolus, inter caetera ejus bona dixit eamet cuncta suffere. ... Quanto ergo major est in sanctis charitas Dei, tanto magis pro eo quod diligitur, et quanto major est in peccatoribus cupiditas mundi, tanto magis pro eo quod concupiscitur, omnia tolerantur. Ac perhoc inde est patientia vera justorum, unde est in eis charitas Dei; et inde est patientia falsa iniquorum, unde est in eis cupiditas mundi."

comes fully prepared with his hermeneutical presuppositions. But as a humanist, he allows the voice of the text to rule, to some extent, his interpretations.

In this instance, one sees the humanist side of Calvin come forward. Treating texts as unities, Calvin was unwilling to allow an atomistic approach in which a word achieves its meaning without regard for the surrounding context. One sees that type of approach, to a small degree, in Augustine's two uses of the text in question. In various needs, the text offers up somewhat different doctrines, based on the key words being considered. Calvin, more interested in the holistic mind of Paul, offers a different approach to the text, but values the message gained by his predecessor. The message is good, but inappropriate to attach to this text.

An extraordinarily important text to consider when describing Calvin's differences with Augustine is Romans 7.14–25.[26] The significance of this text lies in Augustine's shift in interpretation, from an early rendering that stated that the individual that Paul was describing was the pre-grace state,[27] to his later assertion that this statement of anguish was reflective of Paul, and any other believer, demonstrating the divided character[28] of the believer's existence.[29] Calvin approves of the latter interpretation, while bluntly stating that Augustine was in error in the first.[30]

---

[26] The most thorough setting of the sixteenth century reception of the two Augustine's is David Steinmetz's "Calvin and the Divided Self of Romans 7," in *Augustine, the Harvest, and Theology (1300–1650)*, ed. by K. Hagen, (Leiden: E.J. Brill, 1990), 300–313. Steinmetz does a masterful job of setting out the interpretive camps of the early 16th century, and of demonstrating that confessional identity was not a sure predictor of any interpreter's stance vis-à-vis the early or late Augustine.

[27] Augustine, *Ad Simplicianus*, 7–10. Augustine makes clear again and again that the person in question is the individual under the law, not yet having received grace.

[28] Augustine, *Retractationes* II, Cap. 1, §1, PL 32, 629. "In qua illa Apostoli verba, 'Lex spiritualis est; ego autem carnalis sum,' etc, quibus caro contra spiritum confligere ostenditur, eo modo exposui, tanquam homo describatur adhuc sub Lege nondum sub gratia constitutus. Longe enim postea etiam spiritualis hominis (et hoc probabilius) esse posse illa verba cognovi." See also *Contra Pelagianorum* I, chap. X–XI, PL 44, 560–562.

[29] But see also Krister Stendahl's "The Apostle Paul and the Introspective Conscience of the West," *Harvard Theological Review*, 56 (1963):199–215. Stendahl argues that the West, through Augustine, has read the division into the text, and that Paul displays strong evidence of a good conscience.

[30] Comm. Romans 7.15, Ad Romanos 149.33–34. "Augustine was taking part in that same error ..." "In communi errore aliquandiu versatus est Augustinus:".

Calvin claims that this text is not about human nature, and gently chides those who interpret it thus.[31] However, it immediately becomes clear that Calvin does believe that this *is* about human nature, that is, about the nature of believers.[32] Calvin draws a clear distinction between speculation about mere human nature, (*nudam hominis naturam*),[33] and the truth which believers know.[34] This is a special case, of Calvin's accepting the mature Augustine against the earlier Augustine, a decision which parallels that of the Bishop of Hippo himself. For Calvin, the necessity of receiving the later interpretation has to do with the question which Augustine faced, that of the human being before God in the process of salvation. In this case, Calvin has the opportunity clearly to choose a certain tradition, at face value, precisely because the contexts are not significantly different.

In Calvin's exposition of I Timothy 2.1, again we find Calvin taking Augustine to task for making the interpretation not an effort of understanding the mind of the author, but rather of demonstrating the correctness of the ceremonial usage of his time. The pericope in question is "I exhort therefore, first of all, that supplications, prayers, intercessions, thanksgivings, be made for all men." The question arises as to the differentiation between the four modes of prayer. The first three, especially, do not seem easy to distinguish. Calvin states as much, saying, "I confess that I do not fully understand the difference between three of the four kinds of prayer Paul enumerates."[35] However, Calvin's uncertainty about the correct interpretation does not hinder his abil-

---

[31] Comm. Romans 7.15, Ad Romanos 149.25–30. "The inexperienced, who do not follow the subject with which the apostle is dealing or the plan to which he is holding, believe it is human nature which he is here describing. It is the case that among the Philosophers we find such a description of human capacity. Truly, Scripture is much higher in its philosophy, because it sees nothing remaining in the heart of man but perversity since Adam was plundered of the image of God." "Imperiti qui non reputant qua in re versetur Apostolus, aut quam agendi oeconomiam teneat, putant hominis naturam hic describi. Et sane talis est apud Philosophos descriptio humani ingenii. Verum Scriptura longe altius philosphatur, quia videt nihil in corde hominis remansisse praeter perversitatem, ex quo Adam imagine Dei spollatus est."

[32] Ad Romanos 149.33 "quanta sit fidelium infirmitas"

[33] Ad Romanos 149.32.

[34] Susan Schreiner has considered how Calvin uses the evidence of personal experience of the power of the Christian life as a factor in his theology. See her "'The Spiritual Man Judges All Things': Calvin and Exegetical Debate about Certainty in the Reformation." *Biblical Interpretation in the Era of the Reformation*, edited by Richard A. Muller and John L. Thompson (Grand Rapids: Eerdmans, 1996), 189–215.

[35] Comm. I Timothy 2.1, CO 52.265. "Porro quid inter se different tres species ex quatuor quas Paulus enumerat, fateor me non penitus tenere."

ity to criticize one which he feels quite incorrect. He continues, "This is childish, that Augustine twists (*detorquet*) Paul's words to fit the ceremonial usage of his own time."[36] Augustine has found in this text a reflection of the worshipping community in his own day.[37] That seems too facile an explanation to Calvin, unwarranted by the text, and he is willing to critique it without a strong positive alternative.

Calvin was also willing to take Augustine to task for over-discussing a passage, or for considering too subtly. This is the case in his comment on II Timothy 1.9, when he comments that "He calls times eternal, just as in Titus chapter 1, the perpetual series of years from the foundation of the world. The subtle disputation (*subtilior disputatio*) over this matter which Augustine raises in many passages is alien to Paul's mind. Therefore the sense is that before the times began to take their course from all past ages."[38] Again, the reader finds the characteristic desire for plainness, and the method of considering the mind of the author for finding the most likely interpretation. Augustine has taken the words "before eternity" (*ante tempora aeterna*), as license to consider the nature of eternity![39]

A similar criticism of Augustine comes in Calvin's comment upon Hebrews 1.5. Calvin finds Augustine reasoning too subtly again. "Briefly we must consider that the word begotten should be taken here relatively. Augustine's subtlety here is frivolous in fabricating the idea that today means eternity or forever. Christ certainly is the eternal Son of God, because he is his Wisdom, born before time was. But this

---

[36] Comm. I Timothy 2.1, CO 52.265. "Puerile quidem est, quod Pauli verba Augustinus ad ritus suo tempore usitatos detorquet."

[37] Augustine, *Epistolae Secundum Ordinem Temporum nunc Primum Dispositae, et Quatuor in Classes Digestae*, II.10. "Item quod ait ad Timotheum, Obsecro igitur primum omnium fieri obsecrationes, orationes, postulationes, gratiarum actiones pro omnibus ominibus, quaeso exponas mihi, quod discrimen sit in hac diversitate verborum, cum omnia mihi quae gerenda dixit, orationis officio convenire videantur." PL 33.465–466.

[38] Comm. II Timothy 1.9, CO 52.353. "Tempora saecularia hic nominat, sicuti ad Titum capite 1, perpetuam annorum seriem a mundo condito. Nam illa subtilior disputatio, quam agitat pluribus locis Augustinus, aliena est a mente Pauli. Sensus ergo est: antequam ab omnibus retro saeculis tempore fluere inciperent."

[39] Augustine, *Ad Orosium Contra Priscill. Et Origen*, Cap. V. 6, PL 42.672–673. "Ita enim, ne longius abeam, dicimus aeternum Deum, non utique istas duas brevissimas syllabas, sed quod eis significatur. Et dixit Apostolus aeterna tempora priora et antiqua, quod in graeco legitur πϱο χϱονοιν αιωνιων. Ad Titum enim scribens ait: Spem vitae aeternae quam promisit non mendax Deus ante tempora aeterna. Cum autem retrorsum tempora a constitutione mundi habere videantur initium, quomodo sunt aeterna, nisi quia aeterna dixit quae ante se non habent ullum tempus?"

says nothing to the present passage which is given concerning men, by whom Christ was recognized as the Son of God only after the Father made him manifest."[40] Augustine's doctrine is essentially correct, his attaching it to this particular passage of scripture is fallacious.

Another consideration for brevity and for doctrine comes from Calvin's comment on Titus 1.2, where Augustine uses the phrase "before eternal times" to consider the eternity of time. Calvin reviews Augustine's arguments, but eventually offers another.

> *Which God promised.* Because Augustine reads here 'before eternal times' he gets into difficulties about the eternity of time, till at last he explains eternal as meaning time that goes beyond all antiquity. In this sense, he and Jerome and other commentators agree that before the foundation of the world God determined to give the salvation which he has now manifested through the gospel. Thus Paul, would have used the word 'promised' inaccurately to mean 'decreed', since before the creation of humans there was no one to whom he could make any promise. For this reason, although I do not reject this interpretation, when I examine the whole issue more closely, I am compelled to accept a different reading— that eternal life was promised to men many long ages ago, and not only to those who were alive at that time but for those also in our age also. It was not solely for Abraham's benefit that God said 'In your seed all nations will be blessed' (Gen. 22,18): but he has in view all who lived after him. There is no difficulty in the fact that in II Timothy 1.9 he says that salvation was given to men 'before times eternal' in a different sense. For the meaning of the word is the same in both passages. For since the Greek word αἰών means the uninterrupted succession of time from the beginning to the end of the world, in the Timothy passage Paul is saying that salvation was given or ordained to God's elect before the passage of time began. But in this passage where he speaks of a promise he does not include all ages so as to lead us back beyond the creation of the world, but says simply that many ages have passed since salvation was first promised. If anyone wants to take 'times eternal' as a concise mode of expression for the ages themselves, he may do so. But since salvation was given by God's eternal election before it was promised, in Timothy the act of giving salvation is put before all ages, and thus we have there to understand the word 'all'. But here his meaning is simply that the promise is more ancient than a long succession of ages, because it began immediately from the foundation of the world. In this sense he shows in

---

[40] Comm. Hebrews 1.5, Ad Hebraeos 22.33–23.5. "De generatione sic breviter habendum est, relative hoc loco accipi. Frivola enim Augustini argutia est, qui hodie aeternum et continuum fingit. Christus certe aeternus est Dei Filius, quia Sapientia eius est ante tempus genita. Sed hoc nihil ad praesentem locum, ubi respectus habetur ad homines, a quibus agnitus fuit Christus pro Filio Dei, postquam eum Pater manifestavit."

Romans 1.2 that the gospel which was proclaimed only when Christ had risen from the dead was promised in the scriptures through the prophets, for there is a significant difference between the exhibition of grace in the present era and the promise given of old to the patriarchs.[41]

Calvin subjects Augustine and Jerome to the judgment of a conflation of two texts, both of which he believes are problematic if the interpretation they provide is accepted.[42] Here we encounter both a philologist as well as a suspicious hearer of philosophy. Calvin clearly indicates that the unsatisfactory solution offered by Augustine comes out of Augustine's being too concerned about the eternity of time. Eventually, this causes a moment of absurdity, in which a promise is made to non-existent beings. Calvin explicitly ***does not*** reject the interpretation, but instead attempts to persuade his readers of a different solution, which he believes makes better sense of God's promise. Again, a slight doctrinal variance is proposed, but Calvin himself makes it clear, by not denying the truth of Augustine's position, that either position leads toward right religion.

---

[41] Comm. Titus 1.2, CO 52.405–406. "*Quam promisit Deus*. Quoniam Augustinus aeterna pro saecularibus tempora hic legebat, multum se torquet in temporum aeternitate: nisi quod aeterna tandem exponit, quae omnem antiquitatem superant. In sensu vero ipse et Hieronymus et alii consentiunt, quod Deus ante mundi creationem statuerit salutem dare, quam nunc per evangelium manifestavit. Ita promittendi verbo abusus esset Paulus pro decernere: si quidem ante homines natos nemo erat cui promitteret. Ego sicuti non reiicio hanc expositionem, ita, dum omnia propus expendo, aliter sentire cogor: nempe quod a multis retro saeculis vita aeterna hominibus promissa fuerit: neque iis modo qui tunc vivebant, sed in nostram quoque aetatem. Neque enim soli Abrahae consulit Deus, quum dicit (Gen. 22.18): In semine tuo benedicentur omnes gentes, sed posteros omnes respicit. Nec obstat quod secundae ad Timotheum primo capite datam fuisse salutem dicit ante tempora saecularia, diverso sensu. Eadem enim nihilominus est verbi significatio utroque loco. Nam quum αἰών Graecis continua sit temporis series ab initio ad finem usque mundi, illic Paulus datam vel ordinatam fuisse salutem electis Dei tradit, antequam fluere coeerint tempora. Hic vero quia de promissione tractat, non omnia saecula comprehendit, ut nos abducat extra mundi creationem: sed docet multa saecula praeteriisse ex quo salus fuit promissa. Si quis brevius malit, saecularia tempora pro saeculis ipsis accipere licet. Sed quoniam prius aeterna Dei electione data fuit salus quam promissa: ideo in loco illo epistolae ad Timotheum prior omnibus saeculis donatio statuitur: et ita subaudienda est nota universalis. Hic vero nihil aliud significat quam promissionem longo saeculorum ordine antiquiorem esse: quia statim a condito mundo coepit. Eodem sensu ad Rom. capite 1,2 evangelium, quod suscitato demum ex mortuis Christo publicari debuit, promissum in scripturis per prophetas fuisse docet. Plurimum enim a praesenti gratiae exhibitione differt patribus facta olim promissio."

[42] Augustine, PL42 672–673, see above.

The instrument of the mind of Paul was a favorite argument of Calvin's. In his comment upon Galatians 3.1, Calvin again employs this device to chide Augustine.

> *Before whose eyes.* This pertains, as already suggested, to making clear their guilt. For the better Christ is known to us, the more grave is the crime in leaving him. Therefore he says that his teaching was so clear that it was not actually bare doctrine, but was more truly the living and express image of Christ. Therefore they had a knowledge that could bring before them his appearance. Augustine's interpretation is harsh and far from Paul's mind. He says that Christ was pre-scribed, as if he were to be pushed out from possession. Others read pro-scribed. That reading would not be inappropriate, if "proscribed" were taken to mean 'openly proclaimed'. This is the reason that the Greeks use the word προγράμματα, for boards on which property for sale was advertised, so that everyone should see it. But the participle 'pictured' is less ambiguous, and in my opinion, the most appropriate. For Paul is demonstrating, in order to characterize how energetic his preaching had been, he first compares it with a picture which showed them the image of Christ to life.[43]

Here Calvin simply did not feel Augustine's interpretation can be tolerated by the meaning of the text.[44] In his experience of Paul's thought, Calvin cannot find the requisite thought-world to match Augustine's interpretation.

Calvin was not above proposing answers to Augustine's questions that relate to an underlying philosophical sophistication. In his comments on I Thessalonians 4.16, that the dead in Christ shall rise first, Calvin notes Augustine's discomfort, and proposes a solution.

---

[43] Comm. Galatians 3.1, Ad Galatas 59.25–60.7. "*Quibus ante oculos.* Pertinet hoc (quemadmodum iam attigi) ad culpam exaggerandam. Nam quo notior nobis fuit Christus, eo gravius crimen est defectionis. Dicit igitur tantam fuisse doctrinae suae perspicuitatem, ut non tam fuerit nuda doctrina quam viva et expressa imago Christi. Eam igitur habuerant notitiam, quae aspectui conferri posset. Dura est Augustini expositio et a mente Paule remota, qui praescriptum dicit Christum, quasi a possessione depulsus foret. Alii legunt: ›proscriptus‹. Quae vox non male conveniret, si ›proscribi‹ accipias pro ›palam publicari‹. Unde et προγράμματα vocant Gaeci tabulas, quibus possessiones venales publicantur, ut sit res exposita omnium oculis. Sed participio ›depictus‹ minus est ambiguitatis et meo iudicio optime quadrat. Nam ut ostendat Paulus, quanta suae praedicationis energia fuerit, primum picturae ipsam comparat, quae imaginem Christi ad vivum illis expresserit."

[44] Augustinus, CSEL 84, 75f. "hoc est, quibus videntibus Churstus Iesus hereditatem suam possessionemque suam amisit ... Illud enim ita sonat, tanquam non pervenerit ad possessionem, pro qua sanguinem dedit."

He says that those who survive will be *caught up* together with them. [the dead in Christ]. In their case he makes no mention of death, so appears to suggest that they will be exempt from death. Augustine, both in his *City of God*, XX, and his *Answer to Dulcitus*, has great difficulty on this point, because Paul appears to contradict himself. He states elsewhere that the seed cannot grow again unless it dies (I Cor. 15.36). The solution, however, is easy, since a sudden change will be like death. Ordinarily death is the separation of the soul from the body, but this does not prevent the Lord from destroying this corruptible nature in a moment in order to create it new by his power, and this is the way that implements what Paul teaches must take place, that what is mortal may be swallowed up by life (II Cor. 5.4). The phrase which occurs in our Confession that Christ will be 'Judge of the dead and of the living', is recognized by Augustine to be true, rather than figurative language. His only hesitation is how those who have not died are to rise again. As I have said, however, it is a kind of death when this flesh is destroyed, even as it is not subject to corruption. The only difference is that those who sleep put off the substance of the body for a space of time, while those who will be suddenly made new will put off nothing but the quality.[45]

Calvin's answer depends on an Aristotelian understanding of substantial change. It was possible, according to Aristotle's doctrine, for substantial change to occur without the passage of time.[46]

Here is an example that demonstrates Calvin's allegiance to the Christian religious tradition, and to the interpreted scripture. It would

[45] Comm. I Thessalonians 4.16, CO 52.167. "Superstites dicit cum illis simul raptum iri: in his nulla mortis mentio: quare innuere videtur mortis fore expertes. Hic multum se torquet Augustinus, tum libro De civitate vicesimo, tum in responsione ad Dulcitium: quia secum pugrare videatur Paulus, qui alibi (1. Cor. 15,36) negat renasci posse semen nisi moriatur. Verum solutio facilis est, quia subita immutatio mortis instar erit. Mors quidem ordinaria separatio est animae a corpore. Verum nihil obstat quominus aboleat Dominus momento corruptibilem hanc naturam, ut novam sua virtute creet: sic enim impletur quod fieri oportere idem Paulus docet (2. Cor. 5,4), ut absorbeatur mortalitas a vita. Quod in confessione nostra habetur, Christum iudicem mortuorum fore ac vivorum, Augustinus sine figura verum esse agnoscit: tantum in illo scrupulo haeret, quomodo resurgant qui non sunt mortui. Verum (ut dixi) illa est mortis species, dum in nihilum redigitur haec caro, ut nunc est corruptioni obnoxia. Tantum hoc est discrimen, quod qui dormiunt aliquo temporis spatio, corporis exuunt substantiam: qui autem subito innovabuntur, non nisi qualitatem exuent."

[46] For more on Calvin's understanding of Aristotle, see Charles Partee's *Calvin and Classical Philosophy*, (Leiden: E.J. Brill, 1977), 97–99. Partee considers Calvin's knowledge of Aristotle mostly in regards to the doctrine of providence, where Calvin would have been at significant loggerheads with the Philosopher. However, this particular doctrine, that of substantial change occurring without time, raises no such objections. Moreover, it is a commonplace, which Calvin could have come across in his arts course, without needing to have been studying Aristotle with one of the Parisian philosophical masters.

have been easier to slough off the reference to Augustine's difficulties than it was to include them. Through the use of Augustine's discussions, Calvin wished to demonstrate that the unity of testimony of the scriptures is a long-accepted key to Christian doctrine. Augustine, as Calvin notes, was extremely troubled by the interpretation of these passages, and several times suggested the solutions which Calvin adopted, but without Calvin's force and brevity.[47] Both Calvin and Augustine were at pains to recognize that scripture, and likewise Paul, speak with one voice on this matter.

Calvin could acknowledge Augustine as the most perspicacious ecclesiastical writer on a particular passage, while still finding him wanting. This is the case with I Corinthians 6.7, the putative prohibition against lawsuits. Calvin will not permit this passage to become a general proscription of complaints. Calvin reasons that Paul permits judges, enough indication is given for Christians to pursue their rights with moderation.[48] Calvin sees the problem as concerning the virtue of endurance. If someone can pursue a lawsuit without improper attitudes

---

[47] Augustine, *Civitate Dei*, XX.20, Corpus Christianorum, (Turnholt: Brepols, 1955), 733–736. "Sed hic apostolus tacuit de resurrectione mortuorum; ad eosdem autem scribens in epistula prima: *Nolumus*, inquit, *ignorare uos, fratres, de dormientibus, ut non contristemini, sicut et ceteri, qui spem non habent. Nam si credimus, quod Iesus moruus est et resurrexit: ita et Deus eos, qui dormierunt per Iesum, adducet cum illo. Hoc enim uobis dicimus in uerbo Domini, quia nos uiuentes, qui reliqui sumus in aduentum Domini, non praeueniemus eos, qui ante dormierunt; quoniam ipse Dominus in iussu et in uoce archangeli et in tuba Dei descendet de caelo, et mortui in in Christo resurgent primo; deinde nos uiuentes, qui reliqui sumus, simul cum illis rapiemur in nubibus in obuiam Christo in aera, et ita semper cum Domino erimus.* Haec uerba apostololica resurrectionem mortuorum futuram, quando ueniet Christus, utique ad uiuos et mortuos iudicandos, praeclarissime ostendunt.

Sed quaeri solet, utrum illi, quos hic uiuentes inuenturus est Christus, quorum personam in se atque illos, qui tunc secum uiuebant, transfigurabat apostolus, numquam omnino morituri sint, an ipso temporis puncto, quo cum resurgentibus rapientur in nubibus in obuiam Christo in aera, ad inmortalitatem per mortem mira celeritate transibunt. Neque enim dicendum est fieri non posse, ut, dum per aera in sublime portantur, in illo spatio et moriantur et reuiuescant. Quod emim ait: *Et ita semper cum Domino erimus*, non sic accipiendum est, tamquam in aere nos dixerit semper cum Domino esse mansuros; quia nec ipse utique ibi manebit, quia ueniens transiturus est; uenienti quippe ibitur obuiam, non manenti; sed *ita cum Domino erimus*, id est, sic erimus habentes corpora sempiterna, ubicumque cum illo fuerimus. ... Resurrectionem quippe mortuorum futuram et in carne, quando Christus uenturus est uiuos iudicaturus et mortuos, oportet, si Christiani esse uolumus, ut credamus; sed non ideo de hac re inanis est fides nostra si, quem ad modum futura sit, perfecte conprehendere non ualemus."

[48] Comm. I Corinthians 6.7, CO 49.391. "I however answer simply, that since he has just given permission to have judges, he has thereby given enough indication that it is not wrong for Christians to pursue their rights with moderation, so long as offense is not done to love." "Ego autem simpliciter ita respondeo, quum permiserit nuper

of mind, it is permissible. Calvin lists these unacceptable attitudes as lack of self-control, desire for revenge, hostility, obstinacy, and others.[49] Calvin then criticizes the ecclesial exegetical tradition for not having more carefully investigated this issue.

> It is extraordinary that this question has not been more assiduously discussed by ecclesiastical writers. Augustine has worked more diligently than the others, and approaches nearer the scope. But even his work is not free from obscurity, though he does teach truth. Those who want to teach clearly admonish us that a distinction must be made between public and private retribution. For since retribution belongs to the magistrate by God's ordination, those who seek its aid are not irresponsibly taking retribution into their own hands, but are having recourse to God as avenger. That is prudently and aptly said, but we must go further. For if we are not allowed to seek vengeance, even from God, it follows that we are not allowed to have recourse to the magistrate for retribution. Therefore I admit that all revenge is ruled out for the Christian, and he must not practise it either by himself or through the medium of the magistrate; no, and he must not even desire it! If a Christian therefore wants to prosecute his rights in a court of law, without giving offense to God, he must take care not to come into courts with any desire for revenge, any bad feeling, any anger, or in a word any poisonous thing. In all this love will be the best governor.[50]

Calvin the lawyer is evident. He proposes a solution that is theoretically possible, though he himself acknowledges the difficulty of putting it into

---

arbitros, satis eo indicasse, non esse illicitum Christianis, ius suum moderate citraque caritatis offensionem persequi."

[49] Comm. I Corinthians 6.7, CO 49.391–392. "If therefore a Christian man wants to prosecute his rights in a court of law, without going against God, he ought to take care first not to come into court with any desire for revenge, any bad feeling, any anger, or in a word any poisonous thing." "Si ergo ius suum prosequi vult homo christianus iudicio absque Dei offensa, cavere in primis debet ne quam ultionis cupiditatem, ne quem pravum animi motum, ne iracundiam, ne ullum denique venenum in forum afferat."

[50] Comm I Corinthians 6.7, CO 49.391–392. "Mirum est hanc quaestionem non fuisse exactius discussam a scriptoribus ecclesiasticis. Augustinus plus diligentiae impendit quam reliqui, et propius ad scopum accessit. Sed est ipse quoque nonnihil obscurus, utcunque verum doceat. Qui clarius docere volunt, admonent, distinguendum esse inter publicam et privatam vindictam: nam quum vindicta magistratus a Deo sit ordinata, qui ab ea petunt auxilium, non usurpant ipsi temere vindictam, sed ad Deum confugiunt ultorem. Prudenter id quidem et apte: sed ultra progrediendum est. Nam si ne a Deo quidem vindictam licet expetere, ita nec ad magistratus vindictam confugere liceret. Fateor ergo, christiano homini prohibitam esse omnem ultionem, ne vel per se, vel per magistratum eam exerceat, imo ne appetat quidem. Si ergo ius suum prosequi vult homo christianus iudicio absque Dei offensa, cavere in primis debet ne quam ultionis cupiditatem, ne quem pravum animi motum, ne iracundiam, ne ullum denique venenum in forum afferat. Huius rei caritas optima erit moderatrix."

practice. His position comes from his own historical situation, in which this passage had to be addressed in order to refute Anabaptist objections. Thus, although Calvin was aware of the impact of contextual-historical factors on others, he was less willing to apply that sense evenly for his own age.

Calvin could explicitly grant the correctness of Augustine's teaching, while asserting that his teaching has been incorrectly attached to a particular pericope. This is the case with Romans 8.28.

> It is to be held, however, that Paul is not speaking of anything but adversities, as though he had said, 'All the things that happen to the saints is so controlled by God that what the world sees as injurious to them finally shows as tending to their good use.' Augustine says that even the sins of the saints are far from doing them harm because of the ordaining providence of God, that they are able to serve their salvation. This statement, however, though true, does not pertain to this passage, where the cross is considered. It should be noted that the whole summary of piety is tied up in the love of God. The whole practice of righteousness, indeed, depends on this.[51]

Calvin clearly (*verum est*) notes the worthiness of Augustine's statement, but feels that it is inappropriately appended to this discussion of Paul's.[52]

Calvin uses several techniques to examine and transform Augustine's exegetical material. He may chastize Augustine for over-philosophizing, as he did in the case of Romans 1.1, in II Timothy 1.9, and tacitly does in his comments upon Titus 1.2. In these cases, he demonstrates not only a desire for simplicity and brevity, but also a zeal for edification. As well, Calvin implicitly criticizes the directions that human philosophy may lead in the interpretation of scripture. On the other hand,

---

[51] Comm. Romans 8.28, Ad Romanos 181.21–28. "Tenendum vero est, Paulum non nisi de rebus adversis loqui: acsi dixisset Divinitus sic temperari quaecunque sanctis accidunt, ut quod mundus noxium esse putat, exitus utile esse demonstret. Nam tametsi verum est quod ait Augustinus, peccato quoque sua, ordinante Dei providentia, sanctis adeo non nocere, ut potius eorum saluti inserviant: ad hunc tamen locum non pertinet, ubi de cruce agitur. Notandum vero quod pietatis summam sub dilectione Dei complexus est: ut revera inde pendet universum iustitiae studium."

[52] Augustine, *De Correptione et Gratia*, 9,23. PL 44.929–930. "Propter hoc Apostolus cum dixisset, Scimus quoniam diligentibus Deum omnia cooperatur in bonum; sciens nonnullos diligere Deum, et in eo bono usque in finem non permanere, mox addidit, his qui secundum propositum vocati sunt. Hi enim in eo quod diligunt Deum, permanent usque in finem; et qui ad tempus inde deviant, revertuntur, ut usque in finem perducant, quod in bono esse coeperunt. Ostendens autem quid sit secundum propositum vocati, mox addidit ea quae jam supra posui, Quoniam quos ante praescivit ... (Rom. viii.28)."

Calvin may turn to the mind of Paul, as he does in Romans 5.5 and Galatians 3.1. In both cases, his own readings and experience in the thought-world of the apostle make him suspect Augustine's interpretations, even when he wishes to support the pious intent of the father's explanation. Occasionally, Calvin's own doctrinal concerns obliterate the possibility of an uncritical reception of Augustine, as in the case of Romans 3.21. This may also be the case with Augustine's changing interpretations of Romans 7, although this is a difficult case, as the bishop's own mind changed. In that instance, Calvin is merely choosing his Augustine, as must everyone who interprets this passage.[53] Calvin is finding the "correct" historical precedent, and applying it to his own age. Calvin also attempts to guard the unity of the whole Bible, as he illustrated in his comments on Romans 4.19 and Titus 1.2. Here, however, the case seems to be of different weights emphasis, also a crucial concern to Augustine. The two theologians use different weights for different texts. Finally, Calvin will use his knowledge of history to investigate possible interpretations, and will not generally allow time-specific interpretations to stand unchallenged.

Enough citations from Calvin's exegetical critical reception of Augustine have been given to clarify several points. First, Calvin differs from Augustine. Any theory of Calvin as the "true receiver" of Augustine cannot be supported on the basis of the textual evidence, if "true receiver" means one who accepts uncritically and without change. Calvin's was guided by a desire to instill the same Christian religion as Augustine taught, although in an extraordinarily different set of circumstances. Calvin was uncomfortable with some of Augustine's answers, though he believed he understood the reasons behind them.[54] Calvin

---

[53] Steinmetz makes it clear that the choice is not driven wholly by confessional guidelines. See his "Calvin and the Divided Self of Romans 7."

[54] Comm. I Tim. 6.16, CO 52, 332–333. "There is a long dispute in the writings of Augustine of this statement because it seems to contradict what is in the first epistle of John (3, 2), 'Then we shall see him as he is, for we shall be like him.' This is a discussion that he considers in many passages, none are better than his answer found in his letter to the widow Pauline. As far as the meaning of the present passage is concerned, the answer is simple, that we cannot see God in this nature, as it is said elsewhere, 'Flesh and blood cannot inherit the kingdom of God.' (I Cor. 15.50) For we have to be renewed and made like God before we are able to see Him. And so that our curiosity does not go beyond limits, let us always remember the manner of living is more important than the manner of speaking in this inquiry. Simultaneously, let us also remember the prudent caution Augustine gives us, to be on our guard, so that while we are disputing about how God can be seen, we do not lose that peace and sanctification without which no one can ever see God at all." "Longa est disputatio apud Augustinum de hac

chose from among Augustine's answers. But the portion of Augustine which he wanted his readers to know, was the caution against an over-disputatious faith. In this, Calvin represented a principal concern of Augustine's, the living of the Christian life which leads toward God.

Calvin, Transforming Tradition

If the case for Calvin's critically transformative reception of Augustine is considerable, can the same be said for the wider ortho-religious tradition of which Augustine was only one, albeit central, figure? When one begins to delve into the specific differences between Calvin and the other figures mentioned in his comment on I Corinthians 3.15 the suspicion grows that Calvin was not listing particular persons, but rather illustrating his method of receiving the religious tradition through paradigmatic figures. This is illustrated by Calvin's references to Cyprian in his Pauline commentaries.[55] Of these five references, two do not speak specifically to Cyprian's own exegesis. The first is I Corinthians 1.17, where Calvin quotes Augustine's statement about Cyprian in support of the service of eloquence to the gospel.[56] The second reference is Calvin's statement about the patristic author's mixture

---

sententia: quia videtur pugnare cum eo quod habetur in prima epistola Iohannis (3,2), Tunc videbimus eum sicuti est, quia similes ei erimus. Eam disputationem quum agitet pluribus locis, nullibi melius videtur expedire quam in epistola ad Paulinam viduam. Quod tamen ad sensum praesentis loci attinet, simplex est responsio, nos videre Deum non posse in hac natura, quemadmodum alibi dicitur: Caro et sanguis regnum Dei non possidebunt (I Corin. 15,50). Renovari enim nos oportet, ut simus Deo similes, priusquam eum videre nobis detur. Et ne simus ultra modum curiosi, semper illud succurrat, plus in hac inquisitione valere videndi quam loquendi modum. Simul et illud cavere meminerimus quod prudenter Augustinus cavendum praecipit, ne dum altercando vestigamus quomodo posit Deus videre, ipsam pacem sanctificationemque perdamus, sine qua nemo Deum videbit unquam."

[55] The CNTC vv. 8–12 list a total of five references. This agrees with Parker's critical edition of Romans, and Feld's editions of II Corinthians and the Galatians group. There are no references in Romans, three references in I Corinthians, at 1.17, 3.15, and 4.7. There are no references in II Corinthians or Galatians, there is one reference in Ephesians 4.11. There are no references in Philippians, Colossians, the letters to the Thessalonians, Timothy, Philemon or Hebrews. The final reference is in Titus 1.7.

[56] Comm. I Corinthians 1.17, CO 49.322. "For, just as Augustine said, 'He who gave Peter, the fisherman, also gave Cyprian, the orator.'" "Nam, sicut ait Augustinus, qui Petrum dedit piscatorem, dedit et Cyprianum rhetorem."

of straw with gold in I Corinthians 3.15.[57] Again, there is no specific reference to Cyprian's interpretation of any given passage.

In each of the three cases where Calvin names Cyprian as his source he presents the Carthaginian bishop as a friendly authority whose message supports the reformer's own interpretation. For instance, in commenting upon I Corinthians 4.7, "what do you have that you did not receive?", Calvin states that "Finally, we should never glory (just as Cyprian said), because nothing is ours."[58] Clearly, Calvin mentions Cyprian as a source with whom he is in agreement, rather than demonstrating how straw has become mixed with the gold.

This is also the case in the other two instances of citation by Cyprian's name. In the first case, Calvin uses Cyprian's interpretation of the episcopacy to validate his interpretation of Ephesians 4.11. Calvin writes

> There is no place in Scripture which more strongly overturns that tyrannical hierarchy, in which one earthly head is constituted. Cyprian followed Paul and defined briefly and clearly what is the legitimate monarchy of the Church. There is, he says, one episcopate, 'a part in which is held by individuals in solidarity.' This episcopate he claims only for Christ. In its administration he assigns a part to individuals, and that in solidarity, so that no one will exalt himself above others.[59]

Clearly, Calvin is more than pleased to receive Cyprian's authority in this case, although it may be noted that again he transforms Cyprian in the application of old doctrine to new circumstance. The other citation to Cyprian in the Pauline commentaries is a quotation from Augustine's approval of Cyprian's statement about the need for bishops to be patient learners as well as skillful teachers.[60] All of the particular citations to Cyprian are approving, rather than critical.[61]

---

[57] Comm. I Corinthians 3.15, CO 49, 357.

[58] Comm. I Corinthians 4.7, CO 49.367. "Denique in nullo gloriandum (sicuti ait Cyprianus), quia nihil nostrum sit."

[59] Comm. Ephesians 4.11. Ad Ephesios, 231.23–30. "Nullus ergo locus est in Scriptura, qui tyrannicam illam hierarchiam, in qua unum terrenum caput constituitur, fortius evertat. Paulum quoque sequutus Cyprianus, quae legitima sit Ecclesiae monarchia, breviter et praeclare definit. Unus, inquit, est eposcopatus, ›cuius a singulis in solidum pars tenetur‹. Episcopatum uni Christo vendicat. In eo administrando partem singulis assignat, et quidem in solidum, ne quis supra alios se extollat."

[60] Comm. Titus 1.7, CO 52, 411. "Augustine praises Cyprian's saying, 'Let him patiently learn as he knowledgeably teaches.'" "Celebratur ab Augustino Cypriani sententia, Tam patienter discat, quam scienter doceat."

[61] This is generally true of some of the other figures as well, there are no citations to Bernard in the Pauline commentaries, and very few to Gregory and Ambrose.

Calvin's reception through fire was a formula for the reception of tradition. Calvin did not frequently speak about "tradition", it was a term which had become too polemically difficult to handle. However, he was unafraid of "religion." For Calvin, the Christian religion, the right relating of humanity to God, remains unchanging across the centuries. What changes are the outward forms, or accidents, of that observance, and the specific remedies for each people and age. The task of the theologian remains constant, it is always to provide nourishing doctrine for the edification of the Church. But the order of right teaching may change, due to the needs of the people, or the nature of the challenges which the Church faces. Thus, Calvin offers that even the most holy fathers must be received as through fire, not that all their substance will be burnt, but that the human weaknesses, the contextual dross, must be continually purged. In this manner, *"ecclesia reformata, semper reformanda"* rings true.[62] The circle of interpretation stands as an existential norm for the Church, the various historical expressions represent concrete examples of the outcome of that norm, but are always historically contextual, responding to specific circumstances that are not permanent. The picture remains the same, but the canvas is continually shifting. Thus, though the search for the disposition to piety (*pietas*) remains constant, the continually shifting circumstances demand constant reform.

Other passages of Calvin's reception of religion demonstrate this dynamic. One example comes from Calvin's commentary on II Corinthians 4.4. This passage of textual exposition provides another excellent example of Calvin's reception of traditional doctrine and exegesis, while differentiating between the two. Calvin criticizes four of the fathers for twisting the meaning of Paul's mind for the laudable intention of protecting the (to speak from a later viewpoint) orthodox faith. To facilitate ease of reading, here is the entire passage.

> *In whom the god of this world.* He means that no weight should be given to the perverse stubbornness of his opponents. 'They do not see the midday sun', he says, 'because the devil has blinded their understanding.' Nobody of sound judgment can have any doubt that here the Apostle is speaking of Satan. Because Hilary had to deal with Arians who mis-

---

[62] However, *"Ecclesia Reformata, Semper Reformanda"* was not Calvin's slogan. Philip Benedict has traced it to Johannes Hoornbeeck in the middle of the seventeenth century. *Christ's Churches Purely Reformed: A Social History of Calvinism* (New Haven: Yale University Press, 2002), xvi.

used this passage in support of their view that Christ was God, though they denied his true divinity, he twists the text to mean that it is God who has blinded the understanding of this world. Later he was followed by Chrysostom in this reading in order to avoid conceding to the Manichaeans their dualistic view of two first principles. Why Ambrose accepted it is not clear. However, Augustine's reason was the same as Chrysostom's for he also was involved with the Manichaeans. We thus see what the heat of controversy can do in disputes. If all these men had read Paul's words with a calm mind it would never have occurred to them to twist them into a forced meaning in this way. But they were being harassed by their opponents, so they became more concentrated upon disputing them than to inquire into the mind of Paul. But why make such work? It was a puerile subterfuge for the Arians to argue that because the devil is called the god of this world, the word God as applied to Christ does not express true, eternal and unique divinity. Paul says in another place that 'many are called gods', and David declares that 'the gods of the nations are demons'. Thus when the devil is called a god because he has dominion over the impious and is worshipped by them instead of God, how can this detract in any way from the dignity of Christ? As for the Manichaeans this title lends no more substance to their views than when the devil is called the prince of this world. Thus there is no reason why we should be afraid to interpret this passage as applying to the devil for that can be done without any danger.[63]

Here we see one of Calvin's methods of dealing historically with problems, that is, arguing with the exegetical tradition. While it is unlikely that Calvin had the time to do significant research for its own sake into

---

[63] Comm. II Corinthians 4.4, Secundum Ad Corinthos, 70.14–71.15. "*Quibus deus seculi huius.* Significat, quam nihili fieri debeat perversa illorum obstinatio. Non vident, inquit, solem in meridie, quia diabolus eorum sensus excaecavit. Quin de Satana loquator Apostolus, nemini recte iudicanti dubium esse potest. Hilarius, quia negotium habebat cum Arrianis, qui hoc praetextu abutebantur, ut Christum confitendo Deum veram eius divinitatem negarent, sic contextum torquet: Deus excaecavit huius seculi sensus. Id postea sequutus est Chrysostomus, ne Manichaeis duo principia concederet. Quid Ambrosium impulerit, non apparet. Augustino eadem ratio fuit quae Chrysostomo, quia cum Manichaeis erat illi certamen. Videmus, quid faciat contentionis fervor in disputationibus. Si composito animo legissent illi omnes Pauli verba, nemini eorum in mentem venisset ita in coactum sensum torquere. Sed quia urgebant adversarii, magis de illis propulsandis quam de inquirenda Pauli mente soliciti fuerunt. Sed quid opus fuit? Puerile enim erat effugium Arrianorum: Si diabolus vocetur deus seculi, nomen Dei in Christo non exprimere veram et aeternam et unicam divinitatem. Multi enim dii, inquit alibi Paulus, nominantur. Sed dii Gentium daemonia, occinit ex altera parte David. Diabolum ergo vocari deum impiorum, qui illis dominetur, qui ab illis colatur Dei loco, quid hoc ad extenuandum Christi honorem? Manichaeis vero nihilo plus suffragatur haec appellatio, quam quum dicitur: ⟩princeps mundi⟨. Non est igitur, quod vereamur de diabolo hunc locum interpretari, quum sine periculo fiat."

the texts or authors whom he quotes,[64] his use of them suggests broad familiarity with the patristic exegetical tradition.[65]

For Calvin, the meaning of the text is clear, that the phrase "God of this world" must be referred to the Devil. He then concludes that some of patristic comment upon it is flawed. He uses a historical contextualization to argue the reasons for the patristic authors who go astray. He sets out the incorrect opinions of Hilary, Chrysostom, Augustine and Ambrose. His text for Hilary seems to be the *Glossa ordinaria*.[66] Whatever the source, Calvin was not off the historical track in conjecturing Hilary to be consumed with the Arian controversy. Chrysostom was a great favorite of Calvin's and he knew the father well.[67] This citation is taken from the sermons on II Corinthians.[68] Chrysostom's concern with both Marcionism and Manichaeism is clear from his text, and Calvin hardly stretches too far in drawing that historical conclusion.[69] Chrysostom's sermons were probably preached outside of Constantinople, and probably after 391,[70] a time when Manichaeanism was a threat in the East as it was in North Africa. The Augustine text comes from *Contra Faustum*.[71] Augustine's revulsion with the Manichaeans, and particularly with Faustus, hardly needs to be rehearsed. As Faustus was putting forward a "reformed Christianity,"[72] Augustine needed to silence him. The resulting *Contra Faustem*, written around 397, was the source of Calvin's

---

[64] Parker thinks the commentary on I Corinthians was finished by late November, and the dedication is dated January 24, 1546. Parker, 19. The II Corinthians commentary's dedication to Melchior Wolmar is dated August 1, 1546. Thus, the time for composition can not reasonably be deemed to be more than six months, during a time at which Calvin was fully engaged in the work at Geneva.

[65] Irena Backus, *Historical Method and Confessional Identity in the Era of the Reformation (1378–1615)* (Leiden: Brill, 2003), 117. Backus seconds this for Calvin's work on Trinity and Free Will.

[66] Feld, 70, n. 14. If such was the case, it would fit Backus' finding that Calvin takes some of his sources from florilegia.

[67] See Alexandre Ganoczy and Klaus Müller, *Calvins handschriftliche Annotationen zu Chrysostomus. Ein Beitrag zur hermeneutik Calvins* (Wiesbaden: Franz Stein Verlag, 1981).

[68] Feld, 70, n. 15. Hom. 8.

[69] Chrysostom, Migne, PG 61, 455. "Quid sibi vult illud, *Deus hujus saeculi*? Qui Marcionis morbo laborant, de rerum Opifice, justo quidem illo, sed non item bono, haec dicta esse contendunt: aiunt enim Deum quemdam justum esse, qui non sit bonus. Manichaei autem his verbis diabolum significari asserunt; hinc nimirum alium rerum conditarum effectorem, praeter eum qui vere est, perquam stolide inducere cupientes."

[70] Johannes Quasten, Patrology, vol. 3 (Utrecht: Spectrum, 1960), 437–447.

[71] Feld, 71, n. 17.

[72] Peter Brown, *Augustine of Hippo: A New Edition with Epilogue* (Berkeley: California, 200), 48.

citation.[73] In all of these cases, Calvin used a single historical method, contextualization, to argue that the heat of demonstrable battle had led the fathers astray. To call this a historical method is rather generous, as Calvin simply matched historical problems faced by the fathers with the general time of their texts; we have no evidence that he trolled through histories to examine the exact contexts of their controversies.

That method seemed to fail him when he turned to Ambrose, for whom Calvin could supply no reason for the Bishop of Milan to take such a position. This point in his text stands out like a sore thumb, Calvin has "vanquished" the tradition in all of those issues which he has raised, but of Ambrose, simply says, "Why Ambrose accepted this, is not apparent." Calvin had happily worked through the issues of the other patristic sources, but can offer no reason for Ambrose. Here, we have some evidence of Calvin as a fairly astute historian. Yes, Calvin finds no explanation for Ambrose's acceptance of a position. The problem is solved by later scholarship—this is not Ambrose, but Ambrosiaster.[74] As early as 1527, Erasmus had suggested that this text was not Ambrose, but that was not fully accepted in Calvin's day. Calvin's refusal to ram this text into a Procrustean ideal of the bishop of Milan represents a victory of historical judgment, rather than a failure. His contextualizing method provides an actual moment he arrived at a correct, albeit unfinished, historical conclusion.

In the case of I Corinthians 14.14, Calvin again takes the named ecclesiastical writers to task. At issue is the praying in tongues.[75] Calvin notes that praying in a tongue means praying in a foreign language, but wonders about the meaning of "spirit", in the following phrase, that "my spirit prays, but my understanding is unfruitful." In his consideration, he takes on several of the Church fathers.

> What is meant by praying in a tongue is clear from that which comes above, to express a prayer in a foreign language. What is meant by 'spirit'

---

[73] Augustine had high hopes for Faustus' ability to clarify the doctrines of Mani which had so troubled him when he met him in 383. Faustus' inability to do so, and his use of rhetoric to avoid the issues, so annoyed Augustine that he contributed to Augustine's departure from Manichaeism. In 397 and 398, Augustine wrote Contra Faustum. Brown, 47–48, 178.

[74] Feld, 70, n. 16. Ambrosiaster states "Deum dicit saecularium hominum, quia malivoli sunt erga fidem Christi, sensus obcaecare, ne videant veritatem evangelii maiestatis Christis. Hoc ergo illis praestat quod volunt." Corpus Scriptorum Ecclesiasticorum Latinorum, vol. 81, part 2, 221.

[75] It should be noted that Calvin's understanding of the spiritual gift of glossalalia is quite specific, and dis-allows some of the common modern understandings.

is not so easy to explain. An idea that has no particular reason, and not even the appearance of a reason, is Ambrose's reference to the Spirit which we receive in baptism. Augustine more subtly takes it to mean the apprehension which grasps ideas and the signs of realities, so that it is a faculty of the soul inferior to mental intelligence. More probably, is the opinion of those who understand it as the breathing of the throat, in plainer terms the breath. However, this interpretation conflicts with the way that Paul constantly uses the word in this discussion. Even more than that, the word appears to have been repeated so often by way of concession. For they were taking a pride in that title, which Paul certainly allows them to have; but he, on the other hand, is pointing out how dangerous it is to make wrong use of a good and wonderful thing. It is as if he said: 'You are boasting to me about this spirit of yours. But why, if it is useless?' This reason is why I am led to assent to Chrysostom's understanding of this word, for he gives it the same meaning as it had before, a spiritual gift. Thus 'my spirit' will mean exactly the same as 'the gift given to me.'

But here a new question is raised. For it is incredible (at least we do not read of any instance) that there were any people who spoke by influence of the Spirit, in a language they did not know themselves. The gift of tongues was not conferred merely for a way of making noise, but to make communication possible. For how ridiculous it would have been had the tongue of a Roman been directed by the Spirit of God to utter Greek words, when he himself had no knowledge of Greek whatever. He would have been like the parrots, magpies and crows which are trained to make human sounds! But if someone endowed with the gift of tongues spoke sensibly and intelligently, it would have been pointless for Paul to say that 'the spirit prays but the understanding is unfruitful', for the understanding must have been acting together with the spirit.

I respond that for the sake of illustration Paul is taking a purely hypothetical situation, as follows: 'If the gift of speaking in a tongue is kept distinct from the understanding, so that the speaker is a barbarian to himself as well as others, what good will he do by babbling along like that?' For it is not correct to describe the understanding as ἄκαρπον, unfruitful, on the grounds that the Church derives no benefit, in view of the fact that Paul is speaking about the private prayers of individuals here. Let us therefore remember that things which are really bound together are kept separate here for the sake of teaching, and not because it can or usually does fall out that way. The meaning is now plain. 'If I devise prayers in a language that is unknown to me, and the spirit provides me with a rich flow of words, it is clear that the spirit itself, which controls my tongue, will indeed be praying, but my understanding will be wandering elsewhere, or at any rate will not be involved in that prayer.[76]

---

[76] Comm. I Corinthians 14.14, CO 49.521–522. "Quid sit lingua orare, ex superi-

Setting aside Calvin's ingenious solution to the difficulty, what is at hand is his treatment of the patristic authorities. Simply put, there is a confused tradition regarding this passage. Calvin delineates between the various options available, and demonstrates the validity of his choice.

In Ambrose (Ambrosiaster), Calvin objects to the departure from Paul's argument for the purpose of identifying the Spirit with the Spirit given in baptism.[77] Calvin makes the point that there is no textual warrant for this assertion. Further, when Ambrosiaster makes this interpretation of "*spiritus*", he allows the Spirit that has been given to a believer to pray without fruit, at least without fruit for the mind!

---

oribus liquet: nempe concipere precationem idiomate peregrino. Quid sit autem spiritus, non ita facile est explicatu. Omni non ratione tantum caret, sed etiam colore, quod Ambrosius ad spiritum refert, quem accepimus in baptismo. Augustinus subtilius pro apprehensione accipit, quae ideas concipit et signa rerum: ut sit animae facultas inferior mentis intelligentia. Probabilior est eorum opinio qui spiritum gutturis interpretantur, hoc est, flatum. Verum huic interpretationi repugnat perpetua in hac Pauli disputatione verbi significatio. Quin etiam apparet repetitum saepius fuisse per concessionem. Superbiebant enim honorifico isto titulo, quem Paulus illis quidem permittit: sed rursum indicat quam praeposterus sit rei bonae et praeclarae abusus. Ac si diceret: Tu mihi spiritum iactas, quorsum, si est inutilis? Hac ratione adducor ut in sensu huius verbi assentiar Chrysostomo, qui exponit sicuti prius de spirituali dono. Ita spiritus meus perinde valebit ac donum mihi collatum. Sed hic nova quaestio exoritur: neque enim credibile est (saltem nusquam legimus) loquutos fuisse ullos spiritus impulsu lingua sibi incognita. Linguarum enim donum conferebatur non ad resonandum modo, sed potius ad communicandum. Quam enim ridiculum fuisset, linguam hominis romani formari a Dei spiritu ad pronuntiandas voces graecas, quae loquenti essent prorsus ignotae: qualiter psittaci et picae et corvi humanas voces fingere docentur? Quod si praeditus dono linguarum non sine sensu et intelligentia loquebatur: frustra dictum fuit a Paulo, spiritum orare, mentem fructu carere: nam mentem cum spiritu coniunctam esse oportuit. Respondeo, Paulum hic hypothesin sumere docendi causa, quae non erat, hoc modo: si donum linguae ab intelligentia separetur, ita ut qui pronuntiat, sit ipse sibi barbarus, quemadmodum aliis: quid proficiet, sic balbutiendo? Mentem enim vocari ἄκαρπον, quia utilitas nulla perveniat ad ecclesiam, minime convenit: quum hic Paulus loquatur de privatis cuiusque precibus. Retineamus ergo, disiungi res inter se coniunctas, docendi causa: non quia id vel possit, vel soleat contingere. Nunc sensus planus est. Si ergo idiomate mihi incognito preces concipiam, ac spiritus mihi verba suppeditet: ipse quidem spiritus, qui linguam meam gubernat, orabit: sed mens mea vel alibi vagabitur, vel saltem non erit orationis particeps."

[77] Ambrosiaster, *Commentaria in Epistolam B. Pauli Ad Corinthios Primam*, Caput XIV, PL, 17.255. "Nam si oravero lingua, spiritus meus orat, mens autem mea sine fructu est. Manifestum est ignorare animum nostrum, si lingua loquatur, quam nescit, sicut adsolent Latini homines Graece cantare, oblectati sono verborum; nescientes tamen quid dicant. Spiritus autem qui datur in baptismo, scit quid oret animus, dum loquitur, aut perorat lingua sibi ignota: mens autem qui est animus, sine fructu est. Quem enim potest habere fructum, qui ignorat quae loquatur?"

In Augustine, Calvin finds his spiritual ancestor shifting the conversation from a consideration of the meaning of "spirit" that has immediate reference both to the context of Paul's speech, and has concrete significance for application in the Church, seeing *spiritus* as a spiritual gift received. Augustine states that "There is likewise said to be a spirit in man which is not mind, to which belong the images formed according to the likeness of bodies; and he speaks about this to the Corinthians where he sais: 'But if I pray in a tongue, my spirit prays, but my mind is unfruitful.'"[78] Augustine has taken this text as a basis for considering the human psychology, a point which Calvin does not specifically dispute, but rather gives the damning appellation of subtlety (*subtilius*). Augustine's point may be correct, but this is not, in Calvin's opinion, what Paul intended to convey. Chrysostom receives Calvin's praise for the way in which he attacked the problem.[79] Chrysostom immediately notes that the spirit is a gift, which can be accompanied by the gift of understanding. The Corinthians, as well as the Constantinapolitans, are to pray for both. Thus, Chrysostom fulfills both Calvin's desire for simplicity, and his drive for application of the text.

The Ephesians text on the breadth, height, length, and depth of the love of Christ (Eph. 3.18) provides Calvin ample opportunity to lecture at some length to Augustine and others who would stray too far from the plain metaphorical sense. In doing so, Calvin was not only taking on Augustine and Ambrose, but also a significant medieval tradition concerning this text. Bonaventure, in particular, had used this text as an allegorical guide to the preparation for the reading of scripture.[80]

---

[78] Augustine, *De Trinitate XIV*.xvi. *De Trinitate*, in *Aurelii Augustini Opera*, Corpus Christianorum, series Latina, edited by W.J. Mountain, (Turnholt: Brepols, 1968), 452. "Dicitur etiam spiritus in homine qui mens non sit, ad quem pertinent imaginationes similes corporum, de quo dicit ad corinthios ubi dicit: Si autem orauero lingua, spiritus meus orat; mens autem mea infructuosa est."

[79] Chrysostom, Homily 35, In Epist. I Ad Cor. Homil., PG 61.300. "Nam si quis loquatur solum Pesarum lingua, aut aliqua alia aliena, nesciat autem quae dicit, certe etiam sibi ipsijam erit barbarus, non alii solum, eo quod nesciat vim vocis. Erant enim antiquitus ulti qui orationis donum habebant cum lingua; et orabant quidem, et lingua loquebatur, aut Persarum aut Romanorum voce orans; mens autem nesciebat quod dicebatur. Ideo icebat, Si orem lingua, spiritus meus orat; id est, charisma quod datum est mihi et movet linguam; mens autem mea sine fructu est. Quid ergo optimum et utile est? et quomodo faciendum, quid petendum a Deo est? Ut et spiritu, id est charismate, et mente oretur."

[80] Bonaventure, *Breviloquium*, Prologue. The Breviloquium, Vol. II in The Works of St. Bonaventure, translated by José de Vinck, (Paterson, NJ: St. Anthony Guild Press, 1963), 1–16.

But Calvin takes little time to enumerate what he considers the errors of those earlier interpreters, saying only that the text's meaning has been "obscured by a variety of interpretations." There can be little doubt, however, that the interjection against speculative philosophizing can and should also be referred to speculative exegesis.

> *May be able to comprehend.* The second fruit is that the Ephesians should perceive the greatness of Christ's love to humans. Such an apprehension or knowledge comes from faith. By associating them with all the saints, he shows that it is the supreme good that can be obtained in the present life, that it is the highest wisdom, to which all the children of God aspire. Therefore what follows is sufficiently clear, but has been obscured by a variety of interpretations. Augustine is very pleased with his subtlety, which has nothing to do with the subject. For he seeks here I know not what mystery in the figure of the cross; he makes the breadth to be love, the height, hope, the length, patience, and the depth, humility. All these please with subtlety, but what do they have to do the mind of Paul? No more, certainly, than the opinion of Ambrose, that it denotes the shape of a sphere. Leaving aside the views of others, I shall state what all will acknowledge to be simple and true. By these dimensions Paul understands nothing other than the love of Christ, of which he speaks afterwards. The meaning is, that he who knows it truly and perfectly is in every respect a wise man. As if he had said, 'In whatever direction humans may look, they will find nothing in the doctrine of salvation that should not be related to this.' The love of Christ contains within itself every aspect of wisdom. The meaning will be clearer if we paraphrase it like this: 'In order that you may be able to comprehend the love which is the length, breadth, depth, and height, understand it as the complete perfection of our wisdom.' The metaphor is taken from mathematics, denoting the whole from the parts. Almost all are infected with the disease of desiring useless knowledge. Therefore this admonition is very useful: it is what is necessary for us to know, and what the Lord desires us to contemplate, above and below, on the right hand and on the left, before and behind. The love of Christ is held out to us to meditate on day and night and to be wholly immersed in. The one who holds on to this alone, has enough. Beyond it there is nothing solid, nothing useful, nothing, in short, that is right or sound. Go abroad in heaven and earth and sea, you will never go beyond this without overstepping the legitimate bounds of wisdom.[81]

---

[81] Comm. Ephesians 3.18. Ad Ephesios 215.23–216.22. "*Quo valeatis comprehendere. Secundus fructus, ut percipiant Ephesii, quanta sit erga homines Christi dilectio. Talis autem apprehensio vel notitia ex fide est. Quum in ea re sanctos omnes illis socios adiungit, indicat praestantissimum esse bonum, quod possint in praesenti vita consequi, supremam esse sapientiam, ad quam omnes filii Dei aspirant. Caeterum quod sequitur, quum per se clarum sit, hactenus variis interpretationum opinionibus obscu-*

Here, Calvin is disagreeing with Augustine's position in his *De Doctrina Christiana*. Augustine writes

> Thus 'rooted and founded in charity,' we 'may be able to comprehend, with all the saints, what is the breadth, the length, and height, and depth,' which things make up the Cross of Our Lord. Its breadth is said to be in the transverse beam upon which the hands are stretched; its length extends from the ground to the crossbar, and on it the whole body from the hands down is affixed; its height reaches from the crossbar to the top where the head is placed; and its depth is that part which is hidden beneath the earth. In the Sign of the Cross the whole action of the Christian is described: to perform good deeds in Christ, to cling to Him with perseverance, to hope for celestial things, to refrain from profaning the sacraments.[82]

Again, this difference can be seen as a paradigmatic instance of agreement of doctrine, coupled with significant difference in exegetical application. Calvin would not disagree with any of the morals that Augustine derives from this pericope. The Christian is called upon to do the

---

ratum fuit. Augustinus in argutia nihil ad rem pertinente sibi valde placuit. Quaerit enim hic mysterium nescio quod in figura crucis. Deinde ex latitudine facit charitatem, ex altitudine spem, ex longitudine patientiam et ex profunditate humilitatem. Haec subtilitate sua placent. Sed quid ad Pauli mentem? Nihilo certe magis, quam quod Ambrosius sphaericam formam designari putat. Verum aliorum interpretationibus omissis dicam, quod omnes simplex et verum esse agnoscent. Paulus enim nihil per istas dimensiones intelligit quam Christi charitatem, de qua continuo post, significans eum, cui vere et perfecte cognita est, undequaque sapere, acsi dixisset: Quaquaversum respiciant homines, nihil reperient in salutis doctrina, quod non huc referendum sit. Continet enim una Christi dilectio omnes sapientiae numeros. Ideo quo facilior sit sensus, ita resolvi debent verba: Ut valeatis comprehendere Christi dilectionem, quae est longitudo, latitudo, profunditas et altitudo sapientiae nostra, hoc est: tota perfectio. Similitudinem enim sumit a mathematicis, ut a partibus totum disignet. Quoniam hic omnium fere communis est morbus: rerum inutilium studio ardere, utilis valde est ista admonitio: quid scire nobis expediat et quid Dominus considerare nos velit sursum, deorsum, ad dextram et sinistram, a fronte et a tergo. Dilectio Christi nobis proponitur, in cuius meditatione nos exerceamus dies ac noctes et in quam nos quasi demergamus. Hanc unam qui tenet, satis habet. Extra eam nihil est solidum, nihil utile, nihil denique rectum aut sanum. Circumeas licet caelum, terras, maria: non altius transcendes, quin legitimum sapiendi finem transilias."

[82] De Doctrina Christiana, II.xli.62. *On Christian Doctrine*. Translated by D.W. Robertson, Jr. Library of Liberal Arts, Indianapolis: Bobbs Merrill, 1958, II.xli.62. "Ut in caritate radicati et fundati possimus comprehendere cum omnibus sanctis, quae sit latitudo et longitudo et altitudo et profundum, id est crucem domini; cuius latitudo dicitur in transuerso ligno, quo extenduntur manus; longitudo a terra usque ad ipsam latitudinem, quo a manibus et infra totum corpus affigitur; altitudo a latitudine sursum usque ad summum, quo adhaeret caput; profundum uero, quod terrae infixum absconditur. Quo signo crucis, omnis actio christiana describitur, bene operari in Christo et ei perseueranter inhaerere, sperare caelestia, sacramenta non profanare."

good in Christ, to cling always to the Lord, to hope for heaven, and
to maintain a proper attitude toward the sacraments. The question is
not whether Calvin and Augustine generally agreed upon these issues.
Rather, for Calvin, the issue is whether this interpretation passes the
test of being true to the mind of Paul. In Ephesians, does Paul suggest a cruciform stance, or is he using a metaphor for the wholeness
of Christ's love? The appearance of the term both preceding and following the contested portion of the text would seem to support Calvin's
view as the *sensus germanus*.

The Ambrose text in this case is again Ambrosiaster. Ambrosiaster
has taken the position that this represents a sphere.[83] The dimensions of
a sphere, with its equidistance from a center point, suggest to him the
equality of the immensity of God's perfections. However Calvin might
agree with the desire to point out God's excellencies, his view of this as
a model for demonstrating the mind of Paul is that it is sadly lacking.
Again, context has ruled out the possibility of an allegorical reading. It
should be quite easy to see that Calvin thus applies the same standards
to other traditional exegetes that he has to Augustine. The Church is
held together across the ages by the inculcation of Christian piety. Of
course, that leads to a final question.

Calvin's transformation of the Christian exegetical and doctrinal traditions represents at best a form of a-historical optimism, and at worst
a Machiavellian pragmatism. In either case, the truth of transformation cannot be proven, either as genuine development, or as doctrinal
equivalence in a changed historical circumstance. The idea of a genuine development begs the question of judgment, and it seems that no
one can state what doctrinal equivalence in radically different circumstances would be.[84]

There are two answers to be given. One attempts to stand outside of
Calvin's complex of thought, the other inside. Outside of Calvin's position, it has not been the effort of this study to demonstrate that Calvin

---

[83] Ambrosiaster, Ad Efesios, (CSEL 81 III.93.5.) "hoc significat, ut sicut in spera
tanta longitudo est quanta latitudo et tanta altitudo quantum profundum, ita et in deo
omnia aequalia sint inmensitate infinitatis."

[84] In fact, George Lindbeck's *The Nature of Doctrine: Religion and Theology in a Postlib-
eral Age*, (Philadelphia: Westminster Press, 1984), argues for the incommensurability of
cultural-linguistic specimens with each other. That is to say that cultural-linguistic settings are created in language which permits expression of ideas, and truly different
cultural-linguistic communities cannot break the barriers between them. Though Lindbeck's point is made about different cultures that are synchronous, the historical implications are obvious for two cultures widely separated in time.

was right, or correct, or godly. Rather, it has been an effort to follow the coherence of a hermeneutical approach to both history and scripture. Occasionally, Calvin's project proves unconvincing, or fails. Having said that, it is possible to state that Calvin assumes, rather uncritically, a particular stance as the correct sum of Christian teaching. Further, he recognizes that his own stance is historically situated, and therefore subject to reform. Having accepted this reality, he relegates other issues to the hegemony of that stance, and occasionally that hegemony can become a tyranny. This analysis does a better job of maintaining Calvin as a coherent thinker in his own day than some other options which would find him unable to see blatant contradictions in his thought, or caught between his medieval and Renaissance sides.

From within Calvin's thought-world, the question melts away. Calvin, in wide agreement with Augustine and many other orthodox thinkers, held that faith, or the experience of the Holy Spirit in one's life, is the guarantor of the correct living of right religion. Both Calvin and Augustine made the work of the Holy Spirit the condition for the understanding of the scriptures. Even the prince of the scholastics, Thomas Aquinas, will note that the nature of the theological task as a subordinated science makes it finally reducible to a position of faith.[85]

---

[85] Aquinas, Summa Theologiae, Ia. I, 2. Blackfriars edition (London: Eyre & Spottiswoode, 1964), 10–11. "Dicendum sacram doctrinam scientiam esse. Sed sciendum est quod duplex est scientiarum genus. Quaedam enim sunt quae procedunt ex principiis notis lumine naturali intellectus, sicut arithmetica, geometria, et hujusmodi; quaedam vero sunt quae procedunt ex principiis notis lumine superioris scientiae, sicut perspectiva procedit ex principiis notificatis per geometriam et musica ex principiis per arithmeticam notis.

Et hoc modo sacra doctrina est scientia, quia procedit ex principiis notis lumine superioris scientiae, quae scilicet est Dei et beatorum. Unde sicut musica credit principia sibi tradita ab arithmetico ita sacra doctrina credit principia revelata a Deo." "Christian theology should be pronounced to be a science. Yet bear in mind that sciences are of two kinds: some work from premises recognized in the innate light of intelligence, for instance arithmetic, geometry, and sciences of the same sort; while others work from premises recognized in the light of a higher science, for instance optics starts out from principles marked out by geometry and harmony from principles indicated by arithmetic.

In this second manner is Christian theology a science, for it flows from founts recognized in the light of a higher science, namely God's very own which he shares with the blessed. Hence as harmony credits its principles which are taken from arithmetic so Christian theology takes on faith its principles revealed by God." Thomas has set out theology as a subordinated science, subordinated by the knowledge (scientia) of God and the blessed. But the only access to some of this is through the scriptures, whose authority is accepted on faith. Without rehearsing each step of the argument necessary

Thus, Calvin has good company when he claims that the Spirit is the seal of the Christian experience, and the guide, both above and through the scriptures, to the Christian life.

Religionis per Ignis

We must note now that Calvin's reception and transformation of the tradition does not represent a new practice in Christianity. Gregory the Great transformed Augustine through the needs of his own ministry.[86] It has been widely acknowledged that Aquinas' vision of Augustine is at least a transposition. The whole formation of a "monastic theology" represents an amalgamation of classical and patristic sources, drawn through the collander of monastic life.[87] Calvin stands out against this backdrop because of the fact of the Reformation, not because of the project he proposed.

However, Calvin was intentional about his interpretation of both scripture and history. He does supply a rationale for this transformative reception, the reception *per ignis*. That which is not founded directly and only upon Christ is as dross. It is to be cleansed, through the trial of fire, which will make those good buildings stronger, and will free later generations from having to hold onto accretions to the Christian religion that are not genuine.

For Calvin, this was neither an exercise in theology, nor an effort to make a satisfying argument. It was instead a process ordained by God, who directs the children of the Lord again and again to the scriptures to search out a more clear and pure piety. Calvin finds difficulties in Paul's confusion of convention with nature, in the same way that he finds difficulties with early exegesis and its signification of a biblical passage against the simple sense of the text so as to use it more effectively for the maintenance of orthodoxy. In each case, a later viewpoint, a different horizon, supplies the necessary stance for seeing the difficulty, and for cleansing it away.

---

to arrive at the final step, the final step must be that theology, as a science, must begin with a step of faith.

[86] G.R. Evans, *The Thought of Gregory the Great* (Cambridge: Cambridge University Press, 1986), x.

[87] See Jean LeClercq, *The Love of Learning and the Desire for God: A Study of Monastic Culture*, translated by Catharine Misrahi (New York: Fordham University Press, 1961), esp. ch. 4–7, "The Sources of Monastic Culture."

In transforming tradition to maintain religion, Calvin followed an time-honored approach. The historical accident of his living in the first half of the sixteenth century has blurred that truth. Had Calvin been a reformer in a different time, that is to say any earlier period of Christian history than the Reformation, it is quite possible that his work would have been seen as a broad reform within the wide stream of the Church's life.[88] Such is not the case. Thus, inter-confessional strife has made the recovery of Calvin's reception of the Church's tradition a matter of "true or false inheritance" of Augustine, or the patristic authors, or Paul, or the Bible. Those frameworks, as well as the attempt to see Calvin as a fore-runner of historical-critical exegetical method, must finally be set aside. It is more appropriate to see Calvin as an ecclesial interpreter, guided by a passion for the edification of the Church.

Conclusion

The mechanics of interpretation, moving through hermeneutical principles to exegetical practices, have been considered. The horizon toward which that interpretation moves has been covered. The nature of Calvin's theological enterprise, edification, has been discussed at some length, as well as how edification determined his efforts at building a Christian body, and how that body functions as a discerning textual community. Now, we have seen Calvin struggle to recover the gold from traditional readings, while purifying the dross of historical accidents. What remains to be discussed is the nature of Calvin's hermeneutical project. It was earlier stated that Calvin should not be named as an exegetical theologian, but rather a hermeneutical theologian, and in the final chapter, I will argue why this is the case. We will see that Calvin turned to the search for Christian truth through a hermeneutical process of interpretation of scripture, history, and the Church.

---

[88] Certainly, this is not to say that his thought would have been accepted by all of the faithful as salutary. One need only recall the difficulties caused by the Cistercian reform among the Cluniacs, or the difficulties some bishops had with the concept of friars who were in some sense not answerable to their authority during the 13th century. The point is, Calvin's historical place in the 16th century has guaranteed a confessional difference in the way we view his efforts to grasp Christian truth in concert with the earlier portions of the Church's tradition.

CHAPTER SEVEN

TRADITIONS RENEWED

> Even the most lively originality cannot aim at anything higher than to set the common doctrine in the clearest light; just as, again, for the common element there is no higher aim than to encourage the peculiar and original development of doctrine without disturbing the communion, by establishing as definitely as possible the Protestant character of the system. The more the two elements thus interpenetrate each other, the more ecclesiastical, and at the same time the more favourable to progress, is the presentation. The more they are detached from each other, and merely stand side by side as unconnected, the more does the element which clings to the historical, and is set up as of common acceptance, appear to be of merely antiquarian interest, and the original element to be simply ultra-modern.[1]

Through this study, I have traced Calvin's approach to scripture, and the tools he used in that interpretive effort. I have demonstrated a set of hermeneutical categories and exegetical rules that are more helpful than either the historical-critical or the purely doctrinal efforts of earlier attempts to understand Calvin's approach to scripture. I have attempted to display that Calvin understands himself as maintaining the religious tradition, while re-setting its exegetical framework, and some of its doctrinal significations to fit the needs of the faith community to which he ministered.

Calvin's theological effort stands as a testament to what Schleiermacher attempted to state, with one great difference. Calvin knew of no Protestant character to the theological task, and denied its possibility. For him, the Church was always catholic, always Christ's indivisible body. Instead, he grasped a Christian religion that is everywhere and always essentially the same, though masked under different historical circumstances and challenges. He molded this Christian religion through the interpenetration of what I have called the transformational reception of tradition, and the particular pedagogical presentation of doctrine to a single set of contemporary historical circumstances. This interpenetration encompassed the effort to train the Church toward her

---

[1] Friedrich Schleiermacher, *The Christian Faith*, edited by H.R. Mackintosh and J.S. Stewart (Edinburgh: T. & T. Clark, 2001), §25, 110.

final engrafting in Christ which was Calvin's aspiration. Schleiermacher described, in the interpenetration of the common and the peculiar, the work of an ecclesiastical theologian. For Calvin, there was no other kind of doctor.

Calvin's Tasks

Calvin saw the first, last, and only task of theology as the edification of the Church.[2] Serving as the pastor of Geneva and Strasbourg between 1536 and 1564, several realities were brought home to him. The first was that his main community of discourse consisted of the bourgeoisie and artisans who populated these cities. He was not attempting university discourses with learned colleagues, at least not primarily.[3] He had the care for souls laid upon him, and that burden was one he keenly felt.[4]

The literacy of his congregations was spectacularly high by previous standards. Figures as high as 50% adult literacy have been posited, and Bible and catechism reading were both desired and possible.[5] This is demonstrated by Calvin's 1537 *Articles concerning the Organization of the Church*, which make the singing of psalms and the instruction of infants in the faith obligatory; no possibility of this structure would have been possible without widespread literacy.[6] The people of Geneva were to be steeped in the language and logic of the Bible, and to be knowledgeable enough to differentiate between the doctrine of the word of God and

---

[2] See Brian Armstrong's "*Duplex cognitio Dei*, Or? The Problem and Relation of Structure, Form, and Purpose in Calvin's Theology," in *Probing the Reformed Tradition: Historical Studies in Honor of Edward A. Dowey, Jr.*, edited by Elsie Anne McKee and Brian G. Armstrong (Louisville: Westminster John Knox Press, 1989), 135–153.

[3] See Serene Jones *Calvin and the Rhetoric of Piety*, Columbia Series in Reformed Theology (Louisville: Westminster John Knox Press, 1995), for a reconstruction of the audiences whom Calvin was trying to reach.

[4] This is Cadier's point, that Calvin's life was lived under a sense of God's mastery of his life, which sent it in a direction Calvin had not desired. See Jean Cadier, *Calvin, the Man God Mastered*, translated by O.R. Johnston (Grand Rapids, MI: Eerdmans Publishing Co., 1960).

[5] John Hale, *The Civilization of Europe in the Renaissance* (New York: Atheneum, 1994), 399.

[6] *Articles Concernant L'Organisation de L'Église et du Culte a Genève*, CO 10.1–13. *Articles concerning the Organization of the Church and of Worship at Geneva 1537, Calvin: Theological Treatises*, edited by J.K.S. Reid, Library of Christian Classics (Philadelphia: Westminster Press, 1954), 48.

false innovations and inventions.[7] This was necessary for them to take their place both as adolescents progressing in the *schola Dei*, and to fulfill their duties as members of the community of discernment of the meaning of the scriptures.[8]

I have argued that for Calvin, the task of theology is the edification of the Church. From this stance, two advantages are retained. First, some of the more common and inspired efforts at divining the organizational coherency of Calvin's thought can be grasped together. Bauke's *complexio oppositum*, Gerrish's eucharistic theology, Dowey's *duplex cognitio Dei*, and Jones' rhetorical dispositional efforts can be subsumed under this effort. Secondly, this understanding of theology as edification can explain some of the seemingly opposed positions which Calvin's own theology took. It does edify the Church to have a strong self-abnegating strand, which is tied into the regeneration of the believer. On the other hand, it also edifies the Church, and the believer, to understand that it is only through God's merciful act that salvation is possible. Thus, salvation *sola gratia* is paired with a working faith; seen from one angle this is logically inconsistent, from another vantage point this tension offers the edification and education of the body of Christ, and acceptance of the paradox of the Christian faith in this land away from home for the believer.

We must note carefully that for Calvin, this theological enterprise was not a new task, not a new religion, for the gospel was not new. The perennial question that faces the Christian community in any age is that of discernment, of finding the proper way to God's truth as it applies in a new set of historical circumstances. Calvin solved this problem in a manner which is both conservative of the doctrinal legacy which he received, and flexible enough to withstand new historical circumstances. He based the curriculum of the *schola Dei* on the interpretation of scripture. Here we must keep in mind a critical point, that Calvin did not interpret scripture in order to establish a place

---

[7] The allusion to Gillian Evans book is intentional. In her *The Language and Logic of the Bible: The Road to Reformation*, (Cambridge: Cambridge University Press, 1985), Evans makes it clear that the late medieval habit was to withhold the text of the Bible from the laity in its "bare completeness." (152) For more, see Evans, 144–157.

[8] Karin Maag has examined the role of education in the Swiss cities, and its important links to the formation of the members of the community in true religion. See her "The spectre of ignorance: the provision of education in the Swiss cities," *Fear in Early Modern Society*, edited by William Naphy and Penny Roberts (Manchester: Manchester University Press, 1997), 137–149.

of authority for the Church. That was a by-product, but was not the reason for turning to the scriptures.[9] Rather, following his model of the curriculum of the *schola dei*, he believed that the experience of the gathered community of interpreters grasping the gospel through the scriptures, was the substance of the Christian life. Thus, Christians interpret the Bible because that is the key task of the Church. In setting up this dynamic, Calvin devised a grounding of interpretation based on a hermeneutical circle made up of three elements, scripture, history, and the Church. It is to this circle we now turn.

Calvin's Circle: Scripture, History, and Church

Calvin sets out the importance of finding the truth of God's wisdom in his commentary on John's Gospel. Writing on 5.39,

> Again, we are taught in this passage that the knowledge of Christ must be derived from the Scriptures. For those who imagine what they like about Christ will finally have nothing but a shadowy spectre in his place. First, therefore, it must be held that Christ cannot be rightly known other than from the Scriptures. If that is the case, it follows that the Scriptures should be read in this spirit, in order to find Christ in them. Whoever turns aside from this goal (*scopo*), even though he wears himself out his whole life in learning, will never come to the knowledge of the truth. For how can we be wise apart from the wisdom of God?[10]

The knowledge of the truth (*scientia veritatis*), which leads to the wisdom of God (*sapientia Dei*), is the goal. To find this, Calvin sets out a hermeneutical circle, made up of the three elements of scripture,

---

[9] I am not disagreeing with G.R. Evans in her *Problems of Authority in the Reformation Debates* (Cambridge: Cambridge University Press, 1992), 2–34, but rather agreeing with her pointing out of the habits of mind that were active in the sixteenth century, and how those affected the search for authority. Calvin did not turn to the scriptures to find authority, but rather because of his belief in a model of Christian progress through growth in the life of the gospel.

[10] Comm. John 5.39, *Ioannis Calvini Opera Exegetica, In Evangelium Secundum Johannem Commentarius Pars Prior*, edited by Helmut Feld, (Geneva: Droz, 1997), 180.11–18. "Caeterum docemur hoc loco ex Scripturis petendam esse Christi notitiam. Nam qui de Christo imaginantur, quod ipsis libuit, tandem nonnisi umbratile spectrum eius loco habebunt. Primo igitur tenendum est non aliunde quam ex Scripturis Christum rite cognosci. Quod si ita est, sequitur hoc animo legendas esse Scripturas, ut illic inveniamus Christum. Quisquis ab hoc scopo deflectet, utcunque discendo se fatiget tota vita, nunquam ad scientiam veritatis perveniet. Quid enim sapere absque Dei sapientia possumus?"

history, and the Church. These should not be considered as three segments of the circumference of a circle, but rather three intertwining cords, as one might see in a braid, or Celtic circle. They intertwine because they are constantly in conversation and tension with each other; each continually leads the eye to another, together persistently speaking to the richness of the truth that the seeker pursues.

Because of this intertwined character of the three elements, the following exposition may seem to repeat themes frequently. This is intended, for the finding of truth from different angles necessarily gives different vantages upon its substance, and allows different facets of that truth to appear.

Scripture

Scripture is the first part of Calvin's hermeneutical circle. It acts as a guiding source, a repository where God has accommodated the divine being to human consciousness. It stands as an objective whole, proclaiming the gospel. It stands over against the vagaries of time, taking up the function of the classic, accepting the mantle of the founding rule against which all other standards are gauged. Insofar as it is accepted as speaking to all generations because of its very nature, it exercises dominion over the consciousness of later generations, and is resistant to criticism, especially a deconstructing critique.

However, here Calvin's genius for the foundation of the meaning and truth of the scripture transcends some later formulations.[11] By appealing to the Holy Spirit who is part of the very creation of the human subject, Calvin claimed that the classical nature of scripture is not only a reflection of basic humanity, but independently calls to the deepest created reality in the believer. It exceeds the importance of reflection, advancing toward a level of identity with the human as another creation of God, one that carries meaning about the purpose and end of humanity. Scripture is not an artifact of the religious consciousness of Paul. It is not even an extraordinarily felicitous consideration of the human condition, but contains the message of truth about humanity

---

[11] I include here Han-Georg Gadamer's theory of the classical. See his *Truth and Method*. 2nd rev. edition, translated and revised by Joel Weinsheimer and Donald G. Marshall (New York: Crossroad Publishing, 1989).

before God. In the end case, scripture is a movement of the Creator toward the created. As such, scripture reveals something that transcends time and change.

However, the question is posed, does Calvin escape the danger of ossification? This is the peril facing all who assert the classical. If he does, it is only in part. The claim of a classical nature tends to deny a further living voice that can critique the authoritative claim. Here, though, Calvin's explicit placement of the understanding of scripture in a living textual community answers the question. Believers are by nature readers and hearers; they are a textual community.

This is Calvin's crucial move. Through the interpretation of the scriptures under the power of the Holy Spirit, the community acknowledges its subservience to the reign of finitude, while denying that this is the domain of the truly real. Instead, this consensus professes a different world, proclaims a new reality, claims the absolute truth of II Corinthians 5.17 "If anyone is in Christ, he is a new creation. The past is finished and gone, and everything has become new." The scripture's meaning stands over against all ideologies, and points toward a reality outside of the believing community.

Finally, for Calvin, scripture demands response. Again and again he rails at "head-knowledge".[12] One has had no taste of true religion for Calvin until one begins the life commanded by the scripture. Here, application is everything, the living of this knowledge is urgent. The power communicated through the proclamation of the message of the scriptures can only be seen by the human observers in the obedience of the community to that gospel message. We see the meaning of the scripture in the living of the textual community, the society that has chosen to define itself in the living out of this message. For Calvin, with his emphasis on faith-experience, the scripture is only understood when it makes a claim upon the believer, and the believer responds.

History

Calvin wishes to spiral into history, where the characters of the New Testament are real to the citizens of Geneva. He takes a two-tiered stance, both standing above history in substantial matters, and within

---

[12] For Calvin against knowledge which does not touch the heart, see OS 3.53.10–14. ICR I.v.9., and Chapter 1.

history in those of accidental nature. The Genevans are to find themselves in that historically separated, yet essentially connected world. This differs from the approach of some later Renaissance exegetes for whom the historical character of the scriptures was more decidedly a distancing function.[13] This two-sidedness was to define the historicity of that community's understanding of the biblical world, and of its self-understanding as the rightful heir of that world.

This section could have been labeled "Calvin's sense of history." Several questions revolve, like a small solar system, around the dual suns of Calvin and history.[14] These are not easy to answer, nor has this study attempted to do so in either a full or systematic fashion. That study, though possibly fascinating, will have to wait.[15] However, to avoid some provisional answer would leave Calvin in one of two predicaments. Either he would be seen as a divided figure with some brilliant anticipations of future thought while maintaining some hopelessly outmoded suspensions from former times, or he could be seen as simply unable to corral his enthusiasm when useful historical material is available, thus more ahistorical in his outlook, and by implication more firmly

---

[13] Deborah Kuller Shuger, *The Renaissance Bible: Scholarship, Sacrifice, and Subjectivity*, notes that "exegesis becomes an occasion for anthropology. This sort of inquiry stands in sharp, if implicit, tension to the Reformation program for restoring modern society on the basis of Holy Scripture. Grotius's notes defamiliarize and denaturalize biblical culture–without, however, questioning the sacred authority of the biblical text." (42).

[14] The judgment of Irena Backus, that Calvin, in his use of Eusebius, was capable of sensitivity, but at other times too concerned with other (theological) issues, is not insignificant. See her "Calvin's Judgment of Eusebius of Caesarea." *Sixteenth Century Journal* 22 (1991):419–437, for more details. However, Backus is attempting to assess whether Calvin is a historian, rather than the question of this study, that of whether Calvin's historical consciousness allowed him to separate between human nature, and historically conditioned material. A more positive view of Calvin's use of history, concentrating upon his sermons, comes to us from Daniele Fischer, "L'Element Historique dans la Predication de Calvin." *Revue d'histoire et de philosophie religieuses*, 64, (1984), 365–386, where Fischer finds Calvin using various aspects of history always to serve his congregations. "Le souci d' instruire son auditoire est, visiblement, sa première préoccupation pastorale." (386) Fischer even goes so far as to state that "Or, l'élément historique était, pour le peuple, une composante essentialle de l'instruction religieuse." (386).

[15] Fascinating for several reasons, but especially for Calvin's heightened awareness of history, and the development of human knowledge of the historically-conditioned appearance of the nature of reality, which seems at odds with his psychology, which does not give a particular mental faculty to memory.

medieval.[16] He was neither, but rather a careful interpreter of human history for theological and ecclesiastical lessons.[17]

As we have seen, Calvin did have an active historical consciousness whereby he solved reception problems of the interpretive teachings of patristic authors by reference to their historical circumstances. He would point out issues which may have led them to emphasize points which are either unhelpful in the interpretation of a text, or simply incorrect.[18] We see this in the case of his conclusions about

---

[16] For one such reading, see Annette Zillenbiller's "Calvin's Uminterpretation Cyprians bei der Beantwortung der Fragen: Auf wen ist die Kirche gegründet und Von wem wird der Bischof gewählt?," *Calvinus Sincerioris Religionis Vindex*, edited by Wilhelm Neuser and Brian Armstrong (Kirksville, MO: Sixteenth Century Journal Publishers, 1997), 323–333. One quotation should suffice to give a feel for her evaluation of Calvin's use of history. "Aus diesem Grund kann man auch bei Calvin von einer Uminterpretation der von ihm so geschätzen Quelle sprechen. Dies verbindet ihn, wie anfangs erwähnt, mit den meisten seiner Zeitgenossen. Die True zum Quellentext behält er nur solange bei, wie dies seinen Argumenten zu größerem Gewicht verhilft. Greift er in die ursprüngliche Aussage durch eine Veränderung des Textes oder des Kontextes ein, so erfolgt dies stillschweigend. Dadurch bleibt der Eindruck bestehen, daß ein Kontinuum zwischen der Kirche des Cyprian und der des Reformators existiert." (332–333). Another such critique comes from James R. Payton, who states that "Calvin's interest in Church history was neither that of an antiquarian nor a historian; rather, he approached it as a reformer and polemicist. He embraced the authority of the past when it corroborated his views; he readily rejected the witness of the past when he disagreed with its perspective." (467) This statement comes in an article which details Calvin's use of a medieval text before its publication. In fact, the article points out how Calvin had noted, on the basis of very short study, the critique of II Nicaea in the *Libri Carolini*. This would seem to have been a testimony for the sensitivity of Calvin to historical sources, rather than evidence for his overtly polemical uses. See Payton, "Calvin and the Libri Carolini," *Sixteenth Century Journal* 28 (1997): 467–480.

[17] Susan Schreiner has considered Calvin's cautious reception of the lessons of history in her *The Theater of His Glory: Nature and the Natural Order in the Thought of John Calvin*, Studies in Historical Theology (Durham: Labyrinth Press, 1991), 107–114. Though she finds Calvin reluctant to learn empirical lessons of providence from history, Calvin does freely pull upon the Church's history, in a hermeneutical fashion of matching particular lessons to a previously held framework.

[18] Calvin seems to be heir to the historical school of the *Schola Augustiniana Moderna*, with its reliance on whole texts. Leland Saak, considering the contribution of Damasus Trapp, writes, "Trapp argued that the Schola Augustiniana Moderna was characterized by a historico-critical, as opposed to a logico-critical, attidtude toward citing Augustine. The 'happy quoters' were no longer satisfied with the stock Augustine quotations culled from Lombard, Canon Law, and florilegia, but went directly to the original source." Saak, "The Reception of Augustine in the Later Middle Ages," *The Reception of the*

some of Augustine's exegetical offerings, as well as those of Jerome, Hilary, Chrysostom, and others. This even extended to the human writer of the scriptures. As we have seen, Calvin twice found Paul's words to be factually untrue, either for reasons of historical situation or of pastoral need. In his exegetical corpus on the Pauline epistles, Calvin displays a measure of historical sensitivity remarkable for his time.

However, John Calvin used history for his own purposes. His mind was far removed from the Rankean ideal and belonged to the sixteenth-century world of thought. For Calvin, the reading of history belonged to the sphere of theology. The last fifteen years have seen an increasing interest in Calvin as a historian, ranging from seeing history for Calvin as another venue of providence's proof,[19] to seeing Calvin with a polemic interest in history, but not a true interest in history for its own sake.[20] In his commentaries, however, we find him struggling to discern a way to make sense of the lessons of history in the human search for God, which is subordinated to the biblical witness as he understood it.

Writing in 1991, Susan Schreiner noted that for Calvin, history represented the realm of salvation, and the past cannot be rejected without falling into the errors of the Anabaptists.[21] While this is a trenchant insight, important follow-up questions were not asked because her monograph dealt primarily with providence, not history or tradition.

Church Fathers in the West: From the Carolingians to the Maurists, 2 vols., edited by Irena Backus (Leiden: Brill, 1997), 379. Compare this wih the conclusions of Johannes van Oort, writing about Calvin's use of the fathers, who claims that Calvin's knowledge of the fathers depended upon reading them in new editions rather than *florilegia* which allowed him to know the context of the arguments, and that his critical facility allowed him to differentiate, on occasion, between true and pseudonymous works of the fathers. "John Calvin and the Church Fathers," *The Reception of the Church Fathers in the West: From the Carolingians to the Maurists*, 2 vols., edited by Irena Backus (Leiden: Brill, 1997),661–699.

[19] Susan Schreiner, *The Theater of His Glory: Nature and the Natural Order in the Thought of John Calvin* (Durham, North Carolina: Labyrinth Press, 1991), 107–109.

[20] Irena Backus, *Historical Method and Confessional Identity in the Era of the Reformation (1378–1615)* (Leiden: Brill, 2003), 5.

[21] Schreiner, 108.

Other scholars have looked at Calvin as a historian. This approach
has been tried by James Payton,[22] A.N.S. Lane,[23] and Irena Backus.[24]
With varied judgments,[25] a common theme linking these judgments
of Calvin's grasp of history is to judge how well he did history. One
can find evaluations of how well he read texts, or how he did or did
not consider the issues of historical context. For instance, James Payton
points out that Calvin inserted statements into the acts of the II Council
of Nicaea, in his 1550 edition of the *Institutes*, which are repeated in the
1559 edition. There is an implied critique, that Calvin was not acting
as a good historian when he mistook his own notes for material which
he had copied out from a manuscript[26] of the *Libri Carolini*.[27] Likewise,
A.N.S. Lane's comment upon Calvin's use of Bernard notes that "The
one serious example of quotation out of context concerns the *Sermones in
Cantica*, from which Calvin quotes without reference to their monastic
and mystical setting. This raises a significant question about Calvin's
interpretation in two of his citations."[28] Apparently, Lane is concerned
that Calvin did not avoid quoting Bernard here because of the monastic

---

[22] James R. Payton, "Calvin and the Legitimation of Icons: His Treatment of the
Seventh Ecumenical Council." *Archiv für Reformationsgeschichte* 84 (1993): 222–241; "His-
tory as Rhetorical Weapon: Christian Humanism in Calvin's Reply to Sadoleto, 1539."
In *In Honor of John Calvin, 1509–1564*. Edited by E.J. Furcha. Montreal: Faculty of Reli-
gious Studies, McGill University, 1987, 96–132; and "Calvin and the Libri Carolini."
Sixteenth Century Journal 28 (1997): 467–480.

[23] A.N.S. Lane, "Calvin's Use of the Fathers and the Medievals." *Calvin Theological
Journal*, 16 (1981): 149–200; several of his other contributions to the question are contained in his *John Calvin: Student of the Church Fathers* (Grand Rapids: Baker Book House,
1999).

[24] Irena Backus, "Calvin's Judgment of Eusebius of Caesarea." *Sixteenth Century Jour-
nal* 22 (1991): 419–437; "Calvin and the Greek Fathers." In *Continuity and Change: The
Harvest of Later Medieval and Reformation History*, edited by Robert J. Bast and Andrew
C. Gow (Leiden: Brill, 2000), 253–276.

[25] Obviously, there are others. The work of Jill Raitt, Charles Partee and David
F. Wright should not be ignored in this consideration, and the entire Calvin wing of the
history of exegesis school represents, technically, a type of historical investigation into
Calvin's thought and work of selecting historical sources for consideration.

[26] Payton, "Calvin and the Libri Carolini." *Sixteenth Century Journal* 28 (1997): 479.

[27] If one wanted to joust with Payton, one could note that according to Payton's
reconstruction of the facts, Calvin's access to the manuscript was "brief," and yet
dealing with a manuscript source, Calvin immediately was able to discern that the
source supported his theological position, and worked against that of his enemies. As
for the sloppiness of mistaking his own notes for copying out from the text, this is
exactly what Doris Kearns Goodwin claims to have done at the end of the 20th century,
with far greater technical resources at her command. In fact, the details point to Calvin
being a very good historian.

[28] Lane, *Calvin and Bernard of Clairvaux*, 87–88.

and mystical setting which sets Bernard's composition of this work.[29] Again, the issue is how good a historian Calvin[30] may or may not be.[31]

The latest and most significant research into Calvin and history comes from Irena Backus. Her *Historical Method and Confessional Identity*

---

[29] Bernard, *Sancti Bernardi Opera*, (Rome: Editiones Cistercienses, 1957), II.148–149. Bernard of Clairvaux, *On the Song of Songs*, v. 2, 23.15, 38–39. "But there is a place where God is seen in tranquil rest, where he is neither Judge nor Teacher but Bridegroom. To me—for I do not speak for others—this is truly the bedroom to which I have sometimes gained happy entrance. Alas! How rare the time, and how short the stay! There one clearly realizes that the Lord's love for those who fear him last forever and forever. It is there that one may happily say: 'I am a friend to all who fear you and observe your precepts.' God's purpose stands fast, the peace he has planned for those who fear him is without recall. Overlooking their faults and rewarding their good deeds, with a divine deftness he turns to their benefit not only the good they do but even the evil. He alone is happy whom the Lord accuses of no guilt. There is no one without sin, not even one. For all have sinned and forfeited God's glory. But could anyone accuse those that God has chosen? I ask no further pledge of righteousness if he is on my side whom alone I have offended. If he decrees that a sin is not to be imputed to me, it is as if it never existed. Inability to sin constitutes God's righteousness; God's forgiveness constitutes man's. When I grasped this I understood the truth of the words: 'We know that anyone who has been begotten by God does not sin, because a heavenly birth protects him.' Heavenly birth is eternal predestination, by which God loved his chosen ones and endowed them with spiritual blessings in his beloved Son before the world was made." "*Sed est locus ubi vere quiescens et quietus cernitur Deus: locus omnino, non iudicis, non magistri, sed sponsi, et qui mihi quidem,—nam de aliis nescio—, plane cubiculum sit, si quando in illum contigerit introduci. Sed, heu! rara hora et parva mora! Clare ibi agnoscitur MISERICORDIA DOMINI AB AETERNO ET USQUE IN AETERNUM SUPER TIMENTES EUM. Et felix qui dicere potest: PARTICEPS EGO SUM OMNIUM TIMENTIUM TE, ET CUSTODIENTIUM MANDATA TUA. Stat propositum Dei, stat sententia pacis super timentes eum, ipsorum et dissimulans mala, et remunerans bona, ut miro modo eis non modo bona, sed et mala cooperentur in bonum. O solus vere BEATUS, CUI NON IMPUTABIT DOMINUS PECCATUM! Nam qui non habebit peccatum, nemo. OMNES ENIM PECCAVERUNT, ET OMNES EGENT GLORIA DEI. QUIS ACCUSABIT TAMEN ADVERSUS ELECTOS DEI? Sufficit mihi ad omnem iustitiam solum habere propitium cui soli peccavi. Omne quod mihi ipse non imputare decreverit, sic est quasi non fuerit. Non peccare, Dei iustitia est: hominis iustitia, indulgentia Dei. Vidi haec, et intellexi illius sententiae veritatem: OMNIS QUI NATUS EST EX DEO, NON PECCAT, QUIA GENERATIO CAELESTIS SERVAT EUM. Generatio caelestis aeterna praedestinatio est, qua electos suos Deus dilexit et gratificavit in dilecto Filio suo ante mundi constitutionem*" Obviously, in connecting this text to his support for divine election, Calvin is not wandering too far from its original intent.

[30] Again, prescinding from entering fully into the fray, one might ask what other interpretations living in a mystical or monastic context could place upon these words? The text in question comes from Sermon 23.15, where Bernard states, *Non peccare, Dei iustitia est: hominis iustitia, indulgentia Dei.* "Inability to sin constitutes God's righteousness; God's forgiveness constitutes man's." Theologically, the question of context is not germane—or if it is, then the theological reading of the scriptures, separated from the 16th century by far greater chronological and cultural difference, is impossible.

[31] Sancti Bernardi. *Sancti Bernardi Opera*, (Rome: Editiones Cistercienses, 1957), II.149. Bernard of Clairvaux, *On the Song of Songs*, 4 volumes, translated by Kilian Walsh and Irene Edmonds (Kalamazoo, MI: Cistercian Publications, 1971–1980), v. 2, 23.15, 39.

in the Era of the Reformation (1378–1615)[32] represents a considerable step forward, both for her insights into the previous literature, and her own research. She aims to correct the notion that the sixteenth century thinkers were not motivated by an interest in history itself, arguing that "the creative role of history in the Reformation era [w]as a decisive factor in the affirmation of confessional identity."[33]

As the title implies, Backus looks especially at the historical method of the figures she surveys. In considering Calvin, and the doctrines of the Trinity and the bondage of the will, she finds his history as regards the patristic witness to be rather medieval, finding a "sentential" approach to his history rather than thoroughgoing contextual research.[34] Only in his evaluation of exegesis does Backus note that Calvin "actually show[s] active awareness of the patristic corpus ..."[35] This latest work makes great strides in pushing our knowledge forward about Calvin's historical method. Backus does concentrate upon method, and finds Calvin rather uninterested in history for its own sake. However, she adds to that the notion that history, for some of the Reformers (including Calvin), was determined by scripture, and argues strenuously against the idea that Calvin's interest in history was purely motivated by polemical need.[36]

We have thus far been taking history in its sense of *Historie*, the history of historians. This was necessary, for much of the conversation about Calvin and history has come from that perspective. However, it is more fruitful to consider this topic under the category of *Geschichte*, which is more broadly the flow of life within history, or

---

[32] Irena Backus, *Historical Method and Confessional Identity in the Era of the Reformation (1378–1615)* (Leiden: Brill, 2003).

[33] Backus, 5.

[34] Backus, 115–116. "... Calvin conserves something of the Mediaeval approach to the fathers. Callimg them as witnesses in the matter of free will, he tends to rely on isolated phrases which he takes either from florilegia as is the case with 'Augustine's' definition of free will or in some cases from original works, Gregory's statement about the Trinity being probably a case in point. This sentential approach means that Calvin can point up very clearly what he perceives to be contradictions in patristic teaching and also give the fathers the benefit of the doubt which he never gives to the pagan philosophers on the question of autonomy of human will and reason."

[35] Backus, 117. "... but even then his evaluation of it is so radical that he reduces it to one writer, Chrysostom." I give the whole so as not to fail in my historical task. This statement must be taken to refer only to bondage of the will and Trinity, because Calvin's knowledge and approval of other patristic exegetes in other issues is amply demonstrated.

[36] Backus, 2.

rather the current of linkage within time.[37] Here, history takes on more of a philosophical character, and less of the technical quality, in which Calvin suffers from critiques from later ideals of historical attitude. Here, Calvin moves easily into the nature of interpretation from within a given stream. First, there is Calvin's discovery of the contextual nature of truth claims, even claims made by scriptural authors.[38] This is an illustration of the positive function of distanciation. Naturally, this same function of distanciation is at work in the reception of the patristic and medieval authors. At a greater distance, one is able to see issues that were less clear to those who were engaged in those activities.

Calvin proposes this distance as one (less familiar) end of an axis to which Calvin's audiences are accustomed, the other being the familiarity of the tradition in which they live. To the twenty-first century observer, Calvin spends too much time considering the opinions of exegetes whose own age is almost as different from Calvin's as that of the Pauline epistles. To his contemporaries, this was a simple acceptance of the tradition which had formed the whole society in its relation to its God, a point about which all were in agreement for the very maintenance of society. Calvin accepted this strangeness and familiarity, re-claiming texts and meanings by moving back and forth between a new strangeness of his interpretation, and the familiarity of the textual substrate.

Finally, in attempting to recover the exegesis of the patristic and medieval authors, Calvin was always conscious of the effect of particular teachings upon the life and teaching of the Church. He saw God testing doctrines by fire, and purifying the Church from erroneous teachings under which it suffers for a time.[39] Implicit in his comments about Paul's mistaking convention for nature, is the knowledge that this can creep into the scriptures as well. Here, Calvin was the interpreter of self-in-tradition, seeking to differentiate between that which is useful, and that which must be purged away. Calvin consciously attempted to mediate between the historically-effected nature of the Church as an institution, and the unchanging nature of the will of God for believ-

---

[37] I accept these definitions from Paul Ricoeur, "Hermeneutics and the Critique of Ideology," 298–334 in *The Hermeneutic Tradition: From Ast to Ricoeur*, edited by Gayle L. Ormiston and Alan D. Schrift (Albany: SUNY Press, 1990), 326.

[38] See Calvin's comment on I Corinthians 11.14.

[39] See Calvin's interpretation of I Corinthians 3.15.

ers. We can argue about his success in this effort, but his acceptance of
the task demonstrates the clarity he had achieved about the nature of
finding God's truth for living as the Church.

Church

It is always helpful to remember that although Calvin defined the
Church both as visible and invisible, his emphasis, especially after 1539,
lay upon the visible Church.[40] That corresponded to a desire to hold
onto the Church as the number of the elect, which is the Church
across the ages, while placing the greater part of his concern upon the
Church of the congregation, the Church that is the present culmination
of the stream of history.[41] This visible Church is that which constantly
is making sense of the texts available to it.[42] These include scripture
and history, but the Church's own experience of the living out of Christ
is also present and part of the self-understanding upon which it acts.
To comprehend how the Church works in Calvin's tripartite circle of
interpretation, both the visible and invisible Church, which correspond
to the Church across the ages and the contemporary congregation,
must be kept in mind.

The Church's first contribution to the process of finding God's truth
is found in its function as the community that accepts the application
of scriptural meaning.[43] That is to say, the Church is that group, both

---

[40] I. John Hesselink, *Calvin's First Catechism*, Columbia Series in Reformed Theology
(Louisville: Westminster John Knox Press, 1997), 157, "In the final edition of the
Institutes the church is still defined in terms of election; but Calvin's main concern
is with the visible church: its marks, authority, ministry and organization."

[41] For a consideration of some of the practical effects of Calvin's doctrine of the
invisible Church, see David N. Wiley's "The Church as the Elect in the Theology of
Calvin," *John Calvin and the Church*, edited by Timothy George (Louisville: Westminster
John Knox Press, 1991), 96–117.

[42] Even a Roman Catholic, Alexandre Ganoczy, writing with Stefan Scheld, could
write "Unter den reformatorischen Theologen des 16. Jahrhunderts hat diesen Sachverhalt vielleicht keiner so klar durchschaut wie Johannes Calvin. Seine Auslegung will
kirchlich sein, sowohl was deren Voraussetzungen als auch was deren Zwech und Ziel
angeht." *Die Hermeneutik Calvins: Geistesgeschichtliche Voraussetzungen und Grundzüge* (Wiesbaden: Franz Steiner Verlag GMBH, 1983), 89.

[43] Balke notes that experience of the faithful is a hermeneutical key for Calvin,
claiming "In the Bible he sees no collection of dogmas, he sees the doctrines embedded
in the life and faith of the church and of the individual, in the natural habitat of the
verification of faith in Christia and ecclesiastical experience. It is a mark of appropriate
handling of scripture, therefore, when so much of the life of his own church appears
in the commentary of Chrysostom." Willem Balke, "The Word of God and *Experi-*

through history and at this instant, which has bound itself to a way
of life which it reads out of the scriptures.[44] This willingness to be
the society of application has tremendous power. First, it supplies the
self-identity of the communion of the faithful. The faith community
is that one which accepts the dispositional formation in accordance
with the application of the doctrine of the gospel.[45] Thus, the focus
on healing discipline in such a community seems obvious, rather than
scandalous. Secondly, this willingness creates a power and urgency in
the very process of understanding the traditionary text.[46] If we grasp
this, we can begin to understand the importance of preaching, how
it takes on a character of enunciating life-giving law. The community
gives itself over to hearing and considering the Word with a vitality that
denies the possibility of hearing and understanding without obeying.
Thus, the contemporary community, the congregation, opens itself to
the truth claim of its historical self, which is the Church across the ages.
It opens itself to the truth claim of the text, the scriptures of the Old
and New Testaments, received through a tradition of interpretation.
And it claims that this search for truth is not dead dogma, but the
living experience of the truth of God (*veritas Dei*), or at least the living
search for that truth.

It is important to note that this function must be performed by
the living congregation, or wider immediate faith community.[47] That is
because of the dialogical nature of the posing of questions and listening

---

entia According to Calvin." *Calvinus Ecclesiae Doctor*, International Congress on Calvin
Research, edited by Wilhelm Neuser (Kampen: J.H. Kok, 1980), 22.

[44] It is worthy of note that within Calvin's theology, this Church would extend back
to the patriarchs, who also bound themselves to living out the codes of God's truth.
Adding to that, David Steinmetz has observed that Calvin offers a vision of universal
monasticism to the Church, that the *status perfectionis* is, in Calvin's thought, widened to
include all the faithful following lawful vocations. "Calvin and the Monastic Ideal," In:
Calvin in Context (Oxford: Oxford University Press, 1995), 196.

[45] Heiko Oberman writes, "... the Reformation sermon is not legalistic but redemp-
tive, not only directed to individual souls but especially to the corporate existence of the
congregation, not elevating but mobilizing, not a refuge but a starting point and, finally,
not holy and vertical but secular and horizontal: time, space, and dust." "Preaching
and the Word in the Reformation." *Theology Today* 18 (1961/1962): 24. Understanding
the broader context of Oberman's remarks permits us to see that his lack of vertical
notion does not truly conflict with my own inclusion of it.

[46] Perhaps this explains the centrality of preaching in Reformed traditions—the
interpretation of scripture drives toward application in life, making the sermon always
an existential experience.

[47] For instance, a national synod, or ecumenical council.

to claims of the tradition and traditionary text. The questions that are posed are not boundless, but real and urgent. They are shaped by the present horizon of the questioning community. This helps to explain the immediate and provisional character of Reformed ecclesiology and, to a lesser extent, biblical interpretation. The horizon of an actual historical community, representing a particular moment in time, is implicit in the questioning, and thus the answers have an intentional *ad hoc* character. This is a process of learning from the past, an answer of sufficient truth for the present, and a projecting forward toward the future.[48] This is not a weakness, but a strength, allowing flexibility for the life of the community, and its relationship to its foundational understandings and documents.

The Church's final contribution to the hermeneutical circle of the search for God's truth is its service as the community of discernment. We have considered this at some length before, so may move directly into analysis here. The dynamic between the preaching and hearing of the Word acts as a continuing conversation about the meaning of God's truth, enacted in the present. This depends upon the increasing knowledge of the pastor and congregation of the scriptures, mediated through the best available interpretations and the increasing conformity of the body of the faithful to Christ, which more and more lives in it.[49] Here is the answer to the question earlier posed by Harold Bloom's "mis-reading". The strong interpretation of the preacher or doctor is not dropped into a vacuum, but is proffered to the textual community, for discussion, and possibly even correction in accordance with that

---

[48] This cannot be too strongly emphasized. The Roman Catholic critique of Protestant individualism, strongly represented by George Tavard's *Holy Writ or Holy Church: The Crisis of the Protestant Reformation* (Westport, CT: Greenwood Publishers, 1959), must either be eschewed or heavily nuanced. Heiko Oberman demonstrated the difficulty with Tavard's position in his "Holy Spirit-Holy Writ-Holy Church: The Witness of the Reformation." *Hartford Quarterly* 5 (1964–1965): 43–71; but the tendency still persists. One can see this echoed in Ralph Keen's "The Fathers in Counter-Reformation Theology in the Pre-Tridentine Period" *The Reception of the Church Fathers in the West: From the Carolingians to the Maurists*, 2 vols., edited by Irena Backus (Leiden: Brill, 1997), 705–706, where Keen links seeing Christianity as historical as incompatible with the Reformation conception, and the Church as the necessary context for faith. While Calvin does not argue explicitly that point, it is clear that the Church as *schola dei* is the only context for faithful reading of scripture, guided by the Spirit which has guided the true Church across the ages, and which inspired the writers of the scripture.

[49] That this is true even of the congregation is pointed out by Estienne's publishing of the *Nova Glossa Ordinaria* in both Latin and French.

which is already known of God's word.[50] In doing so, Calvin achieves a union of interpretation and critique. When one considers Calvin's hermeneutical circle, with its dependence on scripture and history and Church, and realizes the two-fold nature of that Church, with its acceptance of the contemporary community's position in the correct searching for God's truth, one can see a possible answer to the concerns of those who would see the act of interpretation as politically powerful and ideologically driven, such as the use of particular texts to entrench particular power groups. Further, as a concrete historical example of acceptance of the import of a traditionary stream and text, while radically critiquing a particular ideology—that of the Roman hierarchy, Calvin's project stands highlighted by its real-world application.

Understanding or Eisegesis?

Now, after so much work tearing down a wrong-headed notion of *sola scriptura*, and so much time spent in building a case for hermeneutical and exegetical processes in Calvin's approach to the scripture, this study must answer whether it has argued Calvin, and by implication a whole strand of tradition, into an unpalatable corner. That is to say, is the upshot of understanding Calvin's hermeneutical emphasis necessarily seeing him as accepting an eisegetical structure, which finds not a guide for life in the scriptures, but rather a reflection of what is desired?

This is the most significant worry to any orthodox understanding of the hermeneutical task, and of uncovering it in a given author, or in adopting one for use in the contemporary life of faith. Two answers are possible. The first is that some form of eisegesis is inevitable, that all interpreters bring their prejudices with them, and that the various schema arc ways of arguing for the "rightness" of one approach to the scriptures over the others. As abrupt as that statement may seem, much can be learned from it. For instance, a modern historical-critical scholar dismisses the possibility of the "miracles" of the New Testament

---

[50] Irena Backus points out that Calvin's unfinished project of an edition of Chrysostom may have in its conception been "part of a larger plan to make the works of the fathers available in the vernacular in so far as they helped the faithful understand the Bible. Calvin choise Chrysostom first and foremost because, like the Genevean reformer and several other Church Fathers, he abided by Paul's rule of communicating God's mysteries to the common people." "Calvin and the Greek Fathers," *Continuity and Change: The Harvest of Late Medieval and Reformation History* (Leiden: Brill, 2000), 256.

because of the impossibility of their happening, and looks for other layers of meaning situated in the theology of the text, the clues that it gives to the religious psychology of its community of origin, and the history of its transmission which may be discerned from its redaction history. But in doing so, that scholar dismisses what was precisely the point of the miracle stories, namely that impossible things were possible around Jesus, and occasionally the apostles.[51] In the same way this is the case when an interpreter is unwilling to follow the best scriptural text, or is unwilling to correct an obvious mis-interpretation when new knowledge becomes available; in both cases because of the fear of what it might do to the "faith;" that interpreter is following a particular model of interaction with the biblical text that must be examined for its truth, and its helpfulness to the faith that states that its Lord is named the "Truth".[52]

However enthralling such a position may be, it does not contain the coherent strength to function as a faith-bearing hermeneutic on its own. It may act wonderfully as a cautionary admonition, or even perform a valuable service of bearing tidings of humility to any interpreter, but as a stance which acts alone, it moves inevitably toward utter relativism. Neither the Christian religion, nor any other, can stand a truly relativistic stance in one of its core pillars, and as a "religion of the book," the Christian religion stands upon the interpretation of its central text as a foundational pillar.

But if not the radical acceptance of pragmatic eisegesis, what stance exists, which does nurture faith while allowing a place for a robust hermeneutic, such as that which Calvin employed? The answer is to grasp and accept the circular nature of the interpretive enterprise. We have considered the nature of the hermeneutical circle. What must be fastened upon, if the community of faith or the individual interpreter is not to throw up the hands in disgust, is the caution that although the hermeneutical circle is a circle, it is not a vicious circle!

This is exactly what the reader of Calvin sees in action. Although he did not write a treatise on the nature of interpretation, there is a clear

---

[51] Brad Gregory has argued this point about of privileged biases in his consideration of the historiography of early modern studies in his *Salvation at Stake: Christian Martyrdom in Early Modern Europe* (Cambridge: Harvard University Press, 1999), 1–29.

[52] Jerry H. Bentley gives a fascinating example in his study of the editorial choices made by the scholars working on the Complutensian Polyglot. See his *Humanists and Holy Writ: New Testament Scholarship in the Renaissance* (Princeton: Princeton University Press, 1983), 91–111.

indication of a hermeneutical circle that we have been considering. Ponder again the function of the prefaces to the *Institutes*. On the one hand, they seem clearly to be indications that the audience will find therein the ways to understand the scriptures, the ways to avoid labyrinthine passages and confusion, and the meanings to which it should refer the texts of the Old and New Testaments. This seems an outline of hermeneutical forestructures open to the charge of being guides to eisegesis. However, the final arbiter to which Calvin turns is not the authority of a council, not the patristic consensus, not the authority of a bishop.[53] Instead, Calvin turns to the reading of scripture, and asks only that his book be judged by that court. He writes that his book is a summary of Christian doctrine, and an opening for those who would be aided well in the reading of the Old or New Testament. But that was not the final word. After setting out a doctrinal hermeneutic for the reading of the scriptures, Calvin turned to the judgment of the scripture. He ended his message to the reader by saying "Above all, I must urge him to have recourse to Scripture in order to weigh the testimonies that I adduce from it."[54] Here, Calvin referred once more to the power of the Holy Spirit to speak through the scriptures to provide a common basis for discernment. Scripture speaks in judgment of Calvin, or of any other interpreter.

This stance of the strength of the Holy Spirit's voice, speaking through the scriptures in all ages to a lived reality in the hearts of the believing community, stands as the strength and weakness of Calvin's approach to the scriptures, and to his theology. If this perspective is accepted, then the system works. Calvin has final access to the Holy Spirit's power to make the scriptures, and the Church's interaction with those scriptures, a continual re-freshening of the call of the gospel. This continually clarifies the Church's mission in the world within these circumstances, and her journey out of the world. If, however, this stance cannot be embraced, then Calvin's interpretive practices assume the appearance of merely strong maintenance of the status quo, and the problem of an ancient text speaking trans-historically will be opened again, with all the attendant problems that entails. Though Calvin would not see it as a problem, his is specifically not a universal hermeneutic. For the purposes of this study, it is not necessary to con-

---

[53] Obviously, these solutions had been tried previously.

[54] OS 3.8.25–27. "Sur toutes choses, il fauldra auoir en recommandation, de recourir a l'Escriture, pour considerer les tesmoignages que i'en allegue."

clude whether Calvin is correct, but rather to point out how this stance allows both his strong hermeneutical principles, and his strong biblicism, while maintaining a level of coherence that propelled him into the front rank of the theologians of his own day. It has also made his theology a continuing source of fascination, if at times bewilderment, for generations of theologians.

Conclusion—The Reception of Tradition

What then may we say about Calvin's interpretive process, and its treatment of the scripture, history, and the Church? In the service of the search for God's truth, Calvin constructs a hermeneutical circle, in which three foci existed in creative tension. Perhaps a better way to state this is that these three are cords in an intertwining rope wained into a circle without beginning or end.

These three constantly interpenetrate each other. The history of the Christian Church is filled with the history of scriptural interpretation, the contemporary community sees itself as the momentary culmination of a historical "handing-down" that spans ages, the scripture is the fount of doctrine for the contemporary church which pours through the spout of tradition, and each of these foci continuously and dynamically effects the other two. This is seen above, where material from the scripture section could have as easily been placed in the Church exposition. The three are not accidentally placed together, but are intentionally woven so, so as to make a stronger, more existential cord. This also defines a division within humankind, at least as far as the search for God's truth goes. To be part of that inner band, one must accept an openness to the truth claims of the scripture, must adopt the correct teachings of the Christian religion, found most clearly spoken in the history of the Church, and must embrace membership in the community which is defined externally by application of the teachings of this religion, and internally by continual growth into Christ. Those who do not accept this, according to Calvin, are either foolish enthusiasts, stubborn dogmatists, or foolish academics or atheists who seek something from scripture foreign to its true purpose. These are not the people to whom Calvin spoke. This was not the problem in his age which it may be in later eras, but Calvin's concentration upon this process accomplished two tasks for later ages. First, his effort illuminated how specificity of community provides greater cohesiveness of interpretation, and demonstrates the necessity of that self-understood community as the arena of the application which completes understanding. Secondly, this interpretive endeavor posed the question of how diverse communities may even enter into the process of interpretation. That is to say, Calvin's hermeneutical underpinning and drive toward a particular horizon which is shared through an interpretive community grants us a particularly sharp historical example of shared interpretation, which stands over against both theories of laissez-faire multi-culturalism, and optimistic theories of textual clarity.

Note also that the three strands of the braid of interpretation are three specific areas of the action of the Holy Spirit.[55] Both Calvin and Augustine claim the Holy Spirit as the key to biblical interpretation, our analysis demonstrates that Calvin wrote that into his interpretive procedures and principles. Warfield's classical contention that Calvin is "the theologian of the Holy Spirit," is supported by Calvin's grounding of interpretation.[56] This specific emphasis on the work of the Holy Spirit creates an interpretive space for the living faith community. The Holy Spirit's work in the areas of scripture, history and Church creates the necessary condition for faith-giving life in the Christian community.

Finally, this study has demonstrated a possible avenue for coming to grips with Calvin's theology. Just as Calvin had to move through a hermeneutical process and the fusion of horizons to recover the lessons of the past, this same model is incumbent upon theologians who would wish to use Calvin's thought as a source for the building of contemporary theological models. While the unaccommodated Calvin actually does exist, the theologian, as opposed to the strict historian, must be interested in some manner of recovery for a later age with different challenges. Calvin's own method demonstrates one methodological possibility.

In Calvin's search for the truth of God (*veritas Dei*), we see him enter a circle of scripture, history, and the Church. Each factor is constantly acting upon the other two, each is constantly engaging the others, each is representing to the Christian community both its thrown-ness into this time and moment, and in its acknowledging the circumstances

---

[55] Heiko Oberman trenchantly observed almost thirty years ago that "... one of the most important aspect of Reformation thought is best described as the rediscovery of the Holy Spirit, the present Christ." "Preaching and the Word in the Reformation." *Theology Today* 18 (1961/1962): 21.

[56] Benjamin Breckenridge Warfield, "John Calvin the Theologian," in *Calvin and Augustine* (Philadelphia: Presbyterian and Reformed Publishing Co., 1956), 484.

which have led to this point. These elements which carry the traditionary weight are brought into conversation with living realities, and these critical elements are interlaced in the life of a faith community, which points toward the future. This is Calvin's reception of the Church's history, and the scripture's history, which moves the body of Christ forward in Christian progress, which is the intermediate future, and ever onward toward a divine horizon.

SELECTED BIBLIOGRAPHY

Primary Readings

John Calvin—early editions

Iohanne Calvino. Institutio Christianae religionis: in libros quatuor nunc primum digesta, certisque distincta capitibus, ad aptissimam methodum: aucta etiam tam magna accessione vt propemodum opus nouum haberi possit. Iohanne Calvino authore. Genevae: Oliua Roberti Stephani, XVII Cal. Sept. [16 Aug] 1559. Meeter Center

———. The institvtion of Christian religion / wrytten in Latine by Maister Ihon Calvin, and translated into Englysh according to the authors last edition. Translated by Thomas Norton. London, Imprinted by Reinalde Wolfe & Richard Harison,1561. Meeter Center.

———. Ioannis Calvini Commentarii in Epistolam Pauli ad Romanos. Argentorati: Vuendelinum Rihelium,1540. Meeter Center.

———. In omnes D. Pauli epistolas, atque etia in epistola ad Hebraeos commentaria luculentissima; ex postrema authoris recognitione. Cum indice copiosissimo sententiarum & locorum omnium. Genevae, Apud Ioannem Gerardum,1551. Meeter Center.

———. Iacobi Sadoleti Romani cardinalis Epistola ad senatum populumque: Geneuensem qua in obedientiam Romani pontificis eos reducere conatur / Ioannis Caluini Responsio. Argentorati: per Vuendelinum Rihelium,1539. Meeter Center.

———. Catechismus, sive Christianae religionis institutio: communibus renatae nuper in Evangelio Genevensis Ecclesiae suffragijs recepta, & vulgari quide prius idiomate, nunc vero Latine etiam … in lucem edita / Joanne Calvino, autore. Basileae: In officina Roberti Winter,1538. Meeter Center.

John Calvin—modern editions

Calvini, Ioannis. *Opera Quae Supersunt Omnia.* 59 volumes. Edited by Wilhelm Baum, Edward Cunitz, & Edward Reuss. Brunswick: Schwetschke and Sons, 1895.

———. *Opera Selecta.* 5 volumes. 3rd ed. Edited by Peter Barth and Wilhelm Niesel. Munich: Christian Kaiser, 1967.

———. *Iohannis Calvini Commentarius in Epistolam Pauli ad Romanos.* Edited by T.H.L. Parker. Leiden: E.J. Brill, 1981.

———. *Ioannis Calvini Opera Exegetica, Commentarii in Secundum Pauli Epistolam ad Corinthios.* Edited by Helmut Feld. Geneva: Droz, 1994.

——. *Ioannis Calvini Opera Exegetica, Commentarii in Pauli Epistolas ad Galatas, ad Ephesios, ad Philippenses, ad Colossenses.* Edited by Helmut Feld. Geneva: Droz, 1992.

——. *Ioannis Calvini Opera Exegetica, Commentarius in Epistolam ad Hebraeos.* Edited by T.II.L. Parker. Geneva: Droz, 1996.

——. *Ioannis Calvini Opera Exegetica, In Evangelium Secundum Johannem Commentarius Pars Prior.* Edited by Helmut Feld. Geneva: Droz, 1997.

——. *Registres du Consistoire de Genève au Temps de Calvin.* Tome I (1542–1544). Edited by Thomas A. Lambert and Isabella M. Watt. Geneva: Droz, 1996.

Calvin, John. *Institutes of the Christian Religion.* 2 volumes. Translated by Ford Lewis Battles, edited by John T. McNeill. *Library of Christian Classics.* Philadelphia: Westminster Press, 1960.

——. *Institutes of the Christian Religion: 1536 Edition.* Translated and annotated by Ford Lewis Battles. Grand Rapids: Eerdmans, 1975.

——. *Calvin's New Testament Commentaries.* 12 volumes. Edited by David W. Torrance and Thomas F. Torrance. Grand Rapids: Eerdmans, 1960.

——. *Calvin: Commentaries.* Edited by Joseph Haroutunian. *Library of Christian Classics.* Philadelphia: Westminster Press, 1958.

——. *Calvin: Theological Treatises.* Edited by J.K.S. Reid. *Library of Christian Classics.* Philadelphia: Westminster Press, 1954.

——. "Calvin's Latin Preface to His Proposed French Edition of Chrysostom's Homilies: Translation and Commentary." Translated by W. Ian P. Hazlett. In *Humanism and Reform: The Church in Europe, England, and Scotland, 1400–1643* (Cambridge: Basil Blackwell, 1991), 129–150.

——. "John Calvin: Preface to the Homilies of Chrysostom." Translated by John H. McIndoe. *Hartford Quarterly* 5, 2, (1965): 19–26.

——. and Jacopo Sadoleto. *A Reformation Debate: Sadoleto's Letter to the Genevans and Calvin's Reply.* Edited by John C. Olin. San Francisco: Harper and Row, 1966.

Other Primary Works

Augustine. *Confessions.* Translated by Henry Chadwick. Oxford: Oxford University Press, 1991.

——. *The Trinity.* Translated by Edmund Hill. New York: New City Press, 1991.

——. *On Christian Doctrine.* Translated by D.W. Robertson, Jr. Library of Liberal Arts, Indianapolis: Bobbs Merrill, 1958.

Aurelii Augustini. *De Doctrina Christiana.* Editd by Martin Joseph. Turnholt: Brepols, 1962.

——. *Confessions.* 3 volumes. Edited by James J. O'Donnell. Oxford: Oxford University Press, 1992.

Bernard de Clairvaux. *Oeuvres Completes.* 20 volumes. *Sources Chretiennes* 367. Paris: Editions du Cerf, 1992.

——. *Sermons sur le Cantique.* Vol. 1. *Sources Chretiennes* 414. Paris: Editions du Cerf, 1996.

Sancti Bernardi. *Sancti Bernardi Opera*. Vol. I-II. Rome: Editiones Cistercienses, 1957.

Bernard of Clairvaux. *On the Song of Songs*. 4 volumes. Translated by Kilian Walsh and Irene Edmonds. Kalamazoo, MI: Cistercian Publications, 1971–1980.

———. *Selected Works*. Translated by G.R. Evans. *The Classics of Western Spirituality*. New York: Paulist Press, 1987.

Erasmus. *Paraphrases on Romans and Galatians*. Edited by Robert D. Sider. Translated and annotated by John B. Payne, Albert Rabil, and Warren S. Smith. CWE 42. Toronto: University of Toronto Press, 1984.

Gregorii Magni. *Expositione in Canticum Canticorum*. Corpus Christianorum, Series Latina, CXLIV, Turnholt: Brepols, 1963.

———. *Moralia in Job*. Corpus Christianorum, Series Latina, CXLIII, CXLIIIA, CXLIIIB. Turnholt: Brepols, 1979.

Gregory the Great. *Forty Gospel Homilies*. Translated by David Hurst. Kalamazoo: Cistercian Publications, 1990.

Origen. *On First Principles*. Translated by G.W. Butterworth. London: SPCK, 1936. Reprint edition, Gloucester: Peter Smith, 1973.

William of St. Thierry, *Exposition on the Epistle to the Romans*. Translated by John Baptist Hasbrouck. Kalamazoo: Cistercian Publications, 1980.

Guillelmi S. Theodorici Abbatis. *Expositio in Epistolam ad Romanos*. Migne, PL, vol. 180, 548–694.

Secondary Readings

Amador, J.R.H. "Feminist Biblical Hermeneutics: A Failure of Theoretical Nerve." *Journal of the American Academy of Religion* 66, 1, (1998): 39–57.

Anderson, Luke. "The *Imago Dei* Theme in John Calvin and Bernard of Clairvaux." In *Calvinus Sacrae Scripturae Professor*. International Congress on Calvin Research. Edited by Wilhelm Neuser. Grand Rapids: Eerdmans, 1994, 178–198.

Anderson, Marvin Walter. "John Calvin: Biblical Preacher (1539–1564)." *Scottish Journal of Theology*, 42, (1989): 167–181.

Armstrong, Brian G. "Exegetical and Theological Principles in Calvin's Preaching, with Special Attention to his Sermons on the Psalms." *Ordenlich und Fruchtbar. Festschrift fur Willem van't Spijker Anlasslich seines Abschieds als Professor der Theologische Universitat Apeldoorn*. Leiden: J.J. Groen en Zoon, 1997, 191–209.

———. "Report on the seminar: An investigation of Calvin's principles of Biblical interpretation." *Hervormde teologiese studies*, 54, No. 1–2, (1998): 133–142.

———. "The Changing Face of French Protestantism: The Influence of Pierre Du Moulin." In *Calviniana: Ideas and Influence of Jean Calvin*. Edited by Robert V. Schnucker. Kirksville, MO: Sixteenth Century Journal Publishers, 1988, 131–150.

———. "*Duplex cognitio Dei*, Or? The Problem and Relation of Structure, Form, and Purpose in Calvin's Theology." In *Probing the Reformed Tradition: Historical Studies in Honor of Edward A. Dowey, Jr.* Edited by Elsie Anne McKee and Brian G. Armstrong. Louisville: Westminster John Knox Press, 1989.

———. "The Pastoral Office in Calvin and Pierre du Moulin." In *Calvin: Erbe und Auftrag: Festschrift für Wilhelm Heinrich Neuser zum 65. Geburtstag.* Edited by Willem van Spijker. Kampen: Kok Pharos Publishing House, 1991, 157–167.

Augustijn, Cornelius. "Calvin in Strasbourg." *Calvinus Sacrae Scripturae Professor.* International Congress on Calvin Research. Edited by Wilhelm Neuser. Grand Rapids: Eerdmans, 1994, 166–177.

Ayers, Robert H. "The View of Medieval Biblical Exegesis in Calvin's Institutes." *Perspectives in Religious Studies* 7 (1980): 188–193.

———. "Language, Logic and Reason in Calvin's *Institutes.*" *Religious Studies* 16 (1980): 283–297.

Backus, Irena. *Historical method and confessional identity in the era of the Reformation, 1378–1615.* Leiden: Brill, 2003.

———. "L'Exode 20, 3–4 et l'interdiction des images L'emploi de la tradition patristique par Zwingli et par Calvin." Nos Monuments d'art et d'histoire, Vol. 3, (1984): 319–322.

———. "'Aristotelianism' in some of Calvin's and Beza's expository and exegetical writings on the doctrine of the trinity, with particular reference to the terms ουσια and υποστασις." *Histoire de l'exégèse au XVIe siècle. Textes du Colloque International tenu a Genève en 1976.* Rèunis par Olivier Fatio et Pierre Fraenkel. Genève: Librairie Droz, 1978, 351–360.

———. "L'Enseignement de la Logique à L'Académie de Genève entre 1559 et 1565." *Revue de Théologie et de Philosophie* 111 (1979): 153–163.

———. "Patristics." III.223–226 in *Oxford Encyclopedia of the Reformation.* 4 volumes. Edited by Hans J. Hillerbrand. Oxford: Oxford University Press, 1996.

———. "Calvin and the Greek Fathers," *Continuity and Change: The Harvest of Late Medieval and Reformation History.* Leiden: Brill, 2000, 253–276.

———. "Calvin's Judgment of Eusebius of Caesarea." *The Sixteenth Century Journal* 22 (1991): 419–437.

Bagchi, David and Steinmetz, David C. *The Cambridge Companion to Reformation Theology.* Cambridge: Cambridge University Press, 2004.

Bainton, Roland H. *Erasmus of Christendom.* New York: Crossroad, 1969.

———. "The Immoralities of the Patriarchs According to the Exegesis of the Late Middle Ages and of the Reformation." *Harvard Theological Review* 23, (1930): 39–49.

Balke, Willem. "The Word of God and *Experientia* According to Calvin." In *Calvinus Ecclesiae Doctor.* International Congress on Calvin Research. Edited by Wilhelm Neuser. Kampen: J.H. Kok, 1980, 19–31.

Barnard, Leslie W. "To Allegorize or not to Allegorize?" *Studia Theologica* 36 (1982): 1–10.

Barnett, S.J. "Where Was Your Church before Luther? Claims for the Antiquity of Protestantism Examined." *Church History* 68 (1999): 14–41.

Baroni, V. "De Calvin a Oltramare: Deux commentaires genevois de l'epitre aux ephesiens." *Revue de Theologie et de Philosophie* 20 (1932): 191–210.

Battles, Ford Lewis. "God Was Accommodating Himself to Human Capacity."
    Interpretation 31 (1977): 19–38.
——. "The Sources of Calvin's Seneca Commentary." In *Interpreting John
    Calvin*. Edited by Robert Benedetto. Grand Rapids, MI: Baker Book House,
    1996, 65–89.
——. "*Calculus Fidei*: Some Ruminations on the Structure of the Theology
    John Calvin." In *Interpreting John Calvin*. Edited by Robert Benedetto. Grand
    Rapids, MI: Baker Book House, 1996, 139–248.
——. "Calvin's Humanistic Education." In *Interpreting John Calvin*. Edited by
    Robert Benedetto. Grand Rapids, MI: Baker Book House, 1996, 47–64.
Bell, Theo. "Calvin and Luther on Bernard of Clairvaux." *Calvin Theological
    Journal* 34 (1999): 370–395.
Benedict, Philip. *Christ's Churches Purely Reformed: A Social History of Calvinism*.
    New Haven: Yale University Press, 2002.
Benin, Stephen D. *The Footprints of God: Divine Accomodation in Jewish and Christian
    Thought*. Albany, NY: SUNY Press, 1993.
——. "Sacrifice as Education in Augustine and Chrysostom." *Church History*
    52 (1983): 7–20.
Bentley, Jerry H. *Humanists and Holy Writ: New Testament Scholarship in the Renais-
    sance*. Princeton: Princeton University Press, 1983.
Bernard, Robert W. "The Rhetoric of God in the Figurative Exegesis of
    Augustine," In *Biblical Hermeneutics in Historical Perspective*. Edited by Mark
    Burrows and Paul Rorem. Grand Rapids: Eerdmans, 1991.
Berthoud, Jean-Marc. "La formation des pasteurs et la predication de Calvin."
    La revue reformee 49 (1998): 19–44.
Berthoud, Pierre. "La Connaissance De Dieu Chez Jean Calvin." *La revue
    reformee* 47 (1996): 43–50.
Bloom, Harold. "The Necessity of Misreading." In *Kabbalah and Criticism*. New
    York: Seabury Press, 1975.
Boer, Erik A. de. "Hermeneutische Schlüssel zur alttestamentlichen Prophetie
    in Calvins Hesekiel predigten." In *Calvinus Sacrae Scripturae Professor*. Inter-
    national Congress on Calvin Research. Edited by Wilhelm Neuser. Grand
    Rapids: Eerdmans, 1994, 199–208.
——. "The book of the Revelation in Calvin's Geneva." In *Calvin's Books:
    Festschrift dedicated to Peter De Klerk on the occasion of his seventieth birthday*. Edited
    by Wilhelm H. Neuser. Heerenveen: J.J. Groen en Zoon, 1997, 23–62.
——. "Pagina Obscura in Geneva: A Fragment from a Sermon by John
    Calvin." *Calvin Theological Journal* 34 (1999): 162–179.
Bohatec, Josef. "Calvin et l'Humanisme." *Revue Historique* 183, (1938): 207–241;
    185, (1939): 36–69.
Bouwsma, William. *John Calvin: A Sixteenth Century Portrait*. Oxford: Oxford
    University Press, 1988.
——. "The Spirituality of John Calvin." In *Christian Spirituality: High Middle
    Ages and Reformation*, edited by Jill Raitt with Bernard McGinn and John
    Meyendorff. World Spirituality: An Encyclopedic History of the Religious
    Quest, vol. 17. New York: Crossroad, 1988.
——. "The Spirituality of Renaissance Humanism." In *Christian Spirituality:*

High Middle Ages and Reformation, edited by Jill Raitt with Bernard McGinn and John Meyendorff. World Spirituality: An Encyclopedic History of the Religious Quest, vol. 17. New York: Crossroad, 1988.

———. "Calvinism as *Theologia Rhetorica*." In Wilhelm Wuellner, ed., *Calvinism as **Theologia Rhetorica***. Berkeley: Center for Hermeneutical Studies in Hellenistic and Modern Culture, 1986: 1–21.

———. "Calvin and the Renaissance Crisis of Knowing." *Calvin Theological Journal* 17 (1982): 190–211.

———. "The Two Faces of Humanism: Stoicism and Augustinianism in Renaissance Thought." In ***Itinerarium Italicum***: *The Profile of the Italian Renaissance in the Mirror of its European Transformations*. Edited by Heiko Oberman and Thomas A Brady, Jr. Leiden: E.J. Brill, 1975.

Breen, Quirinus. *John Calvin: A Study in French Humanism*. 2nd ed. New York: Archon Books, 1968.

Brown, Peter. *Augustine of Hippo, A New Edition withan Epilogue*. Berkeley: University of California Press, 2000.

Bru, Vincent. "La notion d'accommodation divine chez Calvin: Ses implications theologiques et exegetiques." *La Revue Reformee* 49 (1998): 79–91.

Bruns, Gerald L. "The Problem of Figuration in Antiquity." In *Hermeneutics: Questions and Prospects*. Edited by Gary Shapiro and Alan Sica. Amherst, Massachusetts: University of Massachusetts Press, 1984.

Burrows, Mark S. "Jean Gerson on the 'Traditioned Sense' of Scripture as an Argument for an Ecclesial Hermeneutic." In *Biblical Hermeneutics in Historical Perspective*. Edited by Mark Burrows and Paul Rorem. Grand Rapids: Eerdmans, 1991.

———. *Jean Gerson and De Consolatione Theologiae*. Tübingen: J.C.B. Mohr, 1991.

Büsser, Fritz. "Bullinger as Calvin's Model in Biblical Exposition: An Examination of Calvin's Preface to the Epistle to the Romans." In *In Honor of John Calvin, 1509–1564*. Edited by E.J. Furcha. Montreal: Faculty of Religious Studies, McGill University, 1987, 64–95.

———. "Zwingli the Exegete: A Contribution to the 450th Anniversary of the Death of Erasmus." In *Probing the Reformed Tradition: Historical Studies in Honor of Edward A. Dowey, Jr.* Edited by Elsie Anne McKee and Brian G. Armstrong. Louisville: Westminster John Knox Press, 1989.

Cadier, Jean. *The Man God Mastered*. Translated by O.R. Johnston. Grand Rapids, MI: Eerdmans Publishing Co., 1960.

———. "L'autorite de Saint Augustin." Revue d'histoire ecclesiastique, Vol. 45, (1950): 670–687.

Cameron, Euan. *The European Reformation*. Oxford: Oxford University Press, 1991.

Chul-Ha, Han. "Theology of Ministry in John Calvin. Jes. 59,21; Rom. 10,17; Rom. 1,16." In *Calvin: Erbe und Auftrag: Festschrift für Wilhelm Heinrich Neuser zum 65. Geburtstag*. Edited by Willem van Spijker. Kampen: Kok Pharos Publishing House, 1991, 95–105.

Copeland, Rita. *Rhetoric, Hermeneutics, and Translation in the Middle Ages: Academic Traditions and Vernacular Texts*. Cambridge Studies in Medieval Literature. Cambridge: Cambridge University Press, 1991.

Cottret, Bernard. *Calvin: A Biography*. Translated by M. Wallace McDonald. Grand Rapids: Eerdmans, 2000.

Davies, Rupert E. *The Problem of Authority in the Continental Reformers: A Study in Luther, Zwingli and Calvin*. Westport, CT: Greenwood Press, 1946.

Davis, Thomas J. *The Clearest Promises of God: The Development of Calvin's Eucharistic Teaching*. New York: AMS Press, 1995.

De Jong, James A. "'An Anatomy of All Parts of the Soul': Insights into Calvin's Spirituality from His Psalms Commentary." In *Calvinus Sacrae Scripturae Professor*. International Congress on Calvin Research. Edited by Wilhelm Neuser. Grand Rapids: Eerdmans, 1994, 1–14.

Demura, Akira. "Two Commentaries on the Epistle to the Romans: Calvin and Oecolampadius," In *Calvinus Sincerioris Religionis Vindex*. Edited by Wilhelm Neuser and Brian Armstrong. Kirksville, MO: Sixteenth Century Journal Publishers, 1997, 165–188.

DeVries, Dawn. "The Incarnation and the Sacramental World: Calvin's and Schleiermacher's Sermons on Luke 2." In *Toward the Future of Reformed Theology: Tasks, Topics, Traditions*. Edited by David Willis. Grand Rapids, MI: Eerdmans, 1999, 386–405.

Dickens, A.G. and Tonkin, John M. *The Reformation in Historical Thought*. Cambridge: Harvard University Press, 1985.

Douglass, Jane Dempsey. "Calvin's Use of Metaphorical Language for God: God as Enemy and God as Mother." *Princeton Seminary Bulletin* 8 (1987): 19–32.

———. *Women, Freedom, and Calvin*. Philadelphia: Westminster Press, 1985.

Dowey, Edward A. Jr. *The Knowledge of God in Calvin's Theology*. 3rd ed. Grand Rapids, MI: Wm. B. Eerdmans, 1994.

———. "The Structure of Calvin's Thought as Influenced by the Two-fold Knowledge of God." *Calvinus Ecclesiae Genevensis Custos*. International Congress on Calvin Research. Edited by Wilhelm Neuser. New York: Peter Lang, 1984, 135–148.

———. "The Old Faith: Comments on One of Heinrich Bullinger's Most Distinctive Treatises," In *Erbe und Auftrag: Festschrift für Wilhelm Heinrich Neuser zum 65 Geburtstag*. Edited by W. van 't Spijker. Kampen, Netherlands: J H Kok, 1991, 270–278.

Ebeling, Gerhard. "Church History Is the History of the Exposition of Scripture." In *The Word of God and Tradition: Historical Studies Interpreting the Divisions of Christianity*. Translated by S.H. Hooke. Philadelphia: Fortress Press, 1968.

———. "Sola Scriptura, and Tradition." In *The Word of God and Tradition: Historical Studies Interpreting the Divisions of Christianity*. Translated by S.H. Hooke. Philadelphia: Fortress Press, 1968.

———. "The Word of God and Church Doctrine." In *The Word of God and Tradition: Historical Studies Interpreting the Divisions of Christianity*. Translated by S.H. Hooke. Philadelphia: Fortress Press, 1968.

———. *Wort Gottes und Tradition*. Göttingen: Vandenhoeck & Ruprecht, 1964.

Eire, Carlos M.N. "'True Piety Begets True Confession': Calvin's Attack on Idolatry." In *John Calvin and the Church*. Edited by Timothy George. Louisville: Westminster John Knox Press, 1991, 247–276.

———. *War Against the Idols: The Reformation of Worship from Erasmus to Calvin.* Cambridge: Cambridge University Press, 1986.

Engel, Mary Potter. *John Calvin's Perspectival Anthropology.* American Academy of Religion Series, no. 52, edited by Susan Thistlethwaite. Atlanta: Scholars Press, 1988.

Engammare, Max. "Calvin connaissait-il la Bible? Les citations de l'Ecriture dans ses sermons sur la Genese." *Bulletin de la Societe de l'Histoire du Protestantisme Francais* 141 (1995): 163–184.

———. "Cinquante ans de revision de la traduction biblique d'Olivetan: Les Bibles reformees genevoises en francais au XVIe siecle." *Bibliotheque d'Humanisme et Renaissance: Travaux et Documents.* 50 (1991): 347–377.

———. "Calvin: A Prophet without a Prophecy." *Church History* 64 (1998), 643–661.

———. "Joannes Calvinus Trium Linguarum Peritus? La Question de L'Hebreu." *Bibliotheque d'Humanisme et Renaissance: Travaux et Documents.* 58 (1996): 35–60.

———. "Le Paradis A Geneve: Comment Calvin Prechait-il la Chute aux Genevois?" *Etudes Theologiques et Religieuses* 69 (1994): 329–347.

Esser, Hans Helmut. "Die Lehre vom 'testimonium Spiritus Sancti internum' bei Calvin innerhalb seiner Lehre von der Heiligen Schrift." Verbindliches Zeugnis. Vol. 2: Schriftauslegung-Lehramt-Rezeption. Edited by Wolfhart Pannenberg. Dialog der Kirchen 9. Freiburg im Breisgau: Herder; Gottingen: Vandenhoeck & Ruprecht, 1995, 246–258.

Evans, G.R. *Old Arts and New Theology: The Beginnings of Theology as an Academic Discipline.* Oxford: Oxford University Press, 1980.

———. *The Language and Logic of the Bible: The Earlier Middle Ages.* Cambridge: Cambridge University Press, 1984.

———. *The Language and Logic of the Bible: The Road to Reformation.* Cambridge: Cambridge University Press, 1985.

———. *Problems of Authority in the Reformation Debates.* Cambridge: Cambridge University Press, 1992.

———. "Calvin on signs: an Augustinian dilemma." *Renaissance Studies* 3 (1989): 35–45.

———. "*Absurditas* in Augustine's Scriptural Commentary." *Downside Review* 99 (1981): 109–118.

———. "*Cur Deus Homo*: St. Bernard's Theology of the Redemption. A Contribution to the Contemporary Debate." *Studia Theologica* 36 (1982): 27–36.

———. *The Thought of Gregory the Great.* Cambridge Studies in Medieval Thought and Life. Cambridge: Cambridge University Press, 1986.

Farrar, Frederic W. *History of Interpretation.* New York, Dutton, 1886. Reprint edition, Grand Rapids, Baker Book House, 1961.

Febvre, Lucien. *The Problem of Unbelief in the Sixteenth Century: The Religion of Rabelais.* Translated by Beatrice Gottlieb. Cambridge: Harvard University Press, 1982.

Feld, Helmut. "Hermeneutische Voraussetzungen und Theologische Leitideen der Johannes-Interpretation J. Calvins." In *Calvin's Books: Festschrift dedicated to Peter De Klerk on the occasion of his seventieth birthday.* Edited by Wilhelm H. Neuser. Heerenveen: J.J. Groen en Zoon, 1997. 105–116.

Fischer, Daniele. "L'Element Historique dans la Predication de Calvin." *Revue d'histoire et de philosophie religieuses*, 64, (1984), 365–386.

Forstman, H. Jackson. *Word and Spirit: Calvin's Doctrine of Biblical Authority.* Stanford, CA: Stanford University Press, 1962.

Fraenkel, Pierre. "Quelques observations sur le 'tu es petrus' chez Calvin, au colloque de worms en 1540 et dans l'institution de 1543." *Bibliotheque d'humanisme et renaissance: travaux et documents*, 27, (1965), 607–628.

Frei, Hans. *The Eclipse of Biblical Narrative: A Study in Eighteenth and Nineteenth Century Hermeneutics.* New Haven, Yale University Press, 1974.

Froehlich, Karlfried. *Biblical Interpretation in the Early Church.* Sources of Early Christian Thought. Edited by William G. Rusch. Philadelphia: Fortress Press, 1984.

———. "Church History and the Bible." Princeton Seminary Bulletin 1 (1978): 213–224. Reprinted in *Biblical Hermeneutics in Historical Perspective*, 1–15. Edited by Mark Burrows and Paul Rorem. Grand Rapids: Eerdmans, 1991.

———. "'Always to Keep the Literal Sense in Holy Scripture Means to Kill One's Soul': The State of Biblical Hermeneutics at the Beginning of the Fifteenth Century." In *Literary Uses of Typology from the Late Middle Ages to the Present*, ed. Earl Miner. Princeton: Princeton University Press, 1977.

———. "Johannes Trithemius on the Fourfold Sense of Scripture: The *Tractatus de Inuestigatione Scripturae* (1486)." In *Biblical Interpretation in the Era of the Reformation*. Edited by Richard A. Muller and John L. Thompson. Grand Rapids: Eerdmans, 1996, 23–60.

———. "Justification Language and Grace: The Charge of Pelagianism in the Middle Ages." In *Probing the Reformed Tradition: Historical Studies in Honor of Edward A. Dowey, Jr.* Edited by Elsie Anne McKee and Brian G. Armstrong. Louisville: Westminster John Knox Press, 1989.

———. "Aminadab's Chariot: The Predicament of Biblical Interpretation." 1996 Warfield Lecture, Princeton Theological Seminary.

———. "The Fate of the *Glossa Ordinaria* in the Sixteenth Century." In *Die Patristik in der Bibelexegese des 16. Jahrhunderts*. Edited by David C. Steinmetz. Wiesbaden: Harrassowitz Verlag, 1999, 19–47.

Frye, Roland M. "Calvin's Theological Use of Figurative Language." In *John Calvin and the Church*. Edited by Timothy George. Louisville: Westminster John Knox Press, 1991, 172–194.

Gadamer, Hans-Georg. *Truth and Method.* 2nd rev. ed. Translated and revised by Joel Weinsheimer and Donald G. Marshall. New York: Crossroad Publishing, 1989.

Gamble, Harry Y. *Books and Readers in the Early Church: A History of Early Christian Texts.* New Haven: Yale University Press, 1995.

Gamble, Richard C. *Calvin and Hermeneutics.* Articles on Calvin and Calvinism, v. 6. New York: Garland Publishing Co., 1992.

———. *Calvin and Calvinism:The Organization Structure of Calvin's Theology.* Articles on Calvin and Calvinism, v. 7, edited by Richard J. Gamble. New York: Garland Publishing Co., 1992.

———. "*Brevitas et Facilitas*: Toward an Understanding of Calvin's Hermeneutic." *Westminster Theological Journal* 47 (1985): 1–17.

———. "Exposition and Method in Calvin." *Westminster Theological Journal* 49 (1987): 153–165.

———. "Current Trends in Calvin Research, 1982–1990." In *Calvinus Sacrae Scripturae Professor*. International Congress on Calvin Research. Edited by Wilhelm Neuser. Grand Rapids: Eerdmans, 1994, 91–112.

———. "The Sources of Calvin's Genesis Commentary: A Preliminary Report." *Archiv für Reformationsgeschichte* 84 (1993):206–221.

———. "Calvin's Theological Method. The Case of Caroli." In *Calvin: Erbe und Auftrag: Festschrift für Wilhelm Heinrich Neuser zum 65. Geburtstag*. Edited by Willem van Spijker. Kampen: Kok Pharos Publishing House, 1991, 130–137.

———. "Calvin as Theologian and Exegete: Is There Anything New?" *Calvin Theological Journal* 23 (1988): 178–194.

Ganoczy, Alexandre. *The Young Calvin*. Translated by David Foxgrover and Wade Provo. Philadelphia: Westminster Press, 1987.

———. "Das Amt des Lehrens in der Kirche Nach Calvin." In *Lehramt und Theologie im 16. Jahrhundert*. Edited by Remigius Baumer. Munster: Aschendorff, 1976, 22–33.

———. "Hermeneutische Korrelationen bei Calvin." *Reformatio Ecclesiae*. Beitrage zu Kirchlichen Reformbemuhungen von der Alten Kirche bis zur Neuzeit. Festgabe fur Erwin Iserloh, hrsg. von Remigius Baumer. Zurich: Schoningh, 1980, 615–627.

———. "Forschungsansatze zur Hermeneutik Calvins: Calvin als paulinischer Theologe." Lecture given at the Europaischer Kongress fur Calvinforschung, Amsterdam, Sept. 16–19, 1974.

———. "Calvin." I.234–240 in *Oxford Encyclopedia of the Reformation*. 4 volumes. Edited by Hans J. Hillerbrand. Oxford: Oxford University Press, 1996.

———. and Müller, Klaus. *Calvins Handschriftliche Annotationen zu Chrysostomus: Ein Beitrag zur Hermeneutik Calvins*. Wiesbaden: Franz Steiner Verlag GMBH, 1981.

———. and Scheld, Stefan. *Die Hermeneutik Calvins: Geistesgeschichtliche Voraussetzungen und Grundzüge*. Wiesbaden: Franz Steiner Verlag GMBH, 1983.

Gerrish, Brian. *Grace and Gratitude: The Eucharistic Theology of John Calvin*. Philadelphia: Fortress Press, 1993.

———. "The Mirror of God's Goodness: A Key Metaphor in Calvin's View of Man," In *Readings in Calvin's Theology*. Edited by Donald K. McKim. Grand Rapids, MI: Baker Book House, 1984, 107–122.

———. "From Calvin to Schleiermacher: The Theme and Shape of Christian Dogmatics." In *Continuing the Reformation: Essays on Modern Religious Thought*. Chicago: University of Chicago Press, 1993.

———. "The Pathfinder: Calvin's Image of Martin Luther." In *The Old Protestantism and the New: Essays on the Reformation Heritage*. Edinburgh: T.&T. Clark Limited, 1982.

———. "The Word of God and the Words of Scripture: Luther and Calvin on Biblical Authority." In *The Old Protestantism and the New: Essays on the Reformation Heritage*. Edinburgh: T.&T. Clark Limited, 1982.

————. "Theology within the Limits of Piety Alone: Schleiermacher and Calvin's Notion of God." In *The Old Protestantism and the New: Essays on the Reformation Heritage*. Edinburgh: T.&T. Clark Limited, 1982.

————. "Schleiermacher and the Reformation: A Question of Doctrinal Development," In *The Old Protestantism and the New: Essays on the Reformation Heritage*. Edinburgh: T.&T. Clark Limited, 1982.

Gilson, Etienne. *The Mystical Theology of Saint Bernard*. Translated by A.H.C. Downes. Kalamazoo, MI: Cistercian Publications, 1990.

Girard, Benoît. *Rhétorique et Théologique: Calvin, Le Commentaire de L'Epître aux Romains*. Paris: Éditions Beauchesne, 1979.

Godfrey, William Robert. "'Beyond the Sphere of our Judgment': Calvin and the Confirmation of Scripture." *The Westminster Theological Journal*, 58, No. 1, (1996): 29–39.

Goudineau, Hubert. "Luther et Calvin commentatuers de l'epitre aux Romains: Une comparaison." *Positions Lutheriennes*, 44, (1996): 16–52.

Graafland, C. "Hat Calvin einen Ordo salutis gelehrt?" In *Calvinus Ecclesiae Genevensis Custos*. International Congress on Calvin Research. Edited by Wilhelm Neuser. New York: Peter Lang, 1984, 221–230.

Greef, Wulfert de. "Calvin on Prophecy." In *Ordenlich und Fruchtbar. Festschrift fur Willem van't Spijker Anlasslich seines Abschieds als Professor der Theologischen Universitat Apeldoorn*. Edited by Wilhelm H. Neuser. Leiden: JJ. Groen en Zoon. 111–128.

Gregory, Brad S. *Salvation at Stake: Christian Martyrdom in Early Modern Europe*. Cambridge, Massachusetts: Harvard University Press, 1999.

Greene-McCreight, Kathryn. "Restless Until We Rest in God: The Fourth Commandment as Test Case in Christian 'Plain Sense' Interpretation." *Ex Auditu* 11, (1995): 29–41.

————. "'We are Companions of the Patriarchs' or Scripture Absorbs Calvin's World." *Modern Theology* 14 (1998): 213–224.

Grin, Edmond. "L'Unite des deux Testaments Selon Calvin." *Theologische Zeitschrift*, 17, (1961): 175–186.

Grislis, Egil. "Calvin's Use of Cicero in the Institutes I:1–5-A Case Study in Theological Method," *Archiv für Reformationsgeschichte* 62 (1971): 5–37.

Grosclaude, Pierre. "La Place de Calvin dans la Litterature Francaise." *Societe de l'Histoire du Protestantisme Francais*, 110, (1964): 160–174.

Haire, J.L.M. "John Calvin as an Expositor." *Irish Biblical Studies* 4 (1982): 2–16.

Hale, John. *The Civilization of Europe in the Renaissance*. New York: Atheneum, 1994.

Hall, Basil. "Calvin and Biblical Humanism." *Proceedings of the Huguenot Society of London* 20 (1960): 195–209.

Hasler, Richard A. "The Influence of David and the Psalms upon John Calvin's Life and Thought." *Hartford Quarterly* 5 (1965): 7–18.

Haslett, Ian. "Scripture, Tradition, and Intolerance: an introduction to the critique of Sebastian Castellio (1515–1563)." *Irish Biblical Studies* 6, (1984): 106–119.

Hazlett, Ian. "Calvin's Latin Preface to his Proposed French Edition of Chrysostom's Homilies: Translation and Commentary." In *Humanism and Reform*.

The Chruch in Europe, England and Scotland, 1400–1643. Essays in Honour of James K. Cameron. Edited by James Kirk. Oxford: Blackwell, 1991, 129–150.

Heidegger, Martin. *Being and Time.* Translated by John Macquarrie and Edward Robinson. San Francisco: Harper and Row, 1962.

Heim, S. Mark. "The Powers of God: Calvin and Late Medieval Thought." *Andover Newton Quarterly* 19 (1979): 156–166.

Hendrix, Scott H. "The Use of Scripture in Establishing Protestantism: The Case of Urbanus Rhegius." In *The Bible in the 16th Century.* Edited by David Steinmetz. Durham: Duke University Press, 1990, 37–49.

Heron, Alasdair I.C. "Die Widmungen der neutestamentlichen Kommentare Johannes Calvins." In *In der Wahrheit bleiben: Dogma-Schriftauslegung-Kirche.* Festschrift fur Reinhard Slenczka zum 65. Geburtstag. Edited by Manfred Seitz. Gottingen: Vandenhoeck & Ruprecht, 1996, 72–78.

Hesselink, I. John. *Calvin's First Catechism.* Columbia Series in Reformed Theology. Louisville: Westminster John Knox Press, 1997.

——. "Calvin's understanding of the relation of the church and Israel based largely on his interpretation of Romans 9–11." *Ex Auditu* 4 (1988): 59–69.

——. "John Calvin on the Law and Christian Freedom." *Ex Auditu* 11 (1995): 77–89.

Higman, Francis M. "Calvin and Farel." In *Calvinus Sacrae Scripturae Professor.* International Congress on Calvin Research. Edited by Wilhelm Neuser. Grand Rapids: Eerdmans, 1994, 214–223.

——. *The Style of John Calvin in his French Polemical Treatises.* Oxford: Oxford University Press, 1967.

——. *Piety and the People: Religious Printing in French, 1511–1551.* Brookfield, VT: Ashgate Publishing, 1996.

——. "Theology in French: Religious Pamphlets from the Counter-reformation." *Renaissance and Modern Studies* 23, (1979): 128–146.

——. "Calvin's Works in Translation." In *Lire et Découvrir: La circulation des idées au temp de la Réforme.* Geneve: Librairie Droz, 1998, 545–562.

——. "The Reformation and the French Language." *Esprit Createur* Winter (1976): 20–36.

——. "I Came Not to Send Peace, but a Sword." In *Calvinus Sincerioris Religionis Vindex.* Edited by Wilhelm Neuser and Brian Armstrong. Kirksville, MO: Sixteenth Century Journal Publishers, 1997, 123–138.

——. "Linearity in Calvin's Thought." In *Lire et Découvrir: La circulation des idées au temp de la Réforme.* Geneve: Librairie Droz, 1998, 391–402.

——. "Luther, Calvin et les Docteurs." In *Le Controle des Idees a la Renaissance.* Actes du colloque de la Fisier tenu a Montreal en septembre 1995. Etudes de philologie et d'histoire 49. Edited by J.M. De Bujanda. Geneve: Droz, 1996. 93–111.

——. "Genevan Printing and French Censorship 1520–1551." In *Cinq Siécles D'Imprimerie Genevoise*: Actes du Colloque International sur l'Histoire de l'Imprimerie de du Livre à Genève 27–30 Avril 1978. Edited by Jean-Daniel Candaux. Geneve: Société d'histoire et d'archéologie, 1980, 31–53.

——. "Calvin and the Art of Translation." *Western Canadian Studies in Modern Languages and Literature* 2 (1970): 5–27.

————. "Calvin et L'Expérience." In *Experience, Coutume Tradition au Temps de la Renaissance*. Edited by Marie T. Jones-Davies. Paris: Editions Klincksieck, 1992, 245–256.

————. "Ideas for Export: Translations in the Early Reformation." In *Lire et Découvrir: La circulation des idées au temp de la Réforme*. Geveve: Librairie Droz, 1998, 531–544.

————. "The Origins of the Image of Geneva." In *The Identity of Geneva: The Christian Commonwealth 1564–1864*. Edited by John B. Roney and Martin Klauber. Westport, CA: Greenwood Press, 1998, 21–38.

————. "Theology for the Layman in the French Reformation 1520–1550." *The Library* 9 (1987): 105–127.

————. "Calvin, le polar et la propagande: l'Histoire d'un meurtre exécrable." In *Lire et Découvrir: La circulation des idées au temp de la Réforme*. Geneve: Librairie Droz, 1998, 289–304.

Hobbes, R. Gerald. "Hebraica Veritas *and* Traditio Apostolica: Saint Paul and the Interpretation of the Psalms in the Sixteenth Century." In *The Bible in the 16th Century*. Edited by David Steinmetz. Durham: Duke University Press, 1990, 83–99.

Hoffmann, Manfred. *Rhetoric and Theology: The Hermeneutic of Erasmus*. Toronto: University of Toronto Press, 1994.

Holder, R. Ward. "*Ecclesia, Legenda atque Intelligenda Scriptura*: The Church as Discerning Community in Calvin's Hermeneutic." *Calvin Theological Journal*, 36 (2001): 270–289.

Hörcsik, Richard. "John Calvin in Geneva, 1536–1538—Some Questions about Calvin's First Stay at Geneva." In *Calvinus Sacrae Scripturae Professor*. International Congress on Calvin Research. Edited by Wilhelm Neuser. Grand Rapids: Eerdmans, 1994, 155–165.

James, Frank A. III. "A Late Medieval Parallel in Reformation Thought: *Gemina Praedestinatio* in Gregory of Rimini and Peter Martyr Vermigli," In *Via Augustini: Augustine in the Later Middle Ages, Renaissance and Reformation. Essays in Honor of Damasus Trapp, O.S.A.* Edited by Heiko Oberman and Frank James, III. Leiden: E.J. Brill, 1991.

Jardine, Lisa. *Worldly Goods: A New History of the Renaissance*. New York: Doubleday, 1996.

Jeanrond, Werner G. *Theological Hermeneutics: Development and Significance*. New York: Crossroad, 1991.

Jellema, Dirk W. "God's 'babytalk': Calvin and the 'errors' in the Bible." *Reformed Journal* 30, 4 (1980): 25–27.

Johnson, David W. "The Myth of the Augustinian Synthesis," In *Biblical Hermeneutics in Historical Perspective*. Edited by Mark Burrows and Paul Rorem. Grand Rapids: Eerdmans, 1991.

Jones, Serene. *Calvin and the Rhetoric of Piety*. Columbia Series in Reformed Theology. Louisville: Westminster John Knox Press, 1995.

Kingdon, Robert M. "Augustine and Calvin." In *Saint Augustine the Bishop: A Book of Essays*. Edited by Fannie LeMoine and Christopher Kleinhenz. New York: Garland Publishing Co., 1994, 177–178.

————. "A New View of Calvin in the Light of the Registers of the Geneva

Consistory," In *Calvinus Sincerioris Religionis Vindex*. Edited by Wilhelm Neuser and Brian Armstrong. Kirksville, MO: Sixteenth Century Journal Publishers, 1997, 21–34.

———. "Popular Reactions to the Debate between Bolsec and Calvin." In *Calvin: Erbe und Auftrag: Festschrift für Wilhelm Heinrich Neuser zum 65. Geburtstag*. Edited by Willem van Spijker. Kampen: Kok Pharos Publishing House, 1991, 138–145.

———. *Adultery and Divorce in Calvin's Geneva*. Cambridge: Harvard University Press, 1995.

———. *Geneva and the consolidation of the French Protestant movement, 1564–1572: a contribution to the history of Congregationalism, Presbyterianism, and Calvinist resistance theory*. Madison: University of Wisconsin Press, 1967.

———. *Geneva and the Coming of the Wars of Religion in France, 1555–1563*. Geneve: Librairie E. Droz, 1956.

———. "The Business Activities of Printers Henri and Francois Estienne." In *Aspects de la Propagande Religieuse*. Edited by A.O. Berthoud. Librarie E. Droz: Geneve. 1957: 258–275.

———. "Anticlericalism in the Registers of the Geneva Consistory 1542–1564." In *Anticlericalism in Late Medieval and Early Modern Europe*. Edited by Peter A. Dykema and Heiko A. Oberman. Leiden: E.J. Brill, 1993, 617–623.

———. "Calvin and the Government of Geneva." In *Calvinus Ecclesiae Genevensis Custos*. International Congress on Calvin Research. Edited by Wilhelm Neuser. New York: Peter Lang, 1984, 49–67.

———. "Calvin's Ideas About the Diaconate: Social or Theological in Origin?" In *Piety, Politics, and Ethics. Reformation studies in honor of George Wolfgang Forell*. Sixteenth Century Essays & Studies, 3. Sixteenth Century Journal Publishers, 1984, 167–180.

Kok, Joel E. "Heinrich Bullinger's Exegetical Method: The Model for Calvin?" In *Biblical Interpretation in the Era of the Reformation*. Edited by Richard A. Muller and John L. Thompson. Grand Rapids: Eerdmans, 1996, 241–254.

Kraeling, Emil G. *The Old Testament Since the Reformation*. London: Lutterworth Press, 1955.

Kraus, Hans-Joachim. "Calvins exegetische Prinzipien." *Zeitschrift fur Kirchengeschichte*, 79, (1968): 329–341. Translated as "Calvin's Exegetical Principles." *Interpretation* 31 (1977): 8–18.

Kreck, Walter. "Parole et esprit selon Calvin." *Revue d'histoire et de philosophie religieuses*, 40, (1960): 215–228.

Kristeller, Paul Oskar. *Renaissance Thought: The Classic, Scholastic, and Humanist Strains*. New York: Harper & Row, 1961.

Lane, A.N.S. "Calvin's Sources of Saint Bernard." *Archiv für Reformationsgeschichte* 67 (1976): 253–283.

———. "Calvin's Use of the Fathers and the Medievals." *Calvin Theological Journal*, 16 (1981): 149–200.

———. "John Calvin: The Witness of the Holy Spirit." *Faith and Ferment* (London: The Westminster Conference, 1982): 1–17.

———. *Calvin and Bernard of Clairvaux*. Studies in Reformed Theology and History, new series #1. Princeton: Princeton Theological Seminary, 1996.

——. "Calvin and the Fathers in 'Bondage and Liberation of the Will'" In *Calvinus Sincerioris Religionis Vindex: Calvin as Protector of the Purer Religion.* Sixteenth Century Essays & Studies Vol. 36. Kirksville, MO: Sixteenth Century Journal Publishers, 1997, 67–96.

——. *John Calvin: Student of the Church Fathers.* Grand Rapids: Baker Book House, 1999.

LeClercq, Jean. *The Love of Learning and the Desire for God: A Study of Monastic Culture.* Translated by Catharine Misrahi. New York: Fordham University Press, 1961.

Lee, Sou-Young. "Calvin's Understanding of *Pietas.*" In *Calvinus Sincerioris Religionis Vindex.* Edited by Wilhelm Neuser and Brian Armstrong. Kirksville, MO: Sixteenth Century Journal Publishers, 1997, 225–240.

Leith, John H. *John Calvin's Doctrine of the Christian Life.* Louisville: Westminster John Knox Press, 1989.

Lienhard, Marc. "Luther et Calvin commentateurs du notre pere." *Revue d'histoire et de philosophie religieuses,* 72, No. 1, (1992): 73–88.

Lindberg, Carter. *The European Reformations.* Cambridge: Blackwell Publishers, 1996.

Linder, Robert D. "Calvinism and Humanism: The First Generation." *Church History* 44 (1975): 167–181.

Lobstein, P. "La Connaissance Religieuse d'apres Calvin: Etude d'histoire et de dogmatique." *Revue de Theologie et de Philosophie* 42 (1909): 53–110.

Loewen, Howard J. "The Use of Scripture in Augustine's Theology." *Scottish Journal of Theology* 34 (1981): 201–224.

Lose, David J. "Luther & Calvin on Preaching to the Human Condition." *Lutheran Quarterly* 10 (1996): 281–318.

Maag, Karin. *Seminary of University? The Genevan Academy and Reformed Higher Education, 1560–1620.* Brookfield, Vermont: Ashgate, 1995.

Mays, James Luther. "Calvin's Commentary on the Psalms: The Preface as Introduction." In *John Calvin and the Church.* Edited by Timothy George. Louisville: Westminster John Knox Press, 1991, 195–205.

McGinn, Bernard; Meyendorff, John; and LeClercq, Jean, editors. *Christian Spirituality: Origins to the Twelfth Century.* New York: Crossroad, 1987.

——. *The Growth of Mysticism.* New York: Crossroad, 1994.

McGrath, Alister E. *A Life of John Calvin: A Study in the Shaping of Western Culture.* Cambridge, MA: Blackwell Publishers, 1990.

——. *Iustitia Dei: A History of the Christian Doctrine of Justification.* Cambridge: Cambridge University Press, 1986.

——. "John Calvin and Late Mediaeval Thought: A Study in Late Mediaeval Influences upon Calvin's Theological Development." *Archiv für Reformationsgeschichte* 77 (1986): 58–78.

Margerie, Bertrand de. *An Introduction to the History of Exegesis.* Vol. I, St. Augustine. Vol. II, The Latin Fathers. Petersham, MA: St. Bede's Press, 1995.

Margolin, Jean-Claude. "Epistle to the Romans (Chapter 11) According to the Versions and/or Commentaries of Valla, Colet, Lefevre, and Erasmus." In *The Bible in the 16th Century.* Edited by David Steinmetz. Durham: Duke University Press, 1990, 136–166.

McKane, W. "Calvin as an Old Testament Commentator." *Nederduitse Gere-formeerde Teologiese Tydskrif* 25 (1984): 250–259.

McKee, Elsie Anne. "Some Reflections on Relating Calvin's Exegesis and Theology," In *Biblical Hermeneutics in Historical Perspective*. Edited by Mark Burrows and Paul Rorem. Grand Rapids: Eerdmans, 1991.

———. "Calvin's Teaching on the Elder Illuminated by Exegetical History.'" In *John Calvin and the Church*. Edited by Timothy George. Louisville: Westminster John Knox Press, 1991, 147–157.

———. *John Calvin on the Diaconate and Liturgical Almsgiving*. Genève: Librairie Droz, 1984.

———. *Elders and the Plural Ministry: The Role of Exegetical History in Illuminating John Calvin's Theology*. Genève: Librairie Droz, 1988.

———. "Calvin's Exegesis of Romans 12:8–Social, Accidental, or Theological," *Calvin Theological Journal* 23 (1988): 6–18.

———. "Exegesis, Theology, and Development in Calvin's *Institutio*: A Methodological Suggestion." In *Probing the Reformed Tradition: Historical Studies in Honor of Edward A. Dowey, Jr.* Edited by Elsie Anne McKee and Brian G. Armstrong. Louisville: Westminster John Knox Press, 1989.

———. "Les Anciens et l'Interpretation de 1 Tm 5, 17 chez Calvin: Une Curiosite dans l'Histoire de l'Exegese." *Revue de Theologie et de Philosophie* 120, (1988): 411–417.

McKim, Donald K. "John Calvin: A Theologian for an Age of Limits." In *Readings in Calvin's Theology*. Edited by Donald K. McKim. Grand Rapids: Baker Book House, 1984, 291–310.

———. "Calvin's View of Scripture." In *Readings in Calvin's Theology*. Edited by Donald K. McKim. Grand Rapids: Baker Book House, 1984, 43–68.

Midelfort, H.C. Erik. "Social History and Biblical Exegesis: Community, Family, and Witchcraft in Sixteenth-Century Germany." In *The Bible in the 16th Century*. Edited by David Steinmetz. Durham: Duke University Press, 1990, 7–20.

Millet, Olivier. *Calvin et la dynamique de la parole: Etude de Rhétorique réformée*. Paris: H. Champion, 1992.

———. "*Docere/Movere: Les catégories rhétoriques et leurs sources humanistes dans la doctrine calvinienne de la foi*." In *Calvinus Sincerioris Religionis Vindex*. Edited by Wilhelm Neuser and Brian Armstrong. Kirksville, MO: Sixteenth Century Journal Publishers, 1997, 35–52.

———. "Exegese Evangelique et Culture Litteraiere Humaniste: Enttre Luther et Beze, L'Abraham Sacrifiant Selon Calvin." *Etudes theologiques et religieuses*, 69, (1994): 367–380

———. "Le premier 'Catechisme' de Geneve (1537/1538) et sa place dans l'oeuvre de Calvin." *Catechisme et Confessions de foi: Actes du VIIIe colloque Jean Boisset*. Edited by Marie-Madeleine Fragonard. Montpellier: Unversite Paul Valery (1995): 209–229.

———. "Geneve, Capitale Litteraire de la Reforme au XVIe siecle." *Paris et le phenomene des capitales litteraires: carrefour ou dialogue des cultures*. Actes du Premier congr'es international de C.L.R.C., 22–26 mai 1984. Vol. 2 Paris: Presses de l'Universite de Paris-Sorbonne 1986, 911–922.

————. "L'Humanite De Calvin." *La revue reformee* 47 (1996): 9–24.

Moehn, Willhelmus T.H. *God Calls Us to His Service: The Relation Between God and His Audience in Calvin's Sermons on Acts.* Geneve: Droz, 2001.

Monheit, Michael L. "Young Calvin, Textual Interpretation and Roman Law." *Bibliotheque d'humanisme et renaissance: travaux et documents.* 59, No. 2, (1997): 263–282.

Muller, Richard A. "The Hermeneutic of Promise and Fulfillment in Calvin's Exegesis of the Old Testament Prophecies of the Kingdom," In *The Bible in the 16th Century.* Edited by David Steinmetz. Durham: Duke University Press, 1990, 68–82.

————. *The Unaccommodated Calvin: Studies in the Foundation of a Theological Tradition.* Oxford: Oxford University Press, 2000.

————. "Fides and cognitio in relation to the problem of intellect and will in the theology of John Calvin," *Calvin Theological Journal,* 25 (1990): 207–224.

————. "The Foundation of Calvin's Theology: Scripture as Revealing God's Word." *Duke Divinity School Review* 44 (1979): 14–24.

————. "Biblical Interpretation in the Era of the Reformation: The View from the Middle Ages." In *Biblical Interpretation in the Era of the Reformation.* Edited by Richard A. Muller and John L. Thompson. Grand Rapids: Eerdmans, 1996, 3–22.

————. "Calvin's 'Argument du livre' (1541): An Erratum to the McNeill and Battles 'Institutes.'" *The Sixteenth Century Journal* 29 (1998): 35–38.

————. "In the Light of Orthodoxy: The 'Method and Disposition' of Calvin's 'Institutio' from the Perspective of Calvin's Late-Sixteenth-Century Editors." *The Sixteenth Century Journal* 28 (1997): 1203–1229.

————. "Calvin, Beza, and the Exegetical History of Romans 13:1–7." In *The Identity of Geneva: The Christian Commonwealth 1564–1864.* Edited by John B. Roney and Martin Klauber. Westport, CA: Greenwood Press, 1998, 39–56.

————. and Thompson, John L. "The Significance of Precritical Exegesis: Retrospect and Prospect." In *Biblical Interpretation in the Era of the Reformation.* Edited by Richard A. Muller and John L. Thompson. Grand Rapids: Eerdmans, 1996, 335–345.

Murphy, Roland. "Patristic and Medieval Exegesis—Help or Hindrance?" *Catholic Biblical Quarterly* 43 (1981): 505–516.

Naphy, William G. "Baptisms, Church Riots and Social Unrest in Calvin's Geneva." *The Sixteenth Century Journal* 26 (1995): 86–97.

————. *Calvin and the Consolidation of the Genevan Reformation.* Manchester: Manchester University Press, 1994.

Neuser, Wilhelm H. "Calvins Verständnis der Heiligen Schrift." In *Calvinus Sacrae Scripturae Professor.* International Congress on Calvin Research. Edited by Wilhelm Neuser. Grand Rapids: Eerdmans, 1994, 41–71.

————. "Calvin's Teaching on the *notae fidelium*: An Unnoticed Part of the *Institutio* 4.1.8." Translated by Mark S. Burrows. In *Probing the Reformed Tradition: Historical Studies in Honor of Edward A. Dowey, Jr.* Edited by Elsie Anne McKee and Brian G. Armstrong. Louisville: Westminster John Knox Press, 1989.

Nicole, P.D. "De l'exegese a l'hometique. Evolution entre le commentaire de

1551, les sermons de 1558, et le commentaire de 1559 sur le prophet Esaie."
In *Calvinus Ecclesiae Genevensis Custos*. International Congress on Calvin Research. Edited by Wilhelm Neuser. New York: Peter Lang, 1984, 159–162.

Niesel, Wilhelm. *The Theology of Calvin*. Translated by Harold Knight. Philadelphia: Westminster Press, 1956.

Oberman, Heiko A. "*Initia Calvini*: The Matrix of Calvin's Reformation."
In *Calvinus Sacrae Scripturae Professor*. International Congress on Calvin Research. Edited by Wilhelm Neuser. Grand Rapids: Eerdmans, 1994, 113–154.

——. *The Harvest of Medieval Theology: Gabriel Biel and Late Medieval Nominalism*. Cambridge: Harvard University Press, 1963.

——. "Preaching and the Word in the Reformation." *Theology Today* 18 (1961/1962): 16–29.

——. "Reformation, preaching and ex opere operato." In *Christianity Divided, Protestant and Roman Catholic theological issues*. Edited by Daniel J. Callahan, Heiko A. Oberman and Daniel J. O'Hanlon. New York, Sheed and Ward, 1961, 223–239.

——. "Calvin and Farel The Dynamics of Legitimation in Early Calvinism." *Journal of Early Modern History*. 2 (1998): 32–60

——. "Europa afflicta: The Reformation of the Refugees." *Archiv für Reformationsgeschichte* 83 (1992): 91–111.

——. "Calvin's critique of Calvinism." *The Dawn of the Reformation. Essays in Late Medieval and Early Reformation Thought*. Edinburgh: T & T Clark, 1986, 259–268.

——. "Holy Spirit-Holy Writ-Holy Church: The Witness of the Reformation." *Hartford Quarterly* 5 (1964–1965): 43–71.

——. "The Pursuit of Happiness: Calvin Between Humanism and Reformation." In *Humanity and Divinity in Renaissance and Reformation: Essays in Honor of Charles Trinkaus*. Edited by John W. O'Malley, Thomas M. Izbicki, and Gerald Christianson. Leiden: E.J. Brill, 1993, 251–283.

Opitz, Peter. *Calvins Theologische Hermeneutik*. Neukirchen-Vluyn: Neukirchener, 1994.

——. "Ein Thorapsalm als ABC des christlichen Glaubens-Beobachtungen zu Calvins Predigten uber Psalm 119." In *Calvin's Books: Festschrift dedicated to Peter De Klerk on the occasion of his seventieth birthday*. Edited by Wilhelm H. Neuser, Heerenveen: J.J. Groen en Zoon, 1997, 117–132.

Ozment, Steven. *The Age of Reform 1250–1550: An Intellectual and Religious History of Late Medieval and Reformation Europe*. New Haven: Yale University Press, 1980.

——. *Protestants: The Birth of a Revolution*. New York: Doubleday, 1992.

Parker, Thomas D. "A Comparison of Calvin and Luther on Galatians." *Interpretation* 17 (1963): 61–75.

Parker, T.H.L. *Calvin's Preaching*. Louisville: Westminster John Knox Press, 1992.

——. *Calvin's New Testament Commentaries*. 2nd ed. Louisville: Westminster John Knox Press, 1993.

——. *Calvin's Old Testament Commentaries*. Edinburgh: T. & T. Clark, 1986.

———. *Commentaries on Romans: 1532–1542*. Edinburgh: T. & T. Clark, 1986.

———. *Calvin: An Introduction to His Thought*. Louisville: Westminster John Knox Press, 1995.

———. "Calvin the Biblical Expositor." *Churchman* 78 (1964): 23–31.

———. "Calvin's Commentary on Hebrews." In *Church, Word, and Spirit: Historical and Theological Essays in Honor of Geoffrey W. Bromiley*. Edited by James E. Bradley and Richard A. Muller. Grand Rapids: Eerdmans, 1987.

———. "Calvin's Concept of Revelation." *Scottish Journal of Theology* 2 (March 1949): 29–47.

———. "The sources of the text of Calvin's New Testament." *Zeitschrift fur Kirchengeschichte* 73 (1962): 270–297.

———. "Calvin the Exegete: Change and Development." In *Calvinus Ecclesiae Doctor*. International Congress on Calvin Research. Edited by Wilhelm Neuser. Kampen: J.H. Kok, 1980, 33–46.

———. "Calvini Opera sed non Omnia." *Scottish Journal of Theology*. 18 (1965): 194–203.

Partee, Charles. *Calvin and Classical Philosophy*. Leiden: E.J. Brill, 1977.

———. "Calvin's Central Dogma Again." *The Sixteenth Century Journal* 18 (1987): 191–199.

———. "Calvin's Polemic: Foundational Convictions in the Service of God's Truth." In *Calvinus Sincerioris Religionis Vindex*. Edited by Wilhelm Neuser and Brian Armstrong. Kirksville, MO: Sixteenth Century Journal Publishers, 1997, 97–122.

Paul, Maarten J. "Genesis 4:17–24: A Case-study in Exegesis." *Tyndale Bulletin* 47 (1996): 143–162.

Payne, John. "Erasmus on Romans 9:6–24." In *The Bible in the 16th Century*. Edited by David Steinmetz. Durham: Duke University Press, 1990, 119–135.

———. "Erasmus's Influence on Zwingli and Bullinger in the Exegesis of Matthew 11:28–30." In *Biblical Interpretation in the Era of the Reformation*. Edited by Richard A. Muller and John L. Thompson. Grand Rapids: Eerdmans, 1996, 61–84.

Payton, James R. "Calvin and the Legitimation of Icons: His Treatment of the Seventh Ecumenical Council." *Archiv für Reformationsgeschichte* 84 (1993): 222–241.

———. "History as Rhetorical Weapon: Christian Humanism in Calvin's Reply to Sadoleto, 1539." In *In Honor of John Calvin, 1509–1564*. Edited by E.J. Furcha. Montreal: Faculty of Religious Studies, McGill University, 1987, 96–132.

———. "Calvin and the Libri Carolini." *The Sixteenth Century Journal* 28 (1997): 467–480.

Pelikan, Jaroslav. *The Christian Tradition: A History of the Development of Doctrine*. 5 volumes. Chicago: University of Chicago Press, 1971–1984.

Peter, Rodolphe. "Rhétorique et prédication selon Calvin." *Revue d'Histoire et de Philosophie Religieuses* 55 (1975): 249–272.

———. "Geneve dan la Predication de Calvin." In *Calvinus Ecclesiae Genevensis Custos*. International Congress on Calvin Research. Edited by Wilhelm Neuser. New York: Peter Lang, 1984, 23–48.

Peter, Rodolphe and Gilmont, Jean-François. *Bibliotheca Calviniana: Les œuvres de Jean Calvin publiées au xvie siècle*. 2 volumes. Geneve: Droz, 1991.

Pitkin, Barbara. "Imitation of David: David as a Paradigm for Faith in Calvin's Exegesis of the Psalms." *The Sixteenth Century Journal* 24 (1993): 843–863.

———. *What Pure Eyes Could See: Calvin's Doctrine of Faith in Its Exegetical Context*. Oxford: Oxford University Press, 1999.

———. "Seeing and Believing in the Commentaries on John by Martin Bucer and John Calvin." *Church History* 68 (1999): 865–885.

———. "Nothing But Concupiscence: Calvin's Understanding of Sin and the *Via Augustini*." *Calvin Theological Journal* 34 (1999): 347–369.

Pont, Adrianus D. "Citizen's Oath and Formulated Confession: Confession of Faith in Calvin's Congregation." In *Calvinus Sacrae Scripturae Professor*. International Congress on Calvin Research. Edited by Wilhelm Neuser. Grand Rapids: Eerdmans, 1994, 237–239.

———. "Confession of Faith in Calvin's Geneva." In *Calvin: Erbe und Auftrag: Festschrift für Wilhelm Heinrich Neuser zum 65. Geburtstag*. Edited by Willem van Spijker. Kampen: Kok Pharos Publishing House, 1991, 106–116.

Pranger, M.B. *Bernard of Clairvaux and the Shape of Monastic Thought: Broken Dreams*. Brill's Studies in Intellectual History, no. 56. Leiden: E.J. Brill, 1994.

Preus, James S. *From Shadow to Promise: Old Testament Interpretation from Augustine to the Young Luther*. Cambridge: Harvard University Press, 1969.

Puckett, David L. *John Calvin's Exegesis of the Old Testament* Columbia Series in Reformed Theology. Louisville: Westminster John Knox Press, 1995.

Quistorp, Heinrich. *Calvin's Doctrine of the Last Things*. Translated by Harold Knight. Richmond: John Knox Press, 1955.

Raitt, Jill. "Calvin's Use of Bernard of Clairvaux." *Archiv für Reformationsgeschichte* 72 (1981): 98–121.

———. "Calvin's Use of Persona." In *Calvinus Ecclesiae Genevensis Custos*. International Congress on Calvin Research. Edited by Wilhelm Neuser. New York: Peter Lang, 1984, 273–288.

———. "The Person of the Mediator: Calvin's Christology and Beza's Fidelity." *Occasional Papers of the American Society for Reformation Research*. 1 (1977): 53–80.

Ravenswaay, Lange van. *Augustinus totus noster: Das Augustinverständnis bei Johannes Calvin*. Göttingen: Vandenhoeck & Ruprecht, 1990.

Reid, W. Stanford. "John Calvin, John Knox, and the Scottish Reformation." In *Church, Word, and Spirit: Historical and Theological Essays in Honor of Geoffrey W. Bromiley*. Edited by James E. Bradley and Richard A. Muller. Grand Rapids: Eerdmans, 1987.

———. "Bernard of Clairvaux in the Thought of John Calvin." *Westminster Theological Journal* 41 (1978): 127–145.

Reulos, Michel. "Les juristes en contact avec Calvin." *Calvin et ses contemporains*. Actes du colloque de Paris 1995. Edited by Olivier Millet. Cahiers d'Humanisme et Renaissance 53. Geneve: Droz, 1998, 213–218.

———. "Le Décret de Gratien chez les Humanistes." *Studia Gratiana* 2 (1954): 679–696.

Reventlow, Henning Graf. "Weisung in der Schrift suchen: Johannes Calvin." In *Epochen der Bibelauslegung. Vol. 3: Renaissance, Reformation, Humanismus.* Munchen: C.H. Beck, 1997, 188–140.

Reynolds, Stephen M. "Calvin's View of the Athanasian and Nicene Creeds." *Westminster Theological Journal* 23 (1960–1961): 33–37.

Rhee, J.S. "Five Views of History." In *Calvin: Erbe und Auftrag: Festschrift für Wilhelm Heinrich Neuser zum 65. Geburtstag.* Edited by Willem van Spijker. Kampen: Kok Pharos Publishing House, 1991, 3–17.

Ricoeur, Paul. *Essays on Biblical Interpretation.* Edited by Lewis S. Mudge. Philadelphia: Fortress Press, 1980.

———. *From Text to Action: Essays in Hermeneutics, II.* Translated by Kathleen Blamey and John B. Thompson. Evanston: Northwestern University Press.

———. "Hermeneutics and the Critique of Ideology," In *The Hermeneutic Tradition: From Ast to Ricoeur.* Edited by Gayle L. Ormiston and Alan D. Schrift. Albany: SUNY Press, 1990.

———. *Interpretation Theory: Discourse and the Surplus of Meaning.* Fort Worth, TX: Texas Christian University Press, 1976.

Roelker, Nancy Lyman. *One King, One Faith: The Parlement of Paris and the Religious Reformations of the Sixteenth Century.* Berkeley, CA: University of California Press, 1996.

Runia, Klaas. "Hermeneutic of the Reformers." *Calvin Theological Journal* 19 (1984): 137–149.

Russell, S.H. "Calvin and the Messianic Interpretation of the Psalms." *Scottish Journal of Theology* 21 (1968): 37–47.

Scholl, Hans. *Calvinus Catholicus: Dis Katholische Calvinforschung im 20. Jahrhundert.* Basel: Herder, 1974.

Schreiner, Susan E. *The Theater of His Glory: Nature and the Natural Order in the Thought of John Calvin.* Studies in Historical Theology. Durham: Labyrinth Press, 1991.

———. "'Through a Mirror Dimly': Calvin's Sermons on Job." *Calvin Theological Journal* 21 (1986): 175–193.

———. *Where Shall Wisdom Be Found? Calvin's Exegesis of Job from Medieval and Modern Perspectives.* Chicago: University of Chicago Press, 1994.

———. "'The Spiritual Man Judges All Things': Calvin and Exegetical Debate about Certainty in the Reformation." In *Biblical Interpretation in the Era of the Reformation.* Edited by Richard A. Muller and John L. Thompson. Grand Rapids: Eerdmans, 1996, 189–215.

———. "Exegesis and double justice in Calvin's sermons on Job." *Church History* 58 (1989): 322–338.

Schulze, Ludolf Ferdinand. "Calvin on preaching." *Hervormde teologiese studies* 54 (1998): 50–59.

———. "Preaching as Topical Communication: The Case of Calvin." *Die Skriflig.* 32 (1998): 115–126.

Schulze, Manfred. "*Contra Rectam Rationem*: Gabriel Biel's Reading of Gregory of Rimini, versus Gregory," In *Via Augustini: Augustine in the Later Middle Ages, Renaissance and Reformation. Essays in Honor of Damasus Trapp, O.S.A.* Edited by Heiko Oberman and Frank James, III. Leiden: E.J. Brill, 1991###∎

Selinger, Suzanne. *Calvin Against Himself: An Inquiry in Intellectual History*. Hamden, CT: Archon Books, 1984.

Shepherd, Victor A. *The Nature and Function of Faith in the Theology of John Calvin*. Macon: Mercer University Press, 1983.

Shuger, Deborah Kuller. *The Renaissance Bible: Scholarship, Sacrifice, and Subjectivity*. Berkeley: University of California Press, 1994.

Smalley, Beryl. *The Study of the Bible in the Middle Ages*. 2nd edition. Notre Dame: Notre Dame University Press, 1952.

Smits, Luchesius. *Saint Augustin dans L'œuvre de Jean Calvin*. Assen: Van Gorcum & Comp., 1957.

Soulie, Marguerite. "Signes et Sacrements dans la Théologie de Jean Calvin." *Les signes de Dieu aux XVIe et XVIIe siecles*. Actes du Colloque organise par le Centre de Recherches sur la Reforme et la Contre-Reforme avec le concours du C.N.R.S. Reunis et presentes par Genevieve Demerson et Bernard Dompnier. Clermont-Ferrand: Publications de la Faculte des Lettres et Sciences Humaines, 1993. 27–36.

Spijker, Willem van't. "Bucer's influence on Calvin: church and community." In *Martin Bucer: Reforming Church and Community*. Edited by D.F. Wright. Cambridge: Cambridge University Press, 1994.

Spinks, Bryan D. "Calvin's Baptismal Theology and the Making of the Strasbourg and Genevan Baptismal Liturgies 1540 and 1542." *Scottish Journal of Theology* 48 (1995): 55–78.

Stauffer, Richard. "Dieu, la Creation et la Providence dans L'oeuvre Homiletique de Calvin." *La revue reformee*, 28, 1977: 196–203.

———. "Les Discours à la Premiére Personne dans les Sermons de Calvin." *Revue d'Histoire et de Philosophie Religieuses* 45 (1965): 46–78.

Steenkamp, Johan J. "A Review of the Concept of Progress in Calvin's Institutes." In *Calvin: Erbe und Auftrag: Festschrift für Wilhelm Heinrich Neuser zum 65. Geburtstag*. Edited by Willem van Spijker. Kampen: Kok Pharos Publishing House, 1991, 69–76.

———. "Calvin's Exhortation to Charles V (1543)," In *Calvinus Sincerioris Religionis Vindex*. Edited by Wilhelm Neuser and Brian Armstrong. Kirksville, MO: Sixteenth Century Journal Publishers, 1997, 309–314.

Steinmetz, David. *Calvin in Context* Oxford: Oxford University Press, 1995.

———. "John Calvin on Isaiah 6: A Problem in the History of Exegesis." *Interpretation* 36 (1982):156–170.

———. "The Superiority of Pre-critical Exegesis." In *Ex Auditu* 1 (1985): 74–82.

———. "Calvin and Melanchthon on Romans 13:1–7" in Ex Auditu 2 (1986): 74–81.

———. "Calvin and Abraham: The Interpretation of Romans 4 in the Sixteenth Century." *Church History* 57 (1988): 12–35.

———. "Calvin and the Divided Self of Romans 7." In *Augustine, the Harvest, and Theology (1300–1650)*. Edited by K. Hagen. Leiden: E.J. Brill, 1990.300–313.

———. "Calvin and the Patristic Exegesis of Paul." In *The Bible in the 16th Century*. Edited by David Steinmetz. Durham: Duke University Press, 1990, 100–118.

———. "Calvin Among the Thomists: Exegesis of Romans 9." In *Biblical Herme-*

neutics in Historical Perspective. Edited by Mark Burrows and Paul Rorem. Grand Rapids: Eerdmans, 1991.

———. "Calvin as an Interpreter of Genesis." In *Calvinus Sincerioris Religionis Vindex.* Edited by Wilhelm Neuser and Brian Armstrong. Kirksville, MO: Sixteenth Century Journal Publishers, 1997, 53–66.

———. "Divided by a Common Past: The Reshaping of the Christian Exegetical Tradition in the Sixteenth Century." *The Journal of Medieval and Early Modern Studies* 27 (1997): 245–264.

———. "Calvin and the Irrepressible Spirit." *Ex Auditu* 12 (1996): 94–107.

———. "The Reformation and the Ten Commandments." *Interpretation* 43 (1989): 256–266.

———. "Calvin and the Monastic Ideal." In *Anticlericalism in Late Medieval and Early Modern Europe.* Edited by Peter A. Dykema and Heiko A. Oberman. Leiden: E.J. Brill, 1993, 605–616.

———. "The Judaizing Calvin." In *Die Patristik in der Bibelexegese des 16. Jahrhunderts.* Edited by David C. Steinmetz. Wiesbaden: Harrassowitz Verlag, 1999, 135–145.

Stephens, Peter. "The church in Bucer's commentaries on the Epistle to the Ephesians." In *Martin Bucer: Reforming Church and Community.* Edited by D.F. Wright. Cambridge: Cambridge University Press, 1994.

Stock, Brian. *The Implications of Literacy: Written Language and Models of Interpretation in the Eleventh and Twelfth Centuries.* Princeton: Princeton University Press, 1983.

———. *Listening for the Text: On the Uses of the Past.* Philadelphia: University of Pennsylvania Press, 1990.

Strehle, Stephen. *The Catholic Roots of the Protestant Gospel: Encounter Between the Middle Ages and the Reformation.* Leiden: E.J. Brill, 1995.

Stroup, George. "Narrative in Calvin's Hermeneutic." In *John Calvin and the Church.* Edited by Timothy George. Louisville: Westminster John Knox Press, 1991, 158–171.

Stuhlmacher, Peter. *Historical Criticism and Theological Interpretation of Scripture.* Translated by Roy A. Harrisville. Philadelphia: Fortress Press, 1977.

Tamburello, Dennis. *Union with Christ: John Calvin and the Mysticism of St. Bernard.* Columbia Series in Reformed Theology. Louisville, KY: Westminster John Knox Press, 1994.

Tatarenko, Yves. "Les 'Sorbonnistes' face a Geneve. La perception de Calvin et de la Reforme genevoise par les theologiens catholiques parisiens (1536–1564)." *Calvin et ses contemporains*: Actes du colloque de Paris 1995. Cahiers d'Humanisme et Renaissance 53. Geneve: Droz, 1998, 135–148.

Tavard, George H. *Holy Writ or Holy Church: The Crisis of the Protestant Reformation.* Westport, CT: Greenwood Publishers, 1959.

Thiselton, Anthony C. *New Horizons in Hermeneutics: The Theory and Practice of Transforming Biblical Reading.* Grand Rapids: Zondervan Publishing House, 1992.

Thompson, Bard. "And the Word became Word: An Essay on the Relationships between the Renaissance and the Reformation." *The New Mercersburg Review: Journal of the Mercersburg Society* 5 (1989): 7–18.

300   SELECTED BIBLIOGRAPHY

Thompson, John L. "The Immoralities of the Patriarchs in the History of Exegesis: A Reappraisal of Calvin's Position." *Calvin Theological Journal* 26 (1991): 9–46.

———. *The Daughters of Sarah: Women in Regular and Exceptional Roles in the Exegesis of Calvin, His Predecessors, and His Contemporaries.* Geneve: Librairie Droz, 1992.

———. "'So Ridiculous a Sign': Men, Women, and the Lessons of Cirumcision in Sixteenth-Century Exegesis." *Archiv fur Reformationsgeschichte* 86 (1995): 236–256.

———. "Hagar, Victim or Villian? Three Sixteenth-Century Views." *The Catholic Biblical Quarterly* 59 (1997): 213–233.

———. "Patriarchs, Polygamy, and Private Resistance: John Calvin and Others on Breaking God's Rules." *The Sixteenth Century Journal* 25 (1994): 3–27.

Torrance, James. "Interpreting the Word in the the Light of Christ of the Light of Nature? Calvin, Calvinism, and Barth." In *Calviniana: Ideas and Influence of Jean Calvin.* Edited by Robert V. Schnucker. Kirksville, MO: Sixteenth Century Journal Publishers, 1988, 255–268.

Torrance, Thomas F. *The Hermeneutics of John Calvin.* Edinburgh: Scottish Academic Press, 1988.

———. "Knowledge of God and Speech about Him according to John Calvin." *Revue d'Histoire et de Philosophie Religieuses* 44 (1964–1965): 402–422.

———. *Calvin's Doctrine of Man.* London: Lutterworth Press, 1949.

———. *Kingdom and Church: A Study in the Theology of the Reformation.* Fair Lawn, NJ: Essential Books, 1956.

———. "The Hermeneutics of John Reuchlin, 1455–1522." In *Church, Word, and Spirit: Historical and Theological Essays in Honor of Geoffrey W. Bromiley.* Edited by James E. Bradley and Richard A. Muller. Grand Rapids: Eerdmans, 1987.

———. "The Hermeneutics of Erasmus." In *Probing the Reformed Tradition: Historical Studies in Honor of Edward A. Dowey, Jr.* Edited by Elsie Anne McKee and Brian G. Armstrong. Louisville: Westminster John Knox Press, 1989.

Tracy, James D. "*Ad Fontes*: The Humanist Understanding of Scripture as Nourishment for the Soul." In *Christian Spirituality: High Middle Ages and Reformation,* edited by Jill Raitt with Bernard McGinn and John Meyendorff. World Spirituality: An Encyclopedic History of the Religious Quest, vol. 17. New York: Crossroad, 1988.

Trinkaus, Charles. "Renaissance Problems in Calvin's Theology." In *The Scope of Renaissance Humanism.* Ann Arbor: University of Michigan Press, 1983, 317–339.

Valeri, Mark. "Religion, Discipline, and the Economy in Calvin's Geneva." *The Sixteenth Century Journal* 28 (1997):123–142.

Verhoef, Pieter A. "Luther's and Calvin's Exegetical Library." *Calvin Theological Journal* 3 (1968): 5–20.

Vignaux, Paul. *Justification et Prédestination au XIVᵉ Siècle: Duns Scot, Pierre D'Auriole, Guillaume D'Occam, Grégoire De Rimini.* Paris: Ernest Leroux, 1934.

Vos, Arvin. *Aquinas, Calvin, and Contemporary Protestant Thought: A Critique of Protestant Views on the Thought of Thomas Aquinas.* Grand Rapids, MI: Christian University Press, 1985.

Wallace, Ronald S. *Calvin's Doctrine of the Word and Sacrament.* Edinburgh: Oliver and Boyd, 1953.

———. *Calvin, Geneva, and the Reformation.* Grand Rapids: Baker Book House, 1988.

Walt, Bennie J. van der. "The Idea of Reform." In *Calvin: Erbe und Auftrag: Festschrift für Wilhelm Heinrich Neuser zum 65. Geburtstag.* Edited by Willem van Spijker. Kampen: Kok Pharos Publishing House, 1991, 18–30.

Warfield, Benjamin B. *Calvin and Augustine.* Philadelphia: Presbyterian and Reformed Publishing Co., 1980.

Watt, Jeffrey. "The Marriage Laws Calvin Drafted for Geneva." In *Calvinus Sacrae Scripturae Professor.* International Congress on Calvin Research. Edited by Wilhelm Neuser. Grand Rapids: Eerdmans, 1994, 245–255.

Weiss, James Michael. "Humanism." II.264–272 in *Oxford Encyclopedia of the Reformation.* 4 volumes. Edited by Hans J. Hillerbrand. Oxford: Oxford University Press, 1996.

Wendel, François. *Calvin: Origins and Development of His Religious Thought.* Translated by Philip Mairet. Durham, NC: Labyrinth Press, 1987.

White, Robert. "Women and the Teaching Office According to Calvin." *Scottish Journal of Theology* 47 (1994): 489–509.

David N. Wiley. "The Church as the Elect in the Theology of Calvin." In *John Calvin and the Church.* Edited by Timothy George. Louisville: Westminster John Knox Press, 1991, 96–119.

Wilcox, Peter. "The Restoration of the Church" in Calvin's "Commentaries in Isaiah the Prophet." *Archiv für Reformationsgeschichte* 85 (1994): 69–95.

———. "The Lectures of John Calvin and the Nature of his Audience, 1555–1564." *Archiv für Reformationsgeschichte* 87 (1996): 136–148.

Williams, Donald T. "John Calvin: Humanist and Reformer." *Trinity Journal* 5 (1976): 67–78.

Willis, E. David. *Calvin's Catholic Christology: The Function of the So-Called Extra Calvinisticum in Calvin's Theology.* Studies in Medieval and Reformation Thought. Leiden: E.J. Brill, 1966.

———. "Calvin's Use of Substantia." In *Calvinus Ecclesiae Genevensis Custos.* International Congress on Calvin Research. Edited by Wilhelm Neuser. New York: Peter Lang, 1984, 289–302.

———. "Rhetoric and Responsibility in Calvin's Theology." In *The Context of Contemporary Theology.* Edited by Alexander J. McKelway and E. David Willis. Atlanta: John Knox Press, 1974, 43–63.

———. "The Unio Mystica and the Assurance of Faith According to Calvin." In *Calvin: Erbe und Auftrag: Festschrift für Wilhelm Heinrich Neuser zum 65. Geburtstag.* Edited by Willem van Spijker. Kampen: Kok Pharos Publishing House, 1991, 77–84.

Woudstra, Marten H. "Calvin Interprets What 'Moses Reports': Observations on Calvin's Commentary on Exodus 1–19," *Calvin Theological Journal* 21 (1986): 151–174.

Wright, David F. "Calvin's Pentateuchal Criticism: Equity, Hardness of Heart, and Divine Accommodation in the Mosaic Harmony Commentary." *Calvin Theological Journal,* 21 (1986): 33–50.

———. "Accomodation and Barbarity in John Calvin's Old Testament Commentaries." In *Understanding Prophets and Poets: Essays in Honor of George Wishart Anderson*. Edited by A. Graeme Auld. Sheffield: Journal for the Study of the Old Testament Press, 1993, 413–427.

———. "The Ethical Use of the Old Testament in Luther and Calvin: A Comparison." *Scottish Journal of Theology* 36 (1983):463–485.

———. "Robert Estienne's *Nova Glossa Ordinaria*. A Protestant Quest for a Standard Bible Commentary." In *Calvin: Erbe und Auftrag: Festschrift für Wilhelm Heinrich Neuser zum 65. Geburtstag*. Edited by Willem van Spijker. Kampen: Kok Pharos Publishing House, 1991, 40–54.

———. "Calvin's Accomodating God." In *Calvinus Sincerioris Religionis Vindex*. Edited by Wilhelm Neuser and Brian Armstrong. Kirksville, MO: Sixteenth Century Journal Publishers, 1997, 3–20.

Zachman, Randall C. *The Assurance of Faith: Conscience in the Theology of Martin Luther and John Calvin*. Minneapolis: Fortress Press, 1993.

———. "'Do You Understand What You Are Reading?' Calvin's Guidance for the Reading of Scripture" *Scottish Journal of Theology* 54 (2001): 1–20.

Zillenbiller, Anette. "Calvin's Uminterpretation Cyprians bei der Beantwortung der Fragen: Auf wen ist die Kirche gegründet und Von wem wird der Bischof gewählt?" In *Calvinus Sincerioris Religionis Vindex*. Edited by Wilhelm Neuser and Brian Armstrong. Kirksville, MO: Sixteenth Century Journal Publishers, 1997, 323–333.

INDEX OF TERMS

accommodation, 29, 36, 44, 45–50, 85, 88, 167
  as hermeneutical principle, 45–50
aedificatio, see also edification, 81, 171, 208
  as hermeneutical principle, 81–82
  as theological-doctrinal principle, 163–168
allegory, 3, 15, 25, 26, 32, 46, 52, 77 127, 128, 129, 130, 133, 136, 207
anagoge, 113, 129, 130
application, 9, 10, 11, 13, 22, 23, 71, 80, 92, 179, 189, 200, 207, 210, 240, 247, 249, 260, 268, 269, 271, 274, 275
atheism, 200, 201, 202
Augustine
  biblical interpretation, 186–198
Augustinian, 3, 24, 25, 26, 27, 137, 139, 164, 185, 186, 190, 196, 199, 205, 223
Augustinianism, 3, 137, 186, 199, 223
authority, 13, 16, 18, 19, 20, 33, 36, 40, 42, 43, 44, 60, 85, 101, 116, 117, 120, 128, 129, 137, 175, 177, 182, 194, 195, 197, 198, 200, 202, 203, 204, 205, 207, 214, 215, 217, 221, 225, 240, 251, 253, 258, 261, 262, 268, 273

Bible
  containing the gospel, 20–23
  see also scripture
biblicism, 22, 163, 274

Calvin
  and Augustinianism, 24–26, 137–138, 199–208
  and the Church, 268–271

  and philosophy, 36–40
  theological center, 163
  view of history, 260–268
caritas hermeneutic, 193
Christ
  end of Christian teaching, 157
  end of the Christian life, 143–156
  end of scripture, 140–143
  engrafting into, 150, 155
Christian life, 3, 9, 23, 68, 81, 117, 140, 143, 146, 150, 154, 159, 161, 180, 185, 191, 196, 210, 219, 229, 239, 252, 258
Church, 268–271
  as faith community, 10, 255, 269, 275, 276
  as textual community, 168–177
  as community of discipline, 177–179
Consistory of Geneva, 176, 177, 178, 179
context, use of, 6, 7, 59, 65, 68, 71, 75, 77, 78, 86, 88, 95, 98, 99, 100, 101, 102, 104, 106, 107, 108, 121, 124, 125, 127, 129, 130, 131, 186, 191, 213, 219, 222, 228, 247, 250, 262, 264, 265, 269, 270
Contextual interpretation, 98
  as exegetical rule, 98–108
  argument use, 99, 100
  authorial use, 102
  cultural use, 104
  vocabulary use, 102

discernment, 20, 33, 204, 215, 217, 257, 270, 273
doctor (teacher), 84, 114, 120, 132, 166, 168, 169, 170, 184, 203, 212, 256, 270

INDEX OF CLASSICAL, PATRISTIC
AND EARLY MODERN NAMES

INDEX OF BIBLICAL CITATIONS

Studies in the History of Christian Traditions

(formerly Studies in the History of Christian Thought)

EDITED BY ROBERT J. BAST

46. GARSTEIN, O. *Rome and the Counter-Reformation in Scandinavia.* 1553-1622. 1992
47. GARSTEIN, O. *Rome and the Counter-Reformation in Scandinavia.* 1622-1656. 1992
48. PERRONE COMPAGNI, V. (ed.). *Cornelius Agrippa, De occulta philosophia Libri tres.* 1992
49. MARTIN, D. D. *Fifteenth-Century Carthusian Reform.* The World of Nicholas Kempf. 1992
50. HOENEN, M. J. F. M. *Marsilius of Inghen.* Divine Knowledge in Late Medieval Thought. 1993
51. O'MALLEY, J. W., IZBICKI, T. M. and CHRISTIANSON, G. (eds.). *Humanity and Divinity in Renaissance and Reformation.* Essays in Honor of Charles Trinkaus. 1993
52. REEVE, A. (ed.) and SCREECH, M. A. (introd.). *Erasmus' Annotations on the New Testament.* Galatians to the Apocalypse. 1993
53. STUMP, Ph. H. *The Reforms of the Council of Constance (1414-1418).* 1994
54. GIAKALIS, A. *Images of the Divine.* The Theology of Icons at the Seventh Ecumenical Council. With a Foreword by Henry Chadwick. 1994
55. NELLEN, H. J. M. and RABBIE, E. (eds.). *Hugo Grotius – Theologian.* Essays in Honour of G. H. M. Posthumus Meyjes. 1994
56. TRIGG, J. D. *Baptism in the Theology of Martin Luther.* 1994
57. JANSE, W. *Albert Hardenberg als Theologe.* Profil eines Bucer-Schülers. 1994
59. SCHOOR, R.J.M. van de. *The Irenical Theology of Théophile Brachet de La Milletière (1588-1665).* 1995
60. STREHLE, S. *The Catholic Roots of the Protestant Gospel.* Encounter between the Middle Ages and the Reformation. 1995
61. BROWN, M.L. *Donne and the Politics of Conscience in Early Modern England.* 1995
62. SCREECH, M.A. (ed.). *Richard Mocket, Warden of All Souls College, Oxford, Doctrina et Politia Ecclesiae Anglicanae.* An Anglican Summa. Facsimile with Variants of the Text of 1617. Edited with an Introduction. 1995
63. SNOEK, G.J.C. *Medieval Piety from Relics to the Eucharist.* A Process of Mutual Interaction. 1995
64. PIXTON, P.B. *The German Episcopacy and the Implementation of the Decrees of the Fourth Lateran Council, 1216-1245.* Watchmen on the Tower. 1995
65. DOLNIKOWSKI, E.W. *Thomas Bradwardine: A View of Time and a Vision of Eternity in Fourteenth-Century Thought.* 1995
66. RABBIE, E. (ed.). *Hugo Grotius, Ordinum Hollandiae ac Westfrisiae Pietas (1613).* Critical Edition with Translation and Commentary. 1995
67. HIRSH, J. C. *The Boundaries of Faith.* The Development and Transmission of Medieval Spirituality. 1996
68. BURNETT, S.G. *From Christian Hebraism to Jewish Studies.* Johannes Buxtorf (1564-1629) and Hebrew Learning in the Seventeenth Century. 1996
69. BOLAND O.P., V. *Ideas in God according to Saint Thomas Aquinas.* Sources and Synthesis. 1996
70. LANGE, M.E. *Telling Tears in the English Renaissance.* 1996
71. CHRISTIANSON, G. and IZBICKI, T.M. (eds.). *Nicholas of Cusa on Christ and the Church.* Essays in Memory of Chandler McCuskey Brooks for the American Cusanus Society. 1996
72. MALI, A. *Mystic in the New World.* Marie de l'Incarnation (1599-1672). 1996
73. VISSER, D. *Apocalypse as Utopian Expectation (800-1500).* The Apocalypse Commentary of Berengaudus of Ferrières and the Relationship between Exegesis, Liturgy and Iconography. 1996
74. O'ROURKE BOYLE, M. *Divine Domesticity.* Augustine of Thagaste to Teresa of Avila. 1997
75. PFIZENMAIER, T.C. *The Trinitarian Theology of Dr. Samuel Clarke (1675-1729).* Context, Sources, and Controversy. 1997
76. BERKVENS-STEVELINCK, C., ISRAEL, J. and POSTHUMUS MEYJES, G.H.M. (eds.). *The Emergence of Tolerance in the Dutch Republic.* 1997
77. HAYKIN, M.A.G. (ed.). *The Life and Thought of John Gill (1697-1771).* A Tercentennial Appreciation. 1997
78. KAISER, C.B. *Creational Theology and the History of Physical Science.* The Creationist Tradition from Basil to Bohr. 1997
79. LEES, J.T. *Anselm of Havelberg.* Deeds into Words in the Twelfth Century. 1997
80. WINTER, J.M. van. *Sources Concerning the Hospitallers of St John in the Netherlands, 14th-18th Centuries.* 1998
81. TIERNEY, B. *Foundations of the Conciliar Theory.* The Contribution of the Medieval Canonists from Gratian to the Great Schism. Enlarged New Edition. 1998

82. MIERNOWSKI, J. *Le Dieu Néant*. Théologies négatives à l'aube des temps modernes. 1998
83. HALVERSON, J.L. *Peter Aureol on Predestination.* A Challenge to Late Medieval Thought. 1998.
84. HOULISTON, V. (ed.). *Robert Persons, S.J.: The Christian Directory (1582)*. The First Booke of the Christian Exercise, appertayning to Resolution. 1998
85. GRELL, O.P. (ed.). *Paracelsus*. The Man and His Reputation, His Ideas and Their Transformation. 1998
86. MAZZOLA, E. *The Pathology of the English Renaissance.* Sacred Remains and Holy Ghosts. 1998.
87. 88. MARSILIUS VON INGHEN. *Quaestiones super quattuor libros sententiarum*. Super Primum. Bearbeitet von M. Santos Noya. 2 Bände. I. Quaestiones 1-7. II. Quaestiones 8-21. 2000
89. FAUPEL-DREVS, K. *Vom rechten Gebrauch der Bilder im liturgischen Raum*. Mittelalterliche Funktionsbestimmungen bildender Kunst im *Rationale divinorum officiorum* des Durandus von Mende (1230/1-1296). 1999
90. KREY, P.D.W. and SMITH, L. (eds.). *Nicholas of Lyra*. the Senses of Scripture. 2000
92. OAKLEY, F. *Politics and Eternity*. Studies in the History of Medieval and Early-Modern Political Thought. 1999
93. PRYDS, D. *The Politics of Preaching*. Robert of Naples (1309-1343) and his Sermons. 2000
94. POSTHUMUS MEYJES, G.H.M. *Jean Gerson – Apostle of Unity*. His Church Politics and Ecclesiology. Translated by J.C. Grayson. 1999
95. BERG, J. VAN DEN. *Religious Currents and Cross-Currents*. Essays on Early Modern Protestantism and the Protestant Enlightenment. Edited by J. de Bruijn, P. Holtrop, and E. van der Wall. 1999
96. IZBICKI, T.M. and BELLITTO, C.M. (eds.). *Reform and Renewal in the Middle Ages and the Renaissance*. Studies in Honor of Louis Pascoe, S. J. 2000
97. KELLY, D. *The Conspiracy of Allusion*. Description, Rewriting, and Authorship from Macrobius to Medieval Romance. 1999
98. MARRONE, S.P. *The Light of Thy Countenance*. Science and Knowledge of God in the Thirteenth Century. 2 volumes. 1. A Doctrine of Divine Illumination. 2. God at the Core of Cognition. 2001
99. HOWSON, B.H. *Erroneous and Schismatical Opinions*. The Question of Orthodoxy regarding the Theology of Hanserd Knollys (c. 1599-169)). 2001
100. ASSELT, W.J. VAN. *The Federal Theology of Johannes Cocceius (1603-1669)*. 2001
101. CELENZA, C.S. *Piety and Pythagoras in Renaissance Florence* the Symbolum Nesianum. 2001
102. DAM, H.-J. VAN (ed.), *Hugo Grotius, De imperio summarum potestatum circa sacra*. Critical Edition with Introduction, English translation and Commentary. 2 volumes. 2001
103. BAGGE, S. *Kings, Politics, and the Right Order of the World in German Historiography c. 950-1150.* 2002
104. STEIGER, J.A. *Fünf Zentralthemen der Theologie Luthers und seiner Erben.* Communicatio – Imago – Figura – Maria – Exempla. Mit Edition zweier christologischer Frühschriften Johann Gerhards. 2002
105. IZBICKI, T.M. and BELLITTO, C.M. (eds.). *Nicholas of Cusa and his Age: Intellect and Spirituality*. Essays Dedicated to the Memory of F. Edward Cranz, Thomas P. McTighe and Charles Trinkaus. 2002
106. HASCHER-BURGER, U. *Gesungene Innigkeit*. Studien zu einer Musikhandschrift der Devotio moderna (Utrecht, Universiteitsbibliotheek, MS 16 H 94, olim B 113). Mit einer Edition der Gesänge. 2002
107. BOLLIGER, D. *Infiniti Contemplatio*. Grundzüge der Scotus- und Scotismusrezeption im Werk Huldrych Zwinglis. 2003
108. CLARK, F. *The 'Gregorian' Dialogues and the Origins of Benedictine Monasticism.* 2002
109. ELM, E. *Die Macht der Weisheit*. Das Bild des Bischofs in der *Vita Augustini* des Possidius und andere spätantiken und frühmittelalterlichen Bischofsviten. 2003
110. BAST, R.J. (ed.). *The Reformation of Faith in the Context of Late Medieval Theology and Piety*. Essays by Berndt Hamm. 2004.
111. HEERING, J.P. *Hugo Grotius as Apologist for the Christian Religion. A Study of his Work De Veritate Religionis Christianae (1640)*. Translated by J.C. Grayson. 2004.
112. LIM, P.C. H. *In Pursuit of Purity, Unity, and Liberty*. Richard Baxter's Puritan Ecclesiology in its Seventeenth-Century Context. 2004.
113. CONNORS, R. and GOW, A.C. (eds.). *Anglo-American Millennialism, from Milton to the Millerites*. 2004.
114. ZINGUER, I. and YARDENI, M. (eds.). *Les Deux Réformes Chrétiennes*. Propagation et Diffusion. 2004.
115. JAMES, F.A. III (ed.). *Peter Martyr Vermigli and the European Reformations*: Semper Reformanda. 2004.
116. STROLL, M. *Calixtus II (1119-1124)*. A Pope Born to Rule. 2004.

117. ROEST, B. *Franciscan Literature of Religious Instruction before the Council of Trent.* 2004.
118. WANNENMACHER, J.E. *Hermeneutik der Heilsgeschichte. De septem sigillis und die sieben Siegel im Werk Joachims von Fiore.* 2004.
119. THOMPSON, N. *Eucharistic Sacrifice and Patristic Tradition in the Theology of Martin Bucer, 1534-1546.* 2005.
120. VAN DER KOOI, C. *As in a Mirror. John Calvin and Karl Barth on Knowing God. A Diptych.* 2005.
121. STEIGER, J.A. *Medizinische Theologie.* Christus medicus und theologia medicinalis bei Martin Luther und im Luthertum der Barockzeit. 2005.
122. GIAKALIS, A. *Images of the Divine.* The Theology of Icons at the Seventh Ecumenical Council – Revised Edition. With a Foreword by Henry Chadwick. 2005.
123. HEFFERNAN, T.J. and BURMAN, T.E. (eds.). *Scripture and Pluralism.* Reading the Bible in the Religiously Plural Worlds of the Middle Ages and Renaissance. Papers Presented at the First Annual Symposium of the Marco Institute for Medieval and Renaissance Studies at the University of Tennessee, Knoxville, February 21-22, 2002. 2005.
124. LITZ, G., MUNZERT, H. and LIEBENBERG, R. (eds.). *Frömmigkeit – Theologie – Frömmigkeits-theologie – Contributions to European Church History.*
125. FERREIRO, A. *Simon Magus in Patristic, Medieval and Early Modern Traditions.* 2005.
126. GOODWIN, D.L. *"Take Hold of the Robe of a Jew".* Herbert of Bosham's Christian Hebraism. 2006.
127. HOLDER, R.W. *John Calvin and the Grounding of Interpretation.* Calvin's First Commentaries. 2006.

Prospectus available on request

BRILL — P.O.B. 9000 — 2300 PA LEIDEN — THE NETHERLANDS